Relationship Response

XRL Relationship

Supportive Responses

XRS Reassurance
XOH Offer of help
XAP Approval

Redirecting Responses

XCA Calling attention
XCH Challenging
XWH Withholding support
XPS Persuasion
XDC Disapproval

Subcategories of Interpretation (XIT) Responses

XIT₇ Therapist uses a preceding client statement to exemplify a process that has been building up during the interview, and of which the client is seemingly unaware.

XIT₈ Therapist speculates as to the possible childhood situation which might relate to current client feelings.

XIT₉ Therapist deals with inferences about material completely removed from the client's awareness.

DEPENDENCY IN PSYCHOTHERAPY

A Casebook

WITHDRAWN

by
William U. Snyder, Ph.D.

*Professor of Psychology and
Director of Clinical Training
Ohio University*

THE MACMILLAN COMPANY, NEW YORK

COLLIER-MACMILLAN, LTD., LONDON

To June

First Printing

Library of Congress catalog card number: 63–7217

The Macmillan Company, New York
Collier-Macmillan Canada, Ltd., Galt, Ontario
Divisions of The Crowell-Collier Publishing Company

Printed in the United States of America

Preface

IN PREPARING THIS BOOK, TWO SPECIFIC PURPOSES WERE kept in mind. First, there was the belief that more case material designed to be used in practicum teaching is greatly needed. Full or nearly full cases are what seem to be most lacking as source material for this sort of instruction; short excerpts or case summaries are not uncommon, but with only a few exceptions there are very few published cases which permit the student to observe the entire therapy process. Also, the published cases that do exist seem to be rather biased in presentation, being oriented around the theories of a specific "school" of psychotherapy, such as psychoanalysis or client-centered therapy. The need was apparent for material of a more eclectic character. The cases of Mr. Quinn and Mr. Jones in this book were counseled by means of a brief, ego-oriented, relationship therapy, drawing theoretical rationale from psychoanalysis, client-centered therapy, and particularly from psychological learning theory.

Furthermore, there is a need for books about therapy in which the authors state specifically what they believe they were doing at a given moment in therapy, and what they believe the results to have been. This we have tried to do by the inclusion of a rather elaborate coding system of client and therapist responses, reproduced in short form on the inside covers of this book.

The second major purpose of this book relates to our observation that problems in the handling of *dependency* are quite common, particularly in the psychotherapy and counseling of young adults. We feel that our particular type of psychotherapy is especially well adapted to handling this sort of problem. We have focused this book on dependency: its nature and its handling by the therapist. This focus has been made especially relevant by our development of a Dependency Scale, which was part of the Client Affect Scale which the clients completed after each interview. That Mr. Quinn and Mr. Jones were more dependent clients than the average of those we work with is evident in Chart 2 of the book. That they also seemed to work through a good bit of their dependency is apparent in the same chart, as well as in the protocols and follow-up material.

This book should be especially useful in the training of psychotherapists or counselors, either as a supplement or as a principal text in a practicum

iii

course. It should also be useful to more experienced therapists as a detailed and systematic presentation of one therapeutic approach to the handling of dependency. Other types of counselors, such as guidance people, ministers, and social case-workers, will find it relevant to their work.

A number of persons have made contributions for which we feel much gratitude. Needless to say, Messrs. Quinn and Jones, although they must remain anonymous, have contributed much, both to the book and to the author's thinking about therapy. These young psychologists have thus made significant contributions to the training of therapists.

The author's wife has given much more than the usually acknowledged support and encouragement. She participated fully in both the research and editorial tasks involved in the dependency study and the writing of the book and in many discussions about the handling of dependency in psychotherapy.

The manuscript was typed by Mrs. R. M. Davis, assisted by Margaret Johnson, Mrs. Joanne Bogaty, and Mrs. Suad Kawar. Statistical help was provided by Dr. Donald T. Laird, Mrs. Anna T. Wink, and Edward Loder. To all these people we express sincere gratitude.

William U. Snyder

Contents

v

LIST OF TABLES

LIST OF CHARTS

Part One

INTRODUCTION

THIS BOOK is concerned with the handling of dependency in psychotherapy. The author's interest in this problem became crystallized during study of the data for the book *The Psychotherapy Relationship,* when he was impressed with the type of relationship he had developed with dependent clients and decided that an intensive analysis of two of the most dependent (of the twenty in the above-mentioned study) would contribute useful information about similarities and differences in psychotherapeutic techniques employed with the same general type of problem, *i.e.,* dependency. (Although similar to each other in being dependent, the two clients were somewhat different in the goals they had for therapy: the one was looking for a substitute father, the other hoped to become independent of father figures.) These two clients have been given fictional Anglo-Saxon names and are referred to throughout the book as Quentin Quinn and John Jones. In the introductory chapter the reader will find a discussion of a number of significant questions relating to the handling of dependency in general, and the character of the dependent relationship established by these two clients in particular. In Parts II and III of the book the individual cases are presented rather fully, with analysis of the therapeutic action which transpired and discussion of its significance.

Therapeutic Dependency: Its Causes, Manifestations, and Treatment

Psychotherapists often use the concept of dependency, but the meaning of this term, as applied to therapy, is not always too clear. As used in this book, *dependent behavior may be defined as behavior involving the need for more help than the average person requires in meeting problem situations.* Maslow and Mittelmann (1941) have stated that

. . . the feeling of helplessness almost automatically carries with it an overvaluation of the strength of other individuals. Thus the patient may seek his restoration by dependence on a stronger person, by blind faith in him, by a desire for his constant presence and his undivided affection and esteem. This seeking may be expressed predominantly in the field of friendship, of professional relationships, or the attitude toward a mate or relative. . . .

3

In terms of its development, dependency is to be expected in children; infants are almost entirely dependent upon others at first for satisfaction of their needs. However, as the child matures, he usually is encouraged to assume responsibilities commensurate with his age so that by the time of adulthood he will be a capable, self-reliant individual. Sometimes circumstances prevent this from occurring. For example, a parent may consistently criticize all efforts at assuming responsibility, accepting only perfection. Or he may warn of the dangers of "misbehavior," so that the child is uncertain as to which actions are safe to perform. Or the parent may constantly solve all of the child's problems for him, so that he obtains little or no experience at handling them himself. Any of these children, as they grow older, may learn to meet problems by use of dependent behavior.

In psychotherapy, dependency manifests itself in different ways. Some of the most common are the client's requesting specific suggestions about how to handle a situation or asking the therapist to remind him of something he wants to talk about in the future (Mr. Quinn did this frequently in interviews reported in this book). Or the client may seek information from the therapist which he could more easily obtain somewhere else. Sometimes he may ask when the objective is not really to obtain an answer but to magnify a condition of dependency or to experience the sense of being helped.

Frequently dependency is demonstrated in the client's asking for reassurance; he may do this in excessive amounts, or he may seek support about things for which most people do not usually require it. For instance, Mr. Quinn at one point made the remark to the therapist: "Do you still love me, Mother?" The psychological meaning of this remarkable statement is discussed later in this book. Both Mr. Quinn and Mr. Jones (like many other clients) frequently sought reassurance regarding the sufficiency of their masculinity.

Another form which dependency takes in therapy is the client's request for the therapist to make certain decisions which most persons prefer to make for themselves. A common example of this type of request is to ask the therapist to decide what the client should talk about. A modification of this behavior is the situation where the client, while actually making a decision himself, later attributes the decision to the therapist. For example, Mr. Quinn said he assumed that the therapist thought that he ought to find more friends of his own sex, whereas this was clearly his own notion or at least a misinterpretation of the therapist's previous reflections of the client's feelings.

Sometimes a client asks for direct assistance unrelated to the therapy situation. Mr. Quinn asked the therapist to help him to obtain a more desirable parking space on the campus, and Mr. Jones considered asking the therapist to come to his college and help him to persuade his colleagues of the value of his work. A modification of this procedure is for the client to arrange some situation in such a manner that the therapist gives help, even though it has not been requested directly. Mr. Quinn wondered whether there were any books available that he could give his mother to read in order to make her more conscious of good mental hygiene practices. And Mr. Jones described at length his difficulties with the therapy case he was conducting, thus putting the therapist in a position of feeling obligated to offer suggestions.

Sometimes the dependency is revealed symbolically in dreams, rather than in real-life actions. Mr. Quinn dreamed that he was fighting with a fraternity man, and the president of the fraternity came to Quinn's assistance and prevented the adversary from retaliating to his aggressive onslaughts. Mr. Quinn easily made the interpretation that the adversary stood for his adviser and that the fraternity president symbolized the therapist.

In handling the client's dependent behavior, the therapist has certain objectives, and these lead him to employ certain procedures. It is the principal purpose of this book to present some of these dependency situations and to demonstrate their therapeutic handling, showing, in the way he handles the cases, the specific objectives of the therapist. In general, it may be said that the therapist has two main objectives: (1) to change the client's *attitudes* about his ability to meet problems, and (2) to help the client to obtain experience in the handling of problem situations. The assumption is generally made that, as the client's attitudes toward himself change and as his experience in solving problems successfully increases, he will become able to function more independently both within and outside of the therapy situation.

To help the client to gain self-confidence, the therapist will frequently deal with the client's self-concept. To help him gain ability in solving his problems, some of the procedures employed include giving instruction in techniques he may use in various situations. Here direct teaching, or what we have classified in this book as giving information, might be said to occur. Sometimes the therapist may assign certain tasks or "homework" for the client to think about or to carry out between interviews; this technique implies giving advice or using persuasion. Sometimes the therapist employs encouragement or reassurance of the client regarding his ability. This will require that the therapist be able to make judgments about the client's readiness to handle a problem of a particular degree of complexity. The therapist will often encourage dependency in the early stages of therapy so as to build up a strong therapeutic relationship which will make it easier for him later to encourage the client to make more and more of his own decisions. The therapist will utilize his own prestige to reinforce the power of his suggestions.

As the therapist provides help, and thus meets the client's needs by reducing anxiety about his capabilities, we believe that the client acquires, by a process of generalization and association, a sense of self-value and an ability to attempt to do that of which he has previously been afraid. But the therapist has, in this process, also acquired rather strong value for the client, much like that of a parent to a child. This is a process similar to that by which a child comes to love his mother. If, however, some person outside of the therapy is simultaneously helping the client to meet his dependency needs, the relationship with the therapist will not be as strong.

Since the therapist is assuming in this situation a role much like that of a parent, he must be careful to avoid repeating the errors that the real parent has made in producing the excessive dependency of the client. For example, he must be careful not to seem patronizing, on one hand, or overly critical, on the other, of the client's efforts to solve his problems. Nor should he allow himself to perpetuate the tendency to solve the client's problems. He will need to encourage all genuine efforts at self-reliance, either with praise or with persuasion. When the client finds "leaning on the therapist" too comfortable, the therapist will need to push him to make some efforts of his own. The therapist must re-condition this dependency into a striving to do things himself.

Throughout all of these activities, the therapist's general attitude must be receptive and permissive, with much reflection of feeling accompanying the more intervening types of therapeutic activity. Only if the therapist really accepts the client and feels positively toward him is the transition from dependency to independence likely to occur successfully. Unless the client is able to perceive the therapist's genuine affection and faith in his ability to become independent, he is not likely to continue making the strong effort necessary to bring about the desired therapeutic change.

Some Other Researches on Dependency

Somewhat surprisingly, dependency, especially as it occurs in psychotherapy, has not been frequently investigated by research methods. We were able to locate only eighty articles written during the past five years which attempted to explore this phenomenon, and less than half of these are significant research studies. More than a quarter deal with the evolution of dependent behavior in young children, usually as studied under observations made in the nursery school or early primary grades. About a dozen are simple descriptions of one or more dependent persons, with an attempt by means of a case study to explore the characteristics or the developmental phases of dependent behavior. A few studies also deal with the treatment of dependent behavior, particularly in psychoanalytic therapy, and with the explanation of the situation in terms of psychoanalytic dynamics. Some of the studies, particularly the more research-oriented ones, deserve mention and are grouped topically below.

Studies of the Characteristics of Dependent Persons in the Psychotherapeutic Situation

Blyth (1960) observed, in studying the reactions of 193 neuropsychiatric veterans, that dependency was the strongest of nine factors in the veterans' decisions to request therapy. In this study, dependency was measured by responses to the Rotter Incomplete Sentences Blank.

The client's expectation that changes will occur in therapy has been shown by Heller and Goldstein (1961) to relate positively to the amount of dependent behavior demonstrated by clients. Also, those clients who thought that therapy would be helpful saw themselves as becoming more independent as the therapy progressed, although they did not, in fact, become more independent during therapy lasting for fifteen interviews. It is interesting, also, that there was a statistically significant relationship between the therapist's early expectation of a client's improvement and the client's expectation of change later in the therapy. Dependency was measured in this study by summing the Edwards PPS scores on succorance and deference and subtracting the score on autonomy. In a different study Heller (1960)

7

hypothesized that the amount of discrepancy between clients' overt and their less conscious expressions of dependency (TAT) would parallel the amount of changes which would occur in overt expressions of dependency during psychotherapy, but this hypothesis was not confirmed.

Our own clients changed only slightly in their manifestations of dependency, as revealed in Table 1.

TABLE 1

Some Dependency Scores of Our Two Clients

	QUINN				JONES			
	Dep*	Def**	Suc**	Aba**	Dep*	Def**	Suc**	Aba**
1st half of therapy	37.5	38.5	62.0	50.0	32.9	35.8	42.3	30.8
2nd half	39.0	37.0	67.0	50.3	30.7	35.0	42.3	24.8

* Dependency Scale on the Client Affect Scale
** On the Edwards PPS

Peterson *et al.* (1958) found in a factor analysis that dependency was one of six areas of psychological problems which therapists considered significant foci for therapeutic activity. Hiler (1959) did not find dependency needs, as revealed on the Michigan Sentence Completion Test, to be related to the length of time that clients remained in therapy; in our own study of twenty therapy clients there was a weak positive correlation of .356, significant at the .06 level. Bernfield and Guthrie (1959) have shown that dependency can be induced hypnotically and that this dependency will affect the dependent character of a pseudotherapeutic situation. The patients who were made more dependent by hypnosis tended, as hypothesized, to discuss fewer topics, to make more emotional statements, to ask more questions, and to show a greater lack of confidence.

Studies Dealing with the Handling of Dependency in Therapy

A considerable amount of work has been done on the phenomenon of verbal conditioning, or so-called "operant conditioning," and a little of it has related to the concept of dependency. Caruth (1959) hypothesized that dependent subjects would rely more heavily than non-dependent ones upon verbal reinforcement cues for guiding their response patterns, even though this reliance was unconscious, but this hypothesis was not sustained. Similarly Hardison and Purcell (1959) failed to confirm the hypothesis that under stress conditions involving negative verbal reinforcement, independent persons would show less performance deficit than would dependent persons. (Dependency in this study was measured by the deference score on the EPPS, while in the Caruth study it was measured by an MMPI scale derived by Gordon.) However, Hardison and Purcell did find that independent flexible subjects tended to improve their performance during negative verbal reinforcement while dependent constricted subjects showed a performance deficit. Both needs and mode of cognitive control were significant in differentiating responses to stress.

A rather significant study was described in a dissertation by Williams (1960). She investigated the effect of the therapist's commitment to the client on the therapeutic progress. Two types of patients were studied: overtly dependent and counter-dependent (three of each). Measures were made of the degree of the therapist's commitment and depth of interpretation and the clients resistance under different therapeutic approaches (Rogerian and non-Rogerian). Williams concluded that, for patients who have problems in the area of dependency, the therapist's demonstrations of his willingness to help are more important determinants of resistance than are his interpretations. Increased therapist commitment led to greater oppositional behavior in *all* patients, but this opposition was necessary in giving the dependent person the confidence to explore his actions and motivations.

Jones, Wells, and Torrey (1958) reported that "feedback" behavior on the part of the therapist which tends to reinforce independent behavior is more effective in changing clients' level of conformity than is the feedback which merely reinforces the conformity.

In this regard, with reference to Messrs. Jones and Quinn, the therapist followed somewhat different procedures. Jones seemed to be fighting his expressions of dependency (counter-dependency?), while Quinn was eager to establish a dependent role and showed little inclination to attempt to be independent. This is slightly evident in the scores found in the table above: Jones shows some reduction in two of the measures of dependency between the first and second halves of the therapy, while Quinn shows no decrease in dependency scores but rather a moderate increase in his succorance score. For this reason, the therapist treated the two cases differently with regard to their dependency expressions. Both clients were allowed to be dependent early in their therapy, as usual. In fact, Mr. Jones was actually encouraged to allow himself to feel dependent. In the latter half of therapy the therapist pushed Mr. Quinn about the necessity of being less dependent, arousing some irritation and hostility in the client. This action was not at all necessary with Mr. Jones, who, despite his rather marked dependency needs, showed a strong desire to free himself of this trait.

Various Measures of Dependency

Some measures of dependency have been discussed previously; others have been developed and should be mentioned. One of the most widely used is the MMPI dependency scale developed by Navran (1954). This is the scale which we have used in our present study as one of the criteria in validating a therapeutic measure of dependency. Navran was able to produce a promising amount of evidence for the validity of his scale, although he did encounter the problem that experienced clinicians could not reliably rate dependency from the study of case histories. It was necessary to have judges choose MMPI items which appeared to reflect dependency and then to compare different diagnostic groups with regard to their responses to these items.

Campbell (1960) performed a factor analysis in order to determine the primary dimensions of item ratings on scales designed to measure twenty-four of Murray's manifest needs. Seven personality traits were reported, of which social dependency and conformity were two.

The relationship of two projective measures to a sociometric measure of dependency was studied by Fitzgerald (1959). These measures were a Protection-Dependency behavior score based on frequency of response in the TAT, the Rotter Incomplete Sentences Blank, a sociometric scale of Protection-Dependency responded to by fraternity brothers of the subjects, and a structured clinical interview. All tests were judged reliably, and in general, significant relationships were found to exist between the different measures. However, the two projective devices tended to reveal somewhat dissimilar, although related, predictive information concerning the relationship between projective test responses and overt behavior.

Nelson (1959) has shown that the Navran MMPI dependency scale was a dependable predictor of drop-outs from therapy, although it did not predict the length of therapy nor the character of the behavior of the patients in their therapy, as observed by their therapists. This study was actually another attempt at construct validation of the concept of dependency, and a number of different tests were used. Dependency was found to be a concept which had a high degree of meaningfulness to the therapists, and the theoretical correlates to dependency were confirmed at a statistically significant level.

Gisvold (1958) performed a validity study of the autonomy and deference scales of the EPPS and was able to establish a fairly high negative correlation (—.54) between the autonomy scale and a criterion of conformity based on use of Asch's group situation. However the deference subscale, perhaps the one that would usually be considered the dependency scale of the EPPS, did not reveal significant correlations with the criterion of conformity. Beswick and Cox (1958) have reported that peers' reports of specified behaviors can be used as a valid measure of aggressive and dependent behavior and what the authors call "repute immaturity."

Couch and Keniston (1960) computed correlations between thirty-two MMPI trait scales and the over-all tendency of subjects to answer "yes" to items. The correlation with the dependency scores was .48, but that for achievement was —.44. The correlation with Cattell's scores for dominant-aggressive versus submissive was .22, and that with his self-sufficient versus dependent scores was —.17. There was also a correlation with a set of factorial scales measuring "oral dependency." Kagan and Mussen (1956) found a positive correlation between TAT dependency themes and the tendency to adopt objectively inaccurate group judgments in a situation of strong pressure favoring group conformity. Levy (1959) reported that a group of conformers in an Asch-type experimental situation were persons who obtained high scores on the EPPS scales for affiliation, nurturance, and endurance.

The efforts to correlate EPPS scores with some other criterion of dependency or a similar trait have been fairly frequent, but the results seem to be somewhat confusing. Thus Zuckerman and Gross (1958) reported that more suggestible persons on a sway test also had high scores on the hero's succorance on the TAT, while the less suggestible persons were higher on autonomy. Scheidel *et al.* (1958) reported that the EPPS dominance score related positively to effectiveness in group discussion situations, and these "effective discussers" scored lower on affiliation, succorance, and abasement. There is always some question as to whether in this sort of correlational study some of these findings might not be the result of coincidence; certainly further studies would be desirable, but they usually are not made.

Our clients were administered a number of different measures of dependency: the MMPI dependency (dy) scale and the EPPS deference, succorance, and abasement scores were the more standardized procedures. In addition they were ranked on dependency by two clinical psychologists thoroughly familiar with their cases. Finally they were scored on the new dependency scale of the Client Affect Scale, which we report in this book. On these various measures Messrs. Quinn's and Jones' ranks (out of twenty clients) were as shown in Table 2. The intercorrelations of some of the dependency rankings are given in Table 4.

TABLE 2

Rankings on Different Measures of Dependency *

	MMPI Dy	EPPS def (1st)	EPPS suc (1st)	EPPS aba (1st)	Ranking by 1st Psy'st	Ranking by 2nd Psy'st	Dep on Client Aff. Sc.	EPPS suc + def — aut	Composite Ranking**
Quinn	2.5	13	7.5	2.5	1	3	1	3	1
Jones	9	9.5	9.5	7	6	5	3	11	6

* Total number of cases on each ranking = 20
** Composite = Both psychologists' rankings + MMPI Dy

Description of the Previous Research Project
on the Psychotherapy Relationship

In this book many references are made to an extensive research on the psychotherapy relationship in which we developed scales of affect between therapist and client. We have now also developed a client dependency scale based on data collected in the previous research project, as well as on some new data. In addition, we make frequent reference to our "twenty research clients," who participated in the research project. For these reasons it is necessary to give a short summary of the research study, although for a discussion of the findings the reader is referred to the book *The Psychotherapy Relationship*.[1]

The therapy used in the study was of an eclectic ego-building relationship type, encompassing both catharsis and insight and based on the principles of learning theory and the concepts of psychoanalysis. The therapeutic personality in this research was most similar to that of Apfelbaum's (1958) Type A therapist: guiding, advice-giving, warm, protective, and nurturant. (He was different from Type B therapists (extremely permissive listener) and Type C therapists (cold and hard-boiled).

Twenty therapy cases, of an average length of 25.5 interviews, were recorded on tapes. After every interview, all twenty clients filled out a questionnaire reporting the client's attitudes, or assumed attitudes, toward the therapy and the therapist. The therapist filled out the same questionnaire in the manner he thought the client had filled it out. The therapist also filled out a different questionnaire regarding his attitudes toward the client, and his estimate of the client's feelings toward him, of the client's progress in therapy, and the client's post-interview need-structure. After every fifth interview the client filled out the Edwards PPS test, and at the beginning of therapy he took the MMPI. The therapist took the Edwards twice and at the end of therapy made six *rankings* on the client as to rapport, hostility, dependency, guardedness, success of the case, and amount liked by the therapist. From one to three years after therapy the therapist also *rated* the clients on his estimate of the types of value systems they held; on affect, controllingness toward the therapist, and self-disclosure;

1. New York: The Macmillan Company, 1961.

13

and on affect from the therapist, on estimates of maladjustment present at the beginning of therapy, and on Leary's "circle" of personality traits. The clients were also grouped into "better" and "poorer" clients on the basis of a multiple criterion of the seven measures in Table 3.

TABLE 3

Tests Included in Criterion Measure for "Better" and "Poorer" Clients

1. Intensity of change on Edwards PPS
2. Low scores on the MMPI
3. High rank on "rapport"
4. Increase in Client Positive Affect
5. Increase in Therapist Positive Affect
6. High mean Client Affect (Positive minus Negative)
7. High mean Therapist Affect (Positive minus Negative)

The therapist did not see any of the test scores or rankings on the clients while their therapy was in progress.

The clients were a very homogeneous group, being composed of nineteen graduate students in psychology and one instructor in an allied department. Their mean age was 27.4 years, with a range from 22 to 42 years. Three were women, and thirteen were married. All clients gave evidence of having problems in the areas of social-sexual adjustment and feelings of professional and personal inadequacy. All were judged at the time of therapy to be neurotic rather than psychotic. On the new scales of the MMPI, ten revealed the presence of sexual problems, ten showed problems of dominance-submission, nine of status, and seven of self-control.

The principal form of data treatment in the research was the completion of a series of thirteen inverse factor analyses of the twenty clients' responses on the universe of affect-scale items. On the basis of these, together with point biserial correlations of each item with the various factors, we derived two affect scales. In the factor analysis, from one to four factors were obtained on each of five interviews on both the Client's Affect Scale (PAC-NAC) items and the Therapist's Affect Scale (PAT-NAT) items. Intercorrelations of these factors on different interviews revealed two definite factors on each scale, a positive and a negative one. There was also a considerable amount of evidence that on both Affect Scales two partially correlated negative factors appeared: on the Client's Affect Scale these were active resistance, or hostility, and passive resistance, or withdrawal. On the Therapist's Affect Scale the two negative factors were impatience with the client and anger or irritation with him. In our final scales we used only a positive and a negative subscale for each, and these were combined into the two single scales of affect of the client and affect of the therapist.

Validity and reliability of the scales were demonstrated, as was that of the original rankings made on the clients immediately after therapy. Adequate variability, both between clients and within clients occurred on the scores of the Client's Affect Scale and the Therapist's Affect Scale.

Perhaps our most significant single observation in the research was the correlation between the scores on the Client's Affect Scale and on the Therapist's Affect Scale, which was .70 ± .12. This constitutes a measure of the relationship between transference and countertransference, and thus of the therapy relationship itself. A similar measure was the correlation of the *therapist's* scores on the Client's Affect Scale and on the Therapist's Affect Scale for the various tenths of the therapy process in each case. (Of the sixty possible correlations, all were positive, and fifty-two were significantly correlated. All the non-significant correlations occurred in the cases of four people.) It was evident that there was a tendency for transference and countertransference to co-vary with each other throughout the therapy process. The validity of the transference and countertransference trends was examined by four different tests of significance and in almost every instance they were substantiated.

There was a fair amount of evidence that our clients tended to cluster into two groups, those whose attitudes toward the therapist were primarily positive and those who felt essentially more negative. Analysis of the differences of the mean scores on the Client's Affect Scale shows that about half of the mean scores were not significantly different from each other, the other half being similarly close, and the clients did, in fact, cluster into two groups showing commonality of affect within each group. Likewise, the therapist tended on various measures to cluster clients into these two groups, *i.e.,* better and poorer clients.

Although the therapist tended to "over-evaluate" the better clients and "under-evaluate" the poorer ones, in general the similarity between the amount of affect coming from each client and the amount directed toward the client by the therapist was striking. While therapist and clients differed considerably in the amount of affect shown, a given client and therapist tended not to differ much in the amount of affect shown toward each other. Whenever the therapist tended to exhibit a large variation in the amount of affect shown a given client on different interviews, the client was likely to be a poorer one.

To us it seems that relationship is a basic component of therapy. Without it, techniques are of little value. Our research led us to believe that there are personality characteristics which make it possible for some clients to establish a better relationship with some therapists than with others, *e.g.,* a dependent client will respond well to a nurturant therapist and a sadistic client to a masochistic therapist. When client and therapist are properly matched, they can develop a very effective interpersonal and therapeutic relationship which is reciprocal in character and which grows increasingly positive, making an effective therapeutic outcome probable. With more knowledge, it should be possible to determine at the beginning of therapy which clients and therapists are best suited to each other and most likely to be able to establish a therapeutic relationship.

Derivation of a Dependency Scale
Based on the Post-interview
Client Affect Scale

In the previous section we have described the derivation of the Client Affect Scale. Subsequently we constructed a scale to measure client dependency, based on the client's post-interview scores on this scale. Using our twenty research clients, the following criteria of dependency were first studied:

1. Rankings on client dependency made by the therapist in Dec., 1957.
2. Rankings on client dependency made by the therapist in May, 1959.
3. Rankings on client dependency made by another psychologist who was quite familiar with their cases.
4. Dependency score on the MMPI (Navran scale).
5. Succorance score on the Edwards PPS.
6. A composite score of the rankings by the two psychologists plus the MMPI dependency score.
7. A composite EPPS dependency score based on the sum of the succorance and deference scores, less the score on autonomy.

The intercorrelations of some of these dependency scores are shown in Table 4. It is apparent that the three scores which relate most to each other are the rankings by the two psychologists and the MMPI dependency score. Therefore we used the composite of these scores (#6 above) as the final criterion for the dependency ranking of our twenty clients.

On the basis of this criterion, we then obtained two different sorts of computations. The second, and perhaps the more significant, computation was a series of 200 Pearsonian [2] correlations between the criterion dependency ranking and the ranking of the clients (for each item) on the frequency of interviews on which they gave an affirmative answer to the item. Thus for a given item, a high correlation revealed that, of our twenty clients, the ones who ranked most dependent on the criterion dependency measure also tended to answer the item most often in the positive or dependent direction. Of the 200 items, eighty-one had correlations of .30 or over, and forty-five

2. A Pearsonian correlation was used rather than a Spearman rho in order to facilitate computation. The assumption was made that differences between the two methods would be very slight and would not tend to favor the scale significantly.

TABLE 4

Spearman Intercorrelations of Various Dependency Measures

	Ranking by First Psychologist (5/59)	Ranking by Second Psychologist	MMPI Dependency Scale	EPPS Succorance Scale	Composite (Two Psychologists + MMPI)	Composite EPPS Dep. Score: def + suc − aut
First Psy'st (12/57)	.660** ±.14	.716** ±.117	.733** ±.111	.219 ±.239	.936** ±.042	.038 ±.240
First Psy'st (5/59)		.457* ±.191	.460* ±.191	.086 ±.240	.673** ±.108	
Second Psychologist			.547** ±.169	.455* ±.192	.844** ±.069	
MMPI Dy				.060 ±.240	.818** ±.080	−.039 ±.240

* Significant at the .05 level.
** Significant at the .01 level.

had correlations of .40 or over. Fifty-five of the correlations were significant at the .05 level, and twenty-two at the .01 level.

Items were selected for our dependency scale according to the following criteria:

1. Item correlations should be only *positive* in direction. (Only three items were eliminated because, although having fairly high correlations, they were in a negative direction.)
2. An item was considered a strong item if it had a correlation that was significant at the .01 level.
3. An item was considered strong if it had a correlation significant at the .05 level and had also been indicated on all three of the "*a priori* logical" criteria.[3]
4. An item was considered a weaker item if it had a correlation at

3. These "*a priori* logical criteria" were: (1) originally written as a dependency item, (2) chosen before the correlation as a dependency item by one psychologist, and (3) chosen before the correlation as a dependency item by a different psychologist.

the .05 level and very little evidence of support on the "logical" criteria basis.

5. An item was considered a weaker item if its correlation was almost at the .05 significance level but was considered as an "excellent" item in the *a priori* judgment of both of the psychologist judges.

In all, fifty-five items (including strong and weaker) met the criteria indicated above and were included in the preliminary form of our dependency scale. They are given in Table A-1. Strong items were given double weighting in the scoring of the scale.

After the preliminary form of the dependency scale was derived, a cross-validation was carried out. For this purpose the Client Affect Scale and the MMPI were administered to twenty-two therapy clients in a University psychological clinic and to eight non-psychotic out-patients in a neuropsychiatric hospital. On the cross-validation, a total of thirty-one items satisfied one or both of two criteria of significance.[4] These items have been marked with a dagger in Table A-1.

A final check on the relationship between the dependency criteria and our preliminary dependency measure was demonstrated by a correlation coefficient of .76 $\pm$ .10. On the cross-validation group, the correlation between the MMPI criterion rankings and the final dependency score was .467 $\pm$ .153. The correlation between the supervisor's rankings and the dependency scale scores (final form) for this group was .360 $\pm$ .170. (The correlation between the supervisor's rankings on dependency and the MMPI dependency scores was only .319 $\pm$ .176.)

Description of the Therapy Used
in These Cases

The therapy of Messrs. Quinn and Jones can be characterized as eclectic. Lying near the middle of a continuum of directiveness, its theoretical basis is drawn largely from the learning-theory-oriented system of Dollard and Miller. However, the contents of the interpretations are frequently also influenced by the theories of psychoanalysis. In spirit the therapy is rather client-centered, and it can be described as an ego-oriented relationship therapy. An analysis of a large portion (1123) of the therapist's statements in the Quinn case reveals the following percentages of frequencies of various responses:

Lead-taking responses	**20.0%**
Structuring	1.4
Nondirective leads	0.4
Directive leads	2.7
Direct questions	15.5

4. A chi square at the .06 level or a ratio of 2.0 or better between the positive answers of the more and the less dependent client groups, as measured on the total Dependency Scale score, were the criteria.

Re-educative and reflective responses 54.4
Restating content 7.4
Clarifying feeling 14.2
Interpretation 17.9
Attenuating interpretations 2.8
Giving advice 2.8
Giving information 9.3

Discussing the relationship 8.1

Supportive response 7.1
Giving reassurance 5.7
Offering assistance 0.4
Giving approval 1.0

Redirecting responses 9.5
Calling attention 1.6
Challenging 4.9
Withholding reassurance 0.2
Persuasion 0.8
Disapproving or criticizing 2.0

It is our belief that the primary requisite for psychotherapy is the establishment of a good relationship between client and therapist. The therapist usually achieves this in a variety of ways, such as by being perceptive, trustworthy, competent, sympathetic, and displaying self-confidence. During early interviews and subsequently at intervals, *structuring* is the means of defining the work of therapy, *i.e.*, what roles the therapist and the client shall take and what their tasks shall be. It may also be used to make explicit the goals of therapy.

When a relationship is at least partially established, the client is encouraged to examine his problems, to try to determine the reasons for his behavior and feelings, and eventually to take steps to change unsatisfactory aspects of his way of life. Some therapeutic techniques which may be used to encourage him to examine his problems are *nondirective leads, directive leads,* and *questions.* On the other hand, techniques which encourage analysis of motivation and feelings are *restatement, clarification,* and *interpretation.* At times a client may not be able to face the implications of a specific interpretation, and then the therapist may wish to dilute, or *attenuate,* it. Also, the client may not be aware of information or of courses of action which could be helpful to him. In such a situation the therapist may wish to give *information* or *advice.*

The work of therapy is difficult, and at times the therapist may feel it necessary to bolster the client's motivation to continue, or he may think it appropriate to reward a particularly good effort, by use of such supportive techniques as *reassurance, approval,* or an *offer of help.*

A major aspect of therapy relates to the fact that nonproductive habits of behavior and thought often tend to persist rather stubbornly. These must be interrupted if they are to be replaced by more satisfying and acceptable ones. Procedures which are used to this end are *calling attention, challenging, withholding support, persuasion,* and *disapproval.*

Throughout the therapeutic process a good relationship between client and therapist must be maintained if therapy is to continue.[5] Consequently, as hostilities or misunderstandings develop, they need to be discussed so that a feeling of trust is restored. The therapist will wish to *discuss the relationship* when the client seems to be resistant or appears to be developing overly strong positive or negative transference feelings. Similarly, if the therapist notices strong emotional involvement on his own part and feels that it may help the therapy for the client to know about these feelings, he may decide to discuss them with the client in a therapeutically constructive manner.

5. A somewhat more extended discussion of the nature of the therapy conducted with Messrs. Quinn and Jones is to be found in our book: *The Psychotherapy Relationship* by William U. and B. June Snyder. New York: The Macmillan Co., 1961.

The Coding System Used in This Book
for Classifying Interview Material

Throughout this book, for purposes of instruction, and also for use in some of our research, we have coded various therapist and client statements. These codings of the therapist's responses are based on several modifications of our own previously published system (1945). We have added some new categories, dropped a few, and subdivided others.[6] The most important subdivisions are in the category of interpretation, where we have applied the Raush, *et al.* (1956) scheme for classifying depth of interpretation.

In this book, most of the frequencies of therapist's responses reported are based on the *condensed* interviews as they appear in the book. Thus, the selective process which influenced the condensation may have had some effects on the results. In order to test whether this method of obtaining the frequencies is reliable, we computed Spearman correlations between the frequencies in various categories for three interviews, measured both ways, and obtained the results given in Table 5. The principal responses of the therapist, together with their codes are given in Tables 6 and 6a.

TABLE 5

Correlations between Classifications of Client Responses on Complete Interview Typescripts and Condensed Interview Typescripts

	Client Affect Themes	Client Topic Source
Jones, 2nd Interview (1st Psychologist)	$.654 \pm .214$	$.712 \pm .183$
Jones, 3rd Interview (2nd Psychologist)	$.599 \pm .224$	$.750 \pm .154$
Quinn, 12th Interview (1st Psychologist)	$.749 \pm .154$	$.739 \pm .132$

6. Judges never agree completely when classifying protocol material. The reader should not become alarmed if he attempts to classify some of the responses in this book and finds that he disagrees with the author. Trained judges usually show a high percentage of agreement.

TABLE 6

Coding Symbols and Categories for Therapist Responses

Lead-taking Responses
  XST   Structuring
  XND   Non-directive lead
  XDL   Directive Lead
  XDQ   Question

**Reflective or Re-educative
    Responses**
  XRC   Restatement
  XCF   Clarification
  XIT   Interpretation
  XAT   Attenuation
  XAV   Advice
  XEI   Information

Relationship Response
  XRL   Relationship

Supportive Responses
  XRS   Reassurance
  XOH   Offer of help
  XAP   Approval

Redirecting Responses
  XCA   Calling attention
  XCH   Challenging
  XWH   Withholding support
  XPS   Persuasion
  XDC   Disapproval

Most of our interviews have been somewhat condensed. Sometimes a client, or the therapist, repeats himself unnecessarily, and this repetition has been eliminated in order to save space. Casual, trivial conversations or digressions have usually been omitted or summarized in a short sentence. Connective phrases have been eliminated, although the idea itself has usually been included. Actually, this space-saving tends to make the material read more easily because of the freer flow of the principal ideas.

TABLE 6a

Coding Symbols and Categories for Different Types of Therapist Interpretations

XIT_4 Therapist connects two aspects of the contents of previous client statements.

XIT_5 Therapist reformulates the behavior of the client during the interview in a way not explicitly recognized previously by the client.

XIT_6 Therapist comments on the client's bodily or facial expressions as manifestations of the client's feelings.

XIT_7 Therapist uses a preceding client statement to exemplify a process that has been building up during the interview and of which the client is seemingly unaware.

XIT_8 Therapist speculates as to the possible childhood situation which might relate to current client feelings.

XIT_9 Therapist deals with inferences about material completely removed from the client's awareness.

Our codings of *client* responses are modified from those proposed by Dollard and Auld (1959) based on Murray's need systems. We found it important to classify both the client's principal affect theme and the principal object or source of his affect. The affect themes and their code symbols are given in Table 7.

The needs or concerns are feelings or drives coming from "within" the client himself, while the pressures are, of course, external motivations. Sex *need,* for example, was scored when the client expressed or implied libidinal interest in another person, while sex *pressure* was the feeling that he was being sought sexually by another person.

TABLE 7

Coding Symbols and Categories for Client Need-Responses

Symbol	Category	Symbol	Category
Anx	Anxiety	Dom n	Dominance need
Hos n	Hostility need	Dom p	Dominance pressure
Hos p	Hostility pressure	Aff n	Affiliation need
Dep	Dependency need	Aff p	Affiliation pressure
Ego	Ego need	Voc	Vocational concern
Nur	Nurturance need	Mob	Mobility concern
Sex n	Sex need	Phys	Physical concern
Sex p	Sex pressure		

We also classified the affect themes as plus or minus, depending upon whether or not the client perceived the need or pressure as being fulfilled or satisfied within himself, *i.e.,* tension-reducing versus tension-building. For example, the occurrence of an orgasm was always classified Sex n +, but the occurrence of a seductive overture could be classified Sex p + or Sex p —, depending upon whether the client found the overture gratifying or disturbing.

We also had a parallel classification of the affect themes which constituted descriptions of therapeutic activities which these affect themes also represented. These are given in Table 8.

TABLE 8

Coding Symbols and Categories for Client's Behavior in Therapy

Symbol	Category
Ins	Shows insight
Plans	Makes plans
Res	Shows resistance
Conf	Confirms an interpretation
Rel	Deals with the relationship
Ques	Asks a question
Drm	Reports a dream
Unc	Reveals unconscious material

These latter classifications (in Table 8) were supplementary to the client affect theme classifications and were reported only when they were apparent, *i.e.,* not in all cases.

The objects (or sources, in some cases) of the affect were classified into major and minor categories as listed in Table 9.

In addition to the above, in many client classifications an arrow was used to indicate a transition from one affect theme to another, usually perceived as being in a causal relationship. Some illustrative codes and their "translations," which make this system easier to understand, are given in Table 9a.

TABLE 9

Coding Symbols and Categories of Major and Minor Sources (or Objects) of Client Affect

MAJOR CATEGORIES		MINOR CATEGORIES	
Symbol	**Category**	**Symbol**	**Category**
self	the client	masc	client's masculinity
par	client's parents	enur	client's enuresis
fa	father	phys	adequacy or physique
auth	authority figure (other)	prof	professional adequacy
mo	mother	rival	admirer of spouse
sib	sister or brother	matur	client's maturity
wife	client's wife	intel	client's intelligence
peers	associates	child	client's child
ther	the therapist	nur. peo.	nurturant people in general
het	heterosexual love object	anim	animals of the client
homo	homosexual love object	relig	client's religion

TABLE 9a

Illustration of Method of Translating a Complex of Coding Symbols

Code	Translation
Sex p — homo → Anx — masc → Hos n + peers	Ungratified homosexual pressure upon the client from others leads to anxiety about the client's masculinity, which leads to openly expressed hostility toward the client's peers.
Hos p — fa → Hos n + ther, Res, (unc)	Unpleasant hostility pressure from the client's father leads to hostile feelings directed toward the therapist in the form of unconscious resistance.

The Interaction of the Therapist's Techniques,

the Topics Discussed by the Client,

and the Therapeutic Relationship

Some General Observations about the
Two Clients' Affect toward the
Therapist, and His toward Them

In general, both clients started out by displaying a moderate amount of positive affect toward the therapist (PAC-NAC score around 40) in the first tenth of their therapy. By the fourth tenth they had both achieved very positive affect scores toward him (around 80). Both clients then experienced some regression after this point, but they resumed their general trend of a slow rise in positive affect, so that in the last three tenths both were very high (above 95; see Chart 1).

The therapist started the cases with a moderate amount of positive affect toward the clients (PAT-NAT score around 40); he showed some general fluctuation throughout therapy (scores between 20 and 60); but in both cases the general trend was upward, ending near 80 for Quinn and near 60 for Jones. For Quinn, the fluctuation was more pronounced, with a marked lowering of positive affect around the seventh tenth of the therapy process, at a time when he was showing a great deal of resistance (see Chart 1).

For both clients there is a strong similarity between the amount of affect shown by the client and the amount shown by the therapist at a given point in therapy, as revealed in Table 10 and Chart 1. The Spearman rank order correlations and the DuMas correlations of profile similarity are all at least .77, and significant at the .01 level (see Table 10, part B). It is also indicated in Table 10 (part C) that the therapist was able to estimate the client's affect in each tenth of therapy well enough to produce a Spearman correlation of at least .60 (in the case of total PAC-NAC affect scores) which was significant at the .01 level.

The two clients were not very similar to each other in the trend of affect which they showed throughout the therapy process. Part A of Table

CHART 1

Both Clients' Affect Scores for Each Tenth of the Therapy Process

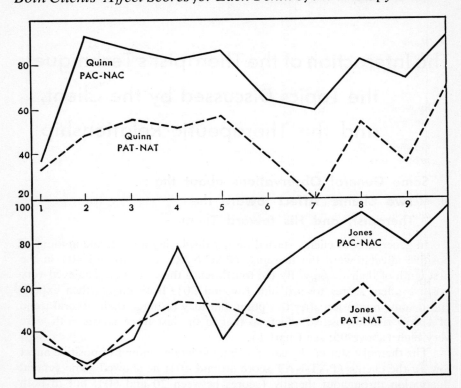

10 indicates that the Spearman correlations and the DuMas coefficients of profile similarity are significant in only one case. However, the rank orders of the Therapist Affect Scale scores correlated .63 $\pm$ .21, which is significant at the .05 level. The correlation of the two clients on the Client Affect Scale was of a zero order, and the DuMas coefficients were not significantly above chance. In other words, in any given tenth of therapy there was as much chance that the two clients were moving in a different direction with regard to affect as there was that they were moving in the same direction. This is true despite the fact that the over-all trend was toward an increment in positive affect.

The data in Table 10 can be interpreted to mean that the therapist felt consistently warm toward the clients, and increasingly so throughout the therapy, but that the two clients' affect toward him differed. The affect of Mr. Quinn was somewhat more positive than was that of Mr. Jones, although later in therapy their positions were reversed slightly. A possible

TABLE 10

Some Measures of Relationship between the Two Clients' Affect Scores

A. Rank Order Correlations and Coefficients of Profile Similarity between Quinn's and Jones' Scores on the Client Affect Scale and the Therapist Affect Scale (for the Ten Deciles of Therapy)

	Client Affect Scale	Therapist Affect Scale
Spearman rank order correlation (rho)	$.01 \pm .35$	$.63 \pm .21*$
DuMas' coefficient of profile similarity (r_{ps})	$-.33 \pm .33$	$.11 \pm .33$

B. Measures of Profile Similarity, or Correlations of Trends, *on Therapist's and Clients' Affect Scores* of Clients Quinn & Jones

	Quinn	Jones
Mean Client Affect Score	76.0	62.4
Mean Therapist Affect Score	48.4	46.5
Rho (Spearman)	$.77 \pm .14**$	$.78 \pm .14**$
r_{ps} (DuMas)	$.78 \pm .33**$	$.80 \pm .14**$

C. Correlations between Clients' and Therapist's Scores on the Client Affect Scale as Filled Out by the Two Clients and by the Therapist as He Thought the Clients Would Fill It Out

	Quinn	Jones
Client Positive Affect	$.47 \pm .19*$	$.40 \pm .20*$
Client Negative Affect	$.69 \pm .13**$	$.58 \pm .16**$
Total Client Affect	$.60 \pm .16**$	$.62 \pm .15**$

* Significant at the .05 level.
** Significant at the .01 level.

reason for this difference may be Quinn's strong succorance needs as contrasted with Jones' pattern of counter-dependence. This behavior constituted one of the most consistently observed characteristics of the relationships between the two men and the therapist.

Was There a Relationship between the Sort of Material Being Discussed by the Client and the Character of His Feelings toward the Therapist?

Answers to this question are found in Table 11. We correlated the Client Affect Scale scores with the scores obtained for responses classified under the categories labeled Anxiety, Hostility Need, Affiliation Need, Sex Need, Dependency, and Ego Satisfaction. Only one of the twelve correlations was significant: Jones obtained a correlation of .391 ± .204 between PAC-NAC scores and Affiliation Needs. This single, low correlation is not sufficient evidence to postulate a relationship between affect score and types of affect, or what we called affect-themes. However, the situation is more significant when we correlated affect scores with the amount of discussion of certain *sources* or *objects* of affect. Correlations were significant, or closely approached significance for both clients, when the discussion dealt with authority figures, mothers, and wives. The correlations were lower when the clients were discussing their fathers, the therapist, or their peers. The direction of the correlations indicates that Quinn felt negative affect toward the therapist when talking about his wife, while Jones felt negative affect toward the therapist when talking about authority figures and his mother.

Did the Use of Any Particular Therapist Technique Seem to Have an Important Effect on the Clients' Feelings toward the Therapist?

Tables 12 and 13 provide some answers to this question. When the client affect score, expressed after various interviews, was correlated with the predominance of different therapeutic techniques in those interviews, the technique of giving education and information (XEI) correlated significantly with positive affect for both clients. There was also a significant correlation with the tendency to attenuate an interpretation (XAT) in the case of Jones. A high correlation between the affect score and the giving of advice (XAV) in the case of Jones was possibly not reliable, since giving advice occurred in only six interviews. If we can draw a conclusion here, it is that the clients felt warmer to the therapist when he was using highly supportive techniques. This is certainly quite consistent with the evidence of rather strong dependency in both of these cases.

TABLE 11

Both Clients: Correlations between Scores on Client's Affect Scale and Certain Measures of Client's Principal Affect Themes and of Client's Source/Object of Affect Responses

	Quinn r PAC-NAC and:	**Jones r PAC-NAC and:**
Affect Themes	Anx $= -.171 \pm .114$	Anx $= -.115 \pm .238$
	Hos n $= .080 \pm .158$	Hos n $= -.126 \pm .238$
	Aff n $= -.164 \pm .117$	Aff n $= .391 \pm .204*$
	Sex n $= -.039 \pm .158$	Sex n $= -.115 \pm .238$
	Dep $= .105 \pm .158$	Dep $= -.138 \pm .236$
	Ego $= -.093 \pm .158$	Ego $= .020 \pm .241$

	Quinn r PAC-NAC and:	**Jones r PAC-NAC and:**
Source/ Object of Affect	Fa $= .263 \pm .149$	Fa $= -.098 \pm .239$
	Auth $= .566 \pm .109**$	Auth $= -.368 \pm .208*$
	Mo $= .382 \pm .127*$	Mo $= -.320 \pm .216†$
	Wife $= -.403 \pm .134*$	Wife $= .330 \pm .215†$
	Ther $= -.070 \pm .158$	Ther $= -.003 \pm .241$
	Peers $= -.299 \pm .147†$	Peers $= .010 \pm .241$

* Significant at .05 level.
** Significant at .01 level.
† Approaches significance at the .05 level.

Was There Any Tendency for Any Particular Therapist Technique Always to Be Used in Conjunction with Other Techniques; i.e., Was There a Therapeutic Pattern?

Tables 12 and 13 again provide some answers to this question. Out of 72 intercorrelations of techniques (36 for each of the two cases), seventeen were significant for Quinn, and eight (or possibly eleven) for Jones. But in studying the character of these correlations it is apparent that a more directive technique is as likely to correlate with a more reflective one as with a directive one. The conclusion may be drawn that for this therapist a balance of directive and reflective techniques seemed to be the most satisfactory approach to the therapy. For example, after the therapist had questioned a client he frequently reflected feelings; however, if reflection did not produce some insight on the part of the client, the therapist tended frequently to intervene with an interpretation or some other more directive procedure.

TABLE 12

Quinn: Correlations between Client's Affect Scores and Certain Therapist Techniques, and Intercorrelations between Rank Orders of Therapeutic Techniques

Therapeutic Techniques	Client's Affect Scores (PAC-NAC)	Therapeutic Techniques							
		XAT	XDQ	XCF	XRL	X Dir	X Sup	XEI	XAV
XIT	−.040 ±.212	.684** ±.063	.573** ±.085	.468** ±.105	.257 ±.147	.126 ±.175	.310* ±.137	.182 ±.162	.075 ±.184
XAT	.195 ±.188		.331* ±.134	.404* ±.118	.273 ±.143	.507** ±.098	.013 ±.192	.331* ±.134	.216 ±.156
XDQ	.180 ±.189			.420* ±.114	−.061 ±.211	.172 ±.164	−.088 ±.215	−.200 ±.238	−.100 ±.217
XCF	−.020 ±.208				−.242 ±.151	.387* ±.126	−.036 ±.225	.260 ±.147	.00 ±00
XRL	{.095 ±.190 / .243 ±.329@}					.322* ±.134	.702** ±.039	.504** ±.098	.132 ±.172
X Dir	.137 ±.181						.180 ±.163	.297* ±.139	.495** ±.101
X Sup	.076 ±.193							.474** ±.104	.074 ±.184
XEI	.300* ±.139								.496** ±.100
XAV #	.249 ±.183								—
X Lead-taking	−.180 ±.241								

@ When correlating only the eleven interviews in which XRL appeared.
* Correlations significant at the .05 level.
** Correlations significant at the .01 level.
# XAV occurs in only five interviews; it may not be valid.

TABLE 13

Jones: Correlations between Client's Affect Scores and Certain Therapist Techniques, and Intercorrelations between Rank Orders of These Therapeutic Techniques.

Therapeutic Techniques	Client's Affect Scores (PAC-NAC)	Therapeutic Techniques							
		XAT	XDQ	XCF	XRL	X Dir	X Sup	XEI	XAV
XIT	−.183 ± .231	.213 ± .230	−.427* ± .197	−.166 ± .234	.075 ± .239	−.341 # ± .213	.090 ± .239	−.077 ± .221	−.063 ± .240
XAT	.365* ± .209	—	−.647** ± .140	.132 ± .237	.174 ± .234	.020 ± .241	−.284 ± .221	.322 # ± .216	.383* ± .206
XDQ	−.030 ± .241		—	−.086 ± .239	−.415* ± .199	−.018 ± .241	−.040 ± .241	−.202 ± .231	.106 ± .238
XCF	.107 ± .238			—	−.161 ± .235	−.331 # ± .215	−.434* ± .195	−.287 ± .221	.458* ± .190
XRL	−.168 ± .234				—	.061 ± .240	−.329 # ± .215	−.039 ± .241	−.063 ± .240
X Dir	.054 ± .240					—	.241 ± .223	−.098 ± .239	.129 ± .237
X Sup	−.076 ± .240						—	.116 ± .238	−.016 ± .241
XEI	.600** ± .154							—	.489* ± .183
XAV	.554** @ ± .167								—
X Leading	−.142 ± .236								

* Correlations significant at the .05 level.
** Correlations significant at the .01 level.
@ Of questionable validity, since XAV occurred in only six interviews.
# Approaches significance at the .05 level.

31

Did Certain Client Behaviors in Therapy Cause the Therapist to Employ Specific Techniques?

Study of Tables 14 and 15 reveals that the answer to this question is affirmative. For both clients a high correlation indicated that when they discussed the therapy relationship, the therapist responded with a discussion of the same topic. With Quinn, the therapist also handled resistance and dependency with a discussion of the relationship, and in addition he dealt with resistance by means of interpretation. With Jones, anxiety was very frequently met with reassurance or other supportive procedures. Perhaps Jones' resistance was not as extensive as Quinn's, and he was more willing and able to face certain unpleasant facts and to try to do something about them. More interpretation was used with Quinn, but this was probably because Jones seemed quite adept at making interpretations, even when they related to rather unpleasant facts. Jones may have been carrying a greater load of anxiety, which would account for the increased use of reassurance when the anxiety occurred in his case. As might be expected, both clients revealed a negative relationship between their own resistance and their dependency feelings. (We are ignoring here the possibility that dependency might be a form of resistance.)

Some Discussion Relative to the Handling of Dependency in the Two Cases

Messrs. Quinn and Jones were the first and third most dependent of our twenty research clients as measured by our own dependency scale (see Table A-8). The mean dependency score of the group was 21.07; Quinn's score was 38.1, and Jones' score was 32.9. On the composite rankings which we computed for dependency (MMPI dependency scale score plus the dependency rankings of two psychologists who knew the cases well) they were first and sixth most dependent, respectively.

The general trend of dependency scores for our nine better clients is reported in Table A-9 and in Chart 2. Their range of mean scores for each tenth of the therapy was from approximately 25 to 33. There was not much variation, but a slight tendency toward an inverted U was apparent; *i.e.,* their dependency was highest near the middle of therapy, as might be anticipated. This trend was even more apparent in the cases of Quinn and Jones. Both started with scores around 32, rose in the middle of their therapy to around 45 and 40 respectively, and then dropped to

TABLE 14

Quinn: Correlations between Certain Therapist Techniques and Certain Client Behaviors, and Intercorrelations between Various Client Behaviors.

VARIOUS CLIENT BEHAVIORS

Therapist Techniques	y Anx	y Dep	y Res	y Rel	y Ins
XRL	.173 ± .155	.284* ± .147	.382** ± .135	.503** ± .119	
XIT	.045 ± .160	.032 ± .160	.457** ± .127		.071 ± .159
X Sup	−.026 ± .160	−.016 ± .160			
XCF		−.179 ± .155			
XAV		−.108 ± .156			

Client Behaviors					
y Res		−.179 ± .155			

* Signif. at approximately the .05 level.
** Signif. at approximately the .01 level.

TABLE 15

Jones: Correlations between Certain Therapist Techniques and Certain Client Behaviors, and Intercorrelations between Various Client Behaviors.

VARIOUS CLIENT BEHAVIORS

Therapist Techniques	y Anx	y Dep	y Res	y Rel	y Ins
XRL	−.111 ± .238	−.025 ± .241	.125 ± .207	.537** ± .172	−.105 ± .238
XIT	.111 ± .211	.227 ± .228	.121 ± .237	.164 ± .195	.080 ± .239
X Sup	.467* ± .188	.217 ± .230			
XCF		.216 ± .230			
XAV		−.130 ± .237			

Client Behaviors					
y Res		−.114 ± .238			

* Correlations significant at the .05 level.
** Correlations significant at the .01 level.

lower scores at the end of therapy—around 29 and 24 respectively (see Chart 2 and Table 16). Quinn's curve was a very smooth one; Jones' was smooth except for one drop in dependency around his eighth interview. It is evident that these two clients were exceptionally high in the amount of dependency they demonstrated and that their trends in dependency followed a curve somewhat similar in shape to the Gaussian distribution.

We think it is worth noting that the groups of nine better clients and eleven poorer clients in our research study did not overlap in the distribution of their mean dependency scores during the different interview segments of therapy. The over-all mean of the poorer clients was 15.34, which is significantly different from that of the better clients, 28.07. The poorer clients' mean dependency scores for each interview segment ranged

TABLE 16

Both Clients: Dependency Scores throughout Therapy
(Based on a Scale from the PAC-NAC)

INTERVIEW-BY-INTERVIEW SCORES			ROUNDED SCORES		
Interview	Quinn	Jones	Interviews	Quinn	Jones
1	33	27	1–3	31.7	34.3
2	30	37	4–6	34.0	35.3
3	32	39	7–9	38.0	31.7
4	32	33	10–12	41.7	40.0
5	34	34	13–15	43.0	35.7
6	36	39	16–18	44.7	26.3
7	36	33	19–21	40.7	24.0
8	36	33	22–24	37.3	
9	42	29	25–27	38.3	
10	38	47	28–29	29.0	
11	40	36*			
12	47	37			
13	45	43			
14	40*	31			
15	44	33			
16	46	27			
17	45	29			
18	43	23			
19	41	25			
20	43	23			
21	38				
22	37				
23	38				
24	37				
25	36				
26	34				
27	45				
28	32				
29	26				
Mean	38.14	32.90			

* A 3-month vacation followed Quinn's 14th interview, and Jones' 11th interview.

CHART 2

Both Clients' PAC-NAC Dependency Scale Scores throughout Therapy, and Also Those of the Groups of Nine "Better" Clients* and Eleven "Poorer" Clients. (Trends Are Rounded into Groups of Three Interviews.)

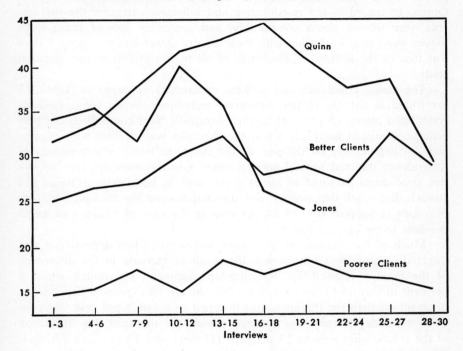

* The apparent rise in the scores of the "Better Clients" at the 25th to 27th interview is largely an artifact. It is due to the fact that by this point in therapy four of the nine better clients had dropped out of therapy and these were persons with somewhat lower dependency scores, and also because one client, Thomas Young, who was then only in the first third of his therapy, happened to have a marked elevation in dependency at that point. The curve of the group of "Better Clients" is probably not reliable after the 24th interview and might appropriately be disregarded beyond that point.

from approximately 15 to 19, as compared with the better clients' range from approximately 25 to 33. It is obvious that the clients who were considered "better" in our research project gave responses on an independent measure (their dependency attitudes expressed on a post-therapy questionnaire) that showed significantly more dependency than did the "poorer" clients.

How Did the Therapist Meet
Expressions of Dependency toward
Himself or toward Other Persons?

Answers to this question are revealed in Table 17. The therapist employed about twice as much of lead-taking procedures with Jones as with Quinn. In regard to the re-educative and reflective category, the two clients were treated about comparably, and somewhat less of these techniques were used in dealing with these clients' dependency responses than was true of the average of responses of all twenty clients in our research study.

The really consistent and striking differences apparent in Table 17 are found in the use of the supportive techniques. While these methods constituted about 15 per cent of this therapist's total counseling, the percentages changed markedly when the therapist was dealing with expressions of dependency on the part of the client. In terms of expressions of dependency directed *toward persons other than the therapist,* the supportive procedures *dropped* to about 8 per cent in both cases (Quinn and Jones). But when dependency was directed *toward the therapist,* the expressions of support *rose* to 34 per cent in the case of Quinn and to 25 per cent in the case of Jones.

Much of the increase in supportive techniques when dependency was directed toward the therapist was the result of increase in the discussion of the therapy relationship. Relationship discussion constituted about 8 per cent of therapist responses, but when the clients expressed dependency upon others than the therapist, this dropped to about 3 per cent. By contrast, when dependency was directed toward the therapist, the discussion of the relationship rose to 23 per cent (Quinn) and 13 per cent (Jones). When the therapist's supportive techniques increased, some other techniques had to decrease in the proportion of their use by the therapist. In general, this decrease was fairly evenly spread among techniques and not concentrated on any specific ones.

Our data suggest the interpretation that Quinn was by nature a more dependent person than Jones and moved toward an independent state less easily than did the latter client. (His therapy lasted half again as long, but the proportion of dependent responses per interview was no greater.) He defined his problem as one of finding persons toward whom to direct his dependency, while Jones obviously was more concerned with diminishing the dependent aspects of his personality. Similarly, Quinn's dependency was more pervasive and directed toward more persons than was Jones'.

The general character of the trends in the therapist's responses to the

TABLE 17

Percentages of Different Therapist Responses to Client Expressions of Dependency upon the Therapist and toward Other Persons in the Cases of Quinn and Jones; Also Total Frequencies of These Responses.

	Total Therapist Responses	Total Therapist's Responses to Client Dep. on Therapist		Total Therapist Responses to Client Dep. on Persons Other than Therapist	
	Quinn	Quinn	Jones	Quinn	Jones
Questioning	15.5%	11.8%	7.7%	9.2%	25.4%
Other Leading	4.5	2.8	16.7	6.9	5.0
Total Lead-taking	20.0	14.6	24.4	16.1	30.4
Clarification	14.2	9.1	20.3	15.5	22.1
Interpretation	17.9	13.0	13.6	15.8	20.4
Other Refl. & Re-educ.	22.3	15.8	8.5	10.8	4.4
Total Refl. & Re-educ.	54.4	37.9	42.4	42.3	46.9
Relationship	8.1	22.4	12.8	3.2	2.8
Reassurance	5.7	8.7	8.1	4.5	4.4
Other Supportive	1.4	2.8	3.9	0.8	1.1
Total Supportive	15.2	33.9	24.8	8.5	8.3
Redirective	9.5	5.1	1.5	9.0	4.4
None	—	8.7	6.6	24.2	9.9

Total Frequencies of Dependency Responses

	Quinn	Jones
Total Dependency Statements	529	394
Total "Dependency on Ther." Statements	177	215
Total "Dependency on Others" Statements	352	179

clients' expressions of dependency upon the therapist is shown in Chart 3. The percentages reported in this chart are not influenced by the number of client expressions of dependency in a given segment of the therapy. It is apparent that the tendency to respond with lead-taking types of responses decreases throughout the therapy in the cases of both clients. Redirective responses remain continuously at a very low level throughout the therapy. Supportive responses remain very consistent in the case of Jones, and somewhat so in that of Quinn. Reflective and re-educative responses tend to increase in both cases, but especially in that of Jones.

Reflective and re-educative responses constitute the largest number, approximately one third, and supportive and lead-taking each constitute around one fourth.

It seems apparent that this therapist's techniques with his two clients tended toward increasing supportiveness and reflective and re-educative procedures as therapy progressed. His tendency to lead and direct decreased concurrently. With Quinn, who made so many demands for support, the increase in supportiveness was more apparent; with Jones, who seemed to move rather easily into insightful types of thinking, the re-educative and reflective responses were the ones the therapist relied upon more heavily. Quinn's greater dependency, then, seemed to elicit a more supportive, less intellectual, therapeutic behavior from the therapist.

CHART 3

Trends in Therapist's Responses to Client Expressions of Dependency As Shown by Percentages *of Responses in a Given Segment of Therapy (Sixths or Fourths) for Each of Four Categories of Therapist Responses.**

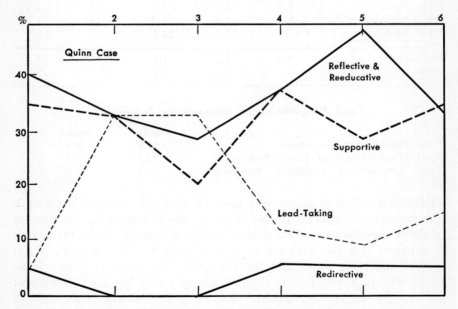

* These percentages are *not* influenced by the total number of client expressions of dependency *in a given segment.*

Chart 3 (Continued)

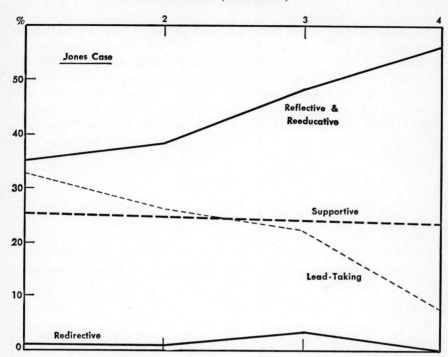

Part Two

THE CASE OF QUENTIN QUINN

Introduction

MR. QUENTIN QUINN [1] was a 22-year-old married graduate student whose problem was primarily one of general immaturity. His main complaint concerned flirting behavior by his wife; he was also bothered by some difficulty in working with maximal efficiency on his professional program, and he believed that the faculty held a low opinion of him. After therapy started, Mr. Quinn showed a great deal of dependency and a fairly strong positive transference toward the therapist. The son of a broken upper-class protestant home, he had experienced a lonely childhood, spending much of his life away from home, and in therapy he placed particular emphasis on his feeling of not having had a close or loving relationship with his father; much of his discussion dealt with this lack or was concerned with how he might find substitute fathers with whom he could build an affectionate, dependant relationship. On a number of occasions he expressed a wish to have homosexual relationships; occasionally these feelings were directed toward the therapist, but it always seemed to be affection, rather than sex, which he craved to share. He reported his wife as saying that she did not love him and found him physically unattractive. His attitude toward her was overly passive. He indicated that he wanted to preserve his marriage at any cost and that the idea of a divorce was totally unacceptable, primarily because of his memories of his own unhappy childhood.

The circumstances which led to Mr. Quinn's coming for therapy were as follows: During the previous semester he had been in a class taught by the therapist and had given the impression of being a bright person who was immature in his attitude and needed something to jolt him into a recognition that undergraduate behavior was not appropriate in the graduate school. After the semester the therapist,

1. Pseudomymns are used for each of the cases in this book, and identifying material has been altered or disguised. Permission was obtained from the clients for the publication of material pertaining to their cases. Brief mention of these cases appears in our previous book, *The Psychotherapy Relationship.*

as instructor, had given Mr. Quinn the lowest possible passing grade and had written him a report in the form of a letter, criticizing his undergraduate behavior, pointing out the attention-getting aspects of it, indicating that he was considered by the faculty to be "on the skids," and announcing that he had been placed on trial for the following semester. The effect was dramatic. The client's wife requested therapy both for herself and her husband. She indicated that she felt that she was responsible for the client's behavior because of their marital difficulties. She said that her husband would like to work with the instructor as his therapist, and she assumed that another therapist would be chosen for her, since she was aware that the therapist never worked with both parties of a couple. It was suggested that Mr. Quinn himself come in to indicate his feelings about the matter. This was done, and it was apparent that he had a sincere desire to obtain help. Arrangements were made for the therapy to take place.

In the cases of Mr. Quinn and his wife, therapy seemed to be relatively successful. The client matured considerably in attitude and took a much more aggressive attitude toward his wife, finally ordering her either to stop her objectionable behavior or to get out. This, along with her own therapy, had a beneficial effect, and she became much fonder of the client. They decided to have children. His professional work improved greatly, and he accepted positions of responsibility and performed very well in them. He gained insight into the fact that a true father-surrogate would never be available, and he lost much of his desire to find one, seeming to be able to meet his affectional needs through his roles as husband and father.

Throughout the period of therapy the client took several personality tests, and after each interview he filled out our Client Affect Scale; the therapist filled out the Therapist Affect Scale and also the Client Affect Scale in the way he believed the client had filled it out on the same day. The therapist also made certain ratings and rankings on the client at various times. These are reported in Table A-2.

Mr. Quinn was diagnosed as a person whose behavior manifested an immaturity reaction; he exhibited strong feelings of inferiority, some anxiety about homosexual thoughts, and evidence of a rather severe maladjustment in his marriage. On the MMPI his high scores were on uninhibitedness (Pd=77), sexual confusion (Mf=77), and ego strength (74) (Table A-3). On the MMPI, among the twenty clients he ranked seventh in the favorable quality of adjustment revealed. On the Edwards PPS (repeated after every fifth interview), he tended to score within normal range; his consistently highest scores were on succorance (61–70); he was consistently low on deference, order, and change (usually under 40). His greatest increases between early and later testings on the PPS were on dominance, heterosexuality, autonomy, and exhibitionism, in that order. His scores decreased most noticeably on affiliation, introception, change, and abasement, in that order (Table A-4).

In terms of affect expressed toward and by the therapist, Mr. Quinn ranked second highest of the twenty clients in positive affect and first in the therapist's positive affect toward clients. In terms of rankings made by the therapist after therapy, Mr. Quinn obtained top or next to top ranks on rapport, amount liked by therapist, dependency, and success of case, and he ranked lowest or next to lowest on hostility, guardedness, and estimate of maladjustment. In terms of post-therapy ratings by the therapist, Mr. Quinn was rated as friendly in affect, passive in controllingness, and open in self-disclosure; he was rated as well-liked in terms of the therapist's affect. When classified by the therapist on Leary's sixteen traits, he appeared to exhibit co-operativeness, conventionality, docility, and dependency (Tables A-2, A-5, and A-7).

On our factor analysis of clients with respect to their MMPI scores, Mr. Quinn's highest weighting (71) was in factor-group I, which contained the more uninhibited (Pd), manic, hysteric type of clients. He also had a weight of 51 in factor-group III, which comprised the more obsessive-compulsive and occasionally schizoid group.

On the factor analysis of the twenty clients with respect to their Edwards PPS scores, Mr. Quinn's only significant weight (84) was in factor-group II, in which the clients were characterized most typically by high scores on succorance and exhibitionism.

On our factor analysis of the Client's Affect Scale, Mr. Quinn had high positive weightings on factor-groups which were interpreted as comprising clients who were trusting, confident, hopeful, companionate, co-operative, relaxed, self-managing, and who viewed the therapist as a friend. He had negative weightings on the factor-groups which were interpreted as comprising clients who were uncomfortable, baffled, taciturn, restrained, and who felt misunderstood and disliked.

On our factor analysis of the Therapist's Affect Scale, Mr. Quinn had high positive weightings on factor-groups which were interpreted as comprising clients who were perceived by the therapist as being relaxed, self-confident, friendly, and open, and by whom the therapist felt appreciated; the therapist felt he understood the clients' problems and enjoyed conducting the therapy sessions with them. Mr. Quinn scored positively on one negative factor, i.e., he was among people who were perceived as wanting an audience, needing to be pushed, and tending to discuss irrelevancies. This perception occurred following the twelfth interview. Mr. Quinn had high *negative* weightings on the following negative factor characteristics: hostile, aggressive, narcissistic, uninsightful, resistant, unmotivated for therapy, unsystematic, unrealistic, distant, and as causing the therapist to feel puzzled, frustrated, uncertain, and resistant toward conducting the therapy interview. To summarize, we see that Mr. Quinn generally showed the attitudes of those clients who were friendly and positive toward the therapist and the therapy. He did not express signs of hostility, aggression, or other more overt forms of resistance and negative affect. Similarly, our factor analysis revealed that Mr. Quinn was perceived by the therapist as being a friendly person who was not especially aggressive or hostile, although during at least one period the therapist reported perceiving some signs of dependency and resistance on the part of Mr. Quinn. Test data on Mr. Quinn appear in the appendix.

On the PAC-NAC Dependency Scale, Mr. Quinn's scores ranged from 26 (in the last interview) to 47, with the mean at 38.14 (see Table 16). His mean dependency score on this scale ranked highest of our twenty research clients.

In order of decreasing frequency, the major sources or objects of Quinn's affect were as follows: his wife, therapist, father, peers, self, mother, masculinity, authority figures, and both parents jointly. The major affect-themes which Mr. Quinn expressed were hostility need, anxiety, affiliation need, ego satisfaction, dependency, sex need, and pressure of hostility from without. These have been covered more specifically in our discussion about each interview. Different types of responses by the therapist, in the order of predominance of occurrence, were lead-taking, interpretation, direct questions, clarification of feelings, redirective responses, giving education or information, discussing the relationship, restatement of content, and reassurance.

Quinn: First Interview (3/2)

IN THE FIRST INTERVIEW the therapist concentrated on allowing the client to tell his story. Mr. Quinn gave a picture of a rather dependent person who hoped that his wife would somehow arrive at the point of being able to show him the love she seemed unable to feel. He reported a pattern of passive concern with no ability to employ aggressive action toward interrupting the flirtatious activities of his wife. Although he felt much resentment about the "snow job" he received from her before his marriage, it was impossible for him to express his hostility in more than an occasional strong outburst of temper and physical aggression, which he then quickly inhibited because of deep feelings of guilt. He did not, in this interview, reveal clues as to the source of his rather strong inhibitions about showing aggression, although the therapist assumed that it was the result of some rather repressive training in childhood. Apparently because of his dependency, he allowed the fear of losing his wife to cause him not to take the usual actions to protect his marriage which might be expected in such a situation.

Even in this first interview, the dependency theme was revealed in the character of Mr. Quinn's relationship with his wife; he responded to her passively, restrained his hostility, and filled a much more domestic role than is characteristic of most husbands. Some dependency was also evident in his turning to his supervisor for some "abreactive" sessions when his difficulties at home became acute. His dependency score was 33 after this interview—near the lower end of his score range.

When the therapist challenged Mr. Quinn's defensiveness about the feminine character of some of his interests, the client revealed definite anxiety about the extent of his masculinity. The therapist did not give reassurance regarding this point, but he did compliment the client regarding his honesty and "hard work" in facing these unpleasant topics. In doing this, the therapist was attempting to start a relationship of trust on the part of the client.

47

In this interview almost all of the client's affect was directed toward his wife, and most of it took the form of suppressed hostility, anxiety, and expression of dependency needs. His affect toward the therapist was at its most negative level (−49), far below that expressed in any other interview. This might have been expected in view of the circumstances which had brought him to therapy. The therapist's affect score (23) was, for this client, also fairly low, being fourth from the lowest score during the therapy.

My wife and I are having difficulties in our marriage. She's not very satisfied with the marriage. She's been necking with another man. However, I haven't blown my stack with him because she asked me not to. (He apparently represses his hostility.) (Dep — wife)

I'm more concerned about *our* relationship than about hers with someone else. Their relationship had dissipated, but then three weeks ago she started another one with a different man. I feel there must be some provocation for this. I asked her to stop seeing him, but she's gone ahead with it. She expects me to get extremely mad, and I do, but I contain it because it is my personal belief that I can do a lot more to help her if I don't blow up. (Repression of hostility may be a life style for this client.) (Hos n — gen)

It's more therapeutic to accept this, even though inside I'm hurt. (Dep — wife) She tells me she wishes sometimes I'd just give her a boot out of the house. (Is his wife expressing guilt, or encouraging aggression?) But we've always found in the past that my acceptance of what I felt was wrong made her feel a lot better, made her feel wanted. But I blew up and gave her a healthy swat across the face. (Apparently he has occasional uncontrollable outbursts of hostility.) She said she thought I did it because she was "asking for it." Actually, I was honestly mad. Then she taunted me about her possibly going farther with this guy, and I suspect that perhaps they may want to. I was disgusted with her. (Hos n + wife)

At the time we were married she gave me a "snow job." I thought she was honestly in love with me at that time, but I realized differently much later. When she told me this, I just went wild; I just started vibrating. (He is under much tension.) (Hos p — wife) After it happened I talked to my supervisor about it, but our conference was just an abreaction and not anything therapeutic. (Dep + auth)

My wife feels guilt, but it's only because she has hurt me, not because she has done something wrong. Maybe the material is too repulsive to her to admit consciously that she feels it's wrong. She says she really married me only because my family had some money. Also, she could not see me hurt by breaking up our engagement at the end of a year. My family has always considered me flighty (Why?), and she wanted to protect me from their criticism, if we broke up. That doesn't seem like enough reason to get married. I think she felt she could talk to me and I wouldn't condemn her. I don't know whether she felt love, or respect, or what, but there must have been something. (Dom p — → Dep n + wife)

I felt disgust and then hate for her, because she had hurt me so much. She said she was the one who started the relationship. Then I hated her boy friend more than her. Probably that was to defend myself. (Hos n + wife; Anx) I wanted to do something about it, but she made me promise not to, and I agreed, because I want to give her the best sort of relationship possible. (Dep + wife) I don't want our marriage to fail. He's still trying to make her. They've been dating during the day, when I'm at school.

Now, recently, she feels that all other men are out of her life, but although she's sincere at the time, her resolution gradually fades off. Although she considers me a good husband, she has this compulsion to flirt with other men. (Aff n — → Anx n — wife)

(Therapist reflected his feelings of hurt and anger; clarification. Asked about further feelings; nondirective lead.)

I felt intense rage, and this is atypical of me. Usually I repress it, or at most I verbalize it rather mildly. (Some self-insight is revealed here.)

What does she see in this other guy? [1] (Question)

If I were a Freudian, I would see an unresolved Oedipal complex on her part. She always loved to hop into bed and cuddle with her father, even shortly before we were married. And she hates her mother. These fellows she liked were *older* guys. Initially she talked with them about her marriage problems. Once she got hurt by being rejected by a guy she'd gone with for three years, so she decided to see how many guys she could make fall in love with her. I was the 92nd or 93rd, I think, and there were 106 altogether. And even after we were engaged there were two or three more. (This compulsively seductive behavior on the part of the wife suggests much insecurity.)

I think she sees me as just a fixture around the house. In her better moods I think she sees me as a companion, and as the guy who does things for her and loves her. We have always had extremely good sexual relations. Our climaxes have occurred at the same time for the most part. Although I notice that sometimes I feel, a day or so afterwards, that it just isn't quite what I want it to be. The more honest she has been with me, the more I have enjoyed the relations. I can sense it when she's holding back things that will hurt me. (Sex n + wife → Ego + masc)

But there's still something lacking; it's the feeling that she is not all mine. Sometimes I'm just a convenience; I drive well, and clean the house. I like to cook. I always make the bed, and usually I wash the dishes, but

---

1. All therapist responses are italicized.

she dries them. She's rather sloppy. That is a cause of some of our discussions. I'm neat. Even if she's next to a closet, she'll drop her clothes on the floor. This bothers me. (It is significant that this young husband participates more than most in household, and more feminine, activities; does this reveal a tendency toward reversal of sex role?)

You seem a little defensive about the housework you do. (Interpretation$_5$)

Well, it's a 51–49 per cent marriage; we help each other, and that's where I can help her most. I can't help her too much with her studies. I sorta' enjoy helping, although I'll admit it's not the normal sort of activity for a husband.

Why did you think I was making something of this? (Question)

I don't know, unless I felt you were asking pretty penetrating questions, which would reveal information that might be a reflection on my masculinity. (Good insight) I don't personally feel that I am particularly feminine, but . . .

You're afraid that I might think so. (Clarification)

Maybe. (Dep + ther)

How does your wife feel about it? (Question)

Well, it's sort of the expected thing, except when she's feeling generous and then she criticizes herself for letting me do so much work. Sometimes it's kind of a battle. She likes to rest and smoke after dinner, and I like to get to the dishes right away before all the food dries on them and makes them twice as hard to wash. The place looks a mess if you get one thing out of line. (The client sounds somewhat compulsive about neatness.) I feel embarrassed if people come in and see the place messed up.

I had meant, how does she feel about your masculinity. Not about your helping with the housework. (Question)

Sexually she thinks of me as very adequate. She acts very immaturely around me; she talks her own private language, a sort of baby talk. I ask her to stop it, but she goes on with it. Sometimes it makes me act or talk in a childish manner, and that makes me disgusted with myself. She may see me as immature, but not as unmasculine. And when I was able to accept her behavior about other guys she felt that I wasn't immature at all.

Sometimes in college if I did something that wasn't a "man's man" way of doing it, and somebody'd poke fun at it, I might feel a little bit anxious about my masculinity. (This sounds like a sensitive area for him.) But I feel quite satisfied that I am the way I am. (Anx — ther)

You've covered quite a bit today, and you're approaching it with a good bit of willingness to think objectively and straightforwardly. (Reassurance)

M-hm. I think first I'll be talking about my wife, and then I want to talk about some of those feelings of lack of comfort in social situations and my immature actions. (Dep + ther) You brought me up short with that report you wrote about my work in your class, and I took a good look at myself, and I now handle social situations better than I did; right now the marriage situation is bothering me more than the other thing.

Quinn: Second Interview (3/9)

IN THE SECOND INTERVIEW the client directed his discussion toward three principal objects: his father, his parents in general, and his peers during his school days. The principal forms of his affect expression were general anxiety, expressions of affiliative needs, and some dependency needs. His affect score toward the therapist (53) jumped by 100 points, coming up to a little below the mean for him. The affect score of the therapist (35) revealed that the latter was still somewhat guarded in his feeling toward the client.

The client spent most of the interview "filling in" on biographical matters, with the principal theme being the intense loneliness he had experienced throughout his life because of the divorce of his parents, and the subsequent circumstance of his spending most of his life out of the home. He brought in a new theme, his feeling of being somewhat rejected by some of his peers because of his physique. The psychosexual implications of his slightly endomorphic body build were not explored at this time.

During the second interview the therapist used predominantly lead-taking procedures, attempting to draw out as much conscious significant material as possible. He used mostly questions directed toward exploring certain information. A mild interpretation that the client might have repressed his feelings about his mother and a single attempt to challenge the client's passive acceptance of his wife's behavior were the only re-educative techniques employed.

Some of the client's dynamics, other than his life style of loneliness, also were revealed in this interview. At one point he admitted readily to having rather strong dependency needs which caused him to feel somewhat jealous of his wife's mothering behavior toward their puppies, but he suppressed his resultant hostility. Later on he reported the misery he experiences when his wife is cold or rejecting toward him. Perhaps most important is the report of his relationship with his parents: his father was perceived as stern and disciplinary, but later he displayed more nurturant behavior toward the son, who then began to question his mother's somewhat biased critical evaluation of the father. From his mother he received affection, but only that of a rather emotionally inhibited person who was never able to give him enough of the security and nurturance that he required; this he received mostly from the maid, in the period of early childhood. Later in his childhood he obtained small but insufficient amounts from peers and parents.

In the case notes, the therapist reported that the client left his pipe and tobacco in the therapy room after the session, a possible sign of positive regard. The therapist also noted having a strong feeling of protectiveness and sympathy toward the client. This was a complete change from his earlier experience of annoyance with the client in his class for the apparent frivolous, superficial, play-boy behavior which Mr. Quinn had displayed there.

The elements conducive to a supportive-dependent relationship are evident in their incipient state in this interview. Many signs are present of a dependent, affection-starved client who is seeking a father-surrogate upon whom to lean for support and affection. Rapid transference and possible countertransference can be anticipated. The dependency score of 30 was quite low for this client, however.

I don't feel well this morning. I notice that although I thought of things during the week, this morning I can't think what to talk about. (Resistance) The home situation right now is pretty good. My wife has not been having as much difficulty restraining herself. But she has been feeling somewhat depressed.

I am jealous of our puppies. My wife calls them her children, and that's the way she treats them. I have certain dependency needs myself (important self-insight), which I like to have gratified. When she cuddles a puppy for the whole evening, I sit there and stew. (Dep — wife) She knows how I feel about that, too. I find myself treating them like people also. Sometimes I'll cuss them out in a displacement of aggression. (Hos n + anim) Sometimes I ask her whether she's trying to please the dogs or to annoy me. (This client is rather psychologically sophisticated.)

Suddenly the other night she started crying and saying that she was so unhappy, and a bad wife, and so on. Her childish behavior gets me down. Perhaps I see myself reflected in it. (Insight)

You're distressed with yourself for being annoyed with her. (Clarification) *What did she mean when she said she was a bad wife?* (Question)

The fact that she couldn't love me enough; she wasn't distressed about meeting these other guys.

Does she feel any guilt? (Question)

Not for what she's done, but if she considers hurting me, I think she does. She would like me to provide her with a rationalization for the behavior, but I'm not willing to do that, because I think it would lead to a complacency on her part. If I act critical, she's cold and icy, and I feel miserable; I can't stand that; I feel lonely and unloved. (The client is very insecure when he feels rejected.)

A lot of that traces back, I think, to the fact that my parents themselves were divorced. My mother is now separated from her second husband. (Dep — par → Anx) So I just won't allow our marriage to break up. If there were children it would be even worse; I can remember how I felt at the time of the divorce. I felt pretty much alone.

I wasn't shaken up at first. I thought we were just going away on a vacation. When mother said they were getting divorced I didn't know what that meant. I hadn't known my father at all well before then. My only real relationship with him was that, when he'd come home from work, if I'd been bad he'd give me a few swats. It was a negative thing, to put it mildly. (Dom p — fa) (This is the first important reference to the father-son relationship.) I was very, very much afraid of him. I'm not afraid of him now (Is this true?), but I was then. (Anx — fa) When mother told us about the divorce, I was only nine, but I got the idea that now I was the man of the family and I should bear up under this, so I didn't cry. I didn't miss my father.

Then I was sent to a very strict private school; from then on I went to many different schools, and I've always felt it was a convenient means of getting me out of the way. (Anx — Par) (Feelings of rejection) Dad would visit me every couple of weeks at the first school; boy, I was lonely there! It was so darn strict; any little infraction and you got beaten with a piece of brake lining. I can remember feeling completely lost. The kids weren't much help. I can still feel miserable just thinking about it. I guess I missed the maid the most, she was my closest family member. (This positive feeling toward the maid suggests important dynamics.) (Dep — mo surrog)

Dad would visit me, and he started treating me as a man and let me make many of my own decisions. Whenever he left, I'd feel all miserable again. (Dep — fa) My one tie to the family had left me. But I began to see him as a human being. (Aff n + fa) I realized that he wasn't as bad as mother had made him out. He could be a mighty nice guy at times, although he could chastize me on vacations, too. (The client came to reject his mother's negative biases toward his father; there were positive feelings.)

Finally I began to work into the school life, and I began to achieve some leadership. Although I'd always hated to fight, I actually learned to box, and was elected dorm captain, and our dorm would win the prize of a cake every month for being the neatest. The second year I won the prize as best student of the year. And I won the music prize and was made captain of the baseball team. I felt lonely, then, but accepted by my peers. (Aff n + peers)

Then mother came home, and she'd visit me too. Then she took me out of that school and brought me home. I went to another school as a day student and lived at home. I enjoyed this school much better, but I felt very *un*consulted about the change. They pushed me ahead a year, so although I was ahead of the kids intellectually, I was way behind them socially. One big guy picked on me because I said "Sir" to the teachers. I got proficiency medals and did well in sports, and most of the kids liked me. I think the military setup represented security, even though it was strict. But you knew exactly what to expect, whereas I couldn't count on the family. (Dep + gen) (Here is evidence of some basic dependency which is satisfied by a consistent regimen, even though strict.)

After three years in that school the family thought I was becoming a behavior problem, so they shipped me off to Blank Academy. I didn't even get consulted about it. I had built up a very strong friendship with a buddy (Aff n + peers), and I felt terrible about leaving. I had never been in a social situation of this calibre, and by this time I was two years younger than most of my classmates. I was still only a kid, and they were young men.

They always pick someone for a scapegoat at that age, and I was somewhat overweight. So my most admired master made the mistake of calling me "Fatso," and the guys picked it up, and from then on, that was my name. That was terribly disturbing. I wasn't close to anybody at first. (Aff n — peers) Finally I built up a friendship with a guy who had all the skills and accomplishments that I seemed to lack. But it was a vacillating relationship; I felt close to him, but I wasn't sure that he felt close to me. Sometimes he'd do things behind my back that would hurt. (His efforts to find acceptance were apparently not frequently gratified.) (Dep + peers)

After I graduated, a friend of mine went with me on a bike trip. We blew hog-wild; I ran my own life. Then I went to a college which I had selected. I felt happy there. But I had been pretty scarred, by that time, as far as lack of self-confidence is concerned. I think lack of self-confidence is the reason I act immaturely at times (Ego — self), which is what you criticized me for in your class. (Dep + gen) (This reveals some fairly significant self-insight.)

(Therapist reflected the pain of the many experiences of deep loneliness, and the client's having related this to his inability to tolerate hostility or rejection from his wife; clarification.)

I have always been my mother's favorite over my sister. (Aff n + mo) Even now she's always turning to me for advice. She's always been dependent on me, ever since the divorce. (Nur + mo)

Why did she agree to have you go away to school (Question); *does it bother you to think about that?* (Question)

I really don't know. I guess she didn't think she could take care of us. They sent my sister away to school, also.

How did she feel about your being away from home? (Question)

I can't remember her saying goodby to me. I'm sure she must have been quite tearful about it, though. I've forgotten about it.

Or repressed? (Interpretation₅)

I don't know.

How did you feel about leaving her? (Question)

I felt bad about leaving that area, but I'm not sure that I felt bad about leaving *her*. I hadn't been close to either of my parents.

Why hadn't you been close to her? (Question)

She never let me. She was a sort of cautious person about showing you any affection, like my father. Their way of being warm was to give you a big stack of presents at Christmas. The maid was the *warm* person. (Dep + mo surrog)

You'd do anything to protect a child of yours from that sort of loneliness. (Direct lead)

Yes, and I firmly believe, without rationalizing, that our relationship can work out.

You said earlier that it was best that you not be hostile with your wife, if you are to make the relationship work. Are you sure? (Challenging)

I'm not sure, no.

We'll have to work on that. (Direct lead)

I think so. Maybe there would be positive results from fighting back. But I'm scared of the results if they were negative, so I avoid the fighting. It's more difficult to decide, because we *both* have inadequacies. (Dep + wife)

Quinn: Third Interview (3/16)

MOST OF THE third interview was devoted to the client's discussion of his sexual development. This discussion evolved from concern he felt over recent compulsive homosexual urges he had been experiencing. He recounted events of a fairly active sex life, which in its early phases had been exclusively homosexual but which in late adolescence had turned largely to heterosexual activities, with occasional homosexual encounters interrupting during periods of rather deep loneliness. The client made the observation that his homosexual interest had been strong only when heterosexual activities were not possible, as in the various boarding schools he attended, and at times when he was very lonely. He indicated that he always preferred heterosexual activities when they were possible and that he felt that it was the companionship rather than the sex that he usually sought. He indicated his belief that his inclinations were predominantly heterosexual rather than homosexual. He believed that his present homosexual interest resulted from his deprivation in the area of heterosexual activities and his strong present loneliness. He indicated, also, that extramarital activity was something he could not condone, particularly if it were heterosexual.

The therapist employed a lot of clarification of feeling (35 per cent) in this interview, and a fair amount of lead-taking (20 per cent) and interpretation (20 per cent). He also spent some time (9 per cent) reassuring the client by agreeing with him that he considered the client's sexual development to be more heterosexual than homosexual.

This third interview again showed the rather strong amount of dependency of which this client was capable. One of the more significant dynamics in his case was also revealed in the large number of times he reported himself to have been seduced; rarely did he admit to being the person to take the initiative in the sexual act. This suggested to the therapist that the client tended to respond passively rather than aggressively in his interaction with other people, particularly in the sexual sphere, and this again bore out the nature of his dependency.

After the interview the client's affect score toward the therapist rose slightly (62), as did that of the therapist (40). Rapport was improving, although not especially rapidly. During the interview the client spoke about his "tremendous need for closeness." This, together with the frequency of his allowing himself to be "seduced" by other males, reveals his marked dependency and his tendency to respond passively toward others. The therapist gave a good bit of reassurance during the interview, a procedure which probably utilized the client's dependency needs, in order to develop the therapeutic relationship. The therapist was quite sincere when he indicated his belief that this client was probably predominantly heterosexual. While Mr. Quinn revealed much homosexual behavior in his psychosexual development, the evidence suggested that his later behavior was more definitely of the heterosexual sort and that he turned to homosexual interests primarily when the heterosexual were not easily available. Nevertheless, we could not say that this client was not a fairly passive person in his sexual life, as well as in other aspects. It is probable that the therapist was correct in reasoning that his general "life-style" was somewhat passive and that he would react in this manner in the therapy situation. The relationship would be built most easily if this principle was kept in mind. However, the dependency score of 32 indicates that the client was not yet ready to admit his dependency needs very overtly.

I'm noticing the same difficulty remembering things I want to talk about. This must be some form of resistance. Perhaps I'm not quite at ease in the situation. My wife had an abreaction again, after her counseling session. She said that our relationship had never been satisfactory; she went so far as to say that even in our intercourse she has only wanted to complete it a couple of times. (Hos p — → Anx — wife) She said she didn't usually love me, and I felt pretty miserable. (Dep — wife)

I guess I was expecting too much of sex. Perhaps she has gone through the same thing that I have, where sex is just something that lets off physical pressure and isn't too deeply satisfying. But still it was a real blow to be presented with this. (Sex n — wife)

(Therapist reflected the feeling) then said, *What did you do about it?* (There is a hint of suggestion in this direct question.)

Accepted it. This time, when she had finished getting it out of her system, she felt better, as she usually does, and she expressed a desire for intercourse then. This time I had decided that I was not going to be at her beck and call. (Hos p — → Sex n — wife) So I said "I'm not subject to orders on this." (The client reveals some ability to show passive resistance.)

Her immediate reaction was "I'm glad." I don't know what she meant by this. She's told her therapist that she has always been able to control her partners in relationships; perhaps she was able to do it too much, and she looks down on people that she can control. Maybe she was more appreciative of me when I refused her, because it showed I had more spunk. (Insight) (Ego + wife)

(Therapist restated), then asked, *Were you just a little surprised with that?* (Question)

Yup! I expected her to try and coax me. The predominant feeling was that of being hurt, though. She had told me numerous times, previously, that she didn't believe anyone could give her the sexual satisfaction that I had, because I was quite patient with her. (Sex n + wife)

I thought I had some insight during the week in the area of my childhood situation, but I can't remember what it was. I think this constitutes some sort of resistance.

One other thing that I would like to bring out this morning. I have no doubt that you were chasing after this in the first interview, in a sense, and at that time it was too threatening to divulge. Now I feel that it is important because it's bothering me a great deal. This is regarding some homosexual experiences that I had during my adolescence. I left this out of last week's biography, too.

When I was at the military school, about eleven to thirteen years old, I had never had any experiences with girls. I didn't know what sex was all about at that time. Anyway I had a friend staying over at my house, and we were taking a shower together, and it was perfectly innocent on my part, he seduced me (denies responsibility), not so that we had a homosexual relationship, but so that he taught me how to masturbate. (Dep + peers → Sex p + homo) I can remember I was very ashamed and unsatisfied with the whole thing. Anyway, at military school I had one other homosexual contact with a friend who stayed overnight at my house. And again this was not really a mutual thing, it was masturbation of ourselves, only in the company of one another. (Sex p + homo)

Then I went to prep school, and I had started to go out with girls, but I didn't know what girls were for. They had a ban on anything to do with girls. Even if you were only caught talking to a girl, you were subject to being bounced out of school. I was at puberty and the drive was starting and I needed some place to let it out. Then I was, I don't like to use the word, "seduced," because I think of it in male-female terms (Is this a threatening self insight?); again I had a homosexual relationship with a guy there. (Dep + peers → Sex p + homo) And I can remember being very dissatisfied with the whole thing. I had complete disgust for it. But I continued it during one year of the three years there. Then after that I just didn't bother with it. I stayed pretty much with self-masturbation.

At college I had two other experiences with a guy who happened to pick me up (seduced again) in the movies, and it was pretty much of an impersonal thing. I didn't like what I was doing. I've noticed this morning that each one of these times that I've had homosexual relationships, it's been when I have felt very much alone. (Dep — gen → Sex n + homo) (He achieves an important insight here.) And female companionship at the time was impossible. At college there were no girls that I went out with that I knew I could get anything out of. All of these experiences seemed to come when I needed companionship, and the only companionship I could get was with males. (Dep — peers → Sex n + homo)

The thing that ties this up with the present is the fact that I have noticed in myself that I have been thinking more about homosexual relationship, again, and I think it is probably very definitely correlated with the dissatisfactions coming from my marriage. These dependency needs I have are not being satisfied. (Dep — wife → Sex n — homo) (Again admits dependency needs.) I have noted it to be increasing in the past few weeks. I still don't think I *will* take any active moves to go find a homosexual partner, because I don't think it would be at all satisfying. (This might be an unconscious homosexual overture to the therapist.)

But the bothersome thing is the fact that I have been having these fantasies. I don't think that I am an invert by nature, who is trying to be bisexual; I think it's definitely a product of this tremendous need for closeness, which I never got in the family, and which I'm not getting now. (Dep — gen → Sex n — homo) (Insight) I know at the beginning of our marriage I had *no* thoughts whatsoever about homosexuality. It didn't enter my mind. But now, I have been thinking more homsexual thoughts. This bothers me, because I don't accept it as being an ideal adjustment. (Sex n — homo) (Reveals some ambivalence about sexual adjustment.)

Why does need of companionship have to take the sexual area? (Dep — gen → Sex n — het) I guess in my feeling, the sexual act is about the most intimate thing that two people can do together. Companionship is wonderful, but sex really draws people together. So that has been bothering me, apparently. Perhaps by having told *you,* I can exercise more brakes on myself. (Dep + ther)

You're distressed by this sort of compulsion toward some other male (Clarification); *you have a fear of it or a disgust for it* (Clarification), *and you hope that telling me about it might make it possible for you to control it a little more.* (Clarification)

Hearing how someone else relates to it would let things settle in my mind a little bit better, I guess. (Dep + ther)

It would give you some catharsis, and also some ego-reinforcement. That is, that you might have to confess it to me, if you did give in to it (Interpretation₇), *and you'd feel a sense of shame about having to tell me.*

(Clarification) *I would in a sense fortify your desire not to do it by providing you with some external inhibition.* (Interpretation₇) *The sense of shame that you'd feel you would have to go through would be enough to help you prevent yourself from doing it.* (Clarification)

Yea, that's probably so. I would like to. (Dep + ther)

A little bit like not having to confess a sin to somebody who might be less accepting of you if he knew about it. (Clarification)

Um-hm. It is threatening to me to tell you these things because I don't know how you would react. I know as a counselor you would accept it, but I don't know how you would react outside of this room. (Dep + ther, Rel → Anx)

Let's review what happened. You were very lonely as a child. You were forced into a strictly homosexual environment almost continuously, with no affection or companionship, or very little that you could receive anywhere else, and a certain amount of it you were offered from boys. (Restatement) *You did, then, the perfectly natural thing of getting involved and being friendly with them, and also the perfectly natural thing of a little sexual exploration, which is entirely understandable. It happens to a great many people. If girls had been around, it probably would have occurred with girls.* (Reassurance) *You make the important point that you were seduced.* (Restatement) *I think this is the most important word in the whole thing. All along the line, you used the word "seduced."* (Interpretation₈) *Then this continued, and it even happened a little bit in college.* (Restatement) *Now how do I feel about it? If that matters, I don't think there's anything wrong about it; it's quite natural, quite understandable.* (Reassurance) *Now the thing that you're more worried about is that you now find some compulsion to engage in some kind of homosexual relationship.* (Clarification) *You recognize also that you're lonely. This has been one form of alleviation of loneliness, or one thing you turned to when you were lonely.* (Clarification) *But you are angry or annoyed with yourself that you could turn this way, because it isn't consistent with your ideal of yourself.* (Clarification) *Your self-image is, well, as a matter of fact you don't even see yourself as a homosexual trying to act like he's bisexual, you see yourself as a person, I think, who's primarily heterosexual, but shows some homosexual tendencies, like many people do.* (Clarification) *And that these are more severe when you're lonely.* (Interpretation₄)

I think another thing that enters into it, too, as I believe I expressed before, I cannot conceive of how anyone can break up a marriage—how anyone can have relations with someone else's wife, or for that matter cheat on his own wife, even with a single girl. That is definitely not in my self-concept. I couldn't do it. So if in looking for this companionship, if I could I might turn to girls; it would definitely be an unmarried one, a younger one. I would always have the idea that I wouldn't want to ruin anyone else's marriage. But for some reason, to me this seems more like cheating on a marriage than a homosexual relationship, even though I think the homosexual relationship would probably be less acceptable to my wife. (He considers heterosexual infidelity more serious than homosexual; this suggests a preference for the latter.) (Sex n — het → Sex n + homo)

Let's see if we can see why that's true. This is a fairly common feeling. (Reassurance) (Then therapist repeats client's last two or three sentences: restatement) *Can you think of why it would seem less like cheating?*

I don't know unless, well, because it's less socially accepted. Society says you don't have affairs with other women when you're married. Society also says you don't have homosexual relationships, but society doesn't talk as much about homosexual relationships. So perhaps that's why I have chosen that, because it was gratifying to me back in the times when I needed someone. (Some insight here) (Dep + peers → Sex n + homo)

It was satisfying, then. You got some affection that way then. Some affection that you could count on. (Clarification) *And now you've been conditioned with regard to your relations with girls. You've gotten affection from them.* (Interpretation$_8$)

I don't quite understand you.

Maybe what I'm saying is threatening. (Interpretation$_9$) *Have you gone through any experiences which would condition you to feel that by turning to girls for a sexual affair you would get any love and affection?* (Question)

Yes I have. After I left prep school, I took this bike trip. And here was my first chance to be on my own and do what I wanted to do. And the first night I was in New York, I headed for Times Square where there were supposed to be hundreds of prostitutes. And I just took off with a bird-dive. I was going to become a man! And this initial contact was just perfectly disgusting. It was just awful! I was so disgusted, disillusioned, and unsatisfied, that even though I had reached a climax I went back to the hotel and masturbated. (This seems like an obvious rationalization of masturbation or of the actual sexual stimulation he received by going to the prostitute.) I was in New York about three weeks, and I had no desire to go back to Times Square. I thought there must be something wrong, because people wouldn't write all these things glorifying sex so highly, if that was all there was to it. (Sex n — het)

Then I went up to New Haven and dated a girl who was an acquaintance of a friend of mine. She was an older girl, and she knew what was coming off, and this was my first real experience with a girl whom I had even kissed. Then we went on our bike trip, and I didn't have intercourse with any of the girls. I can remember being sort of afraid, I didn't know how to go about having intercourse with a girl who wasn't a prostitute.

So I just necked and petted. So I got no real satisfaction out of these relationships. (Sex n — het)

Then I went to college in the fall, and they were college girls, and for the most part pretty high morals. I got satisfaction out of the companionship, but no particular sexual satisfaction. Then that following summer I went to Mexico with a guy who'd just graduated, and one night I was dragging a guy and his wife around town, and he picked up for me a girl who was making sandwiches at one of the bars. I was pretty far gone at this point; I'd had a lot to drink, and he said to come into his bedroom which was behind the restaurant, and, I'm blocking here, here was another homosexual relationship that I hadn't expected. I was completely powerless to do too much about it (seduced again). (Dom + peers → Dep + peers) I was asking him for instructions on how one went about having intercourse with a girl, and unfortunately he demonstrated, and I was completely disgusted. (Dep — peers → Sex p + homo) Anyway I took this girl out on the back road, and I had intercourse with her, and I was still so crocked that I didn't know what I was doing. It was quite satisfying at the time of the climax, and that cost me twenty bucks. (Sex n + het) She wasn't a prostitute, but she did have an illegitimate child to support.

Back at college I continued to have relationships with girls. Although I was looking for more sex than I was getting, I wasn't really working at it. And I enjoyed my dates very much with girls. During my junior summer I took a job as a cook in a restaurant. Cooking had always been a hobby of mine. (Client gives much circumstantial material about the details of this job.) Anyway one of the people who came to our restaurant was a waitress from another restaurant; and she was a pretty good-looking kid, and she was the most forward creature I've ever come across. We went to her house, and she takes off her clothes and says "Come on." (Seduced!) And we had intercourse five times during the night! Although satisfying physically, I had no real attraction for the girl. (Sex + het)

Then I started going with this other waitress who had an illegitimate child, one of the cutest children I've ever come across. I had a relationship with her for the rest of the summer, but I think it was mainly because of this kid; I felt very sorry for her. At any rate this girl allowed me to have sexual intercourse with her. I use the word "allow," because she claimed that she had never allowed anyone to do it before, that she had been raped. I feel that was pretty much of a lie, but she said, "See what I'm doing for you. That shows you how much I love you." Well, I sorta' let my feelings run away with me, and physical passon took over, and I began to think perhaps I was falling in love with her. And so we had intercourse every couple of weeks during the summer. (Sex n + het) At the end of the summer I left, and I kept getting reports that she was making out with just about anybody that would sleep with her. I visited her later, and I just told her "That's all babe, you've had it." I didn't miss her at all, although I missed the little girl; I was very attached to *her.*

During my senior year there weren't any sexual relationships at all, although I went out a lot more than I did before. I was looking for a more permanent relationship, perhaps. Then along came my wife. I had intercourse with her, and this was the first time that I'd been completely satisfied in a relationship. (Sex n + wife) I didn't love her as deeply as I do now, but it was still very satisfying, because there was an expression of positive feeling and not just a physical outlet. So I guess my relationships with girls have been kind of unsatisfying. If they were satisfying from a sexual point of view, they weren't satisfying from the point of view of companionship, and vice versa. How this compares with the homosexual relationships I'm not quite sure. They were satisfying physically, but not mentally.

You felt that you were getting satisfaction from companionship or affection with them, though. (Clarification)

Yes, I did. Not in the two at college, but I did at prep school. They were friends of mine, all of them. (Dep + peers → Sex n + homo)

So actually they were deep friendships; satisfying to the very deep need for companionship and affection and understanding. (Interpretation$_5$)

That's right.

But with the girls, the only one who was satisfying, really, was your wife. (Clarification)

And also, as long as I was getting companionship even to the degree just of normal dating, I didn't consider homosexual relationships. I had no need for it. (Aff n + het)

As long as you could get any affection and companionship in heterosexual situations, you didn't have this need at all. (Clarification)

That's right.

Is your feeling that you wanta be loved by somebody; is that it, would you say? (Clarification)

I think to a great extent, yes. (Client sighs audibly.) (Dep — gen)

And you don't feel that you're getting that, now. (Clarification)

That's right. Sometimes I feel actually disliked. (Hos p — wife)

When she talks the way she did last Wednesday, you must have felt very rejected. (Clarification)

That's right.

She's the only girl that you've ever dated a lot. And so when she tells you that she doesn't love you . . . (Interpretation$_4$)

She's not the only girl that ever really gave me love. For some reason I left out one other relationship. Probably because I feel a great deal of guilt about it. It was with a girl of a different religion. We were very much attracted to each other. (Aff n + het) I felt guilty because I kept trying to have deeper sexual relations with her. (Reveals active heterosexual aggression here.) I even wanted to have intercourse with her, but her religious training was in conflict with the things I would want her to do. Finally I broke it off on those grounds, even though I was interested in other religions. That's something I'd like to square away too. Boy, that was a mixed up period of my life! She wrote this terrible letter to me, actually it was perfectly deserved, saying, "What kind of a guy was I?" I'd gotten satisfaction out of this relationship, but not to the depth that I've gotten it from my wife.

That's why I feel so rejected when she says things like this, because I've thought there was so much depth to it, and I know it could be. (Dep — wife) (Sighs deeply.) We have so many things in common. I'm sure my wife *had* satisfied all my needs for a time. She's the only one, and I did quite a bit of looking around. (Sighs.) (Dep + wife)

I have about five minutes of twelve. What do you make of what we've said today? Can you draw any conclusions? (Directive lead)

Well, I think that the general information from your experience that you have given me on the question of the homosexuality has reinforced what I was thinking and probably hoped would be true. (Dep + ther, Rel) I know, I can admit that I was worried that, actually, homosexuality might be a more basic thing in my personality, deeper than just a situational thing. (He shows some anxiety about his masculinity.) I didn't think so, but perhaps you might conclude, "Well, this guy is just rationalizing, he really is a homosexual," and well . . . (laughs, with embarrassment). I'd be prepared to argue with you till doomsday, probably. (Dep + ther) But with regard to whether homosexual versus heterosexual relationships have been satisfying, to a very large extent, the homosexual ones were satisfying at a point where I needed something, and when I could get something else they dropped in importance. (Aff n — → Sex n + homo) I may think about homosexual relationships, but I don't think I'll *do* anything about it. There's too much to jeopardize by acting on such urges. (Is he expressing a hope rather than a conviction, here?) (Dep — gen → Sex n + homo)

Yes, at this point it would be better, wouldn't it, not to take any action, until you were pretty certain about what is the right action. (Persuasion; the therapist is proscribing any irrevocable actions affecting the client's life situation until therapy is completed.)

I'm convinced that the relationship would just be a pretty poor substitute for what I want, and I think I can hold myself in check until our relationship straightens out. It's just these Wednesday night blows that drop me down. (Dep — wife → Anx)

That would be extremely threatening and depressing, to have that happen. (Clarification) *As a matter of fact I had the feeling that your affect wasn't as strong as could be justified in such a situation, but I also felt that you were not giving full vent to your affect, or not abreacting in the sense that you were really feeling about it.* (Interpretation)

That's another thing that I'd like to go into, the fact that I can't, in front of other people, express what I really feel. Probably it ties into the fact that it was never done in my home life.

You were sort of conditioned to repress your feelings and not to show them. (Restatement)

That's right. Not necessarily repress them, just don't show them.

Well, I'm very much in agreement with your observations about the situation. (Reassurance) *I think we'll have to come back to the question of some of the compulsion toward homosexual ideas, to see whether there is further meaning or whether there are further elements that should be understood.* (Directive lead) *I also think that if you put yourself on a scale of just how much of your drive is homosexual, and how much is hetero-sexual, you'd find yourself on the heterosexual end of the continuum some-where.* (Reassurance) (Pause) *I guess our time's up for today.*

Quinn: Fourth Interview (3/22)

IN THIS INTERVIEW the client divided his time fairly equally among discussion of authority figures (his adviser), peers, his feelings toward the therapist, and professional concerns. Anxiety was his principal type of expression, and dependency was evidenced somewhat. Ego needs and academic concerns occupied much of his thinking; his fears about his academic adequacy were quite intense.

The therapist's activities were principally interpretation (26 per cent), lead-taking (21 per cent), giving information (16 per cent), and reassurance (9 per cent). As in the previous interview, there was a slight rise in client affect toward the therapist to a score of 88, but there was no change in that of the therapist toward the client (41).

Therapeutically, this interview was not a highly productive one, being oriented as it was mostly along lines of academic problems. This may have been an indication of some resistance, or just a reactive response to an increase in situational pressures which tended to preoccupy the client.

Several developments during this interview indicated increasing dependency upon the therapist. At the beginning, the client reported that all of his homosexual compulsions had disappeared, probably as a result of the reassurance about his sexuality which the therapist had given during the previous interview. Later he reported his feeling that his internship supervisors had acted like big brothers, while his adviser had been cold and distant, and that he had felt reassured during the previous semester when the therapist had told him he was capable of better performance than he had been giving. At the end of the interview he expressed appreciation for the advice the therapist had given, stating that he was grateful to the therapist for having shown "this much interest in me," something which had rarely happened in other situations. In this interview the therapist was quite supportive, giving a great deal of reassurance, advice, information, and even persuasion. However the client's dependency score was still remaining rather fixed (32).

I'm having quite a bit of academic trouble; I flunked two exams, and I'm waiting to hear the results of the third.

All homosexual compulsive thoughts have disappeared since our last interview; maybe it's just the effect of your reinforcing my own ideas; (Dep + ther) (Insight?) also, everything is going very well at home. My wife has been very affectionate. (Sex n + het)

I don't know whether to discuss situations as they arise or to try to discuss main issues. What do you think? (Here he reveals his characteristic dependency.) (Dep + ther)

(Therapist encourages talking about whatever seems most important to client.) (Nondirective lead)

I want to discuss what seems to be flippancy on my part, when actually I'm under social stress. I will kid around with a professor with whom I feel safe, and it may seem as though I'm being disrespectful. If the professor accepts it, it shows other people that I am accepted by him. (This may be a rationalization for repressed hostility; he may also be revealing unconscious transference in this idea.) (Anx — auth)

I don't trust my ability around here. At the hospital where I interned, the supervisors acted like big brothers. (Dep + auth) (Dependency need revealed here.) Around here I don't know where I stand. If I flunk this third exam, my whole career here might be in jeopardy. You reinforced my insecurity when you told me last semester in your class that I wasn't doing what I was capable of doing, and I knew it was true. (Dep + ther)

I've been working a great deal more since you said that. But I'm worried, because I feel I'm very much on trial around here this semester. (Anx — prof)

(Therapist reassured him that a third failure would not be too critical. He indicated that he had noticed that the client was working quite hard this semester. He also reflected the client's anxiety.) (Reassurance)

Also, I'm worried about getting my thesis out this semester. I can't understand what my adviser wants me to show, and he seems to have strong ideas about it. And I have two very difficult courses this semester. This morning I learned that I would have to repeat the two exams. It looks like nothing but 48-hour days can get me through this semester. (Anx — prof)

Can you focus your insecurities toward specific people? (Directive lead)

Yes, three in particular. First there is my adviser; I can't figure out his attitudes. At times he's very friendly and at other times he seems very cold and distant. I just try to stay out of his way as much as possible, but I'm afraid he'll blackball me anyway.

Then there's the department head. He seems very austere to me, I don't know why. Maybe he just represents *the* big power around here. And then there's his secretary; she's always shaken me up, for some reason. Perhaps because she keeps delivering these unpleasant messages. (Anx — auth)

Sometimes I actually believe I'm dumb, although I know I can produce when I'm motivated. (Reveals deep insecurity)

Do you think it's true that you are really dumb? (Challenge)

No, I know I'm not, because of the work I can do when I'm really motivated.

How bright do you think you are? (Question)

Well, I took a test in school and had an IQ between 130 and 140. I ended up on the Dean's list for the last two years in college, even though I almost flunked out my first year. In the first year I was bored with my courses, and I accepted too many invitations to goof off at the tavern and the bowling alley. (Ego + intel)

How do you react to these people who seem threatening? (Question)

Quietly. I don't do any of that kidding with them. I say "Yes, sir; No sir." (Dep — auth)

I wondered whether you might tend to avoid them? (Interpretation$_7$)

Oh, definitely. If I meet them I feel nervous. I don't walk away, but I'd just as soon not have the encounter take place.

I always have disliked being in groups. I say silly things just to fill up the silence. I think it goes back to prep school days, where I never got away from being called "Fatso." (Anx — peers)

How does the youngest kid in a class act when he feels insecure all the time? (Interpretation$_5$)

This youngest kid? I don't know, I never really looked at it that way.

Well sometimes they keep real quiet. And sometimes they put on a show. They feel some acceptance in the role, if they amuse people. (Interpretation$_8$)

(Therapist tells about a little boy in a group of adults who couldn't get their attention in any way except by jabbering silly, nonsense phrases.) (Interpretation$_8$)

That sounds like *my* "little brother." (Insight; client laughs; he has no brothers.)

Regarding these three people whom you feel afraid of and avoid, I wonder if there might be a possibility of a kind of straight-forward deliberate approach toward them, rather than trying to escape from them? (Advice)

Well I'm afraid to approach my adviser until I have something concrete to give. (Dep — auth)

Which do you think would make a better impression on him? If he catches you in the hall and presses you about your progress, and you admit you haven't done anything, or if you were to go to him at his office and say, "So far I haven't accomplished much, but I've been extremely busy with the courses I'm taking, and I'm not quite sure what direction we ought to be taking with this thesis." (Advice)

Well, definitely the latter. But when I go to him and ask a question, he seems to think I'm pretty dumb. Sometimes I think he isn't very clear in his own mind about what he wants done. But I think the *positive* approach is by far the best. (Anx — auth)

You see, the difference is between an approach which accepts responsibility but admits that you haven't had a chance to carry it all out yet, and an approach which seems to be trying to escape responsibility, even though you're still being held responsible. (Gives information, but also is somewhat persuasive.)

That's right. I think I do a lot of avoiding of responsibilities.

You see, he may have taken the attitude that I did, that you were goofing off. (Information) *But he's a clinician, and, if he perceives your behavior as motivated by the right sort of motives, he is likely to judge your behavior as clinically understandable rather than academically reprehensible.* (Information) *Maybe all of us have had a lack of understanding of all the factors that have been operating in your case.* (Reassurance) *I don't mean you should tell everyone that you're in trouble and need help, but we may all have been seeing you as immature, or unmotivated, or not caring, when you really do care. Well, I sound like an adviser, today.* (Advice)

No, I appreciate your telling me, because nobody has ever shown that much interest before, except one psychology professor in college. (Dep + ther, Rel)

Quinn: Fifth Interview (3/30)

MUCH OF the fifth interview was taken up with the expression of concern about academic progress, or with the directing of dependency needs toward the therapist or the client's father. There were a fair number of gratified affiliant needs directed toward his wife, with whom the marital relationship had improved considerably. The therapist directed much of his effort toward giving information (18 per cent), and discussing the relationship (18 per cent); there was also a large amount of interpretation (18 per cent) and of reassurance (24 per cent).

The client's affect score toward the therapist (97) rose markedly, making this interview his second most favorable one; the therapist's affect score toward the client rose a little, causing it to reach approximately its mean level.

In this interview the client's dependency toward the therapist began to become rather pronounced, and he started the process of asking the therapist for extra-therapy assistance in his academic affairs. The therapist handled the situation rather cautiously, agreeing to help if necessary, but not without first discussing the possible deleterious effect such help might have on the therapeutic relationship. Mr. Quinn attributed his need for support to the lack of a sufficient amount of such support from his father when he was young. The therapist was endeavoring to build a good relationship with this client and recognized the intensity of Quinn's dependency needs, but he wanted to make a clear discrimination between temporary therapeutic support and general parental support. In this interview Mr. Quinn's PAC-NAC dependency score rose just a little.

It's been quite a week for disappointments. I failed the third exam. But I did go out of my way to get an appointment with my adviser. I know the frontal approach is the best, now, instead of all this goofing around trying to get in the back door. I'm most worried about what the faculty think of me. (Anx — prof)

I told the department head I just want this semester to show what I can do. He didn't commit himself, of course. I would certainly like some reassurance (laughs in an embarrassed manner). (Dep + ther) I'll be on internship full-time this summer.

I feel badly about my performance here so far. I just hope the staff doesn't feel as badly as I do. (Pause) Can you give me some reassurance about it? (Embarrassed laugh) I mean without committing yourself. (Here the dependency needs are apparent again.) (Dep + ther)

It doesn't do much good for me to commit myself, because I have only one vote. (Withholding; the therapist is avoiding the giving of reassurance for reasons which he states below.)

Is it that bad?

Well, as someone hinted to you, there was some real questioning at the last evaluation meeting. What you probably need is some fairly strong support by some of the members. (Information) *The group will take special factors into consideration; in those circumstances they're the softest bunch in the world.* (Information) (Pause) *I could give support as your therapist, if I felt free to use the information, but I don't feel it's legitimate to do that.* (Withholding)

But you, of all the faculty, know me the best. You're in the best position to judge whether I'm sincere. I know you can't violate therapy, but . . . (Dep + ther)

Well I don't have to violate confidences, but I can convey the feeling that there is a reason to give some special consideration, without conveying the reasons. (Offers help) *I would be willing to make that effort in your behalf, and I will do so, because I am convinced that it's appropriate,* (Offers help) *but what I'm concerned about is what this does to our relationship in therapy. Does this make you feel obligated to me, and also perhaps obliged to keep me feeling that you are sincerely trying?* (Relationship) *That's why, when a student is in therapy with me, I try to stay out of those departmental decisions about him. If 25 professors can't make the decision based on performance, it's not my business to give them confidential information, which would contaminate the therapy relationship.* (Relationship) *I'm concerned about the effect on our relationship of your feeling that you have some obligation. Also, could you still speak freely, even if your feeling was that you really didn't give a damn about psychology? I would want you to be able to do so, just as though I weren't a member of the faculty.* (Relationship; here the therapist agreed to give some assistance but not without taking the precaution of discussing its possible adverse effect on the therapy relationship.)

Well, I think I have always been as honest with myself as I could be. And I'd want to be just as honest with you. If I didn't like psychology, I'd do better to leave right away.

Things are going much better at home. My wife's been everything a wife should be. As long as I know she's pulling on my side, I think I'll move ahead without any difficulty. (Dep + wife) I think her therapy is helping her. It's going much better now, except that my compulsive cleanliness is not being gratified quite as much as I'd like. But she's been very attentive and helpful.

I haven't done any woodworking for several months, I've been so busy studying. And we hardly even go to the movies, now.

In therapy, my wife decided that her reason for being so childish is because when we were first married I treated her like a child, making all her decisions for her, and so forth. I hotly denied it, but it may have been true at one time. I probably was pretty possessive and didn't give her a chance to develop a wifely role around the place. She wasn't a good cook, and I was pretty fair at it. *Now,* the kitchen is her province, and I ask to cook one night a week, but just because I enjoy it. (Dom n + wife)

I was making all her decisions for her. But now I let her make all the decisions on food, and so on, and her behavior has changed a lot.

Why do you have a strong need to seek approval in love? (Question)

Maybe because I don't think I've done well enough. I think it's just a *natural* thing to want approval in love. (Dep + gen) Do you mean why do I want it more than most?

Yes.

'Cause I didn't get it when I was younger. (Dep — par → Dep + gen) Let's see, I should be able to connect these two, now. (Laughs; pause.) I'm really blocking, because I can't think about it.

Well, you're getting tense about the fact that you're blocking. (Reassurance) *There might be two possible explanations. The one would be because it had always been the source of great reward for a person, but the other would be when the person felt he never got enough of this behavior as a child.* (Interpretation$_8$)

My wife has been pretty concerned that her father may have had thoughts of incest, which is something that I have wondered about. (Elaborated in much detail.) I don't know why I've gone off on a tangent this way. Is this obfuscation? (Dep + ther)

(Therapist reassures him that the material has not been irrelevant to the question of the marriage adjustment.) (Reassurance)

I think I have to demonstrate to her that I am able to see things from her side, then it will be better. (Aff n + wife)

My father is visiting this week, and we're glad to have him, but it makes us both feel nervous. He has been awfully good to us since we've been married. I feel like a dirty dog, because I treat him sort of offhand. (Dep + fa → Hos + fa → Anx) I just don't know how to relate in any other way with him. He's not warm, but he's good. I've never been able to tell him any of my difficulties. (Dep — fa → Anx) (Although the client has guilt in feeling critical of his father, he is forced to recognize that the latter has not met his dependency needs in a satisfactory manner.)

Quinn: Sixth Interview (4/6)

APPROXIMATELY four-fifths of the discussion of this interview was about the client's feelings for his father; the rest was about a father-surrogate in the person of a somewhat older peer with whom he had developed a dependent relationship. About one-third of the feelings were related to affiliant needs or presses, one-quarter to dependency needs, and one-sixth to the feeling of being the victim of hostility. Perhaps this marked focusing of feelings about his father was a natural sequence to the father's having paid him a visit over the previous weekend, but his attention to this topic cannot be attributed merely to this incident, since the amount of time devoted to the father throughout the *entire* therapy process (one-sixth) was second only to the amount devoted to discussion of his wife (one-fifth) and about equal to the time spent in discussing the relationship with the therapist. It seems entirely safe to say that the matter of the client's relationship to his father was his second most important problem; his main concern in this matter was his father's inability to gratify the client's dependency needs. The latter kept searching for a father-son relationship; his interaction with the older "buddy" (restaurant owner) appears to have been simply an extension of the same need.

Early in the interview Mr. Quinn reported a very significant dream in which he had been about to have intercourse with his wife (before marriage) and his father had interrupted the situation, butchering the wife's body and wrapping it in small bloody packages. Mr. Quinn interpreted the dream in terms of his father's trying to direct his affairs, particularly the dating relationships; he missed any implications of possible Oedipal or castration anxieties apparent in the dream. He perceived his father as an authority figure and a source of financial support. But this was not the father he wished to have; he preferred a relationship with a beneficent, warm, guiding and advising, "big brother" sort of father. This is the sort of relationship he had attempted to build with the restaurant owner with whom he formed a partnership, but the latter, for reasons of financial irresponsibility or character dis-

order, was a severe disappointment to Mr. Quinn. However, he still
hoped to establish some such relationship with his father, although he
recognized, somewhat wistfully, its improbability.

The therapist made some mild attempts to turn this fantasy in a
more realistic direction, or at least to indicate the improbability of its
accomplishment.

The discussion of the client's father gave a very clear picture of the
sort of relationship which Mr. Quinn would probably hope to establish
in therapy. Any alert therapist would have recognized the implications
for therapy of his numerous longings for paternal support and affection.
The therapist was prepared to capitalize on this dependency need and
to provide something of the missing relationship, as a temporary, therapeutic expedient. As a matter of fact, Mr. Quinn's needs fed directly
into this therapist's basic supportive, warm, advising methods. The
therapist recognized that a problem would likely arise later in therapy
when it became necessary to wean Quinn away from this dependency
without destroying the basically favorable elements of the relationship.
One positive aspect of the situation was the fact that Mr. Quinn rejected
in theory the idea of being dependent, calling dependency a "dirty
word" in his vocabulary. Thus, although he expressed many strongly
dependent needs, he was conscious of the undesirability of such a need
pattern being too evident in an adult male. He rationalized that his
dependency needs were greater than normal because of the insufficiency
of their satisfaction in his youth, but he was aware of the appropriate
adult attitude in this regard, and therefore it seemed likely that he
would prove somewhat amenable to encouragement from the therapist
in the direction of independence, after he had achieved more insight
into the character of his need systems, and their sources. His PAC-
NAC dependency score rose a little, again (36), but had not yet
reached his mean.

During the sixth interview the therapist employed mostly the
methods of lead-taking (24 per cent), primarily in the form of direct
questioning (18 per cent), and restatement of content (21 per cent).
The client's affect toward the therapist remained very high (97) in
this interview; that of the therapist toward the client (56) increased
over the previous interview.

I thought I should explore the relationship with my father; it certainly
bothers me, because of the lack of closeness. (Dep — fa) I thought of a
dream I had last year which probably typifies the way I perceived him, in

symbolic form. In the dream I was playing cards with some guys, and some girl was there and beckoned to me, and we went in the back room and were making love, and just as I was starting to have intercourse with her I noticed that she was my wife. This may have suggested some guilt about having had intercourse with my wife before we were married. Then in the dream I had to go out of the apartment, and the guys were still in the living room, so I went out, and when I came back I had a feeling that something terrible had happened. The whole place had changed, and my father was there, and there were some packages lined up in butcher's paper that had something red seeping out of them. They were still warm, and I knew that he had cut up my wife! When I woke up I was pretty worried (laughs nervously), but then I decided that perhaps the dream stood for his having tried to slow down our relationship, or cut it off completely. Probably it went deeper than that even, in that I may have thought he was trying to destroy everything that I loved. (The Oedipal and castrative implications of this dream seem quite obvious.) (Hos p — → Anx — fa; Drm)

His relationship to me, regarding the girls I was going with, was one in which he considered me to be pretty flighty. And he tried to throw some minor monkey wrenches in the way, never very successfully. The dream was a representation of our relationship. It was me against him, whenever I could get any affection from any other people. (Hos p — fa)

(Therapist reflected the client's hostility and feeling of being thwarted.) (Clarification)

I don't think he was consciously hostile, but I'm sure he was unconsciously. He may just have been looking out for my best interests and thinking that perhaps I was more swayed by the heart than by the head. Both of my parents thought I was flighty. They came from the old school, where two dates meant you were engaged. Actually I didn't go out with more than fifty girls, and I wasn't serious about more than five or ten.

This whole relationship had been strained to say the least. When I was only four years old, he was sort of like a playmate with me then. I remember him helping me dig holes in a beach. Also he rode me on his shoulders on a bicycle. (Dep + fa) Then the next memories I have of him are when I was five or six, and I guess I was considered to be a rather wild kid, and they used to tie me up out in the yard, so I wouldn't take off with my friends. This memory still bothers me. Sometimes I'd get lunch and sometimes I wouldn't. I was mortified. I didn't have much bladder control, so it would reach a point where I would have to urinate, or else wet my pants, out in the middle of everywhere. That's probably the worst memory I have of my early childhood. I was horribly embarrassed, because it went against all my toilet training. (Why should this situation remain a major traumatic memory for the client? Is it associated with some guilt feeling?) (Hos p — fa)

I'd never see Dad until dinner time, and then if I had been a bad boy it was my father's duty to spank me when he came home. Occasionally my mother did, but not usually. If there was something at dinner that I didn't like, I had to sit at the table until I ate it, and so I saw my father as being rather stern at this time. I was very afraid of him; he has a stern appearance. (Hos p — fa)

One time before Sunday School I called my sister a swine, and they punished me by keeping me home from Sunday School, which hurt me very much. After my parents were divorced, I was able to like Dad a little better when he came to the school to see me. (Dep + fa) However, I was still afraid of him, and I still am, in a sense.

Even when I was sixteen or seventeen years old, when I'd be home on vacations I had to be in by ten o'clock, which I thought was impossibly early. But he'd stay up till I came in around twelve. He never bawled me out, but I knew he didn't like it.

When I was in college, he still seemed to want to control things. When I took the bike trip and the trip to Mexico, he checked surreptitiously on the guys I was going with, even though he said I could go. When I got my first A in college, he only said, "Well, you've shown you can do it, now I expect every mark to be an A." (Dep + fa)

The next summer I got a job. I didn't want to hurt either parent by going to stay with them and then leaving to spend the rest of the vacation with the other one. This friend invited me to start a restaurant with him, so I worked like a dog, twenty hours a day. This guy didn't have any money, and the bill collectors were pounding on the door daily. We were ready to close, so I went home and tried to borrow money from Dad, (Dep + fa) and he said it was a lousy business deal and he wouldn't lend me the money. Well, for the first time in my life I cried in front of him. (Dep + fa) I thought of this guy I was working with as a big brother, (Dep + fa surrog; theme of dependency on a "big brother") I said I was going to borrow 500 bucks from somebody else if I had to. (Dep + fa) So he saw I was in a pretty sad state at that point, and he said he'd loan me the five hundred on a pay-on-demand note, and he'd expect me to pay it off. Well, the 500 bucks was gone in a day, 'cause this guy was close to 10,000 bucks in the hole. Actually the restaurant was doing fine, with a businessmen and college student clientele, but we were still behind financially.

Anyway, Dad never pressured me for the money particularly, although he always let me know that I was going to pay it back. I had never collected any wages, I had something like $1400 due me, including the $500 that my father had loaned me. Well, I knew the guy was strapped, so I said I'd take a one-year note for a thousand. Well, Dad had told me that money and friends don't mix, and after that summer my relationship was never the same with that guy. Anyway he always has a hard-luck story, and I've only gotten about a hundred bucks out of him. I'm completely disappointed in him as a person. (Dep — fa surrog)

But Dad has not hounded *me* for the money. He just lets me know how much I still owe him. I have never been able to get out from behind that eight-ball. My wife says "Since he gives us money often, why don't you just ask him to cancel the debt, instead of giving us money." But I can't *see* that. I feel it's a debt of honor. If I didn't pay it, he'd be disappointed in me. I've paid several hundred dollars against the account. (The client's struggle to establish his independence is apparent.)

My relationship with my father has been, for the last few years, on a monetary basis. He's been the one that paid the bills. (Dep + fa) I didn't earn much of my keep, although before I came here I worked in a factory to earn money.

In my senior year, I went through a period where I felt a very great need to be close to my family. I'd gone through what I called a "religious renaissance" type of thing. I wrote them warm, confiding letters. (Dep + par) My mother responded very nicely and said she hoped I'd be able to keep coming to her and saying what I wanted to say. I got a letter from my father which was kind of humorous; I think I had embarrassed him. He just can't relate to people this way. (Dep — fa)

Only at one time has he ever really opened up to me, and he told me why he left my mother, and who the other woman was. I think he was a little bit sorry that he'd done that, because he had lost face by doing so. That was the one time where he confided in me, and we've never talked about it since. He'll tell me about how much money he makes but nothing really personal. I've kidded him a lot about his girl friends, and so on. (Aff n + fa)

He's been very lonely for the last year and a half. (Client shows sympathy for his father, in addition to the hostility.) His cousin lived with him till then, but she died. But she wasn't really providing any companionship, because she was an invalid. I felt close to him at this time, 'cause I knew what trouble he was having. He called me up to tell me about it sometimes. (Nur + fa)

I wanted to be close to him, but I felt I'd been rebuffed when I tried, and I just couldn't take the risk again. We talk, but I can't tell him either my victories or my defeats. (Dep — fa)

In childhood he was the source of discipline, and then in your adolescent period he was the source of money and to some extent discipline, but not as much so, because you weren't at home as much. And now there's a distant relationship. (Restatement) *There have been efforts to get close to him, but he's been unable to respond or to reciprocate. You see his psychological needs, but when you've made overtures, he's been aloof.* (Restatement) *So*

*although you'd like to have a close, understanding relationship with him,
you actually feel quite a bit of distance.* (Clarification)

That's right. I know he loves me very much, but he just can't show it,
except financially. He gives me big presents. Before he was leaving last
Sunday he gave me a hundred dollars, and I said I didn't want it. But I
could see he was getting very hurt if I didn't take it. That was his way of
saying "Here, Son, I'm trying to help you, relate to you, and so on." And
so I *took* the money. (Dep + fa) I really didn't want to, but I knew if I
refused he'd be very hurt by that. At one time he thought I'd do just about
anything for money, so he can't understand it when I object to taking money
now. He's surprised by the change. I guess he thinks maybe I've gotten a
little responsibility and a little pride, now. (Ego + self)

*You know that he loves you. The thing he hasn't been able to give you
is affection, is that it?* (Restatement)

That's right.

He can give you checks, and you're pretty sure he loves you. (Clarification)

I know he does, but he can't say it. And I can't say it back, either.

Do you love him, do you think? (Question; the therapist is testing the
limits of the client's positive feelings for his father.)

I'm *sure* I do. I *know* I do, but I can't say it.

*You'd like very much to feel close to him, and yet, when you're around
him you sort of freeze up, in a way, is that it?* (Clarification)

That's right. But I just don't think he can relate to anybody particularly
closely. Which is a tremendous shame, because I know he wants to. But I
don't know why he can't get it out. Maybe his family was the same way, too.
(Aff n — fa)

*You're sort of implying an emotional impoverishment on his part, aren't
you, and you're saying that maybe he never had any love, so it was impossible
for him to be able to give it.* (Restatement)

It may be something that I just have to accept. I don't want to, because
I think one can get an awful lot out of a father-son relationship. (Dep + fa)
I still don't think it's too late, but I don't really know what he'd do if I
really approached him again and said something. It might just embarrass
him. (Aff n — fa)

You said something very significant. (Calls attention) *That in your first
early memories of him he had played with you and helped you build forts
in the sand, or something like that.* (Interpretation$_8$) *And that's the only
time you reported this.* (Calls attention)

That's right. That's the only time it happened. Maybe that's it. I know
that *once* I had something, and that's what I wanted so much. Maybe if it
had never happened I'd just accept it. But *once* he could relate to me, that
way. (Dep + fa)

What you're saying is that when you were a little boy he was companionable, that he accepted you as kind of a pal. On his terms, that is. And then this disappeared, is that it? (Interpretation₇)

That seems like it. I don't know whether his way of doing it now is to just try and be with me, and so forth. He came up last week, and he asked me to go fishing with him. That was fine, we'd go fishing, and have a nice time, and talk about *nothing*. Maybe that's as far as he can come, and it's my job to go further than that. I don't know, but I feel I'm going to get kicked in the teeth. (Aff n — fa)

You really don't want to risk being rebuffed, since that's what happened before. (Clarification)

That's right.

You sort of see that what he can give is limited to these rather distant signs of friendliness and the money that he can give. (Restatement) (Pause) *Why did he come? He came to visit, didn't he?* (Question; trying to get client to see that his father is probably quite fond of him.)

Yes.

And then when he came, you said you were very busy. Was there much interaction at all? Did he spend much time with you? (Question)

Well, he couldn't, because I was out of the house early Sunday morning, and he was still sleeping. I was just working outside all day on this project that I had to finish that weekend because it was the last time this other guy could help me. So naturally, my father had to spend most of his time with my wife. I didn't want it that way, but I couldn't help it. I got a letter from him this last week saying he hoped on the next visit we could spend more time together. (Dep — fa)

It may be significant to think about what you're looking for. (Direct lead) (Pause) *And whether it is available. Whether it can be achieved.* (Challenges; therapist is getting at the matter of the client's prolonged dependency on his father.)

I know what I've always wanted. Somebody I could go to and say "Such-and-such a thing happened, and I feel terrible. What can I do about it? I did well on this. I feel good, and I wanta share it with you." A sharing type of thing, that's what I want. (Dep — fa)

You want a sort of emotional support? (Clarification)

Ah,—if support's the right word. (He rejects the idea of his being dependent.)

Emotional response, at least.

That's what I want. I feel that a father-son relationship should, and could, be a very close thing. A father can guide, and so on. (Dependency) Closely. Not saying, "Don't do that, because it's not good," or "Don't do that, because I say so." It's an emotional *flow,* that's what I want. (Dep — fa)

You didn't want a disciplinary father. You wanted a friendly father, really. (Clarification)

Well, even with a disciplinary father who was *emotionally* close. I mean, if I deserved discipline, fine. And I still want such closeness very badly. (Dep — fa)

It's something that you never got, really, and that's why you feel a lot of need for it. (Clarification)

I sure can't revel in the memories of when I was three or four. (Dep — fa)

In a sense you feel you've been denied a real father-son relationship. You're still looking for it. (Clarification)

Um-hm.

You sort of rejected my word "dependent." (Calls attention) *I think that bothered you.* (Clarification; the word was "support.")

I think it did. But, I don't know whether dependent is quite the right word for what I mean. In my own mind I can't see that wanting a close exchange between people necessarily means you're dependent on them. In that sense, if you use the word dependent, I would think of it as one person being equally dependent on the other. Going both ways. The same as any friendship, or any marriage, or anything. But dependent is probably, I think, a nasty word in my life. (Laughs) I think of it as being a pretty weak thing. (Dep — gen)

Um-hm. We might want to talk about that sometime. (Structuring)

I think so.

Quinn: Seventh Interview (4/13)

MOST OF this interview was concerned with the client's relationships with his parents, and with childhood situations; Mr. Quinn attempted to examine the dynamics of his early behavior in order to discover possible explanations for some of his present difficulties and attitudes. Probably his enuresis and fire-setting were signs of childhood anxieties, and his dreams suggest classical Oedipal concern. Of interest also are his strong attachment to the maid, who was apparently a genuine mother-surrogate, and his pattern of sibling rivalry and of defiance of, and hostility toward, his father. The client's affect-themes in the interview consisted mostly of affiliation need, anxiety, hostility (about 20 per cent of each), dependency, and the pressure of being dominated by his father.

In this interview the therapist engaged in about the usual amount of direct questioning (20 per cent), but he greatly increased the amount of interpretation (33 per cent) over that which usually took place. Much of this was related to the possible significance, in terms of psychoanalytic theory, of childhood events. The client accepted many of these interpretations rather easily; however, he rejected some, particularly any suggestion of the presence of hostility feelings toward his mother, preferring to perceive his father as the "witch" who was always threatening him. Similarly, fears of bears and snakes were also considered by the client to be symbols of the father. The therapist was rather deliberate in making interpretations relating to psychosexual problems; he also pressed the matter of unveiling the client's repressed hostility toward his parents. He felt that each of these themes was close to a major problem area for this client and that he should utilize the manifest content of the interview to bring these matters more into the open.

There was, in the sixth interview, some further discussion of the dependency theme, although his dependency score remained unchanged (36). Early in the interview Mr. Quinn wished to deny dependency, but admitted that this was impossible. When faced with alternative interpretations of enuresis and fire-setting as signs of either dependency or hostility, he chose the latter as the more likely interpretation. He also reported that when he was a child his (older) sister had been quite dominant and sexually aggressive, facts which might have accounted for his somewhat passive behavior toward his wife. He reported a strongly affectionate relationship with "his" maid and also indicated that the maid's boy friends had served in the role of older brothers for him, so that he had affectionate memories of them, whereas he felt he had never "belonged" to his parents.

After this interview, the client's affect score (90) dropped a little but probably not significantly so. The therapist's affect score remained essentially the same (55).

I seem to have reached a plateau, because this morning I can think of nothing in particular that I want to talk about. (This initial resistance seems to be characteristic of Mr. Quinn.)

I tried to think somewhat further about this dependency business. For some reason nothing came. (The subject of dependency seems to be a principal cause of resistance.)

Well, what do you think might be the reason that nothing came? (Direct question)

Well, for one thing, I am not quite sure in my own mind of what way I am dependent. It's a confused area. I'm sure I *am* (dependent), but I'm not sure how. Maybe I should explore it more and try to get it straightened out. I don't know where to begin. (Laughs uncomfortably) Begin at childbirth? (Laughs again) (Dep + gen)

Um-hm. Dependency would appear to be something that you'd just as soon not recognize in yourself, is that it? (Interpretation$_5$)

That may be right. Because, perhaps when I have felt dependent in the past, it hasn't been at all gratified. (Dep — par → Dep — gen) Rather than have to experience the hurt, I stay independent.

So there were some aspects of your behavior that you perceived as independent. Cutting off the family relationship, really. (Clarification) (Pause) *Last week you called dependency a dirty word.* (Interpretation$_4$)

Yeah. In my own vocabulary, that is. (Laughs) Probably this is one area that I haven't done any thinking at all about, and that's probably why I'm confused about it, and just exploring, at present. (Dep n — self; Res)

It's really slow in coming. (Pause; sighs audibly) As a small child, I can never remember particularly feeling that I belonged, although I must have. But as I said last week, I can never remember the positive feelings, only the negative ones. All I can remember is the punishment. But I must have felt I belonged, because I can't remember being particularly unhappy then. I didn't feel too much "in on things." For one thing our family structure was kind of authoritarian and conservative. We children didn't have much say in things. (Dom p — par)

You said you can only remember the punishments. Last week you described being tied out in front of the house. (Restatement) Was there a lot of punishment; did you feel you were punished a good bit? (Question) I think you said, too, that your father usually did the punishing or the spanking. (Restatement)

I don't think I really was punished a lot; when I got older the main punishment was withdrawal of privileges, which didn't seem as much like a punishment to me. I don't know whether punishment was very consistent. I have a tendency to think that my mother was less consistent about it. (Dom p + par)

I did some pretty wild things, as I recall. Once I set a whole stack of newspapers on fire in the basement. I don't know why I did it; I wasn't thinking destructively, I just thought it'd be nice to have a fire. (Describes how he tried to put out the fire with water but had to run upstairs and call for help.) I never saw my father move so fast in his life. (Laughs) I don't know why I think that's funny. I can't remember whether I got punished; I have a strong feeling that I must have. I still can't see why I think it's so funny. (He is confused about his enjoyment of the aggressive aspect of this fire-setting.) (Hos n + par)

If you think it's funny, it must be important. (Calls attention)

It must be; it's not a *funny* thing to do. I don't know.

Might the funny feeling be a certain amount of (Pause) *satisfaction in having succeeded in being hostile? (Interpretation$_8$)*

That's what I was sort of batting around without saying.

But it might, of course, be threatening to you in the sense that this would. . . . (Interpretation$_8$)

Although I can remember I fully expected to be able to put it out myself, when I started it, I can remember I just did it for my own personal satisfaction. But with my background, and seeing how I get a chuckle now, I think maybe it was a way of venting hostility. I don't know. (Hos n + par)

This would be a way of showing the old bastard, wouldn't it? (Encouraging catharsis by reflecting repressed feelings.)

I never called him the old bastard. (Laughs with enjoyment) At times I apparently have felt like it.

Did you enjoy playing with fire? (Question)

That just reminds me of something; not fire particularly, but I enjoyed playing with things that I wasn't allowed to have. My father had a long knife, and I remember I wasn't allowed to play with it. But I remember when I was quite young I took the knife and ran around the neighborhood showing it to my friends and to some workmen on the street. That's two examples of doing something I shouldn't have done. I have a sort of feeling that I may have tried to possess things that were illegal. (Hos n + fa)

So it was a defiance of authority, and it was a possessing of the forbidden. (Interpretation$_4$) *And rather oddly, the two things that you remember are things that are frequently characterized as sexual symbols.* (Interpretation$_9$)

I never thought of them in that way at all. (Laughs) Hum. Although a lot of things in my childhood weren't normal development as I understand them now. For one thing I was enuretic until the age of eight. (An important symptom is exposed here.) I can remember being in a sort of quasi-awake-asleep type of thing. And I used to have the most horrible terrors. The house used to creak in the morning, and I still remember very vividly perceiving big bears walking down the hall. I didn't dare go out in the hall to go to the bathroom, cause they were gonna' get me. And so I just wet the bed. And I remember also if I got the nerve to get up and go to the bathroom I always used to think that there were snakes underneath the bed. (Laughs.) That's kind of a symbol. (Anx — fa; enur)

So are the bears. (Interpretation$_7$)

I remember jumping off the bed as far as I could, and when getting back in I would jump from as far away as I could.

I remember a dream I had that is still extremely vivid to this day. We used to have a maid at that time who was probably—to me I think she represents a mother-father surrogate. She was usually with my sister and myself. I can remember that in my early years my parents were only someone who was around, but *she* was someone to whom we went when we were in trouble. Her bedroom was up in the attic. I can remember dreaming of walking up these stairs and looking for my maid, which probably stands for looking for security. (Dep — mo surrog) And she wasn't there, and I turned around, and just as I turned, I noticed something at the window, and I looked, and then it dawned on me, there was this most horrible witch there. (Anx — mo. surrog; Drm) And I woke up in a cold sweat. That dream is really the only dream that has stuck since childhood that was a real dream. (Deep sigh) I'm stuck.

Well, what do you know about the interpretation of the dynamics of enuresis? (Question)

What obviously comes to mind is that I was scared to death of something.

So, it's the result of fear, actually? (Restatement)

Yeah. I don't know whether unconsciously it stands for something sexual.

Well, there are two general interpretations frequently made for enuresis, and of course there is no proof for either one of these. The one is the dependency interpretation, a kind of regression, and desire to remain at an infantile level of behavior, where you just let it go and you don't have to hold it back. Often children who have been completely toilet trained become enuretic on the birth of a sibling. That's fairly common. (Interpretation$_8$) *Another interpretation that's often made is that this is a form of hostility, where you're getting even in an outwardly aggressive way, rather than in an intropunative way. It's a little bit like the child might be saying, "Piss on you," or something like that. And he also defies the toilet-training wishes of the parent.* (Interpretation$_8$)

I think that the latter might be more appropriate. Dependency doesn't sound quite right, because the persons who would get most mad would be my parents, although it was the maid that would change the sheets. And that means the hostility idea, and they were not satisfying any of my dependency needs, particularly. It *might* have been a way of trying to get at them, although I don't think so. (He seems quite ambivalent.) I wouldn't have kept on so long when I found it wasn't getting me anywhere. It *might* have been a way of being hostile. (Hos n + par; Conf)

That reminds me of something else. I remember there was a tremendous amount of sibling rivalry with my sister. My sister used to push me around, and she took great glee in it. And I just hated her then. I don't know whether she was not prepared for my coming on the scene, but it was pretty rough for a while, I guess. Mother recounts the time when she found my sister had my hobby-horse's reins wound around my neck, and I was gasping and turning purple. And a friend of ours tells of another incident, and she says that my sister had my head in the toilet and was flushing the toilet, trying to flush me down. My sister couldn't have been older than four or five, I guess. I remember I really hated my sister a great deal, but she was the only one, really, that I could play with. There was no boy in our neighborhood, and I used to play with my sister and her girl friend. And my sister was quite dominant. (This may explain his passivity toward his wife.) And frankly it was so bad that they finally took her to a child psychologist. After that, her expression of hostility was not so damaging. It was more a shoving around, and kicking, and that sort of thing. (Anx — sib → Hos n + sib) Then I learned to box, so after that there was a nice threat I could use. (Laughs) The first vacation I was home, I whipped the crap out of her. (Laughs with satisfaction) After that, she took it pretty easy.

I always thought she was the favored one, because my mother didn't particularly take any positive part at that time, and my father would react toward us, and he tended to react more positively toward my sister (Anx — par)

We never had any sex education. I was never, even informally, given any instruction by my parents. The first time I heard anything about sex, my sister had apparently just come into puberty. And my mother had some pamphlet which she was using to explain to my sister about the facts of life.

And I came in and saw the pamphlet, and I wanted to read it, and both of them, but especially my mother, got very embarrassed. She put it in the drawer, so I went back later and read it, but it just didn't make any sense to me. (Sex n — par)

I remember one other incident at this time which my sister and I have never spoken of since it occurred. My sister and I used to do some exploratory play which didn't mean a thing to me, and it hurt me, as a matter of fact. She used to call it "weiner in a bun," where I would stick my penis between her legs. And I guess I was about seven or eight, and she'd be about three years older, about the time I read this pamphlet. (Actually he was probably 11 or 12 years old.) We were at my father's place, spending the night, and she was sleeping on the couch, and I was sleeping on the floor beside her, and she asked me to suck her breasts. And I can remember not thinking a thing about it. and we kept that up for close to an hour, and it became so tasteless to me, I can remember getting a coca-cola and inundating her so it would taste better. But still this meant nothing to me. Then we went in the bathroom and got in the bathtub, and she asked me to urinate between her legs, and I still didn't know what this was. I was confused and not very pleased with it. (He continues to protest innocence in the sex play in which he was involved.) (Sex n + sib)

I didn't know anything about sex until I went to this boarding school. There were these two kids I'd meet in the bushes, and one of them was able to get a prophylactic from his father's closet. I thought it was a white balloon, and I didn't know what they were talking about, but I knew something was not nice. (He recounts other incidents regarding his innocence. Then he mentions his first encounter with masturbatory behavior in a group situation with other boys. Reports that his first orgasm was during the event of mutual masturbation mentioned in a previous interview.) Something tells me I got the feeling that sex was a dirty thing. What led into all this digression, here? (Sex n + homo)

I think it grew out of a discussion of sibling rivalry, and as you thought about your sister, certain elements of aggression and hostility recurred to you, and then you mentioned sex-play types of activity with her. (Restatement) *It was a rather natural progression of ideas.* (Reassurance) *You were rejecting the idea that there was any possibility of regression in your enuresis.* (Restatement)

Well, I never was at a point where I wasn't being enuretic, or broken of it and then went *back* to it.

My lead there, in mentioning a younger sibling, was probably too specific, because it wouldn't necessarily have to be jealousy of a sibling; it could be entirely possible that you'd want to restore a state of more pleasurable attention on the part of your parents. But you *accepted more the idea that it might be hostility toward your parents.* (Interpretation$_8$)

Um-hm. Ah, I knew that in the many families that I knew, the parents were pretty close to the kids, but in our family that wasn't so; our maid was the one that was close to us. (Dep — par; Aff n + mo surrog) My parents' goodness seems to have been in this giving gifts type of thing. (Dep — gen)

You felt that they didn't give you affection, though. (Restatement)

No. (Pause)

We might someday think about that dream about the witch. That might have some significant implications. (Direct lead) *I think it's also somewhat significant that the five symbols that you've described are often given analytic interpretations: the enuresis, the fire-setting, the fascination with the knife, the fear of bears, and the fear of snakes. Several of those are hostility symbols, but also with some Oedipal implications.* (Interpretation₇) *Of course, it's probably literally true that most childhood fantasies have been given analytic interpretations by the Freudians. It may only be a coincidence that these five symbols all seem to have some relationship to psychosexual development.* (Attenuates) *What does the witch usually stand for to the Freudians?* (Question)

Well, what I thought it might stand for in my own case, is, ah (sighs) that it might symbolize my parents. The maid was the security figure, the one that gave me love. (Dep + mo surrog) Seeing this witch looking in the window scaring me half to death might stand for principally my father. I always thought of him as an ogre, which is the male counterpart of a witch. (Anx — fa)

Um-hm. Ogre, or devil, or giant, are the usual mythological male symbols. (Interpretation₇)

And I can remember that my maid was really a pretty sloppy person. She got chewed out many times for being so sloppy, and I used to feel tremendously hurt when she was. I would side with her immediately. (Aff n + mo surrog)

You were very fond of her, and she was a real affectional symbol. (Clarification)

Yeah. She did one thing once, that completely still nauseates me. (The client tells a story of his spitting on one of his little friends.) I remember my maid took me in the bathroom and spat in *my* mouth; it was phlegm and everything, and she made me swallow it. I just about croaked. And that was terrible, that she whom I loved so much would do a thing like that to me. It still nauseates me. (Dom p — mo surrog)

Um-hm. I notice that you call her my maid. (Interpretation₇; the therapist calls attention to his use of the singular possessive here, implying a close personal relationship.)

She *was* my maid. She was more my maid than anybody else's maid.

She and I were closer than she was to my sister. (Dep + mo surrog) And I remember she used to get her boy friends to play with me; they were like my brothers, really. That's interesting. (Dep + fa surrog)

She was really then the mother-figure. (Interpretation$_7$)

And her boy friends sorta' supplied the father-figure. I remember one brought me a baseball. They used to take me for rides, and stuff. (Dep + fa surrog) When my mother took us away, then it broke up, and that's what I missed, really. She was really terrific. (Dep + mo surrog) She died when I was about thirteen; I only saw her twice after we went away, I think. (Reports two encounters.) I still remember I was tremendously attracted to her, but it wasn't quite the same after being away for several years. When she died, I felt sorry, 'cause she was the most important thing in my life up until the time I was married. (Dep + mo surrog)

You identified the witch as your father, but witches are females, not males. (Interpretation$_8$)

Well, of course, you can go through from manifest content to latent content, or something. It may have been a female witch because I didn't know about any male witches, or any devils either, for that matter. For me, witches were the epitome of evil, and they did terrible things to children. It had no male counterpart that I can think of now. (Hos n + fa)

You resist an obvious interpretation. (Challenges)

I do? (Laughs) I must still be resisting it, because I can't think of it. (Res)

You came so close to it. You said it might be your parents. Why weren't you able to say that it might be a bad mother? (Challenges)

I never thought of my mother in a bad light. I thought of her as being weak, perhaps. But she has always been the closer of the two parents to me. (Dep + mo) I can never think of her in a particularly negative. . . . She was the one I could go to. I just can't think of her as being a witch, because she was the most positive of the two parents. (Aff n + mo)

She wasn't as positive as the maid, though. (Restatement)

No. Another thing that makes me think it was my father was that he was the one that usually chewed out the maid. I still resist the interpretation. (Laughs) (Res)

It may not be right. (Attenuates)

Well, consciously I can't think of it as being right. It just doesn't make too much sense. The witch being the most terrible symbol that could ever be, and when I think of the parents, the one terrible parent was my father. (Anx — fa) Although I don't think of him as terrible now; my parents were just the products of their environments, too.

And at that time you were not aware that they tried in their own way, or that they were the product of their environments. (Restatement)

That's right. I just knew that I wasn't satisfied. I remember getting negative sibling-feelings over the fact that my sister used to get the new stuff and I'd get the hand-me-downs. (Anx — sib)

I'm reminded of another incident. Apparently I was toilet-trained quite early; my mother had given the trainer seat away when I was a year old, she said. It's interesting that my earliest memory should have something to do with elimination. I can remember that toilet trainer-seat. I think my toilet training was probably a pretty strict type of thing. I know the reaction when I wet the bed was pretty explosive.

Um-hm. I see our time's up for today.

Quinn: Eighth Interview (4/20)

THE EIGHTH INTERVIEW was another devoted almost entirely to discussion about the client's father. Hostility press, affiliation need, and anxiety were the principal client affect-themes. This discussion of the client's father was touched off by a dream about a professor, who in the dream exhibited a rather threatening, demanding attitude toward the client. This professor was quickly interpreted as being a father and authority symbol.

The client's sense of having been misused by the father and his anger and urge for revenge were strong, although there was some ambivalence, apparent in a yearning for a mutually understanding relationship with his father. Several incidents were reported of the father's administering corporal punishment when the client was old enough to feel intense resentment about such treatment, but characteristically he quickly repressed the resentment and adopted a passive, conciliatory attitude. Mr. Quinn also reported several incidents of what were probably unconsciously directed acts of revenge on his part, carried out in such a manner as to appear to be accidental and innocent of any intent to harm.

The therapist's activity in this interview consisted principally of direct questions (31 per cent), interpretation (22 per cent), and clarification (18 per cent). The therapist was attempting to draw out the material regarding the client's feelings about his father. The interpretations were fairly deep ones pointed toward uncovering some of the more unconscious hostile motivation underlying feelings and actions consciously assumed by the client to be quite innocent. Other interpretations were directed toward helping the client to see that his usual behavior was probably lacking in normal aggressiveness, particularly in situations involving his interaction with his father. The client felt some guilt about criticizing his father or expressing hostility toward him, although at times he expressed a good bit of such hostility.

At one point the therapist tried to arouse some expressions of "normal" hostility on the part of the client toward his father, particularly with regard to the incidents of corporal punishment in late adolescence. Mr. Quinn could admit very little of this; he might have momentary flare-ups of anger, but these were quickly suppressed. In the incidents which he described, however, there were a number of unconsciously hostile acts, such as the client's accidentally spraying paint on his father's shoes, or asking him, when he fell in the lake, whether he got his money wet.

When Mr. Quinn made one strong overture of affection toward his parents, in a letter, his father was not able to respond to this gesture in any but an embarrassed way, and the client was left feeling quite hurt by this lack of affectionate response. Thus, his yearnings for nurturance and acceptance by a father-figure were left almost entirely unsatisfied (except financially), and this need remained one of the strongest drives of this client which had to be worked out in the therapy relationship.

The client's affect toward the therapist remained fairly high (93), and that of the therapist did not change much (54) from the previous interview. There is some possibility that the dream about one of the therapist's colleagues might be interpreted as a sign of a beginning of negative transference feelings toward the therapist, although no interpretation of this idea was made to the client. There was no confirmation of such a trend insofar as the Client's Affect Scale might have revealed such a development, and the dependency score remained at the same level (36) as in the two previous interviews.

(Mr. Quinn started the interview by expressing much concern about whether he could complete the requirements for his thesis by the end of the semester. Although his advisor had previously encouraged him to believe that this was possible, in a recent conference he had told Mr. Quinn quite abruptly that he couldn't possibly finish in time. This had caused him to be alternately worried and depressed. (Voc — prof) After reporting this fact, he switched to telling about a dream.)

I had a funny dream last week. Not so funny; I woke up rather frightened. Had to do with Dr. R.; I can't remember the dream exactly; I just remember a small part of it. Well, apparently a lot of the people around the department have been asking my wife if I'm gonna graduate this semester. And Dr. R. asked her, "Where do you plan to go next year?" It didn't make either of us feel particularly good; it sounded kinda negative, to put it mildly. And anyway in this dream he came over where we were, and I was sitting in the hall, and he came running up to me, which he would never do, (laughs) and he stuck his finger in my face, and said, "You failed." And that was all there was, that I can remember from the dream. And when I thought about it, it wasn't so bad, but I know it woke me up right away, and I was pretty scared. I don't know as there's anything particularly significant; I think that this shows my worry right at this point. (Hos p — → Anx — fa)

Um-hm. General anxiety. (Clarification)

Yeah.

Have you even had any courses with him? (Question)

Yeah. And I heard from someone that his evaluation of me at that time was this laziness business. So he might be my actual protagonist, I don't quite know, but he happened not to be, in the dream.

It might be significant, why you chose him. (Calls attention)

Yeah, well, I've been thinking about it; he reminds me of my father. (Client makes the most obvious interpretation, here.) Yeah, he is the same type of individual, very hard to get to, he seems to be. Probably a very nice person, he seems to be, too. But kinda hard to crack through the veneer. (Dep — fa) I wonder if I could think of any. . . . we could carry this further. My father is this way. That's kind of interesting, too. (Sighs) I'm bogged down. (Laughs in embarrassment) I can't think along this line. (Anx — fa)

Well, you've been studying quite hard. (Reassurance) *Have you been having much chance to think about yourself during the week?* (Question)

No, I haven't. I've wanted to, but I don't dare. We're on sort of a total push. I haven't done a thing about anything. Were you thinking of something in particular?

Well, I was just trying to find one possible explanation for your being bogged down. (Information) *You have probably been pretty preoccupied with your day-to-day activities.* (Reassurance) *You were wondering why you would see Dr. R. as your father.* (Restatement)

Why I should think of my father. I can see on the surface why I might see *Dr. R.* that way.

Why would you think of your father as . . . ? (Question)

Well, I know I certainly wouldn't want him to run up to me and have him stick his finger in my face and say, "You failed." (Anx — fa)

Are you sure about that? (Challenging)

Well, I don't know why he'd want me to fail. Oh, I see what you mean. That might be his way of expressing it or something. But he's never expressed himself that way. The only time I ever did fail anything was a calculus course in college, and I was away that summer and didn't even hear about it till I got back. And by then whatever feeling had been there had sort of dissipated. But he's never reacted that way to grades; he's always said, "Well, try and do better." Still, there is a very great similarity between the two of them. (Anx — fa)

I wasn't thinking so much of the specific situation in the dream, but the feeling that he was the mentor, he was the one that had to be pleased, and who was chiding you for being less competent than he expected. (Interpretation₅)

Yeah. That *would* have been the case a while back, more than now, because now I feel a great deal more responsibility for myself, and my wife, and the department, than I do to him. As I said, I never let the family know whether I do well or I do poorly. I don't think of him as being the one who has to be pleased anymore, particularly.

Well, the things we dream about are often what we learned at one time; that is, much earlier. Our fears and our anxieties in life are things we've picked up at the age of two or the age of seven. (Interpretation₈)

Well, since he was always the chastising one more than my mother, it'd be pretty logical that I'd feel this way about having to satisfy him. I think I told you about the remark he made the time I got my first A in physics; he said, "Well, you've shown you can do it, now do it again." He said it sort of as a joke, but it was sort of a veiled threat, you know. (Laughs) He never pushed me that hard, but I remember that I was always afraid of him, that if I didn't do well, something would happen. But it never did. But I was afraid of him. (Anx — fa)

Well, this dream was enough to cause you to wake up terrified. (Interpretation₇)

Not terrified, but very worried. After the twilight state, it sorta lost its completely negative quality. I suppose the more real feelings are the ones that one feels in the twilight state.

They're the deeper, more real emotions, that's right. And the thought that you had about it after you got yourself more organized, and built up your defenses, would be less basic. (Information)

I don't know why, but I'm still scared of the man. I don't like it in myself. I no longer take any crap; (laughs) he doesn't usually hand out crap; he's got good ideas, but they don't agree with mine. I listened pretty much, even in college, and I wouldn't go against his wishes. I'll stand up for what I think is right and tell him so, but I'm still scared of doing it. (Dep + fa)

You were going to say you no longer will take any crap from him, is that right? (Interpretation₄)

Well, yeah. (Laughs) I was gonna use that phrase, but as I say, what he says usually makes good sense, from his standpoint. But to me, my way of thinking, it may be crap.

The inference is that you once had *to take his crap, is that right?* (Interpretation₇)

That's right.

Now you'll stand up to him. You'll tell him where to get off, and you'll tell him what you think is right or where he's wrong, (Restatement) *but when you do this you're really quite scared.* (Clarification)

I worry about it, that's for sure. (Dep — fa) I know he can't do anything about it. I know he won't do anything about it other than argue, but it's still bucking authority. (Anx — fa)

He'd be displeased, though. (Restatement)

He's THE authority figure, in capital letters, still.

He can't do anything about you now. (Restatement) *What would he have done when you were, say, ten?* (Question)

By that time I'd been on my own at school. Until my parents were divorced, he used physical punishment. After that it was denial of privileges, like some movie I'd particularly want to see. (The discussion then shifted to Mr. Quinn's memories of physical discipline administered by his father. His principal feelings are reported in partially condensed form for the rest of this interview.)

I remember spankings I got after the time my parents were divorced. Once he and my sister and I took a trailer trip when I was fourteen or fifteen. My sister had done something that really was lousy, and I called her a bitch. So she told Dad, and he descended on me like the wrath of God. Cuss words were out, even thinks like "Jeez." So he stopped and cut a nice piece of young sapling, and bent me over and whaled the daylights out of me. Boy, did that hurt! I was miserable. Just about the worst beating I've ever gotten. (Hos p — fa)

Then, about two summers ago he conked me one. I was spray-painting, and the airhose got stuck. I was trying to pump through the hose, and he came along to help me out in his own inimitable fashion. The thing suddenly squirted through and doused his shoe. I don't know whether I thought it was funny, but I laughed. Maybe it was nervous laughter, but then he hauled off and swatted me one, a good conk on the face. He marched out, and I marched out in opposite directions. I was sizzling. A little later I said something about the fact that it was nervous laughter, and he said, "You shouldn't laugh at things like that." (Hos p — → Hos n + fa)

He slapped you on the cheek when you were about 20 years old? (Restatement)

Yeah.

But he didn't apologize? (Therapist is implying in this direct question that the father's behavior was unreasonable.)

No, he couldn't have.

How did you feel when he slapped you? (Question)

I was burned.

How long did that feeling last? (Question)

Just a couple of minutes. I started thinking from the standpoint of how *he* must have felt. It's not nice to have your good clean shoes covered with white paint. (Dep + fa)

Why do you think you laughed? (Question)

I probably felt "You got yours, Buddy." (Hos n + fa)

Um-hm. It was an accident, and you hadn't intended to do it, but nevertheless he got what you felt was coming to him. (Clarification) *And you didn't have to be responsible because you hadn't tried to do it. You felt a real sense of revenge.* (Interpretation$_8$)

Probably so.

You could allow yourself to be aggressive toward him only by accident, (Clarification) *but when the accident happened, you felt so much satisfaction that you were almost overcome with glee, is that it?* (Interpretation$_8$)

That may be phrasing it a little strongly (Laughs) (Res)

I have to admit that the situation was hilarious enough that I couldn't stop chuckling when you told me about it. Probably because I felt the same sense of retaliation, without having to feel responsible. It was a classic "custard pie" incident, but you didn't even have to throw the pie yourself. (Attenuates)

That's right. That kind of incident was very few and far between for me. If he makes a mistake in business, I don't find that amusing. I feel sorry it happened. (Aff n + fa)

This brings to mind another incident. (He recounts how they were rowing on rough water, and his father stood up and fell overboard but pulled himself back on board. Client laughs at this point.) I made the boo-boo of the century. I said, "Did you get your money wet?" (Laughs) I don't know why my first concern was with his money; and they've never let me forget it. (Laughs, again) I could see he was all right, and I didn't think it had *that* much significance. (Hos p — → Hos n + fa)

Why do you think you said it? (Question)

Well, I don't think it was an aggressive type of remark. His money would *have* to have gotten wet. Of course, as I've said, he stands for money to me.

Was this your way of asking if he got completely wet? Almost like asking if he got his soul wet. (Interpretation$_8$) (Pause)

That's pretty strong. (Res) (Laughs apologetically)

Perhaps it is. (Attenuates) *It could seem like a dangerous idea, too.* (Challenges) (Pause) *Did he bawl you out for saying it?* (Question)

As I recall, he emitted some choice words!

Your family's interpretation of the incident was that you didn't give a damn what happened to him, but that you did care about his money, is that it? (Restatement)

Yeah, they never carried it too far, though. They thought it was sort of amusing in a strange way.

How did you feel toward him the time he whipped you with the sapling? (Question)

I was indignant. I didn't think it should have happened in the first place. I tried to explain to him that my sister had done something lousy. So besides the physical pain, which was tremendous, I was mad. I didn't think I deserved it at all. (Hos n — fa)

It made you angry, and sort of humiliated? (Clarification)

Yeah.

Well, what did you do? (Direct question; the therapist is trying to infer that the client's submissiveness was excessive, that some sort of retaliation was to be expected, normally.)

Nothing.

Did you cry? (Question)

I think so. I didn't want to. It was terribly painful. I didn't bawl.

Did you say anything? (Question)

No. I sure wanted to. I wanted to call him every name in the book.

Maybe you would like to have done *things, in addition to saying things.* (Interpretation$_8$)

I wouldn't be surprised. Saying things is just the more socially approved way of doing something. I felt a lotta' times like I wanted to haul off and swat him. But the old mores say one doesn't do that sort of thing. Besides I don't know what the consequences would have been. (Hos n — fa)

How big were you at that time? (Question)

I guess I was shorter than he was. He's a strong man, too. He's always been very active and athletic.

So if you had taken a poke at him, you know who would have lost out? (Question)

(Client laughs.)

In such a case, what might he have done to you? (Direct question; the therapist is inferring the presence of actual fearfulness toward the father.)

I don't know. I never saw him lose his temper uncontrollably. He could be awfully mad, but I don't believe he would have gone into a complete rage.

How about when he slapped you for spraying paint on him? (Question)

Well, that was just spontaneous, and didn't last any time at all.

It was a situation pretty similar to that whipping incident, also, which would be pretty hard for a boy of fourteen to take, wouldn't it, to be physically beaten that way. Quite humiliating. (Clarification)

It was humiliating, all right, but the thing that particularly bothered me was the fact that it wasn't deserved. (Hos n — fa)

And even if it had been deserved, you probably felt that the method of punishment was inappropriate. (Clarification)

That's right. (Pause) This feeling I had at that time was awfully close to the feeling that I had the first time I felt my parents had told me a lie. They promised I could go somewhere, and then they said I couldn't, and I was crushed. (Hos p — par)

You had been betrayed, in a sense. (Clarification)

Yeah. (Discussed his feeling that his father preferred his sister. But then recounted how once when his sister betrayed him and reported something he had told her in confidence, his father criticized his sister for violating the client's confidence.) Boy, that felt good to me, too. I felt I'd been waiting twenty-some years for this. Later he just told me I should tell him when I wanted to take trips out of town from college. And I was pleased that he could speak to me in a nice logical way, rather than emotionally. (Aff p + fa; Ego + fa)

He treated you sort of like an adult, didn't he? (Interpretation$_8$)
Um-hm.

I think it's pretty important that you said that in each of these conditions where you felt that you were treated in a way that made you extremely angry, what you did was to repress it. To try to get over it very rapidly. (Interpretation$_7$; pointing out client's life style.)

Um-hm. I always do that. I think about it and work it through. I think about whether it's really deserved, and whether it'll do me any good, and so on. (Dep + gen) Also, now I let it out much easier. I tell my wife when I get mad. (Hos n + wife)

But your wife is not your father. (Interpretation$_5$; teaching discrimination.)

Nope.

And we were talking about your father, the fact that you still feel afraid of him. (Clarification)

I couldn't do it to him, now. I don't think. I'd argue logically, but if he got me angry, I don't think I could sing out and let him know where to go. I think I might soft-pedal it a bit. (Dep + fa)

(Reports a recent vacation situation when he told his father and sister and brother-in-law that he was tired of doing things the way they wanted to do them.) My dad was both hurt and angry at this, and I just told him I'd had enough of this running around, and I was going to sit tight and enjoy myself. (Ego + self)

So you did sort of stand your ground and declare yourself, there. (Restatement)

Yeah. I've declared myself a lot, but in a nice sort of way. Always in the accepted manner. He still does stuff that burns me up. It's as if he doesn't credit me with much intelligence. (Reports a long account of their arguing about the kind of housing he would try to find on his internship.) That's the sort of direction that I don't need, and don't want. And he also made some derogating remarks questioning how much of my woodworking I had done myself. He never likes anything I do unless it's done *his* way. (Hos p — fa)

It's usually a very directing kind of relationship on his part. (Restatement)

Yes. Never asking, always telling.

You have a good bit of resentment of the fact that this is the way it is. And of the fact that you still have this fear reaction toward him. (Clarification)

Um-hm. There's another feeling that comes out, which is to be expected, too. And that is guilt feelings for sort of shredding him here, because even with what he's done, I still feel the love of a son for his father. And I ask myself whether it was really as bad as I've been saying, but I have to admit that it was. (Dep — fa) So when we talk about stuff like this, if I don't think hard about it, I'll forget what went on in the hour. (Res)

You feel a lot of guilt about saying these things about him. (Clarification) *Two weeks ago, you left expressing the theme that you hoped that you could have a good father-son relationship with him, and you didn't feel it was too late. You're saying today, in a sense, that you still would like to have that.* (Interpretation₄) *You feel some guilt when you recapitulate these instances that were not representative of the kind of relationship that you'd like to have had, when you find that you felt angry with him and he was not warm to you.* (Clarification) *You were pleased to be able to tell me about the situation when he sided with you against your sister.* (Clarification)

This was real positive behavior on his part. Probably the feeling I've always had was as "The Unwanted." I remember asking my mother "Was I wanted?" (Dep — par) And the way the family broke up, and everything.

You didn't feel that you were wanted. (Clarification)

Well, I know I always have been with my mother, but somehow she doesn't count as much as my father. (Dep — fa)

It's wanting to be wanted by him that is more important. (Clarification)

Yeah. I know he does, but it doesn't seem like he does. I always had the feeling that I was tolerated, not that I was wanted. But I wanted to be loved for me, myself. (Dep — fa)

Is it possible that he was actually quite ambivalent? (Interpretation₉)

I wish I could talk more knowingly about him. But the fact is, I just don't know. He's got this façade all the time. Every once in a while it cracks through, usually in a monetary way, but I dont know what his real feeling is.

Well, what would make him make the trip down here? (Question, eliciting persuasive reasoning.)

'Cause he wanted to see *us*. Principally *me*.

You said that when you were staying with him, he would give these orders about not coming in late, and he would always be awake, no matter how late you arrived. What would make him always be awake? (Interpretation₉)

I know *what* would. He was worried about me. I *know* there's a lot of positive feeling there, but maybe I've gotta have it so blunt that it's stated: "I think a lot of you, Son" and "You've done well; you're a good boy." (Dep — fa; wants affectionate, dependent relationship.)

How did you feel when he said he was worried about you? (Question)

He never said that. He usually said either "Good night" or "I asked you to come in at such-and-such an hour." Although I know now that there's an awful lot of positive feeling, it's just that he can't come out with it.

He can't really give love ungrudingly, is that it? (Restatement)

Yeah. Our letters are a riot. They stink! (Imitates reading a letter about the weather.) And I have a lot of big failures and little failures, big successes and little successes that I want to tell about, but I don't. (Dep — fa) I'm afraid of getting laughed at.

One time you tried to tell him, and you were sort of ridiculed. (Restatement)

That's right.

How often does he write? (Question)

At least once a week. *I* don't. I never was good at writing, even with my good friends. But his letters are so damned impersonal. (Dep — fa) Although, actually his letters are warmer than mine are. (Recognizes that he himself is partly responsible for the poor communication.) I sincerely thank him, and everything, whenever he's done something for me. But he tells *me* about his business, so actually his letters are closer than mine. That's funny, because I think that I'm the one who has to make the overtures, and yet I'm afraid to. I guess I'm afraid of another disappointment. (Dep + fa)

You can't depend on how he'd react. (Clarification)

No.

That letter may have been too threatening to him, that he had not been a good father. (Interpretation₉; the therapist is trying to give insight into the father's probable need-system.)

Probably so, 'cause I really laid it on the line. I said everything that I wanted about our relationship (Dep + fa), and how I was feeling, how I felt about religion, how I felt about a girl. I just catharted completely, and it was probably very threatening. He probably appreciated the fact that I'd done it, but he just couldn't take it. At that time I was completely outgoing toward everything. (Dep + fa) So I couldn't do things by half measures.

And you may have shown him his shortcomings, how far he had missed the mark. By telling what you wanted, you were also telling what you hadn't gotten. (Interpretation₉)

That's right.

Quinn: Ninth Interview (4/27)

THE MAJOR TOPICS in the ninth interview were hostility toward the father and concern about the client's masculinity, adolescent homosexual activities, and general adequacy. The analysis of affect themes reveals that about three-fifths of the content related to feelings of adequacy or inadequacy and about a sixth related to sexual needs. The matter of whether or not he had a sufficiently virile physique and a sufficiently masculine personality was a major concern of this client; the relation of these problems to the one of concern about passivity is obvious, although perhaps not readily recognized by the client himself. The therapist considered the passivity problem to be the more causative one, and the masculinity problem to be the more symptomatic. The client's utilization of athletics to prove his masculinity is an obvious dynamic.

Interpretation (27 per cent) and asking leading questions (24 per cent) were the principal activities of the therapist, although there were also some incidents of reassurance (15 per cent) and clarification (10 per cent). Most of the reassurance was directed toward helping the client to feel more comfortable about the examinations he would be required to take in the near future. The interpretations were the chief therapeutic tool utilized to help the client see the connection between his fear of homosexuality and lack of masculinity and his deeper general insecurity. Interpretations were employed for the purpose of connecting some of the symptoms to the dynamics indicated above. An effort was also made to help the client distinguish between having once been a sexually immature youth who engaged in some homoerotic sexplay and being a confirmed homosexual.

A number of events occurring in this interview reveal significant aspects of the therapy relationship. One was the display of a certain cameraderie which made it possible for the therapist and the client to say mildly teasing things toward each other without either feeling injured by this. The therapist was pushing rather insistently an interpretation that the client's fear of fatness was actually a fear of femininity.

The client could accuse the therapist of "catching" him in an evasion of this interpretation, and the therapist could admit laughingly that he was being directive at this point.

The therapist employed quite a bit of reassurance, which for this client was a much desired procedure. Reassurance was given about the client's probable academic ability, about his not really being "a homosexual" because of engaging in some homosexual play when younger, and about his anxiety over his masculinity probably being the result of his father's forcing a certain competitiveness upon him and of his own fear that he was not as adequate a person as his father. For the therapist to be recognizing all of these things, and implying that they were normal and understandable and probably only based on unreal and imagined inferiorities, would be a procedure likely to produce a lot of warmth toward the therapist on the part of Mr. Quinn. Most people react with pleasure to being told complimentary things about themselves, and this positive affect tends to generalize to the person making the favorable evaluation. Thus, while these procedures were entirely sincere on the part of the therapist, they had a very important secondary effect of building up the positive transference which the client felt.

During this interview, the client's affect dropped to 80, making it close to the mean of his usual scores. The therapist's affect remained fairly constant at 59. However, the dependency score rose to 42, well over this client's mean score.

I am completely exhausted from an exam. I passed it, but I'm sure I didn't get honors. I'm very pessimistic about exams. I started nail-biting before exams at the prep school, and I still do it. If I get tense in an exam, I go to pieces. (Dep — gen)

(Therapist tried to reassure the client by suggesting some self-calming procedures which the client could use if he started to blow up. He also pointed out that while failure on exams could possibly limit his graduate career at this university, there were other graduate schools which would take him; Reassurance.)

I know that I have ability in many areas, and yet sometimes I look at myself and call myself a boob. I wonder if I know *anything*. It's an emotional reaction. (Ego — intel)

(Therapist encouraged the client to consider this response an overgeneralized reaction to inferiority feelings in other areas; Reassurance.)

I've always felt socially inferior to my classmates because I was two years younger than most of them. I still cringe when I remember how I was called "Fatso" because of my somatotype. I also was called a fritterer, satisfied to have a good time with no responsibilities. (Anx — phys)

Let's take the phrase "Fatso." Why does it bother you so? (The therapist asks this question because he suspects that this nickname touches off a fear of being perceived as somewhat feminine.)

Well, I was somewhat heavy, and I was pretty touchy about that. Until I was fourteen, I was quite a butterball. Then I went on a really strict diet. And as I started to grow tall, my proportions improved. I'm sensitive about overweight, and no matter how much I diet, I can't avoid some chubbiness. Unfortunately, I like fattening foods, and when I'm depressed, I let go of my self-control and start guzzling a milkshake. I don't know why I'm so sensitive about it. (Anx — phys)

Why do you think it bothers you, though? What elements of it seemed derogatory? (Question; client sighs deeply; it becomes apparent that the client always sighs when pressed to face the question of lack of masculinity, or of passivity on his part.)

Well, to my way of thinking, anybody who is fat is not taking care of himself. I probably equate fatness with general sloppiness. I'm trying to figure out why fatness would have picked up such negative connotations for me. Probably because people use the concept in a derogatory manner.

I wonder if it's deeper than that. You said that fatness is parallel to sloppiness. Is it parallel to anything else? (Interpretation₇)

Yeah. It isn't masculine. The ideal man is the mesomorph. That's my ideal, too. I've always wanted to have muscles and good build. Even now I'm quite embarrassed in a bathing suit, although I'm not that fat, really. (Anx — phys)

You've always wanted to be an inverted triangle. (Clarification) (Both laugh) *So the inference about overweight is that it isn't masculine.* (Pause) *Which makes it what?* (Interpretation₇)

Feminine. (Sighs) You caught me, didn't you. (Laughs)

I had to beat you over the head with it. (Both laugh) (Structuring; there is a camaraderie apparent in the relationship now.)

The next question is why I react so strenuously when I feel feminine. (Sighs) There're so many things that might be a part of it. The male role in society, for one thing, is *the* role. The man is important, and the woman is submissive. And also in my own family situation: the male was the authoritarian, the potent one. I wonder if also the fact that, since my parents' divorce, for some time after that I lived with my mother and might have been reacting against being a "mamma's boy." People might have assumed that I was. (Pause) It was much easier to identify with her, because she was easier to get to. (Anx — masc)

I wonder also if the homosexual behavior might have fit into it, too. I may equate homosexuality with being sort of feminine, perhaps. (Anx — masc)

You mentioned three possible sources of anxiety about seeming feminine. One is the ego concern: the position of the male as dominant in our society, and particularly in your family. And another was the possibility that you might be perceived as identifying with your mother. And third, you mentioned the possibility that people might think you were more homosexual. (Restatement) *Perhaps you were a little bit reaction-sensitive to this because of the incidents that had taken place, is that it?* (Interpretation₄)

Yeah. (Deep sigh)

Does it bother you to think about it now? (Question)

Yeah.

Why do you think that it does? (Question)

Because I don't think it's good. It's not healthy or well-adjusted behavior. Although there are supposedly well-adjusted homosexuals.

But this didn't make *you a homosexual, did it?* (Reassurance; the therapist was attempting to teach correct labels.)

No.

But you still feel embarrassed to think about it, and talk about it. (Clarification)

Yeah. (Deep sigh)

That's a pretty deep sigh. (Interpretation₆)

(Client laughs) It's a very bothersome topic.

Why do you think it is? (Question)

Well, as I expressed one time before, I just don't condone the behavior, and I was worried that perhaps I might be homosexual, or bisexual, or something. I haven't felt that way since that time I talked about it. And it doesn't worry me much, but the memory of past worries is still somewhat sensitive. I have very negative feelings about this departure in myself. (Anx — masc)

Well, what I'm trying to do is to help you become slightly more desensitized. Not so desensitized that you'd walk down the street and say (laughs) *"Did you know that I engaged in a homosexual activity when I was twelve?"* (Structuring; both laugh)

Well, just from a statistics point of view, I know that something like 50 per cent have a homosexual encounter to the point of orgasm sometime in their lives. So I know I'm normal. But it still bothers me. (Anx — masc)

Do you think any of these feelings of insecurity and inadequacy are a fear that you really just aren't any good anyway? (Interpretation₉; the therapist is encouraging an interpretation that the fear of being less masculine has been a generalized response based on deeper feelings of inadequacy.)

It could well be.

If you were real athletic-looking, muscular, and robust, then you could feel pretty good and that you filled the prototype of the masculine, aggressive, athletic male. (Interpretation₇)

Of course they often say that the "man's man" is the homosexual. (Laughs) The physical-culture-boy-type.

He's probably worried about his physique and whether he's masculine or not. (Information)

I'm not disappointed in the way my physique finally developed. Covering my fat, there's quite a bit of strength. I don't have to show my biceps or hoist up cars to prove I've got muscles. (Ego + phys)

So you know there's nothing puny about you. (Restatement)

Yeah. Not at all. (Sighs)

But you weren't always too sure of that. (Clarification)

Yeah. Another thing, too. My father pretty much fills the stereotype of a mesomorph. He's very strong and always was the athlete. I think probably we're about equal now in strength, because as he gets older he's slowed down a bit. But I can remember competing with him. Once when I was about fifteen I wrestled with my father, and I got him in a hold he wasn't used to, and I hurt him. (Laugh) I gave him "the juice." I just laughed now when I said that. That's the way I felt at the time, too. "I got him." (Laughs) (Hos n + fa)

This is what we talked about last week, isn't it. (Interpretation₄)

Yeah. I showed him!

You were showing him that you were as strong as he was, and you were getting revenge, in a sense. (Interpretation₈)

Yeah, by hurting him. I was pleased. It still gives me a good feeling. I say to myself, "You rat." (Hos n + fa → Anx)

You feel a little ashamed of yourself for feeling so triumphant. (Clarification)

Yeah. Like last week, I was ashamed to be tearing my poor father apart here. (Dep + fa)

Well, as long as you're tearing him apart here, and not somewhere else, it's not too difficult a problem for us to handle. (Reassurance) (Pause) *He was pretty athletic. How about you?* (Question; therapist encourages discrimination between discussion of hostility in therapy and acting out hostile impulses outside of therapy.)

I went out for sports a good bit. But I was always afraid of getting hurt. In football, I was captain of our class team. I played pretty decent tennis. I always worked at a sport. I played to win. I still play with every bit of strength I have, even if I have to hurt myself. (Anx — masc)

You play with a sort of desperation? (Interpretation₅)

Yeah. I've sprained more fingers and gotten more wood under my fingernails! I've done above average in sports.

You were actually pretty athletic, then, weren't you. (Reassurance)

Yeah, but I never got any particular recognition for it from my family.

You couldn't come up to your father's expectations. (Restatement)

I don't know. I use to play him in tennis. At first he whopped the tar out of me. But then as he got older, and I got more practice, I could beat him to my satisfaction. (Hos n + fa)

You tried to prove something. (Interpretation₈)

Yeah. I guess, that I was able to do well—that I was masculine enough to do well. (Anx — masc)

Whom were you trying to beat? (Question; the therapist is encouraging insight into the possible dynamics of his competitiveness in sports.)

Myself? (Laughs) I don't quite know what you mean. Do you mean was I trying to beat *him,* or something? (Long sigh) Probably so, although he wasn't competing in sports at the time I was. But still, he had the record of having been very good.

Who was the big athlete of the family? The big man? (Question)

He was.

What I'm getting at is the rivalry between father and son. We talk a lot about sibling rivalry, but I don't think many people realize that often it's quite possible to have very intense rivalry with a parent. And it's often encouraged by the behavior of the parent, who encourages it because of his own need to try to demonstrate his competence. (Interpretation₉)

Yeah. (Sighs) This was very important. To be competent in his eyes. (Dep — fa) Nowadays, I have other values that sort of supersede those, however. But I'd still like to prove myself a man. I don't think I've done it yet. (Anx — masc)

When do you think you will *have proved that you're a man?* (Question)

When I get the buying-power. When I'm established and show I can hold down a job. Money's important, although that's not why I want the Ph.D. Money has been played up in importance in our family so much. (Anx — fa)

It's his criterion of success. (Restatement)

Yes. Even though he doesn't say anything about it, it's the fact that he uses the stuff so much. It's the way he expresses himself. Also, I got quite a bit of criticism at various times because I didn't hold a job. I was sort of flighty. (Anx — fa)

Um-hm. Well, our time's about up for today. I think you're going to do pretty well on those tests. If you find yourself getting tied up, try to remember what we talked about. Tell yourself that you're just being panicky and letting your inferiority feelings generalize. (Reassurance)

Well, I feel a lot better. Maybe it's just talking about other things that's helped. (Dep + ther)

Um-hm.

Quinn: Tenth Interview (5/4)

T HE TENTH INTERVIEW was quite different from most; it could be characterized as being more a sort of guidance or counseling than psychotherapy. Three-quarters of the client's statements were about his mother; as in the case of his father, this preoccupation with discussion of the mother was coincident with a visit which his mother was making. The principal affect-themes of the client were an expression of nurturance toward the mother, hostility, and anxiety.

The therapist directed his remarks toward clarification of feeling (21 per cent) and equal amounts of advice-giving and direct questioning (14 per cent each). He expressed some disapproval of the client's permitting his mother to visit at this rather busy and hectic period, and he also gave a little reassurance. He loaned some mental hygiene books to the client for his mother to read. Perhaps it was somewhat the therapist's fault that the interview concerned itself with the problems of handling the mother, rather than with the more basic question of the client's relationship with her and his concern about seeming to be rejecting in his attitude toward her. However, the client himself was somewhat responsible; his attitude was not one of requesting help in resolving a neurotic relationship with his mother (which he did not really exhibit), but one of asking the therapist for help in finding ways to get his mother out of his way. He was quite willing to keep his life generally free of her influence.

The client's affect toward the therapist became more positive in this interview (93), but that of the therapist toward the client, although in general not given to very much fluctuation, did drop a bit following this interview (51).

The therapist's methods were quite supportive in this interview, as in the lending of books and the offering of advice. Mr. Quinn responded well to support; he did not show excessive dependency at this time, although he was always willing to react passively toward other persons, including the therapist. His dependency score dropped four points to 38.

My mother has presented herself on the scene during the last week, and this has caused me to do a bit of thinking about my relationship with her. She's just been separated from her second husband, and she's at loose ends. We invited her up, hoping it would be in June, but she wrote that she was coming for two weeks, right now. And this is a very bad time, because I'm so very busy. (Hos n + mo)

I'm sorry for her; I never liked her second husband. She may have brought this on herself, but still I'm sorry for her. She's staying at a hotel in town; I guess she realized neither one of us would be very happy having her stay at the house for that long a time. (Nur + mo)

I've told her time and time again I can't help her with her problems, but I know she's going to ask me to. I'm all tied up with my own problems, and besides I don't think you can give your own mother psychotherapy. (Nur — mo)

It almost might have been better to write and say that since you were so terribly rushed right now, couldn't she come in June. (Disapproval; the therapist obviously felt that this visit came at a very inopportune time and that the client could have prevented it.)

Well, it just wouldn't have been convenient with her to do it that way. She's very dependent on me and always wanting me to tell her what to do. I wouldn't be surprised but that she's already started going into a depression anyway. I know I'll have to be true to myself, but I'll feel like a rat, because she's very easily hurt, and I've always been her favorite. (Anx — mo) But I just can't spend much time with her, and I won't put myself in the position of giving her any real advice. (Nur — mo)

There's nothing for her to do around here, and we feel obligated to entertain her. But I can't afford to take the time. We ship her to the hotel in the evening, but I feel awful about doing it. (Nur — mo)

My thesis is going very badly; we can't get any significant results. Both my adviser and I are discouraged about it. And I'm almost sure I can't get the first draft in by the deadline. (Voc — thesis)

I could try to explain to mother about all the problems we're having in getting everything done, but I doubt if she'd understand the situation. Psychology just doesn't make sense to her, I'm afraid. (Nur — mo)

(Therapist suggested that it might be possible to recognize the mother's dependency needs and give her simple answers to her questions without attempting to go into any complex or involved explanations.) (Advice)

I don't know any simple answers to her problems. She's made a mess of her life, and she's terribly lonely. She doesn't even know where she should live. She even thinks about trying to effect a reconciliation with her second husband. She thinks she might try to find a job; she doesn't have much training for anything.

I took another look at my feelings toward her; the relationship is just not as close as it once was. She's kind of a fuddy-duddy. (Hos n + mo)

She's very petty, too. I just can't *take* a close relation to her any more. But that makes me feel guilty. (Anx — mo)

Why do you think it makes you feel guilty? You've grown away from any dependency on her. (Question)

Well, according to the culture, we don't farm out our parents. For another thing we were very close, when I was about eleven and was living at home. She was just about my only parent then, and I was the head of the house, or at least the "man of the house." I feel some guilt that I allowed the relationship to change, (Anx — mo) although I'm not saying that it was a good one.

At the time of the divorce she painted a pretty black picture of my father, but later I realized he wasn't really that bad. Some time ago my aunt told my wife that mother had figuratively broken Dad's back; he just couldn't take it any more. I can see how she might have. Her prattle gets on your nerves. But I can't say, "Shut up." It's pretty hard on my wife when I'm not there. (Hos n + mo)

I think you made a mistake in letting her come for so long. (Disapproval) *I can see that the situation is a very difficult one, though.* (Attenuates)

Well, both of us felt sorry for her, and although I had some reservations about it, I told her to come. (Nur + mo)

This is the problem all along, isn't it, that you hate being unkind to her. (Clarification)

I still feel guilty about it.

You feel guilty about something that you can't do anything about. (Clarification)

That's right.

Then you must think you could *do something about it, if you* would. (Interpretation₄)

Yeah. Or at least I could try. But I'd have to invite her to come and live with us if I were to *really* make her happy. But that wouldn't be fair to either my wife or me. But mother's pretty depressed. She needs psychotherapy, but not with me. And I don't know whether she could take therapy. (Nur — mo)

(Therapist discussed supportive therapy with older persons, as being preferable to a deeper type of insight-therapy.) (Information)

I wish she and Dad would get together again; they might be happy. Probably I'm talking to you as I would talk to her if I had the guts to do it. I just can't hurt anybody, and especially my mother. (Nur + mo) (This may be a basic character trait of this client; it is consistent with his passivity.)

Sometimes people have to be hurt in a gentle way, because it's unavoidable. (Advice)

She's bound to be hurt anyway. It's inescapable. I'm gonna have to break it to her as gently as possible, I guess. If I didn't give her help now, when she needs it, I'd never forgive myself. (Nur + mo)

She reads a lot, and my wife has brought her home some novels.

Do you have any simple mental hygiene books she might read? (Question)

No, I don't. Mine are mostly graduate level books. Are there any books at the library that I might get her? (Dep + ther)

They might have some; Travis and Baruch, for instance. I might have some here that would be suitable. I could lend you a couple. You could just happen to have them lying around the place, where she could find them. (Offers help; both laugh) *Sounds like the "birds and the bees" kind of thing in reverse.* (Both laugh)

I think she would appreciate it. It wouldn't even have to be that subtle; she's looking for information, actually. I feel a lot better about it now, because I feel I know more what to say. (Dep + ther)

It's almost as though you have to reverse the roles, now. In some ways you're now like the parent, and you have to treat her like an unhappy child who has to be helped to face up to a problem. You want to be gentle about it, but also to get the point across. (Advice)

Quinn: Eleventh Interview (5/18)

THE ELEVENTH INTERVIEW was one which reflected the deep discouragement of the client about the fact that his wife was renewing her flirtatious behavior toward other men and had told her husband that she did not love him and found him physically unattractive. The client's principal affect-themes were hostility, anxiety, and a sense of damaged ego-concept. The client expressed a sense of helplessness about being able to do anything to salvage his marriage and mentioned divorce as a possible resolution which might be preferable to the present unsatisfactory situation. He admitted his own immaturity or character defect in being unable to be aggressive enough to satisfy his wife.

In this interview the therapist used many direct questions (37 per cent), which were designed to open up issues or to bring to the client's attention matters or attitudes which he had not yet considered. He also used a considerable amount of interpretation (16 per cent) and some clarification of feeling (12 per cent). A little criticism of the client appeared when the therapist questioned the client's diagnostic discussion about his wife. The therapist himself gave a diagnostic impression, which was somewhat damaging. This interview dealt with a regression in the marriage relationship, so its general tenor was depressed.

In this interview the client showed some dependency in his attitude toward his wife; he was unable to take any strongly positive stand about her behavior, even though it upset him greatly. He tended, also, to lean on the therapist for advice or suggestions. The therapist seemed quite willing to give him both of these. Mr. Quinn asked about having interviews during the summer and indicated his willingness to make a fairly long drive each week in order to have them, if it were possible. (Actually this was not possible because of vacation plans of the therapist.) Although the therapist almost urged the client to be more positive and aggressive in his behavior toward his wife, he also cautioned him against taking any precipitous action, such as a separation, which might endanger the permanence of the marriage. As the relationship with the therapist was quite good at this point, Mr. Quinn apparently was turning to the therapist for much support and advice. The therapist was taking a rather forceful, directing sort of approach, capitalizing on the client's dependency. He was supplying "ego-strength" to bolster the less self-assured ego of this client. Mr. Quinn's dependency score rose a little to 40; he was in the more dependent phase of his therapy.

The client's affect toward the therapist (91) remained almost identical with that of the previous interview; the therapist's affect score increased a considerable amount (58), so that it placed in the upper quintile as far as the therapist's affect scores toward this client were concerned.

Mother never pinned me down. I think she may have taken a hint from the fact that I wasn't paying too much attention whenever the conversation would go vaguely in the direction of her problems. She thumbed through one of those books, but she didn't seem particularly motivated to do any reading in that area. (Hos n + mo)

My wife has dropped another bomb. It's the same business of still not really caring for me; she's actually negative toward me and always trying to get me mad. Sometimes she succeeds quite well. She says she doesn't know why she does it. She walked out on me for a while last Friday, and I told her that sometimes she is extremely childish. I was really burned up. After she came back, I didn't speak to her for an hour. Then she tried to win back my positive feelings. She has these impulses which she says she can't understand. She tells me she doesn't love me. I think she's been on a plateau in her own counseling for quite a while. (Anx — wife)

She attempted a very tearful reconciliation with me. She wants me to tell her what's wrong with her. She even expressed some suicidal thoughts. She said that when we were first married, she actually hated me. Now she doesn't even want to stay around to find out whether we can come to love each other. Also, she said that during intercourse she is repelled by me, although when she gets excited she forgets about me and just enjoys the situation in a physical way. She said that, when she looks at me without clothes on, she thinks I look like a woman. But she admitted that I'm not really womanly looking. (Anx — wife)

It is very difficult not to try to therapize her. I don't know how much more of this I can take. When she says things that are very shattering to me, I have felt it was best for the marriage just to accept it and not blow up. But she complains that I don't tell her how I feel. She doesn't really empathize with my feelings; the most I get is a perfunctory reassurance. (Dep — wife)

When she does well in something, I boast about her, but I don't tell *her* that I'm proud of her. I probably should do that more. I feel pretty miserable. It's damn difficult to carry on activities in a rough semester when I'm also worried as hell about what's going on at home. (Dep + ther)

Did any of these reactions from your wife relate to your mother's visit? (Question)

Well, I think my wife was made tense by her visit, so it really may have precipitated some of the reaction against me.

What's your interpretation of your wife's saying she feels you look like a woman? (Question)

She said she thought she felt that way because I had once had homosexual experiences. I think it was a mistake to have told her about that. (Anx — masc)

The unfortunate part is that her lack of responding to you as a male can be a conditioning factor to make you feel more insecure about your masculinity, and perhaps to increase your homosexual concerns. (Interpretation₇)

Yes, but I'm sure I'd never let that happen.

What do you mean when you say you love her? (Question)

That's a hard thing to define. Aside from the fact that I admire her intelligence and beauty, I also believe I can see what she *could* be. It's sort of an idealized image. (Aff n + wife)

Do you mean you feel tender toward her, or protective, or passionate toward her? (Clarification)

All of those. It's much deeper than anything I've felt for anyone else. I usually feel fond of her, but lately I've been tempted to give her a healthy swat. I can take just so much from anybody, and then I can't take any more. (Anx — wife)

I have the feeling that sometimes you take more than that, anyway. (Challenges)

I do. I probably shouldn't. (Dep + wife)

Do you tell her you feel like socking her? (Question)

I sure communicate that I'm angry. But I'm afraid of endangering the relationship. I don't know whether I should go away, or get a divorce, or what. (Dep + wife)

Well, I'm not trying to encourage you to hit her. I think physical violence is damaging to a relationship. (Advice) *But I have the strong feeling that she's asking you for something that you're not giving her. What do you think it is?* (Interpretation₉)

(Client sighs deeply.) Well, she keeps bringing up that she has a feeling of loneliness. But she won't tell her therapist, because she's afraid she'll cry. That must be the area where I'm not fulfilling her needs. And yet she prefers for me to be out of town if possible; she'd rather live alone. (Anx — wife)

What sort of person is her father? (This question was an attempt to explore the possibility that the client's wife was hoping for a strongly masculine father-surrogate in her husband.)

My first reaction was "He's a dope." (Laughs) That may be what I think. I can't help but keep thinking that he is at the bottom of all this. I don't really think that I have deserved the negative reaction I've gotten. He is an effeminate man, to my way of thinking. His interests are feminine.

What are her feelings toward him? (Question)

I'm still rather sure there's an unresolved Oedipal complex there. She and her father have been pathologically close all her life. She cuddled in bed with him right up until our marriage. She has even fantasied having intercourse with him. I suspect he's fantasied the same thing. It looks like a very sick relationship (Hos n + wife)

I asked you what you thought she wanted from you that she wasn't getting, and you said, "companionship." I wonder if that's it? (Challenges)

(Client sighs very deeply.) Personally I just don't know what she wants. I've tried everything. I've been myself. I've tried to play roles.

What types? (Question)

Oh, the aggressor, the pacificist, the wit.

How have you tried to play the aggressor? (Question)

I've been a little bit rough in handling her. Not just sexually. I might tell her to shut up, or smack her. I just don't know what she needs. And I don't want to try living a role. (Hos n + wife)

Well, I have a theory which may be wrong, but I'll pass it on to you. You don't have to accept it. My theory is that she wants you to fill a strong, masculine, supportive role, to be what you called a "man's man"—positive, self-assured, determined. (Advice) *Of course, I don't know her; I'm just building this theory on the things you've told me.* (Attenuates) *I feel she's trying to goad you into being more assertive and aggressive.* (Interpretation$_9$)

Well, that's right, because passivity, although it's accepting, is not very masculine.

You told me she goaded you into her slapping her once, and I had the feeling that you felt she seemed somewhat pleased by it. (Clarification) *For one thing it would reassure her that you liked her, that you could get jealous, or at least, weren't indifferent to her.* (Interpretation$_9$)

Um-hm. That may be very right. It sounds quite feasible. Unfortunately, right now is a very insecure phase of my life, although I hope to be the kind of person you're describing, eventually. I don't *feel* self-assured, right now. (Dep + gen) At times I fall into a very unsure role with her; I guess I'm not very sure of myself in most areas at times. I feel rather disgusted with myself.

Did you ever try to make a diagnostic description of your wife? (Direct lead; this is a bold maneuver on the part of the therapist, based on a fear that the client must adjust himself to the fact of his wife's having a fairly serious character disorder.)

Yeah. It frightens me. Her reality-testing is poor. And this impulsive behavior; I've sometimes thought of her as being manic-depressive. She has terrific mood-swings. But I don't mean she has a psychosis; it's not that bad. But it isn't good. I resent one thing; I sure got a hell of a snow job before we got married. I would have waited a while before I married her, if I had known then what I know now. (Hos n + wife)

Your diagnosis isn't very good, in my opinion. It's hard to be objective in diagnosing one's wife. (Disapproval)

You aren't thinking she's a paranoid, are you?

No. I was thinking of some character disorder in a person with a pronounced immaturity pattern. (Information)

Yeah. (Sighs)

Why should I bring up this matter of diagnosis? (Structuring; when this therapist takes an unexpected step, he frequently uses this method to give the client some insight into his intention; this prevents allowing a misperception and possible trauma to occur.)

So I could think more objectively about the situation.

Yes. You're confused, and puzzled, and hurt by her behavior. (Clarification) *I feel that you are so close to the situation that you haven't examined its psychological meaning, as you might if she were a case instead of being your wife.* (Disapproval)

But how can one help somebody to grow up? I've tried so many different ways. But I get negative rebuffs. I think she's so mixed up that a lot of it will just have to come out in her therapy. I can't *take* a life full of what's been happening. (Dep + gen) I want a companionate marriage. I'm afraid of rejection, and I don't know what she's afraid of.

I can't take this uncertain existence. It would be better to go one way or the other. Maybe I've got to learn to take a gamble. (Dep + gen)

Once you said you couldn't accept a divorce, that you had no choice. (Interpretation₄)

Well, now I think that a broken marriage would be better than this unpleasant, uncertain sort of situation. But maybe the marriage just hasn't had enough time yet to crystallize. (Sighs, deeply.) Maybe I'm afraid to precipitate things too early. (Anx — wife)

You want to cement the marriage as much as possible. (Clarification)

Um-hm. I suppose that sounds cowardly, and I should be more objective. But a whole home is so darn important to me. Both sets of parents would blame me for a divorce.

You've talked about divorce with her? (Question)

Yeah. I'd like to tell people the kind of things she's done, but I wouldn't. (Hos n — wife)

You're feeling awfully depressed, (Clarification) *but it would be best not to do anything precipitous about changing the marriage relationship, until you've had a good chance to consider it here.* (Advice; again the therapist gives the usual proscription against making any irreversible decisions until therapy is completed.) *Also, she may be in a difficult phase of her own therapy right now, and this could be reflected in the home situation.* (Information)

That's sure true. (Pause) It's noon. Are you going to be available this summer (Dep + ther)

No, but we have a couple more weeks. Then I'll be away for the summer, but we can get started again early in the fall. You'll be on internship most of the time, won't you?

Well, yes, but if you were here, I'd drive up over the weekends. (Dep + ther; obviously the client has developed fairly positive, and perhaps dependent, attitudes toward the therapist.)

I wish it were possible, but I'm going to be away for most of the summer. But we can get started first thing in the fall.

Quinn: Twelfth Interview (5/25)

IN THE TWELFTH INTERVIEW the client spent most of his time discussing his peer relationships and his wife. There was some discussion of the relationship with the therapist and some expression of concern about the client's masculinity. The most prominent client affect themes were ego concerns and general anxiety. Affiliative presses, hostility needs, and dependency needs also each represented about a tenth of the affect themes. The client had made a tentative step in the direction of being more dominant in the marriage situation, and his wife's approval of this, which the therapist expected, had occurred. The client, feeling that his marriage was somewhat improved, shifted the discussion to his feelings of insecurity in group situations. His anxiety seemed to stem partly from a fear of seeming less bright than other men in a group, but perhaps the more basic feeling was a fear of seeming less masculine than the others. He related this to a number of situations during his adolescence when he felt less mature and virile than his peers. He reported not having this problem in groups composed mostly of women.

In this interview the therapist used a rather wide diversity of techniques: direct questions (25 per cent), interpretation (20 per cent), giving information (12 per cent), discussing the relationship (12 per cent), clarification of feeling (9 per cent), reassurance (9 per cent), and disapproval or challenging (9 per cent). The discussion of the relationship, in the amount indicated, was evidence of a new trend in this case. The therapist, believing that the client's resistance stemmed from some concerns he was feeling about the relationship, deliberately focused his attention on that topic, using the matter of the client's sitting next to him in the therapy classes as a topic for launching the discussion. The client recognized his very positive feelings toward the therapist but tended to ignore the reference to possible dependency feelings. He first stated that his sitting near the therapist was accidental, but later he admitted that it probably was not. After this interview his dependency score rose to its highest level (47).

Most of the interpretive statements in this interview occurred in the context of the client's discussion of concern about being insufficiently masculine. It became apparent that the anxiety in groups of males stemmed largely from this concern about his masculinity.

Following this interview the client's affect toward the therapist fell from 91 to 53, a marked drop to the fourth lowest score of the entire series. The therapist's score dropped nine points to 49, which placed it at about his mean for this client. Analysis of the actual items on the Client's Affect Scale shows that this drop in score was general in character; the client felt less sense of affiliation, succorance, and being understood, and more sense that the therapist was rejecting, dominating, and derogatory. He felt more general resistance and fear of self-exposure. Our best conjecture as to the cause of this change in affect is that resistance was developing over the necessity to discuss ego-damaging material and that the client experienced anxiety and some resentment at the therapist's moderately interventional attacks upon this resistance.

Some significant developments in the relationship took place during this interview. Mr. Quinn's more aggressive behavior toward his wife (he hit her) was not unrelated to the therapy relationship, since he actually attributed to the therapist a suggestion (during the last interview) that he be more aggressive, even though he recognized that the therapist had not recommended physical aggression. Shortly after this discussion a resistance phase seemed to develop, and the therapist made a direct interpretation of resistance as occurring at the point where the conscious material had been pretty well worked through. The client then pointedly indicated that he preferred to have the therapist take a more directive role in the therapy. Similarly, later in the interview, he indicated that he liked the therapist best as a teacher when he was taking a very active part in the class discussion and citing information from his own experience. Both of these examples reveal the dependency needs of this client. He also brought up his general anxiety about being in a group of male peers, with whom he feels very inadequate, in contrast to his feelings in a group of females. The therapist interpreted his fear of being conspicuous in a group as a fear of revealing a lack of masculinity, and he accepted this point reluctantly. He also indicated that it was quite important for him to seem virile in the eyes of the therapist, as it was also in those of his wife and his father. Again the anxiety about lack of masculinity showed itself in his discussing his having sung "castratti" in a boys' choir, and how ambivalent he felt about the recognition (and possible conspicuousness) which his solo boy-soprano role had given him. The therapist offered reassurance that he considered Mr. Quinn to be "more toward the masculine end of the continuum."

The therapist called to Mr. Quinn's attention the fact that he usually sat near the therapist in class and offered the interpretation that he found this position somewhat comforting and protecting against primitive fears he might be feeling in a group of male peers. Reluctantly Mr. Quinn admitted that this was true; he also indicated that he felt he could relate easily to people who perceive him as masculine, the way his supervisor in the hospital had.

Although the client's affect score dropped in this interview, we do not feel that the relationship was suffering particularly; as mentioned above, it seems more likely to us that Mr. Quinn's anxieties were aroused by the necessity of discussing rather threatening material. Quite likely, also, the therapist's rather deep interpretations about some of his defense mechanisms and basic insecurities caused some resistance and concern to develop.

At the end of the interview Mr. Quinn asked the therapist to tell him whether he had passed his comprehensive examinations. While this material was clearly outside the scope of the therapy, the therapist deliberately told Mr. Quinn that he had passed. He did this with the definite intention of capitalizing on this situation as a means of helping to build up the warmth of the relationship.

Last week you didn't recommend it, and I didn't think of it, but I hauled off and hit my wife last Saturday. She just kept nagging me, and I got the impulse and just let it go. (Hos n + wife) I was immediately sorry, but I was also glad I'd gotten it out. And her reaction was very surprising; she became extremely positive toward me. I guess it's the fact that she had some sign of feeling from me, even if it was negative. Since then the relationship has been a lot more pleasant, and I started living the type of personality that I would like to live. (Aff n + wife; Despite his denial the client was evidently influenced by the therapist's recommendation that he act more decisively toward his wife; she in turn responded as the therapist had predicted she might.)

What do you think are the dynamics of what happens when you hit her? (Question)

Perhaps it lets her know that I am feeling something. She sees that I care.

I don't know that that's enough to explain it. (Challenging)

Well, maybe also she likes to see me be dominant. That may be something that she needs. But I don't like to be dominant, physically. (Dep — wife; typical upper-class rejection of physical aggression.) I believe in a 51–49 split. I want a companionable marriage. (Aff n + wife)

I think it's been hard for her to accept the restrictions of marriage; she prefers the freedom of her "bachelor" days. She needs a lot of demonstration of affection, just as I do. (Dep + gen) But when I get fed up with her behavior, I just turn cold for a while. She says, too, that she's afraid of me. I don't know what she means by that. She gets nervous with me around; afraid I might do something, but she can't verbalize what. I certainly don't usually show physical violence. If I just look at her a little bit "strongly," she says she gets all fussed up. (He then described at considerable length the characteristics of his wife's family, depicting them as being very neurotic people.)

Um-hm. You sort of pick these topics up and go through them rather quickly, (Disapproval) *and you feel a little panicked that you've covered everything important.* (Clarification) *I wonder if you aren't showing signs of a little bit of resistance—a kind of plateau?* (Interpretation$_5$)

I guess I don't want to dig in, but I don't know what it is I'm afraid to discuss. I went through a counseling relationship when I was an undergraduate that was a real loss. The counselor was the most streamlined non-directive person I've ever seen. I disliked him from the start. Maybe I'm carrying over a few feelings from that. I got nervous *there* when I just had to sit. (Hos n + ther; Rel)

I wonder if you're telling me that you're not sure this is going to work out, either? If I just let you sit, it could go pretty badly. (Interpretation$_5$)

That may be. (Dep — ther, Rel; Laughs embarrassedly) I keep running up against walls and getting stuck.

Well, resistance of that sort very often relates to the counselor or the relationship. (Relationship) *However, do you remember how in class I've discussed the "twelfth interview phenomenon," the level where a person has told his story, or in analytic terms he's gone through the conscious level pretty much, and he has to start working on some of the preconscious or subconscious levels?* (Structuring)

That's a harder nut to crack. I don't want to make this relationship with you a storytelling session. A lot of the surface things that were bothering me have now been worked out positively. But there are other things that I want to square away.

The thing that still bothers me tremendously is my relationships in a group situation. I'm scared to death of being in groups. In a one-to-one relationship, or even a double date, I can be perfectly at ease. But in a class situation, I'm scared to death to say anything. (Dep — gen) I get frustrated in your class because I'll have a number of questions I want to bring up, but I don't feel they are related to what the others are talking about. (Anx — peers)

What do groups mean to you? (Question)

They are just magnified in their threatening aspects. I know these people and like them individually, but in a group I tighten up. I guess I think of the classes as competition, although I don't like that. (Anx — peers)

When did you first feel this way about groups? (Question)

That's what I was about to explore. I know I felt that way at prep school, but *there* I was being rejected by many people. I felt I wasn't worth much, and I also felt that I was misjudged. Even at military school I felt that way. I wasn't a leader, but I did well in my studies. Still I didn't feel particularly accepted, there. (Anx — pers) I was a soprano soloist in the glee club. I stayed soprano till I was thirteen. I finally rebelled and changed to tenor. They were more mature and adult. My voice never really cracked as it does in adolescence. Even when I was 13, I was singing "castratti." (Laughs) That's when I rebelled against singing treble. Some girls were visiting our school, and they looked at me especially, and I was mortified. I was proud that I had such a high-range voice, but also mortified. I think that incident caused me to tighten up in a group. I demanded to be put in the tenor section. Before then, I had liked it, because the solo soprano had the highest status in the choir; I got all the main solos. (Anx — masc)

At that age a boy soprano is a hero in a group, and pleasing to adults, also. (Information) *But I thought it was interesting that you used the term "castratti." Did you use it unconsciously? Or with implied cynicism?* (Interpretation₅)

I was being kind of cynical. (Laughs) I think it signified to me, I'm sure, that I hadn't reached manhood, yet. Also, I looked so much younger than the others. (Anx — masc)

One therapeutic practice that I think is very valuable is the analysis of the sequence of the client's thoughts. If we check your sequence here, we were talking about things about groups that make you feel uncomfortable, and when I asked you when you first felt this way, you focused on the incident of being a boy soprano and suddenly finding yourself a boy among men. And you used a very significant word to describe this. (Interpretation₄) *Now I wouldn't make too much of such a sequence,* (Attenuation) *but I wonder if that doesn't represent a kind of miniature of the important sequence of dynamics.* (Interpretation₅)

It might be, but how? (Sighs deeply) I keep coming back to the same thing in everything I say. This manhood matter.

Are you saying that you feel somewhat emasculated in a group situation, especially with men? (Interpretation₇)

I think maybe I do, sort of. I feel that I'm not going to show myself up as being a man. It's very important for me to show myself as adequate in a masculine way. (Anx — masc)

What are you trying to prove? (Question)

That I was a man.

Actually you probably were more active in sports than most of the boys. (Reassurance)

And I did well.

Have you ever been in groups where you were the only male present? (Question)

Yeah. I took an education course last year. Twenty-three females, and I was the only man! I felt very strange. They were mostly teachers.

Did you have difficulty talking? (Question)

No. I think that may have been a function of the fact that most of them were so stupid they didn't even belong in graduate school.

And also women. (Interpretation$_5$)

Well, I don't look down on women. There are a lot of intelligent women.

What am I trying to contrast in this discussion? (Question)

My relationship in this type of group to that with a group that's principally male, where I *do* feel very inadequate. (Anx — masc)

In the group of men you feel you'll seem less mature or less masculine. (Clarification)

Yeah. And also, less bright. I don't wanta' seem dumb. I'm threatened by some of the female graduate students here, too, whom I consider to be very bright. But I guess I can talk to them feeling more equal than to the guys. Especially some of the guys in *your* class. (Anx — peers)

Who do you feel most uncomfortable with in that group? (Question)

Well, X. is the leader. And maybe Y. Though X. has been very friendly. They're both very bright. They see the global problems, when I'm tied down with the bits and pieces. They have more experience than I. They seem more powerful. But they seem to be nice guys. I don't feel threatened when I relate to them personally. (Anx — peers)

As a teacher with the orientation that I have, I was rather pleased that you listed X. and Y. as the leaders of the group. But as a psychologist I was wondering why you didn't say anything about your feeling toward me in the group. (Relationship)

You're getting threatening. (Laughs) Your participation has been sort of directional, which it should be. Sort of a clarifying thing. It's like a group therapy situation. What I enjoy most is when you give some examples from your own experiences. That contributes a lot. (Dep + ther)

Um-hm. I'm steeped enough in student-centered teaching always to feel a little guilt about doing that, and yet also to have the conviction that some of the teaching has to be by precept and example, both real and vicarious. (Information)

What I was getting at, and I don't want to embarrass you, is that I've noticed where you tend to sit in class. (Relationship)

You mean sitting near you. I don't want to hurt your feelings, (laughs) but it's usually that I arrive a little bit later than most of the others. You *have* something there, though. (Dep + ther)

It's true that the last seats to fill up in a class are usually the ones nearest the "teacher." But in group dynamics a point is made of watching to see which people generally sit near the recognized leader of the group. (Information) *I'm not saying this in a critical way.* (Reassurance) *I perceive this as a sign of identification or of positive transference, or possibly, in terms of your discussion today, identification with me as a kind of, not protector exactly, but someone who would be on your side if anything got rough.* (Interpretation₅) *I'm going back to the primitive sort of instinct that might be felt, for example, by a four-year-old, and is only unconscious in an adult. I'm not implying that you're sitting there in dread or fear that somebody is going to beat the pulp out of you!* (Attenuation; therapist laughs.)

You remember last semester I sat about where G. (female) sits.

I do remember, and that's precisely why I noticed the difference. Perhaps, I thought that the class relationship was paralleling the change that has occurred in our relationship since therapy. (Relationship)

It might be. I find you much less threatening this semester than I did last semester. (Dep + ther, Rel)

Well, we're much more friendly now. You probably saw me then as distant and remote. (Relationship)

Definitely as an authority figure. I've felt quite comfortable sitting next to you in class this semester. (Dep + ther, Rel) Although sometimes I worried if people were looking toward you, and I felt too many eyes pointing in *my* direction.

Why? What might they see? (Question)

I know what you're thinking, but I'm not so sure it's right. (Laughs) Seeing me as not being a man. (Anx — masc)

The fact that you know that I'm thinking it, and you don't think it's right, could mean that I'm crazy as hell, or it could mean that you were resisting. (Challenges) (Both laugh)

Yeah. That may be. This line of discussion is very threatening to me. (Anx — ther)

Makes you nervous. (Clarification) *Why?* (Question)

It's very uncomfortable. I don't know. Probably to you, I've got to look very masculine. (Dep + ther, Rel; transference is revealed here, and probably some dependency.)

I wondered about that. That's why I asked you who threatened you most in the class. (Information) *Well, there's no reason to feel anxious about talking about it. The fact that you can recognize that this is somewhat threatening to you is good.* (Reassurance) *We both know that this is something that bothers you a little, and we'll have to be careful and treat it from that point of view.* (Attenuates)

I think it's the same reason that I react so strongly to my wife's comments about my being fat. (Dep + wife)

You want very much to have people whom you respect think of you as male. Anything that suggested that they didn't would be pretty threatening. (Clarification) *I believe I mentioned once that I saw you as being toward the masculine end of the continuum.* (Reassurance)

A lot of people do think of me as a man in my relationships. I think my supervisor at the hospital did. And the other staff members there. And I feel I can really relate to the people who do. (Dep + auth) The others, I'm so worried about, but I don't know why I should be.

Um-hm. I guess our time's up for today.

(As the client was leaving, he asked the therapist if he knew whether the client had passed his comprehensive exam. (Dep + ther) The therapist told the client that he had passed and gave him his scores. This was a deliberate attempt to build rapport; it tended to utilize the client's dependency feelings to enhance both the relationship and the transference.)

Quinn: Thirteenth Interview (6/1)

IN THE THIRTEENTH INTERVIEW the major topic of concern for the client was the adequacy of his masculinity. He also discussed his wife's feelings toward himself and his own suppressed hostility toward the man who was attempting to interest his wife. There was a brief discussion of a dream which he considered to be revealing of Oedipal feelings toward his mother, although the therapist offered the suggestion that the person in the dream sounded more like the maid than his mother. The client gave numerous evidences of his confusion, during childhood and adolescence, regarding sex-typing and of his participation in typically feminine interests and activities. The principal affect themes of the client during this interview were the expression of ego-needs and sex needs. A little anxiety and dependency were displayed, and his dependency score remained quite high (45).

During the thirteenth interview the therapist did a good bit of direct questioning (45 per cent) and interpreting (32 per cent). This was designed to cause the client to elaborate his own statements about his lack of masculinity or to point out to him elements of which he did not seem to be aware. Some of the interpretations were at a deeper level, pointing out the unconsciously passive feminine nature of some of his behavior.

Whatever negative affect had developed between client and therapist during the previous interview was reversed during the thirteenth; the client's affect score rose to 73 and the therapist's to 58. By its nature the material discussed should have been as threatening as that of the previous interview, but apparently the previous anxiety and resistance were lessening.

We must have run into an area that is still very tight for me, last week, because I haven't been able to do any thinking about it. I've either suppressed or repressed the entire area. The general area of masculinity seems very threatening to me. (Anx — masc; a major area of resistance became evident here.) I wonder if I've internalized some of my father's comments about the fact that I was kind of ineffective. He was always harping on the matter of why I should grow up. My sports participation must have been an attempt to show him that I was mature. (Anx — masc)

Once when I was ten or eleven, I had a big balloon, and I cried when it broke. I had some childhood activities which were somewhat feminine: I sewed handkerchiefs, and I played with my sister and her girl friends. There weren't any boys in our neighborhood. I was the smallest, so I was always the follower. (Anx — masc) I never gave my stuffed animals away. I think they fulfilled a tremendous need for me—something I wasn't getting. I feel all "glued up" inside when I talk about them; I didn't realize that one could build up such dependence on stuffed animals. (Dep + gen; these items of information about the client's childhood all suggest somewhat feminine interests and life-style.)

When did you learn to cook? (Question)

Oh, yeah. Not 'til I was about 13, when I was living with mother again. I remember even during this period in the mornings and on weekends I'd go into mother's room and climb into bed with her, and I kept that up until she got remarried when I was about 12 or 13. She certainly didn't discourage it. (Dep + mo → Sex n — het, mo) (Sighs)

You had almost no masculine ideal to identify with in this period. Your father was distant, and there was no companionship with him. (Interpretation$_8$)

That's right. I couldn't even tell him how lonely I was. (Dep — fa)

I remember one incident when a little girl and I put on a show for everybody in the apartment area by dressing up in each other's clothes. But I was pretty embarrassed by it. I felt terrible wearing a dress; I guess it's very significant of the feminine role. (Anx — masc) Another incident that was mortifying to me was in military school when I had to play the female part in a dramatic performance. I was embarrassed by it; there was even a kissing scene, and I was repelled by it and didn't kiss, but just embraced. (Anx — masc) Nobody ever said anything; they thought it was very nice that I was willing to take the part. (Many boys of his age would have refused even this small amount of identification with a feminine role.)

Why do you think the director chose you? (Question)

I thought you might ask that. (Laughs) Perhaps because I'd had the lead in the play the year before, and they knew I could do it justice. That's the reason I prefer to think. And the other reason is that maybe I walked around looking like a female. I hope that wasn't it. (Anx — masc)

Did any of the teachers ever fill a satisfactory masculine-ideal role for you? (Question)

Well, you were never with them long enough for that to happen. You only saw them for a few minutes in any particular day.

It was easier for you to identify with the warm, sympathetic women who were essentially passive in life-style. (Interpretation$_8$)

Um-hm. (Sighs)

Did you ever wish you were a girl? (Question)

I remember having dreams that were definitely homoerotic in nature. I'm sure I was very young. (Sighs) One dream I still remember. I dreamed I was wrestling with a *sumo* wrestler. I know I was getting a tremendous amount of pleasure in the dream from doing it. (Sex n + homo; Drm) Here's a fat guy, (laughs) but although he's a male, a *sumo* wrestler is as close to a female body type as you can get. Maybe this would just be an Oedipal dream, standing for wrestling with my mother, but I hardly knew my mother, either. (Sex n — mo)

What was the physique of the maid? (Question)

Fat. Hm! Mother substitute. Might well have been.

This discussion arose last week in connection with the marriage. (Interpretation$_4$) *I wonder if you have any further thoughts on the connection between this topic and the marriage?* (Directive lead)

Nope. (Laugh) I can't think of any. (Sighs) Other than the fact that, as we said last week, I may not appear as a particularly masculine figure to my wife, because I may still not be sure of what *I* am (Anx — masc) (Sighs). I don't do anything that's particularly *un*masculine. I do a lot of things that are quite masculine, like my woodworking and building airplane models. (Ego + masc) Maybe she considers my models somewhat childish.

How about cooking? (Question)

Well, I don't actually enjoy that. I don't do it very creatively.

You like to keep the place clean. (Interpretation$_5$)

Um-hm. At least I help. I don't think that's an unmasculine thing. There're an awful lot of husbands in our neighborhood who do the cleaning. It's no different from doing the dishes—just sharing in the responsibility. (Aff n + wife)

I'm not saying that there's something wrong about this. (Reassurance) *I'm simply trying to find out what the roles are.* (Structuring)

They're a little bit mixed. So in that sense she isn't seeing a completely masculine person. (Here he admits that there is some reversal of sex-type roles in his marriage.)

In some ways you show more interest in domestic concerns than she does. For instance it's she who leaves her clothes lying around. (Interpretation$_7$)

Yeah. She was worried last week when she made her first pie; she was afraid it wouldn't be as good as mine are.

How feminine is she? (Question)

She wouldn't be the stereotype of a feminine person at all. She's kind of aggressive. But she strikes me as very female if not very feminine. I wouldn't want a mate who was retiring and shy. She's a *strong* representative of her sex. She's sexually arousing. She isn't at all masculine. Some women would find her too aggressive. I prefer women with a little backbone and not the clinging vine type. (Dep + wife)

Female, but not excessively feminine. (Restatement)

Yes. Maybe because I'm still quite unsure of myself, and I need somebody that I can depend on. (Dep + wife; several times he has admitted this uncertainty about the adequacy of his masculinity, particularly in his marriage.)

Who's the aggressor in the sex behavior? (Question)

Me. I find it a very acceptable role. Once in a while we reverse roles in terms of the dominant position on top, but usually I am the more aggressive one. I don't know why she could think of me as feminine in the sexual role, other than just my body. (Ego + masc) Before we go to sleep we sort of cuddle together. I have to lie on my stomach, I guess it's sort of self-protection, and she sort of cuddles around me. I guess I'm taking the passive role there, and she's taking the more protective role. (Dep + wife) We always make up any differences before we go to bed. I seem to hold a hurt longer than she does, or else I don't compartmentalize. She can usually tell when I'm mad and don't want to have sex. (Hos n + wife)

It almost seems like you would be sort of withholding yourself. (Interpretation$_9$)

Yes. That's kind of feminine. (Anx − masc)

Or passive resistance. (Interpretation$_9$)

I think our roles are companionate; I think it's a mutual courting. We each try to see how the other one feels.

This other guy is still trying to make a play for my wife, even though she won't have anything to do with him. It still makes me mad as hell. I just about plastered him one at a party some weeks ago. The masculine thing to do would be to do something about it, but she's asking me not to. I'd sure love to push my fist right in his mush. (Hos n − rival)

Then why don't you? (Challenges; although this seems to be a challenge, it was actually intended more as a question about his motivation.)

Mainly because she says she doesn't want me to. (Dep + wife) I don't know how I would handle it. He is in a position where he could injure me academically. If he'd said just one thing at that party, I would have let him have it. I had my inhibitions down from quite a number of drinks. I really do hate his guts. (Hos n − rival)

How does she feel about him? (Question)

She says he doesn't mean anything to her, but I'm not sure. She likes very masculine physiques, and he's a mesomorph—a Tarzan type of creature. She seems to get infatuated when she encounters *any* guy with a beautiful physique. Unfortunately, just because of bone structure, I could never achieve a real masculine body-type. (Anx — masc)

Um-hm. I guess our time is about up. There's no school next week, but I can see you, if you want to come in.

Sure do!

Quinn: Fourteenth Interview (6/8)

THE MAJOR OBJECTS of discussion in the fourteenth interview were the adviser, the client's wife, his masculinity, and the therapist. In this interview the client reported an important transference dream which revealed his sense of dependency upon the therapist to protect him when he came into conflict with authority figures. When he dreamed of taking some aggressive steps himself, he also dreamed of a fear of retaliation from the authority person toward whom he showed the aggression. He showed some insight into his fear of other males, not indicating, however, any awareness of the possible implications of a latent homosexual trend in his own behavior, and lack of aggression toward male peers. The client expressed a strong rejection of a colleague who was flagrantly promiscuous in his heterosexual behavior. The principal client affect-themes were anxiety, hostility, dependency, ego needs, and the sense of being the recipient of hostility from others.

In this interview the therapist employed much interpretation (41 per cent) and some direct questioning (21 per cent). There was also a little challenging and persuasion (9 per cent). Much of the interpretation was designed to reveal the origin of the client's passivity in the upper-class conditioning to which he had been subjected as a child. The therapist also challenged the client as to how much aggression he felt he must tolerate before he would fight back, clearly implying that the client was overly passive in his unwillingness to fight back. During this interview the therapist also helped direct the client's interpretation of his dream, which was discussed both at the manifest level of expressing hostility toward his adviser and of feeling the need to be protected by the therapist, and at the deeper level of feeling hostility toward the other men in whom his wife showed some interest. Its Oedipal and latent homosexual implications were not discussed.

The client's positive feelings toward the therapist, as revealed in the dependency elements of his dream, also showed themselves in his score on the Client's Affect Scale, which was 94, his fourth most positive score during the entire treatment. The therapist's score, never showing very much fluctuation, rose two points to 60, which was also his fourth highest score. At this point in therapy, when strong dependency on the therapist was revealed, the affect between client and therapist showed itself to be very high and positive. The post-interview dependency score dropped five points (to 40) however, although only temporarily.

I got two Honors grades in my courses this semester, which is very pleasing. It demonstrates that I am able to do the work if I try. Along with passing the comps quite well, I think this semester has been pretty successful. (Ego + prof)

I had a funny dream last night; I'm not sure that it means much, but I just thought I'd relate it. It was a very long one, and I can interpret part of it, I think. The part that completely confuses me is that I was driving a Corvette, and I parked it outside of a fraternity house, and the top was down. There were four people in it, and I recognized one as being Dr. C. (woman faculty member). Couldn't quite figure what she was doing there, but anyway, I had a box of kleenex in the car, and I went away from the car for a distance, and I was able to picture her with a fiendish gleam in her eye, and she came over and I didn't know what was happening, but I came running back and they took off toward the fraternity house. And what they had done was fill the car full of kleenex, just wadded up. (Hos n — peers) And I said "I'll get you" or something like that. I was pretty mad, and suddenly I reached the toleration point, I just couldn't take any more, and I took off across the street, and they went in the front door of the fraternity house and locked it. So the back door was right down below and I saw one of the three guys heading for the stairway that goes downstairs to lock the back door, so I jumped over the railing and just got inside the back door before he got there. And I proceeded to slug him, many, many times, (Hos n + auth) and then I remember I smiled, and I said "I'm exhausted." I couldn't do any more. And he was about ready to work out on me (laughs) and at this point the house president came up and I explained what they'd done, (Dep + ther surrog) and at that time it seemed terrible, and so the house president forgave me, and he told the guy that he'd done many, many things that were wrong and asked why he did it, and so on. The guy said something to the effect that "Every once in a while I get tightened up inside and I just go wrong, and I can't help myself." At this point I woke up with a tremendous cramp in my leg, which is still with me this morning. I'm trying to figure why Dr. C. would be in the dream as a fiendish person. In the first place I don't know her that well. (Anx — auth)

Well, what have your contacts with her been? (Question)

Strictly at parties. Pretty much small talk, and so on. I can't think that she reminds me of anybody. She doesn't look like anybody.

She might be a screen for someone else, or she might be a role-symbol of some sort. (Interpretation$_5$)

Is it possible that she can be a role-symbol for the psychology department?

That was one that I was thinking of. (Interpretation$_5$)

I wonder if I would think of her as being the least threatening of any of the faculty.

What did the three fellows who were with her seem like? (Question)

I only saw the one that I was slugging. I don't know what he was like. Pretty young. About my age, or so. Bigger than I was; I seemed pretty small in the dream. Nice looking guy. I remember when I was slugging him I felt very impotent. (Anx — masc) I couldn't put power into my punches. And then I sheepishly smiled. That might be that same thing we were talking about last week (concern over seeming less masculine than the wife's current admirer).

What does that tell me about you? (Question)

In other words, the way I have sort of pictured myself as being an impotent male. Here was a demonstration of it in the dream. Sluggin' for all I was worth and just couldn't put any power in my punches. Tried to do a masculine thing, but wasn't able to do it. And it was sort of a woman's way of getting out of the thing to smile at him and say, "Please forgive me. I'm exhausted. Don't hit me now." (Dep + auth) Perhaps going to the house president—I was scared, I know that, and he was right there pleading my case and so on, because I was afraid of getting beaten up. (Dep + ther surrog)

Uh, you were attempting to do something aggressive and masculine, and you just didn't have the strength to finish. (Restatement) *You suddenly lost your nerve, and your only defense was to be apologetic, and in a sense to throw yourself on his mercy and be somewhat humble, and win him over by a smile.* (Restatement)

It wasn't that I had just lost my strength, I lost what little I had been able to muster. Whenever I've gotten into a fight, that has been somewhat characteristic of me. It only happened once. I hated this guy so, I just went wild, and I practically picked him up bodily and threw him outa my room. But I've always been afraid to hit somebody, full power. I don't quite know why. Even in boxing class, I was in the finals but only because of points on defensive. I'd never slug a guy hard. (A possible sign of latent homosexual feelings.) I never could pound anybody. (Anx — peers)

That might be very important to go into sometime. (Calls attention) *Getting back to the dream for a minute, were all three of the fellows that were accompanying Dr. C. young?* (Question)

Yeah.

What was the house president like? (Question)

He was a young good-looking guy. All the guys I guess were good-lookin'. And he seemed pretty much like the epitome of fairness. (Laughs) He was — I was sorta looking up to him, like a God, or something. He'd be a very fair person. (Dep + ther surrog)

He took your side. (Restatement)

Not only that, but somebody I could trust. (Dep + ther surrog)

He called the others off of you. (Restatement)

Um-hm.

Have you been in any situations where you kind of felt the need of someone to defend you? (Question)

Yeah, *you.* (Dep + ther)

Well, that's what I was getting at. You might perceive the four in the car as the clinical faculty. Dr. C. was the key to that. (Interpretation$_7$)

But why should she be threatening? As you said, she might just stand for something. But I can easily see where the house-president might well have been you, because of my feelings toward you in the last month or more. I had thought of you as being a sort of helper and someone I could count on to help me through the situation. (Dep + ther, Rel)

I'll be darned if I can figure out why kleenex in the car. It's a minor thing. I wonder if it might just be a symbol for the over-reacting I've been doing for quite a while. The big things I haven't been reacting to too much, but the little things keep blowing up outa nowhere.

It would be a little hard to trace the specific symbolism. (Attenuates) *It's rather interesting that it was a Corvette, a powerful or speedy car. And notoriously automobiles are . . .* (Interpretation$_9$)

Sex symbols.

Well, and/or libido symbols, particularly for males. (Interpretation$_7$) *One might interpret that they were fouling it up, or messing it up, or jamming it up,* (Interpretation$_9$) *only I don't know what the meaning would be. In fact, all of this is somewhat speculation.* (Attenuates) *However, to my "third ear" it seems reasonable that these four might be faculty members. I might have been the house president, not necessarily older but the recognized leader and adjudicator.* (Interpretation$_7$) *The car might have been a symbol for you, of your potency or power in some way.* (Interpretation$_9$)

I often think that my love for sports cars, besides the fact that I like the way they handle, is as a status symbol. Maybe one always thinks of a "man's man" in a sports car. All the ivy league clothing ads and so on, and standing beside a sports car. (Anx — masc)

Well, you don't need a sports car just for transportation, so it must have some other meaning. (Interpretation$_9$)

Yeah, well, I like them mechanically much better than an American car. There's very good grounds that they're superior, according to most sports car fans.

But they're all a biased sample. (Challenges; both laugh)

I mean the handling and spring, and so on. I feel it's a much safer car. But I still do get a thrill out of a powerful car. I never had one myself, but last week a guy borrowed my Ford, and he lent me his Jag in return, and that was *great.* I love the *power* in that car. (Ego + masc)

So they're really symbols of power, (Interpretation$_9$) *and also their low slim lines are symbols of trimness, fastness, agility.* (Interpretation$_9$)

Which I ain't! (Laughs)

But you might like to be. (Clarification)

Yes. Yes. I would love to be a mesomorph. (Anx — phys)

So that may be what the car symbolizes. Your self-ideal, or your ideal production. (Interpretation$_9$) (Pauses) *The specific meaning of tissue paper or kleenex would be a very hard one to identify.* (Attenuates) *One might postulate that they were insulting your car by filling it with something like toilet paper, but that's pretty analytic.* (Interpretation$_9$) *It's very hard to attach any significance to it, except that it was a disturbance or blemish or insult of some sort.* (Attenuates) (Pause)

There's one more dream interpretation. One could go at it at a lower level. At a deeper level, Dr. C. might have more meaning than she does at the level we discussed. (Interpretation$_9$)

Well, my thoughts about her are just that she's a very nice person. I don't know anything about her. She just seems awfully nice to talk to and a lot of fun at a party. She lets down her hair and becomes one of the girls, Other than that I have no contact with her. At a party she lets you call her by her first name. It makes me feel good that she's trying to integrate herself with the students as well as the faculty. (Aff n + auth)

You were slugging one of these guys? (Question)

(Client laughs) Maybe I know what you're thinking. I wonder if he stands for the guy that had made a play for my wife, perhaps? (Hos n + rival)

Perhaps? (Question)

Oh, I don't think that my wife and Dr. C. are equivalent. Then again, maybe last week my wife *did* seem somewhat like her. (He discusses a characteristic they might have in common.) Maybe that explains this deviltry that was in her eyes in the dream. That's the way I felt my wife was, and the way she has admitted that she was. Devilish, just for the sake of being devilish. But this guy did not look at all like the one she had the flirtation with. (Pause) He might well have stood for him. That makes me mad. (Laughs) That I wasn't able to beat him up. (Hos n — rival) I know in real life if I ever came to that stage—I almost did at that party two weeks ago—

there wouldn't be too much trouble. I know with him I'd be quite mad enough. (Very audible sigh)

I certainly do feel impotent in a lot of situations. I'm not so sure but that my wife's telling me not to do anything about it wasn't a nice excuse for me to avoid doing anything. I don't know why. (Dep + gen)

You're saying that you very easily accepted her request that you not do anything aggressive. (Clarification)

(Client sighs) That's what I'm wondering. Of course, I'll never know. 'Cause I didn't *do* anything. (Dep + gen) When she first told me, I was all set to take off down the road and pay a visit to the guy. But she stopped me from doing that. (Dep + wife) What I wanted to do was go in there and try and make him lie, in other words catch him at it, and then see what happens. (Hos n — rival)

Trap him in a position where he would show no remorse, but be completely culpable, so you would be justified in being aggressive. (Clarification)

I can't think that he did feel sorry, because he kept trying to get her to go out with him after that.

I get very worried about my wife's continuing to show some interest in other men. She was always the rejected child with her mother, and she needs something to keep bolstering her ego. These guys are symbols of acceptance. She's felt rejected by me at times, because I have tended to dominate her the way her mother did. And she felt that I have kept her from going away to college. (Nur + wife)

After we discussed this last night, we felt very much in love with each other and had very satisfying sexual relations. This was the first time that she had felt like it from the beginning. (Sex n + wife)

I have always pulled my punches in fighting; I thought it was because I was afraid of being hurt. I was never able to slug anybody. I am never willing to be the aggressor. But I've often had the desire, as in that dream, to pound somebody in the mush. But appropriate situations seldom arise, and when they do, I still don't do it. (Dep + gen)

Any form of aggression that I showed produced overwhelming counter-aggression from my father. I must have done some aggressive things in disguised form, like setting that fire in the basement. Or throwing stones at streetcar windows. But, so what? (Hos n — fa)

One of your greatest problems is the concern that your self-image causes, because you see yourself as less aggressive than you would like to be. (Interpretation$_7$) *We've traced some of the roots of this in the upper-class conditioning you underwent. And also in your desire to be liked by people whom you felt were rejecting.* (Interpretation$_8$)

I'd do anything to get or to hold friends. Especially someone I idolize, like that restaurant owner. (Dep + fa surrog)

But do you have to adopt a Christ-like role of always turning the other cheek? (Challenges) *Can we find what your values are, and then decide how far to go, aggressively, in achieving them?* (Advises) *How much aggression from others will you tolerate before fighting back?* (Question)

I don't know. I have been disappointed in myself, but I wouldn't want to go to the opposite extreme.

Of course not. (Approval)

I have been afraid to do anything that might make my wife mad at me and cause me to lose her. (Dep + wife)

This shows how neurotic needs can distort situations. (Interpretation$_7$) *In reality, I would predict that doing something aggressive about this other guy might have caused her to increase her respect and affection for you.* (Persuasion)

It might be. (Sighs) It's water over the dam, now.

There's another guy I dislike intensely. He's a student that we see socially. He does everything that I disapprove of. He's married and has children, and yet he flagrantly flaunts his promiscuity before everybody. His values stink! He exploits everything I hold dear. He has an open mind of what he calls the "Greenwich Village type!" That gets me mad. Every time he opens his mouth I think, "Well, here comes some more bull."

Quinn: Fifteenth Interview (9/19)

MOST OF THE CLIENT'S concern in the fifteenth interview was about his wife's behavior, but there was a small amount of reference to his father and to the therapist. The principal affect-themes were anxiety and hostility. There was also some expression of dependency and sex need. The client's principal concern was his wife's continuing tendency to become interested in other men and to talk about leaving him. This caused him to be ambivalent, sometimes anxious and depressed, but sometimes hostile. He decided, however, to spend more time with his wife and to try to increase the expression of those things which she would find positive about himself and the activities in which they shared a mutual nterest.

In this interview the therapist employed much more than his usual amount of redirecting behavior (26 per cent). Several times he called the client's attention to the importance of specific matters, and several times he challenged a statement by the client. Once he expressed disapproval in the form of accusing the client of repressing a feeling.

Although this interview followed a three months' lapse, the client's affect score toward the therapist (92) was about the same as before the summer period. The therapist's score had dropped five points (to 55), which still placed his score near the top third of his affect scores for this client. At one point the client pointed out the strong feeling of affection that he felt for his internship supervisor, and the therapist wondered whether this might have implied an unconscious criticism of himself for not being available to the client during the summer.

Several parts of the interview revealed information about the therapy relationship. At the very beginning the client said, "You act like a good-luck charm!", giving the therapist undeserved praise for the client's wife's recent cessation of her behavior. Late in the interview, Mr. Quinn mentioned that he could never feel critical of his father and that he still wanted to re-establish a dependent father-son type of relationship with him. He indicated that this was the sort of satisfying relationship he had built up during the summer with his internship supervisor;

137

there may have been some implication of criticism of the therapist for not providing enough of the same type of relationship. His dependency score returned to a fairly high level (44).

Although several times he was warmly sympathetic, the therapist was at other times critical of Mr. Quinn's passivity. He also gave advice about ways of making it more difficult for Mr. Quinn's wife to find opportunities to flirt. At one point, Mr. Quinn remarked defensively, "I'm no jailer!" The over-all affect of this interview was quite positive, however, and Mr. Quinn showed few signs of being disturbed by the more directive sorts of activities of the therapist.

As I mentioned last week in the hall, I found out this fall that my wife has been dating different men during the summer while I was on internship. *You* act as a good-luck charm; whenever I tell you about things, the situation changes. (Dep + ther; this statement reveals strong positive transference, certainly in this specific situation unearned.) She's stopped now, but I still have very strong feelings about it. She believed herself to be in love with the last guy. She was all set to leave me. (Anx — wife)

I've taken a lot of walking over because I'm usually a pretty passive guy, but this time I threw caution to the winds and said what I thought about the whole business. (Hos n + wife) I said that I was hurt and angry, but that I still wanted and loved her. (Dep + wife) I've started expressing my feelings more, even in things like commenting on a beautiful tree we would be passing. Her reaction was, "I didn't know you thought about things like that." I have been all wet in my previous policy of keeping all my feelings to myself. In the past I just couldn't show emotion for fear of having my feelings hurt. (Dep + gen)

My wife says she wants to stay with me, but in the past she has never been able to control these impulses to flirt with the boys. I don't think I should beat up the guy; (Dep + gen) she has to be able to show that *she* can stop this herself, without depending on me to break it up for her. After she told me about it and we decided we really loved each other, we had a wonderful intercourse, the finest we've ever had. (Sex n + wife)

I wonder if you remember that you told me the same thing about a reconciliation that took place last spring? (Interpretation$_4$)

I guess every time we have a reconciliation, sex is always better. But this time it was *really* as complete as I can imagine. My wife used to fake passion; usually she actually doesn't want sex, except at certain rare times. She usually thinks sex is a very distasteful thing.

As much as I'd like to, I'm too much of a realist to think that she's all through with her flirtations. I'm reconciled to her tendency toward promiscuity. (Dep + wife)

Are you reconciled? (Challenging)

I don't *want* it to happen, and if it does, I want to do something about it. I think my way of being firm in my opposition, but not hitting her, is the best way to handle it. (Dep + wife)

She keeps a tally of her boyfriends.

Might you call it a score-card of her victories? (Interpretation$_5$)

It's that, all right. She bats 1000. They're all infatuated.

What difficulties can we anticipate that we will encounter in a situation of an essentially monogamous male married to a wife who keeps a score-card, and who, in a little over a year of marriage, has had half a dozen flirtations? (Question) *We're faced with the question of what this means for you.* (Calls attention)

Yeah. It reminds me of the drug addict. Can't taper off.

That's a good analogy. (Approval) *The successful drug addict can't taper off. It has to be a clean break.* (Information)

I'm no jailer! She has actually asked me to give her strength. I've explained to her that it only takes a short conversation to get out of these situations when they start. You seem to feel there's a poor prognosis, and I realize that's true. I want her happiness, and if she really decides it's not with me, I'll feel better than if she just takes off without making a genuine decision. (Dep — wife)

When I try to imagine your feelings, I know you must be unbelievably crushed by it. (Clarification)

That's the way it was. I usually try not to cry, but since this happened, I have. (Dep + gen) I've stopped repressing it, even in front of her. It's been partly my fault in the past, in that I have not kept the channels of communication open enough. There hasn't been enough real mutual interest in each other's feelings and needs. I think she's changed from hating me, first to indifference, and now to really caring for me somewhat. (Aff n + wife) I knew something was happening when I was away this summer.

You may have put your finger on a crucial detail; (Clarification) *her interest in others has usually increased when you were away. The opportunity has been greater then;* (Information) *you can't make yourself a jailer, but when you're available, less of this flirtatiousness occurs.* (Advises)

That's true. I may be filling the vacuum, but if she has this much, can I really satisfy her enough? She seems to have this need to test her own limits. She's been very foolish about it; it was partly the men's fault, but she also told them that she was extremely unhappy and was going to get a divorce. I felt as though there was no point in going on with life. (Dep + gen)

You felt alone, and totally unloved again. (Clarification)

That's right, I knew I had friends; I felt secure with my internship supervisor. (Dep + auth) One thing this has done, it has taught me not to feel so complacent. (Dep + gen)

If I'm constantly available and responsive, she'd have less interest in others. But she has to make the decision for herself. I've made up my mind not to be away from home any more, however. I was a real fool not to insist that she go along with me last summer. (Dom n + wife)

There are two situations, you see, you should always watch; one is to avoid these vacuum situations for her, and the other is always to be as responsive to her as you can. (Advises)

It's hard to be responsive when I get walked on. (Hos n + wife)

What's the best way to respond to being walked on? (Question)

When I get jabbed, I like to jab back. What I actually do is to try to accept things. (Dep + gen)

I think you're clouding over what you've actually done, which has usually been to repress it. Neither the repression, nor the extreme hostility seems to me to be a desirable action. (Disapproval) *The step that you took more recently, of facing it and saying something about it, is the hygienic step, and each time it has produced a better understanding.* (Approving) *In a minor way this was also true about your thesis last year. Avoiding the issue didn't get you anywhere.* (Advises)

I can bear with it if I realize that she can't help herself. She's emotionally gooped up. I have a breaking point somewhere, but I dread a divorce. My father would criticize me for it. (Dep + fa)

Well, isn't he pretty vulnerable, himself? (Challenging)

Yes, but I could never criticize my own father. (Dep + fa) That's one thing I must work on. I still want to build a more positive relationship with him. (Dep + fa) I don't have many really warm relationships. (Dep + gen) My internship supervisor is one person I really feel warm about. (Dep + auth) (Does this constitute a criticism of the therapist for "rejecting" him in the summer or for not being nurturant enough?)

Quinn: Sixteenth Interview (9/24)

IN THE SIXTEENTH INTERVIEW the client was very depressed because his wife had left him for several days, saying that she wanted to find out whether she cared more for another man. She had returned and there had been a reconciliation, but he was still doubtful whether she really loved him. Approximately two-fifths of his discussion in this interview concerned his wife, and a like amount was about his feelings toward the therapist. A small part concerned his own sense of adequacy. His symptoms of dependency and feelings of inadequacy were probably at one of their highest points during this interview; his predominant feeling seemed to be one of despair and impotence about not being able to do much to change the situation with his wife. The principal affect-themes were anxiety and hostility. There were some dependency needs, affiliation needs, and pressure of hostility from others.

In this interview the therapist was very directive, using much interpretation (23 per cent) and challenging and persuasion (25 per cent); however, there was also some use of reassurance (12 per cent), clarification of feeling (9 per cent), and other techniques. Actually, the therapist was pushing the client to take a more aggressive position with his wife and was inferring that Mr. Quinn's inability to do so might be the result of some masochistic need on his part. He criticized the client for offering to arrange for his wife to live away from home so as to decide which man she preferred, saying that the more "normal" male behavior would be to threaten physical aggression if his wife carried out the proposed temporary separation. The therapist suggested that the client's wife might be interpreting his passive behavior as a lack of interest in her. However, he also did express sincere sympathy for the client, and when Mr. Quinn was most depressed, he offered a considerable amount of reassurance.

The client's sense of frustration, combined with the rather strong pressure from the therapist, apparently caused his affect toward the therapist to become less positive, for the score on the Client Affect

141

Scale dropped almost 30 points to 64, placing it in the lowest quarter of his affect scores. The therapist's score also dropped, to 43, or around the thirtieth percentile for his scores toward Mr. Quinn.

Some very important events affecting the relationship transpired in the sixteenth interview. At the beginning Mr. Quinn did two very dependent things. First, he asked the therapist to get him a better parking place than he had. The therapist tried, but was unsuccessful. He did not do this as a therapist but as an administrator, but this distinction may be begging the question, since he could not escape the implications of this act for therapy. Second, Mr. Quinn indicated that he had considered calling the therapist to get his advice about whether to let his wife live away from home for a while. He did not call however; during the interview the therapist was very directive in letting the client know that he considered Mr. Quinn's a very poor decision, perhaps the result of some masochistic need. He described it as "Not normal behavior for a husband." When Mr. Quinn rationalized his behavior as being "clinical," the therapist challenged this rationalization. He asked how long Mr. Quinn was going to allow himself to be "walked on" and "loused up" by his wife. The client admitted his great fears of being aggressive in almost all situations and called himself "backboneless." He had, however, "stood up to" his internship supervisor, but revealed the insightful statement that the only people he could be firm with were gentle people. The therapist recognized his sense of desperation and expressed quite a bit of sympathy for him. The suggestion was made that they would have to try to condition Mr. Quinn to become more aggressive; he felt that this would be difficult because he never had any need to be aggressive toward the therapist. The latter commented that he had been deliberately trying to provoke some hostility, but Mr. Quinn indicated his awareness of this and simply said that he considered the therapist's criticisms justified. Some intention to attempt to be more forceful seemed evident, however, and the therapist began to feel a little concern that Mr. Quinn might go too far with such behavior and counseled not taking too big a step in this direction too rapidly. He again reassured Mr. Quinn of his feeling that the latter had quite a bit of potential for development.

We see in this interview, then, almost the extreme point of Mr. Quinn's neurotic helplessness to take a more aggressive role, with the therapist exhorting, cajoling, encouraging, and persuading him to try. His PAC-NAC dependency score was at 46, one point below its highest level. As the therapist suggested, Mr. Quinn was indeed a Hamlet, and this was his major problem to correct. Undoubtedly the strong pressure from the therapist was somewhat disturbing to Mr. Quinn, and his affect scores became less positive, as indicated above. However, that the techniques were effective is revealed in subsequent interviews. The relationship was strong enough to support this amount of pressure without undue disturbance to the client, and with some positive gains evident. In terms of learning theory, the therapist was applying some punishing behavior for the neurotic responses, and some encouraging and rewarding behavior (reassurance, approval, persuasion) for the "healthy" response, and the learning took place in the desired direction.

(The client had asked the therapist to get him a special parking permit on the campus. (Dep + ther) There was some possibility that he was entitled to it, and the therapist made an inquiry, but the request was rejected. The therapist explained this to the client. (Dep + ther))

Quite a bit has happened since last week. I made a decision which I thought was right, and I wanted to call you up and ask you about it, (Dep + ther) but I decided I had to make it on my own, anyway. (A sign of maturation) On Thursday my wife said she was going to leave me for a couple of weeks so she could think things out. She admitted she would be going out with this other guy. I told her it would be all right with me. (Dep + wife) Then she got scared, so I offered to call the hotel and make her reservations. But she decided to stay with her girl friend in town. Well, she called me four times that night, she missed me so much. At noon the next day she called and said she wanted to come home, but she had a date with the other guy. So she came in at 2:30 in the morning; I was sitting up waiting for her. She missed the security of being at home, but not much of a change has taken place. I expressed the way I felt about it, but I don't think it cut any ice. It's making me damn discouraged. (Anx — wife)

Last night she decided she ought to try to make something of the situation with *me,* rather than trying *first* to work it out with him. I'm getting mighty disgusted and discouraged. (Dep + gen) Several nights ago, after she had returned, we had a very passionate time during intercourse, and afterwards she said it was just physical and there was no love involved. That made me feel terrible. (Sex n + wife)

I should think you would feel very discouraged. (Reassurance) *I was* hoping *that you'd be very disgusted.* (Advice)

I am, but I'm still afraid to do anything. If I throw her out, she's got nothing to hang on to. As long as there's a possibility that we can have a good relationship, I don't want to jeopardize it. (Dep + wife)

Maybe you can only have it if you act in such a way as to demonstrate that you're willing to jeopardize it. (Advice)

Well, I was, when I showed that I was willing to arrange for her to leave for a while. (Dep + wife)

I wonder whether that action might have any deeper significance? (Challenges) *You felt that you were being considerate and thoughtful.* (Clarification; the therapist thought that the offer might have been perceived by the client's wife as a sign of lack of interest on the part of her husband.)

The way you said it made it sound kinda cheap. I don't think it was like my saying, "I've had enough, get out." After she came back, I told her I'd bent over backward to give her a chance to find out which she wanted, and she said, "Well, I didn't ask you for the chance, did I?" I really saw red. I said "Well you ungrateful . . .", and then I started slugging her. (Hos n + wife)

That was the same night you said you had such intense intercourse. And once last spring you said the same thing. You had your best intercourse right after a big fight. (Interpretation$_4$)

She must feel positive when she sees I'm bothered by her behavior. But the intercourse was the passionate animal type of thing; it wasn't with any real feeling of love. (Sex n + wife)

Do you think your behavior in letting her have several weeks to think it over was the normal behavior of a typical husband? To say "Go ahead, and I'll make the arrangements for you?" (Challenges)

No, certainly not. And it wasn't the behavior I would like to have be typical of me. (Dep + gen)

What would you like to have done? (Question)

Clap her in irons and throw her in some room where she couldn't get out. (Laughs) I'm going very much against my own feelings as a person. The clinician and the person comes in conflict. (Dep + gen)

Is it just because you're a clinician? (Challenges)

It's hard to separate the clinician from *me*. I empathize with any client. (Dep + gen → Nur + wife)

But in this case you're a husband. (Challenges)

Well, I'm not trying to go at this thing like a clinician. But my training affects the way I react. The normal thing to do would be to react very strongly to all of this, but when I see how disturbed she is, I hold that back. (Dep + wife → Nur + wife)

Maybe you permit her to do these things to hurt you because you want to be hurt. (Interpretation$_9$)

I've asked myself that. Why should I want to be hurt? It would be because I feel I have done something wrong. (Anx — self)

I wonder if you aren't saying that certain passive elements of your personality tend to dominate at times and that you get some gratification from suffering. (Interpretation$_9$) (Client sighs) *The typical husband would say, "If you see him again, I'll beat the tar out of you."* (Persuasion)

Yeah. That's really what I'd like to say, but if you deny somebody something, they'll want it even more. (Dep + gen)

Sometimes. Unless they want to be told that they can't have it. (Persuasion)

I'm scared to death I'll lose her if I do that. At times I wonder which would be worse, not having her or having her the way she is now. (Dep + wife)

That's a good question. (Calls attention) *It seems to me that when you offered to make the hotel reservation, you were going a lot farther than just giving her time to decide.* (Challenges)

She can think more freely when she's not around me.

She won't think more freely when she's around him. (Challenges)

But I was just getting damn desperate. I thought I had tried everything. (Anx — wife)

Sometimes children interpret extreme permissiveness as being the same as indifference. (Interpretation$_9$)

But I'm afraid if I take a stand, I'll lose her. I guess my dependency is a big factor here. I need to have someone with me. (Dep + wife)

I think you're telling me that because you are a lonely guy, you will let her louse you up. (Interpretation$_7$)

I suppose I am saying that. (Dep + wife)

How long are you going to allow yourself to be walked on? (Disapproval)

I don't know. How long can I take it? I'm paralyzed. For my own mental well-being I should react in a very typical or normal way, but everything clinical says to "hold up." Maybe I'm using "clinical" as a rationalization. (Dep + ther)

You don't have to beat the pulp out of her, but firmness might be the answer. (Persuasion) (Pause) *There is, of course, the interpretation that the husband who lets his wife have affairs wants her to have them.* (This is probably a pretty threatening interpretation; it may even have implications of latent homosexual needs.)

I wouldn't say that is the case with me. (Laughs with embarrassment) I just feel completely nothing. It goes past the point of being hurt. (Dep + wife)

Numb. (Clarification)

Yeah.

I feel very sorry for you. (Relationship) (Pause) *Did you ever read Hamlet?* (Question; interpretation)

Yeah. Three times. I'm the old Danish prince who can't make up his mind. Sometimes I think of myself as being a very backboneless individual. I'm afraid to do things because I might louse up my own sense of security. (Dep + gen → Dep + ther)

But actually you're not all bad. (Reassurance)

I know. But I can't look at it objectively. (Dep + gen)

When you think people are feeling critical, they might be thinking, "Quinn is a nice guy. Why does he always worry so about his mistakes?" (Reassurance)

But I was conditioned to be afraid of making mistakes. I just don't stand up to anybody, unless I feel very secure. (Dep + gen) I've stood up to my internship supervisor occasionally. I even criticized him for reacting to another psychologist passively, which is what I might do myself. (Hos n + fa surrog)

Why could you stand up to him? (Question)

Because we're very much alike. We can each see the other's point of view. It's one of the few close relationships I've ever had. (Dep + auth) Not really close, maybe, but I just felt a certain bond, the way I felt for that partner in the restaurant. I've thought, "Gee, it'd be nice if *he* were my father." I felt more like a son to my supervisor than a brother. (Dep + fa surrog) (He is expressing dependency needs again; is he telling the therapist that the supervisor is a better father-surrogate than the therapist?)

What kind of father would he be? (Question)

A real understanding father you could talk to like a son would. He'd be democratic, although with firmness. He has a strong set of values, but he's completely consistent and totally fair. (Dep + fa surrog) He isn't rigid, like my father was. And he isn't opinionated like my dad. I feel guilty if I express these feelings. (Dep + fa)

All the hostility has been conditioned into guilt, hasn't it? (Interpretation$_8$)

Yes.

So the question for us in therapy is how to condition some of it back. (Information)

That's right. (Pause) How does one do a thing like that? (Dep + ther)

Well, one way would be by permitting aggression and not punishing it, wouldn't it? Or even by rewarding it. (Information)

Yeah, but I have no need to be aggressive in here, because nothing you have ever said has made me mad. I thought you were a little wrong sometimes, but I never have felt mad about it. I thought you were just trying to explore a possible interpretation which I might not agree with. (Dep + ther, Rel) Sometimes I get mad in classes, and if I showed it there, I'd probably get blackballed immediately. (Dep + gen) And if I do it at home, then my wife has to react to it. So where do I get aggressive? (Dep + ther) Toward my dogs? I sublimate some of it into my woodworking. But that doesn't help very much. My wife says I ought to let out my aggression in more gradual ways and not save it all up. (Hos n — gen)

That's the problem, isn't it. If you bottle it all up, then when the bottle bursts, wow! (Interpretation₇)

I just went into a total rage and started beating her up. (Pause) Even when I was a little kid, I was not at all aggressive. (Dep + gen)

So we have to try to help you discover in therapy that fighting can be useful, effective behavior. (Persuasion) *You say I have never done anything to make you mad. But I actually deliberately tried to provoke you a little bit, before.* (Relationship)

I know you did. (Laughs) You sometimes overinterpret deliberately just to exaggerate the situation and make it seem a little absurd. I always realize that there's some truth to what you're saying. (Dep + ther)

Extreme, but in the correct direction. (Restatement)

Yes, and designed to make me think. You haven't said anything that was blatantly no good. (Dep + ther) I feel very frustrated, because you've pointed out what *I* sort of felt. I just can't do anything about it. (Dep + gen) (Pause) Maybe it's only with important people that I can't show aggression. If it's somebody I don't want to lose, I can't be aggressive. (Dep + auth)

You'll take punishment in order to hold onto these relationships which are so important to you. (Interpretation₅)

Yeah. After my wife left me last week, I tried to feel self-secure, but I really didn't. (Dep + wife) (Sighs) If I start letting out this stuff, will I be able to control it? (Dep + gen) Maybe I pick on unimportant things like keeping the house clean in order to displace my aggression. This is a drain on a person. Nobody likes to look at himself and see unpleasant things. (Dep + gen)

It's painful. (Clarification)

I guess I'll have to work at it bit by bit. Making an easy transition will be difficult for me; I don't want to go too far. I need to get feedback, and my wife doesn't usually give that. (Dep + wife) But I guess there's some way out of this mess.

Well, you have more potentialities than you realize. (Reassurance) *You don't want to take any giant steps right away. This aggression thing is a heady potion; it has to be taken in small doses.* (Attenuates)

Quinn: Seventeenth Interview (10/1)

I N THIS INTERVIEW, as reported in the case notes, the client spent about two-thirds of his time talking about his anger with his wife, one-quarter about his unsatisfactory relationship with his peers, and about one-sixth with his dependency upon the therapist and the internship supervisor. Hostility was the predominant theme, but affiliant needs were strongly expressed, and there were some expressions of anxiety and dependency and of a sense of being the victim of hostility from others. His PAC-NAC dependency score remained very high, at 45.

We do not have an adequate report of the therapist's participation in this interview, due to a recording failure.

The client's affect toward the therapist dropped to 49, one of his lowest scores, and the therapist's score on affect toward the client was 53, also a rather low score for him. In view of the fact that the client had taken the therapist's previous advice and told his wife he would "kick her out," this drop in client affect score is somewhat surprising. However, during this interview, the one interpretation which we know that the therapist made was to point out that a therapy relationship is not the same as a friendship. In view of this client's marked dependency, and his desire to build a father-son relationship with the therapist, we can assume that this interpretation by the therapist would be rather disappointing and even threatening to the client. In fact, in a later interview (the 27th) this same effort to teach the client to discriminate between a father-substitute and a therapist produced an identical reaction, a significant shift of his affect in the negative direction.

The therapist noted in his remarks after the interview that he found himself experiencing strong nurturant feelings toward this client, like those he "might feel toward a son who had been hurt." His affect score would not be as likely to reveal these feelings, however, since the Therapist's Affect Scale measures the entire picture of the therapist's perception of the client's maturity and adjustment as well as the therapist's feelings toward the client; the presence of nurturant feelings of the therapist toward a dependent client would usually mean that a state of mature adjustment on the part of the client was not evident, and this would affect the Therapist's Affect Scale in the direction of producing a generally more negative score.

Due to a fault in the recorder, the seventeenth interview recorded at so low a pitch that it was impossible to hear it. The following are the therapist's notes made after this important interview.

Client was very depressed. (Anx — wife) Has learned that his wife has again been flirting with other men. (Hos p — wife) He therefore issued an ultimatum; he will "kick her out" if this ever happens again. Last night they had a terrific fight, and she said that she feels restless and doesn't love him. (Hos p — → Hos n + wife) He is very lonely, (Aff n — wife) but also shows many signs of becoming angry and resentful. (Hos n + wife) He has been considering a legal separation but wouldn't consider a divorce, at least for several years. We talked about his isolation from people; he has no close friends. We discussed some reasons, such as his fear that people would "use" him, as the man in the restaurant did. (Dom p — peers) He has felt very close to two colleagues (both married) on his internship. (Dep — wife → Aff + peers) At the hospital they were quite friendly, as were their wives, but here they have become somewhat distant. He blames this on his wife, whom he feels they find in some way objectionable. (Hos n + wife) He said that his internship supervisor and I are his only real friends. (Dep + ther, auth) I pointed out the difference between a therapy or supervisory relationship and a friendship. (Interpretations) I also encouraged him to turn to his clinical work as a sublimation and an escape from his emotional problems during the present difficult situation. (Advice) I find that he arouses in me strong nurturant feelings; I feel very protective, as I might toward a son who had been hurt.

Quinn: Eighteenth Interview (10/8)

THE EIGHTEENTH INTERVIEW was a rather positive one. The marriage seemed to have stabilized, in that there had been a reversal of roles, with the husband having taken on a more aggressive role and the wife a more submissive one. The therapist had the feeling for the first time that the marriage situation could be viewed with some optimism.

An important trend in this interview was the exploration by the client of his relationships with other persons, particularly when they evidenced some positive expression toward him, and he found himself feeling suspicious of their motives. This trend in the discussion was touched off by one such event in the case of the therapist.

Approximately half of the client's discussion was about his wife, one-fifth about the therapist, and one-sixth about himself. Many of the client's affect-themes were of anxiety, hostility, and expression of ego and affiliation needs. The need to dominate showed itself to be fairly strong, and this was unusual for this client; dependency was also apparent.

On the part of the therapist, also, the procedures in this interview represented something of a change. Some form of discussion of the relationship made up 21 per cent of the therapist's responses. There were also direct questions (18 per cent), clarifications of feeling (18 per cent), interpretations (12 per cent), and challenging or calling attention to some of the client's ideas (12 per cent). This discussion of the relationship is an important technique; this therapist tends to utilize it whenever there is much resistance or when the client himself focuses on the idea. In this case Mr. Quinn brought up the point of having once felt suspicious when the therapist expressed sympathy with his misery; the therapist seized this opportunity to develop the point fairly extensively, because he believed that it represented a good illustration of the client's general difficulties in his interpersonal relationships. The client made constructive use of the theme, seeing in his own behavior a distantiating sort of activity.

Another interesting phenomenon was the ease with which the client appeared to have adopted some of the therapist's previously expressed values regarding appropriate dominance roles in a marriage. He even seemed puzzled as to the origin of his own increase in what he correctly labeled "ego-strength." On the other hand, at one point he somewhat quaintly spoke of a decision which he and the therapist had made jointly to take a more firm stand with his wife; no such joint decision had ever been openly arrived at, although the therapist was delighted to perceive the client's feeling that this was a problem on which they were working together in the search for a solution.

The client's affect toward the therapist rose thirty points in this interview (79); the therapist's changed very little (54). Affect for each was somewhere around his mean for this case. At the end of the interview, the therapist made a special point of stressing the difference between his roles as a therapist and as a teacher and administrator; he was hoping that there might not be too much of a contaminating effect from aspects of the administrative role in which he had been forced to be less nurturant than he had consistently tried to be in the therapeutic relationship.

An important development in this interview was the evidence of the client's beginning to demonstrate real attempts at more dominant and independent behavior, particularly toward his wife, and in his recognition of his lifelong pattern of seeking out "big brother sorts of relationships on which I could rely." This was the sort of insight and more mature behavior which the therapist was hoping to see this client develop. His PAC-NAC dependency score dropped two points, to 43, and this was the beginning of a gradual but persistent decline, which displayed only one relapse (in the twenty-seventh interview).

This is the first morning when I haven't felt like doing much of anything. I know I need to, but I've just gotten bogged down. (Dep + ther; Res) My wife teased me last night about having a date coming up with another guy; I said "Well, you know what the consequences are, if you do. You're not coming back here, and if you do come back, it's just to pack your stuff." Then I asked her why she was being negative, and she said she still wasn't sure whether she loved me or him. (Dom n + wife) But she admitted that the prospective date was fictitious, when I accused her of making it up for the purpose of testing me out. (It appears that the marriage situation is changing; the client is now demanding, and receiving, more loyal behavior from his wife.)

She's started wearing nightgowns rather than pajamas. I was reading in bed, and she came in and actively seduced me. (Sex n + wife) It turned out to be a rather satisfying intercourse. When she's just "doing her wifely duty," I can't enjoy it. (Dep + wife)

What do you think of this apparent change of behavior on her part? (Question)

I know what I'd love to think it means—that she has a real feeling for me. But I think it might more likely be that she feels she has a duty toward me, and she may as well make it as much fun as possible. (Anx — wife)

It's almost as if for the past week or two the roles have been somewhat reversed, and you're the one who's been hard to get. And you've been saying, "Play it my way or get out." (Interpretation$_7$)

Yeah. She doesn't quite know what to make of it. And she's finding that I sincerely mean that I won't take any more of this horsing around that's been going on. (Dom n + wife)

Well, I think this is a very important change in the dynamics of the case. (Calls attention)

Actually, you're right that it's a role reversal, but in the sense that *I'm* now putting on the pants in the family. (Dom n + wife)

You're now taking the dominant role, in the sense of being the one who's determining what goes on in the house, aren't you? You're setting the rules, or the limits. (Interpretation$_7$)

Since I took the first step last week of starting to set the limits, I'm surprised how much more at ease I feel in doing so. I've changed my orientation on the question of whether it's best for my wife if I just "suffer along with her." I'm now thinking more about what's best for *Quentin.* (Dom n + wife) Her parents want to come to visit this weekend, and I said it was O.K. if she was sure she'd still be around, herself. I let her know that I was pulling no punches, and that even if mamma is here, daughter gets thrown out if she tries any funny stuff along this flirting line. (Dom n + wife)

I told her I had given her a chance to think, and she had been completely dishonorable, so she wasn't getting another chance of that sort. She had to do her thinking here in the house. (He seems to have adopted the behavior and values which the therapist suggested recently.) If I'd said that two weeks ago, I'd have scared hell out of myself; now for some reason I've gotten some strength from somewhere, and it doesn't scare me. (Dep + ther → Ego + matur) (The client has apparently borrowed "ego-strength" from the therapist.) If she leaves, she leaves. It's too bad, but I've got a life to live, too. (He now feels that his own self-esteem is of some importance to him, too.)

You've decided that your own self-integrity is the ultimate allegiance. (Clarification)

It sure as hell *should* be, but that isn't what has been true in the past.

The more I think about it, the more I realize that possibly all my life I've tried to get some relationships on which I could rely. (Dep + gen) With this fellow who was a "big brother" to me in the restaurant affair, I probably put more into that relationship than was warranted; I imbued him with characteristics he didn't even have, just because my need was so tremendous. *imagined* (Dep + fa surrog) (This is a healthy insight.) I've always wanted everybody to be my friend, and I've let them walk all over me without complaining. (Dep + gen)

You're saying that you've shifted the balance of power in your family, and you're letting aggression out when you feel it. (Restatement) *I'm just a little bit worried as to whether in this reconditioning process you might go too far, and use all negative conditioning on her rather than employing some positive reward along with the punishing behavior.* (Advice; the therapist is cautioning against an over-reaction which his disinhibitive suggestions might have instigated.)

I don't think I will. I think we have also been having some fun in the sense that we have been tending to do things together more than we used to. We've been entertaining more, and we've started taking up bowling, which we can do together. In the past our only common recreation was going to the movies. (Aff n + wife)

You're starting to share some common interests. (Restatement)

Yeah. We went to a dance, and then she wanted to go to the tavern where she would meet this other guy. I refused to take her, so we went and had a soda at the drug store! (Dom n + wife; this is not the passive, compliant client of several weeks before.) She had been doing a lot of drinking beer with this other guy, and she'd always end up clobbered. She had been hanging around with this Bohemian group; last week they threw their regular party, and I refused to go or to let her go. She says they're the only people she's comfortable with, but I think they're a bunch of beatniks. I think she's always been self-oriented and never tried to see my feelings.

My wife seems to think I'm an old sober-sides, a quiet guy. But my reputation in college was that of a pretty fast guy and definitely on the carefree side. I guess I've *grown* up since graduate school and marriage. (Ego + matur)

Are you saying you don't do much that's social, or you don't do enough for her? (Question)

Well, I don't do as much as she expects. I think if I felt at ease in it, I would do more, but I'm uncomfortable with that kind of crowd. (Anx — peers) I like small parties, though.

I think I've had more ego-strength during the past two weeks; I think there's a definite improvement in our marriage, too. It's not just a truce between us. (Ego + matur) My wife seems to be getting a lot out of her therapy. It was a happy combination of events that you and I decided I should take a stand in my marriage when we did in therapy; (Dep + ther) only the day before, her therapist had said "Under no circumstances should you leave Quen at this time, while you're as confused as you are." I think that helped to hold her down after I issued my ultimatum. She's gonna be under pressure this weekend, too, with her family coming to visit. (Nur + wife) (It is interesting that the client considers that he and the therapist *jointly* made a decision for him to take a more firm stand with his wife.)

It seems as though parents visit you fairly often. (Challenges)

Yeah. Mine are coming the week after hers. Her father's giving me a big deal; he's gonna take me out for a game of golf. (Laughs sarcastically) He's always digging at me. (Hos p + fa surrog)

In what way? (Question)

Lecturing. About stuff he doesn't know a thing about!

What do you do when he lectures? (Question)

I pay attention, (Dep + fa surrog) and if he really goes against the grain, I'll tell him. I don't really pay attention, I just try to look as though I am. (Hos n + fa surrog)

These visits from parents seem to put an added strain on the relationship. (Disapproval)

Just wait till the following weekend for the strain! My father and my mother are coming down together.

I don't want to take refuge in spending time with other people so that we don't have time to see each other. This visiting every weekend has gotta come to a screeching halt pretty soon. We've got homework, if nothing else. (Dom n + wife)

I get the feeling that in a way we're sort of marking time. (Interpretation$_5$) *You used the word truce before. Is it that in a way your marriage was previously deteriorating, and in these past two weeks the decline has decelerated or even stopped, but you're not ready to say that it is yet moving over in the constructive direction?* (Clarification) *Maybe the therapy is dependent on the marriage, and so it is doing the same: stabilized, but waiting to see which way to go from here.* (Interpretation$_7$)

Yes, that's natural. The thing that is pressing me most is my marriage. I know there are other things I want to get into, but the present trouble is so much in the foreground that I find it difficult to get into other areas. (Dep + wife)

And of course some of the other things may be determined in their course by what happens in the marriage. (Interpretation$_7$)

Probably it's reciprocal.

You hinted at one problem when you talked about your difficulties in large groups. (Directive lead)

There's one other thing that I think is pretty important. Several weeks ago, when I said how badly I felt, you said "I really feel *very* sorry for you."

My immediate reaction was "I don't trust that at all." (Dep — ther, Rel)
That's interesting, because my wife has done exactly the same thing. I didn't
think I was like that. When I think back on it, I feel that you meant it when
you said it. That expression of a real warmth is probably about the warmest
thing you've ever said, and immediately I got clutched up about it. (Dep +
ther, Rel)

*Well, let's go into it. I remember after I said it, I felt a little worried that
you might misinterpret the word "sorry."* (Relationship)

Well, I interpreted it as meaning empathy. (Dep + ther, Rel)

*Yes, that's what it was; I was afraid you might interpret it as synonymous
with pity, and I didn't feel that. I felt deeply empathic with the anxiety that
you were undergoing.* (Relationship) *Now you said that you immediately
became suspicious.* (Relationship)

I think this is kind of typical of me in any situation. I did trust my wife
until I found that the trust wasn't well-founded. She is one of the few people
whose statements I have trusted. (Dep + wife)

*Your confidence has often proved to be misplaced, hasn't it? You trusted
your parents, and neither one of them was able to fulfill that trust ade-
quately. And the same with this fellow in the restaurant.* (Clarification)
Have you really ever trusted anybody who didn't later betray the trust?
(Question)

Yeah, the guy who was my best man. He's the only one who never did
anything to violate the trust. It makes me feel very weepy, at the moment.
(Dep + peer)

Well, we're touching the core of deep feeling. (Clarification) *The kind
of feeling that I think most of us keep under control most of the time.* (Reassurance)

The interesting thing is that *I* have not kept up my relationship with him.
He invited us to visit him last summer, and then I couldn't get away.

*And when I expressed a feeling of warmth toward you, you wondered
if it was really genuine. You asked yourself what I was hoping to get out of
it.* (Relationship)

I wondered if you were doing it just so I'd make progress in therapy,
or did you really feel that way. I guess the same form of distrust is shown
in these two relationships. It's terrible. (Dep + ther, Rel → Hos n + ther)

*Your family didn't very well condition you to feeling any trust or con-
fidence in your relationships with people. Your trust in people has proven
misplaced.* (Clarification)

I always thought I entered any relationship trusting the person until he
proved otherwise, but I'm not so sure. In these two relationships the trust
has not been violated, and yet when I get down to real depth, I can't trust it.
That's a hell of a way to be. The only important thing in any relationship is
trust and mutual respect. (Dep + gen) (Pause)

I might tell you that in terms of our relationship, I had been worried by the fact that our relationship in therapy might seem to be threatened by our relationship as student and teacher. Since I've "let you down" there, in that I couldn't use my influence to get you certain privileges, I wondered whether you would perceive this as lack of trustworthiness on my part. (Relationship)

Well, actually I was imposing on *you* with an unfair request. I had no right to ask you to do that. (Dep + ther, Rel)

I just wanted to be sure that you perceived the dual role that I have toward you, and that I hope the academic situations can be kept free from coloring our therapeutic relationship and how I feel toward you here. (Relationship)

I don't think there's any conflict in the two roles. As a teacher you can't be as permissive as you are in this situation. I don't think I'm threatened now by your position on the staff, the way I was when we first started therapy. (Dep + ther, Rel)

Quinn: Nineteenth Interview (10/15)

EELINGS ABOUT the therapist dominated the client's discussion in the nineteenth interview. The therapy was reaching the point at which the therapeutic relationship was becoming the most important aspect. The client criticized the therapist for using the word neurotic about some of his behavior. In this matter the therapist retreated somewhat. He deliberately let the issue become one for some argument, because he felt it was good for the client to be able to argue with him. While he maintained his principle, holding that by his definition some of the client's behavior was neurotic, he also agreed to accept a different word if the client preferred. The client went into a phase of reporting "bad" things about himself; these were what Dollard and Miller call peccadillos; but the client, while telling about them, seemed to feel they were very important. He said that he felt as though he had made "the great confession." The therapist interpreted that the client was probably trying to test the therapist's acceptance of him, a subject which had been begun in the previous interview. This the client accepted and revealed a rather obvious evidence of a transference relationship in his statement, "Mother, do you still love me?" The therapist tried consistently to help the client see that the recognition of his dependency was more important than gaining the reassurance which he was seeking. However, the therapist did give reassurance, but only after he had first focused on the matter of dependency. The client made the self-interpretation that possibly in this questioning behavior he was trying to punish the therapist in advance for anticipated future rejection, which is what he has been conditioned to expect from those he comes to trust. The therapist did everything he could to alter the anticipated response pattern here, while also going farther than just gratifying the client's dependency needs. It was as though he said, "You can be dependent now, but someday we will hope you won't have this need to be so dependent." This was to become a major direction the therapy would take for many of the remaining sessions.

The therapist also interpreted the client's feeling as not being yet prepared to accept the sense of obligation which it would produce in him for the therapist to be showing strong positive regard, and the client accepted this interpretation, basing his feeling on his past conditioning that people who were accepting toward him almost always later betrayed him.

Later, the therapist again attempted to loosen somewhat the cord of the client's dependency, when he indicated that he would not accept full responsibility to remember the topic the client wanted to discuss at the next interview.

During this interview there was also some discussion of the client's wife, father, and his own masculinity. The principal affect-themes were anxiety, hostility, affiliation need, and dependency and ego-needs.

The most unique feature of the therapist's activity in this interview was the large percentage of his reflections which were devoted to the relationship (28 per cent). Clarification of feeling (17 per cent) and interpretation (13 per cent) also made up sizeable portions of the therapist's responses.

Affect in the nineteenth interview remained at about the same fairly high level for the client (80). That of the therapist plummeted severely to a score of 14, the second lowest score on the therapist's affect toward this client. This marked drop in therapist affect was almost entirely the result of lower scores on parts III and IV of the scale, which are ratings on a client's progress in therapy and on his emotional maturity. The therapist's feelings toward the client and his estimate of the client's feelings toward himself (parts I and II) were not too different from previous interviews; the change in parts III and IV was partly the result of the evidence of the client's marked dependency. The client had, of course, also revealed some fairly immature behavior, and part IV of the scale is heavily weighted with items bearing on this question. There is no evidence that the therapist felt less positive affect toward the client; the scale is sensitive to judgments in more areas than affect alone.

Despite the signs of growing independence in Mr. Quinn, there were still some strong evidences of dependency in this interview. At one point he said that he had never found a strong father-figure to relate to, although he had tried very hard; at another point he mentioned that he had always wanted a "male to whom I could look up, and who would accept me as a male" the way his father had never done. He also indicated that three "secondary father-figures" (the therapist, the internship supervisor, and the restaurant owner) had "accepted him as a male," which his father had never done. He had always felt he was competing with his father to try to be more adequate in every skill, particularly those which were signs of masculinity. He wanted the therapist to like him and hoped that the therapist would not reject him for having experienced an extramarital sexual fantasy. It was quite clear that the therapist was being seen by Mr. Quinn as a strong, but benign and loving, father-figure. The PAC-NAC dependency score dropped by two points, to 41.

You suggested last time the idea of going into a little more depth and not getting tied up in the surface things. I can see the value of that, because I'm not gonna make too much progress if we just scratch the surface. It's difficult to avoid talking about my family life. When the situation isn't so bad at home, I start getting defensive about what to talk about in therapy. I guess I'm afraid to see myself too accurately. (Anx — gen) (Reports some progress in the events in his family; the visit of his parents-in-law was a strain; he felt some satisfaction in beating her father at golf; when his wife was under strain, she tended to "short-change" him in front of her parents; his wife has dropped out of school, and the relationship has been better as a result.)

I was going to have it out with her ex-boyfriend while her parents were there so she couldn't do anything rash; but I couldn't get away from the house. Gradually my resolution to do this faded away, partially because my wife has been relating better to me. Also, I'm just scared to do it; he might beat me up. I think that's important.

I want to talk about the fact that I very much want to have children, and my wife would, too. She keeps asking for one, but I say no, because a child is not something to use just to hold a relationship together. It's tough on a kid, and I want to wait and be completely sure that she's going to stay with me. (Dep + wife) When I'm objective, I know I'm not willing to bring a child into an unstable marriage, hoping that the child might stabilize it. I want a kid so much myself, too. My wife has the crazy idea that our child wouldn't be normal. She tries to create a physical composite of our physiques, and the result is some sort of idiotic monster. (Laughs) I tell her we could love a deformed child if we got one. I think she feels the baby may not be pretty because of me, and that if it was ugly, she couldn't stay with me. This made me very angry. I told her, "Beauty is only skin deep, as *you* should know," which is a sarcastic remark if I ever heard one, but she deserved it and she knew it. (Laughs) (Hos n + wife)

She has told me innumerable times that I'm not her type, physically. Her admirers have been physically rather "beautiful," and she can't seem to get beyond the physical. She has told me that I am ugly. Perhaps I am overweight, but since I was ten years old, I haven't thought of myself as being ugly. I want to feel that I'm attractive to my wife. (Dep + wife)

In the past I have gotten back at her, by criticizing specific details of her appearance. Then she started calling me "Fatty," but I don't like it. So I nicknamed her "Baggy Bosom." (Laughs heartily) She said that this bothered her because it was true. Obviously those are hurtful names. (Hos p — wife → Hos n + wife)

A form of teasing, and derogation. (Restatement)

Yeah. My weight has bothered me for many years. I think I hated it so much because my father has such a good physique. According to the charts I'm only ten pounds overweight, but I'd like to be ten pounds *under*weight. I'm certainly not torpid, but I'd have more energy and feel better if I weighed less. It's funny that I've chosen friends around here who have the same trouble; they're overweight. (Anx — phys)

We might consider why it's so threatening to be attacked on grounds of physique. (Directive lead)

We did once before; it's the feminine stereotype. It's interesting that my worries about homosexuality have dropped out; I rarely think about it. I haven't any fear that I'd have any tendency to try it. I know darn well that I wanta be a "man's man" type of thing. I would love to be a mesomorph. (Anx — phys) I suppose I doubt my own masculinity, possibly because I have never really been able to relate to a masculine figure. And I have kept trying so darn hard. (Dep — fa)

What do you mean by "relate?" (Question) *What should you be able to do?*

I always wanted some male to whom I could look up (Dependency), and who accepted me as being a male. (Dep — fa surrog) My father has always made critical comments about my weight, and my being not sufficiently athletic, and how *un*mechanical I was. And these are masculine traits. I've tried to prove him wrong. (Dep — fa → Hos n + fa)

You've wanted to be accepted as masculine by these masculine figures. (Clarification) *I think that's the clue. This is where you've never felt rewarded.* (Interpretation$_5$)

A few of these secondary father-figures haven't indicated that they felt me to be feminine. This guy in the restaurant, and you, and my supervisor. (Dep + ther, fa surrog) But I've never convinced my father. (Dep — fa; note that the client identifies these three males toward whom he has related dependently, as "secondary father-figures.")

He must have some strong need to deny your masculinity. The characteristic father-behavior would be to encourage masculinity in a son and to reward signs of its development. And even to need to see it, when it might be less than real. (Information)

He's never rewarded it. When he saw my woodwork and my models, he implied that someone must have helped me or even done it for me, which is worse. (Hos p — fa)

Trying to prove something to someone who has a neurotic need not to accept it is a kind of hopeless task, isn't it? (Challenges)

Yeah. But I have a need also, to prove it. (Dep — fa → Hos n + fa) I don't think mine's neurotic, though. Maybe it becomes neurotic when one continues to try the impossible.

Is it almost as if you were somewhat in competition with him? (Interpretation₇)

Yeah, I guess it is. Like when I beat him in tennis. And I've built better models than he used to build. (Dep — fa → Hos n + fa)

I think it is wise to differentiate neurotic from appropriate goals. (Advice)

For some reason I object very strenuously to the way you throw around the word neurotic. (Laughs) (He is able to criticize the therapist, but without hostility; this suggests that he is growing out of his dependency a bit; Hos n + ther)

It kind of hurts for me to use the word "neurotic" in reference to any of your behavior. (Clarification)

Yeah. It's realistic, but it's threatening. It's like calling me fat. (Anx — ther)

You see it as a kind of insult or derogation. (Clarification)

Yeah. It isn't, really. It's calling a spade a spade. You're not calling *me* neurotic, you're saying certain behavior is neurotic. (Dep + ther)

Maybe we can find better substitutes for the word. It's a rather hackneyed one. We might say, "Behavior directed toward an unobtainable goal." (Information) (They laugh) *But I'm more concerned with what it does to you, with the fact that you are distressed by using the word. It's not that I'm worried,* (Relationship) *but it may be a general category of fact that anything that seems to indicate that you are less than adequate, or even than the best, may be highly threatening.* (Interpretation₇)

I guess it's threatening to think that someone who is training me to be a clinician thinks that I'm neurotic, or have neurotic traits. (Dep — ther, Rel)

You probably tend to use the word rather inclusively. (Attenuation)

Yes. I think of *a* neurotic, not neurotic traits.

And you consider it bad. (Clarification) *Now I could as easily say, if you didn't have some neurotic traits you wouldn't have come to therapy. By a priori definition we deal with neurotic things in therapy.* (Interpretation₇; the therapist was not willing to back down immediately in this argument, partly because he felt it was good hygiene to let the client argue with him.)

I could use the word maladjusted. (Laughs)

That's probably the sense in which I use the word neurotic, and you probably use it in the sense of some unstable old woman who is about to go off the deep end. (Information)

It's a semantic difference.

Well, I'd be willing to give up the word in terms of application to you. I don't think of you as a very neurotic person. (Reassurance) *But I still would contend that the desire to defeat one's father is a somewhat neurotic drive.* (Interpretation$_7$)

Well, now that we've discussed it, I think it won't bother me if you use it any more. Maybe I was just asking you to say how bad you thought I was. (Dep + ther)

There's something else I've wanted to mention for a number of interviews. I wasn't sure how you'd react to it. (Dep — ther) I don't like what I did. Toward the end of the summer I thought about going out with another married guy and trying to pick up a couple of women, and one night we almost did. As it turned out nothing happened; I couldn't go along, after all. But I had strong ideas of wanting to do it. At that time I was extremely unhappy with my wife, and I felt lonely as hell. (Dep — wife → Hos n + wife) It's quite a change that when I felt lonely I thought about looking for a dame instead of a guy. But I don't like it in myself, and I'll never tell my wife, because she trusts me. (Dep + wife)

Let's see what the meaning of this is. (Calls attention) *You're telling me that you toyed with the idea of some extra-marital activities. You didn't do anything,* (Restatement) *and you were somewhat pleased that in this hour of need you turned to heterosexual rather than homosexual types of activity.* (Clarification)

Um-hm.

You weren't sure whether to tell me, because you thought I might be critical of you. (Relationship)

Um-hm. I'd be critical, if *I* heard it. (Laughs) It's in opposition to what I think is basic to a marriage. I have always kept my wedding ring on. (Dep + wife → Anx) But at that time I was tempted; I thought that perhaps my wife had been running out on me and that "What's sauce for the goose is sauce for the gander." (Hos n + wife)

You sound almost like you were trying to get revenge. (Interpretation$_5$)

Yeah, I was. But actually I found it kind of repulsive. (Dep — wife → Anx)

Let's see how this bears on our relationship, in that you felt some anxiety about whether you should tell me about it. (Relationship)

Well, obviously I want very much that you should like me and respect me, and I don't think extra-marital promiscuity is good. (Dep + ther, Rel) Society agrees, and I feel that you do, too. I felt that you would censure me because of it, even though you might not say anything. (Dep — ther →

Anx) (The client projects some of his own moral standards onto the therapist, who had tried to avoid revealing any value judgments in this matter.)

Would it be possible to see it as being a form of behavior which need not be evaluated but could simply be analyzed in terms of meaning? (Reassurance) *A true* clinician *doesn't make decisions about values, but a* person *does.* (Information)

That's what I was gonna say. You can't be *completely* analytical. (Dep — ther)

And you're wondering whether I could accept you, and still respect and admire you, if you did things that might cross the boundaries of my own personal value system. (Relationship)

That's right. I feel sorta like I've made the great confession, or something. (Dep — ther)

You've confessed to something that is beneath your own standards of behavior, something that you don't respect about yourself. (Clarification) *And you hope I won't reject you for it.* (Relationship)

That's right. Won't you give me any satisfaction about it? (Dep — ther) (Laughs)

I'm trying to work through your feelings, (Structuring) *rather than just give you the reassurance that I don't reject you,* (Withholding) *because I think understanding your feeling of the need to be reassured is more important from the point of desirable mental hygiene.* (Information; the therapist is starting to try to help the client to be less dependent.) *The best form of adjustment would be to be able to tell me that you did something you didn't particularly admire, but that you did it for a reason and that although you hope I won't reject you for it, if I do, it doesn't make too much difference to you, since that would indicate a defect in my own value system. Now that's the ideal, the ultimate in self-assurance, isn't it?* (Relationship)

Yeah. Which I don't have. The thought that cropped into my mind, which is embarrassing for me to say, but I think it's important, was that what I was asking you was, "Mother, do you still love me?" (Dep + ther, Rel; transference here is intense and obvious. The therapist was surprised that at this point he was seen as a mother; but actually most clinical activity is rather maternal in character.)

Um-hm.

That embarrasses me to say that, probably because it's a revelation to me that the transference is pretty deep. (Dep + ther, Rel)

Um-hm. Your preconscious gave you away and let you say something that threatened you (Interpretation$_5$) *because it revealed a lot of transference.* (Relationship)

Yeah, and I don't like to admit it, for fear you'll reject me. (Dep + ther, Rel)

Why should I reject you? (Relationship)

I must be rigid as hell, because although I didn't do anything very bad that night, it seems very bad to me. (Dep — ther, Rel)

Well, you have a pretty strong moral structure, a pretty strong superego. (Disapproval) *You may be attributing to me more super-ego than is there, too. You may be seeing me as more virtuous than I might be.* (Relationship) *Or you may be aware of personality characteristics within me that I don't realize I'm demonstrating.* (Relationship) *I think if a person is really accepting of someone, he's very reluctant to reject that person just because he might have done something that didn't seem wise to the first person.* (Relationship) *I don't think that I disapprove at all of what you felt, actually.* (Reassurance) *There might be enough countertransference that I take a little delight in the idea that you felt it.* (Relationship) *I have the feeling that maybe your wife* deserved *a kick in the pants.* (Approval)

I don't think I'll consider doing it *again.* I seem to have such a strong moral sense in that way, and yet when I was a kid and even now, there are a lot of things I do that are definitely immoral in a psychopathic sense. Even while I was in college, I stole like a fiend, shop-lifted. I don't feel too badly about it, but I wouldn't do it now. I wonder why my moral sense has gotten so strong since then? (Dep + gen)

You're telling me lots of bad things about yourself, today. (Relationship) *Why do you think you're doing it?* (Question)

Maybe I'm trying to test *you.* (Dep + ther, Rel)

To see whether I would reject you. If I really accept you, could I accept some of the really bad things about you that I don't yet know. (Relationship)

Maybe. (Dep + ther, Rel)

That's the interpretation I *make of it.* (Relationship)

I'm bogged down. I want to say something, but I don't quite know what. I don't know whether anybody has known everything that I consider bad about myself, and still accepted it completely. (Dep + ther, Rel; he is describing the core of a good therapeutic relationship.) Even my wife has rejected some of it. (Dep — wife)

You have yet to experience a situation where you could tell the worst things about yourself and not be rejected. (Clarification)

Um-hm. Actually they aren't really very bad. (Laughs) I'd hate to see how I'd react if I'd *really* do something that was bad. (Dep + gen) (Pause) I'm stuck. I wonder why. (Pause) You're not giving me any help. (Laughs) (Dep + ther, Rel)

We're actually working on the very deep subject of our relationship, and you indicated that it threatened you when I showed a deep empathy for you. (Relationship) *In some ways this made you obligated to me,* (Interpretation₅) *and you weren't sure you wanted to carry that obligation. You were saying that you didn't really believe me, that under test that empathy would* *break down, just as it has in all other cases.* (Relationship)

That's right. I'm not ready to accept it yet. I'm not ready to be particularly warm in the relationship, at the moment. (Hos n + ther) But I'm not sure that I go so far as to believe your empathy is not real. It's just that I've never had any experience in the past with real empathy directed toward me. (Dep — ther, Rel)

You're feeling some resistance or hostility to me, at this point. (Relationship) (Pause) *I think I can assure you that I do accept you completely, despite the knowledge that you have given me of these events that you consider transgressions.* (Reassurance)

I just got a funny thought. I just thought that I'm trying to punish you for being nice to me. That doesn't make too much sense. (Dep + ther → Hos n + ther) (Laughs)

It's logical, if in the past, whenever people have been nice to you, they later stopped being nice. It would be a natural conditioning. (Reassurance)

Yes. I'd like to talk more about this next week. I often forget what we talk about, so I'd appreciate a reminder. (Laughs with some embarrassment; this is a dependent sort of request to make; Dep + ther)

If you want me to refer to my notes at any time, I always can. (Structuring)

I wish you would. (Dep + ther)

I'll wait for you to ask me next week, though. (Both laugh; structuring: the therapist refuses here to accept all of the responsibility. He is trying to recondition the client away from some of his more dependent behavior.)

Quinn: Twentieth Interview (10/22)

DISCUSSION IN this interview was divided among the topics of the client's father, the therapist, the client's wife, and his peers. He took very decisive action in ordering his wife out of the house when he found that she was still writing letters to her admirer. Although after a long discussion he relented, he feels that the situation has come entirely under his control. Since the event, his wife has become very devoted.

The feeling about the client's father was mostly anger that he was unable to get his father to express much love toward him; he displayed a considerable amount of repressed hostility toward his father. He did engage in a rather profitable discussion, following the therapist's lead, of ways in which he could gratify some of his dependency needs through nurturant behavior which he might express toward children of his own. He also stated that there were other persons from whom he could obtain gratification of his dependency needs: father-figures, such as the therapist or supervisor, and peers. It took a suggestion from the therapist to remind him that a wife might also serve in this capacity.

The client rejected the therapist's interpretation that he might fear allowing himself to feel obligated to people and therefore kept them at a distance, although he later appeared to have adopted the idea himself.

In this interview the therapist made a number of specific attempts to teach discrimination between past and present, or past and future events, usually by a simple statement of contrast, which took the form of giving information. The therapist also utilized approval and encouragement when he pointed out that the client had thought of a very important point, i.e., that he could find other persons toward whom he might direct his affectional needs. And he remarked that there had been a real gain in the quality of the client's marriage relationship and his academic work.

The principal affect-themes of this interview were affiliation need, hostility, anxiety, and ego needs.

The therapist's techniques consisted primarily of interpretation and clarification of feelings (21 per cent of each), direct questions (14 per cent), supportive procedures (11 per cent), giving information (8 per cent), and restatement of content (10 per cent).

In this interview the client's affect dropped twenty points (60), while the therapist's rose twenty-two points (36).

There was much discussion of the therapy relationship and of dependency. Mr. Quinn made statements like, "Will you help me?" and "You'll have to stimulate me." He indicated that he wanted in no way to endanger the relationship, and he could accept punishment from the therapist and "like a child, still know that his parent loved him." He showed some independence of his father in rejecting offers of money from him, but he also said, "Complete independence will come when he's dead." The therapist tried to "teach" him about how the relationship with his father would inevitably change as they both grew older and his father became somewhat dependent on Mr. Quinn. At one point the client said that he no longer saw the therapist as a father-surrogate, but then he asked why he still had so much need for affection from a father. The therapist tried to describe how he could obtain some satisfaction for his dependency needs by turning to his wife, but Mr. Quinn insisted that the relationship would have to become more ideal for this to happen, although he indicated that he had started to move in that direction and had told his wife how much he needed her. He recognized that he could sublimate some of this need in a relationship with children and that he must not exploit the children by expressions of too much control based on his own needs. He also mentioned again that perhaps he could direct some of his dependency needs into "relationships with friends, older men like yourself and my internship supervisor." His dependency score rose again by two points, to 43.

The therapist's idea of a mature way of handling the dependency needs which Mr. Quinn had toward his father would be for the client to direct some of them toward his wife and to develop nurturance needs toward his children. However, it was apparent that Mr. Quinn was resisting this idea somewhat and was suggesting the method of building relationships with father-surrogates and "big brothers." In fact, Mr. Quinn's need to continue this procedure became apparent during the twenty-seventh interview, when he attributed to the therapist the idea of developing relationships with his peers as a way of handling dependency needs.

Mr. Quinn experienced a good bit of resistance in this interview, often finding it difficult to talk or to remember things. He attributed this to the intensity and depth of the material which he was exploring. The therapist reassured him that this was a natural development in therapy. His resistance may have accounted for the drop in his affect score.

I remember what we were going to talk about again, but I'd like to diverge for a couple of minutes. It gradually came out that my wife has been corresponding with this other guy. I told her to pack her bags and get out. (Hos n + wife) She said "You certainly have guts." She sat and cried, and so we talked for a couple of hours. It turned out that I didn't kick her out. She let out an awful lot of pent-up emotion, and I felt that she showed some remorse for doing it, and has since told him that she wasn't going to write any more. And since then I couldn't ask for a more attentive or more loving wife in the last couple of weeks. (Aff n + wife) I think the real threat, that she would have to get out, shook her up so that she started evaluating her real feeling. I *think* she actually has some feeling for me, now. So I'm not sorry that I went back on my own word and let her stay. (Dep + wife) I warned her that there's never going to be any of this stuff with any other guy; even ten or fifteen years from now, I'll still kick her out. (Dom n + wife) Things have been very positive. She says she still believes that affection and flirting need not be restricted to marriage, but she knows my views, and she's not going over the boundaries.

I guess we've gotten to some basic stuff, because I'm finding it very hard to talk about it, and hard not to forget what we were talking about last time. (Resistance) I remember asking you whether you rejected me, in terms of being a mother-figure. (Dep + ther, Rel) Did our last discussion have something to do with my not trusting those that I came to love? (Dep — gen) I can't quite crystallize it. Will you help me? (Dep + ther)

(Therapist recapitulated the client's previous remarks about having been always conditioned to the idea he would be "let down" by those he trusted. He also reminded the client of his insight that maybe in his hesitation to trust the therapist, he might have been trying to punish him; interpretation$_9$)

I remember I was testing you all during the hour by mentioning things which I considered to be bad in myself. (Dep + ther, Rel) It's funny, already I have pushed that under. (Long pause) I guess you'll have to stimulate me. (Dep + ther)

Was it about the possibility that you might have been trying to punish me? (Question)

Hm. Punish you in advance, before I could get hurt by betrayal. (Dep + ther, Rel)

Or it might be interpreted as trying to punish me so that you will be *punished.* (Interpretation₉)

I can't think of myself as a masochist. (Ego + self) (Laughs)

What might it prove to you if I started punishing you? (Question)

That you didn't really have a good feeling toward me. (Dep + ther, Rel)

It would be showing you that your deeper fears were right—that I really didn't love you. (Interpretation₇) *And if I didn't love you, what does that mean?* (Question)

That I wasn't worthy of being loved and respected. (Dep + ther, Rel)

What about the obligation that love entails? (Interpretation₉)

Yeah, the receiver is obligated to the person who loves him and has to do things for the person who loves him, and shouldn't hurt him, and so on. (Dep + ther, Rel) (Pause) It's tough going. (Dep + ther; the client apparently has an intellectual understanding of the dynamics of this situation.)

If you've proved that people really don't love you, then you aren't much obligated to them. (Interpretation₉)

That would be true. But I like doing things for people. I'm not really an exploitative sort of person. (Aff n + peers) I enjoy feeling obligated to people because that builds up a bond in your personal relationship. (Dep + gen) Your proposal sounds like garbage to me. (Laughs) I hate to say so, to you. (Hos n + ther) (Laughs) (Clearly, Mr. Quinn is not ready to accept the interpretations he verbalized earlier in the interview.)

Why? (Question)

Well, I'm loth to endanger our relationship. (Dep + ther, Rel) All my relationships are tenuous enough without adding anything else to them. I have tended to make myself a doormat for people (Dep − gen) and then withdraw when they expected too much. That fits in with my difficulty in being aggressive, also. I had to internalize it. Maybe this masochistic thing isn't too far off.

Consciously I can see the need for aggression. I think a husband in my circumstances should even take physical measures to punish the sort of thing that has happened. (Hos n + wife)

You feel it would be proper to fight with this guy, (Clarification) *but you don't feel the inclination to do so.* (Clarification) *Why?* (Question)

I'm scared to. I might get the tar pounded out of me. He's a big boy. (Dep − peer → Anx) But in my fantasies, I can beat him up. If I were *really* out to punish myself, I think I would relish getting myself into that situation.

What situation does this replicate? (Interpretation₈)

With my father. But I don't know exactly how. (Laughs) (Dep − fa)

How old were you when your father struck you in the face? (Question)

Twenty-one. (Laughs) I guess it should be obvious, but I don't exactly see it.

What would be the usual inclination of a twenty-one-year-old man? (Interpretation₇)

To strike back. I couldn't do *that*. (Dep — fa → Anx)

Why? (Question)

Because that isn't done. It's not acceptable. But I can also think that I'd be afraid of getting beat up. (Dep — fa → Anx) Although I know that in a fight I could win, physically. (Pause) Maybe if I did that, I'm afraid that he'd *really* reject me. Whatever grounds I had gained would be lost. (Dep — fa → Anx)

That's pretty important, isn't it? Then you could expect no affection. (Calls attention)

Yeah, I guess that's the main motivation. It would kill the relationship. He would completely reject me. (Dep — fa → Anx)

But he struck *you.* (Interpretation₈)

That's legal. It's acceptable to society. He's allowed to chastise me. (Dep — fa)

Until what age? (Question)

Until I'm twenty-one. (Laughs, then sighs several times) But he doesn't consider me as being a man. Or at least he didn't then. (Dep — fa)

When will he concede your manhood? (Question)

(Client sighs deeply) Perhaps the day we have a baby. (Laughs) I think this last weekend he started to get an appreciation of a real independence, a lack of need for him, on my part. He offered me his extra electric razor, but I said "No." He asked me if I needed any money, and I said "No, thanks." (Aff p — fa)

So you've been more independent. (Clarification)

Yeah, although I still take money in the sense that I get the income from some stocks that he put in my name. (Dep + fa)

So the reality of the situation is that you can't feel independent yet, because you aren't *entirely independent.* (Clarification)

Complete independence will be when he's dead. (Dep + fa)

But before that he'll go through a period of becoming more and more feeble, and you'll still be strong. And your income-producing characteristics will be on the increase, while his will probably be waning. (Information) *In reality, some day he must accept the fact that you are a stronger man than he is.* (Information; here the therapist is teaching discrimination between past and future relationships of Mr. Quinn and his father.)

It bothers me to say things like this, because he's a very nice guy. (Dep + fa → Aff n + fa)

You feel a lot of affection for him. (Clarification)

I really do.

Perhaps when I depict him as potentially weak, you can feel more affection for him. (Clarification)

Then he'll be more human, yes. (Pause) I'm having real sticky going, here. (Sighs) I have wanted to hit him at times, very much. But I couldn't do it in any other way than, say competition in sports channels. (Dep — fa)

I'm not advocating that you do. I wouldn't want you to feel that I am. (Advice) *But I'm concerned about the pent-up hostility which you haven't been able to let out.* (Interpretation$_7$)

I can't even really let it out here. And this is a very non-threatening situation. I don't think it's because I continue to see you as my father-figure who would reject me if I did. I must really have shoved it under. (Dep — fa → Dep + ther, Rel) (Sighs)

Your yearning for affection is greater than that for revenge. (Clarification) *Some sons would know that if they got so mad that they hit their father, he would still forgive them.* (Information)

I don't believe that would happen, in my case.

You don't feel sure enough of his love that you know he could accept almost anything from you and still love you. (Clarification)

But why can't I even think about it? Why do I have so much need for affection from a father? (Dep — fa)

From my mother it doesn't worry me so much; she's more demonstrative. But even if she weren't, it wouldn't bother me so much.

You always knew she loved you. (Clarification)

Um-hm. And *he,* I sure didn't. He always did the beating, tying me in the yard, and so on. (Deep sigh) And then he sent me away to school. (Hos p — fa)

The worst of all, maybe. (Interpretation$_8$) *And when you did make a loving overture to him and wrote him that letter, he didn't respond.* (Restatement) (Pause) *But you also know now that he* wants *to love you.* (Clarification; again the therapist is trying to teach discrimination between different aspects of the father's ambiguous behavior.)

But I can't see how he's ever gonna loosen up. I still can't tell him how I really feel about that. (Dep — fa → Anx) Maybe with such a negative relationship in the early part of my life, it's hard to build any other basis for one. He hasn't changed much. (Dep — fa) (Sigh) Stymied again. I'm putting an awful lot of work on you, today. (Dep + ther) (Laughs)

I think you're saying you doubt whether he ever can give you the love you want. (Clarification)

That's right. I have to resolve in my own mind the fact that I'm not gonna get it. It's rough to have such a need for it. I used to be able to say I didn't give a damn. But I did, really. It's a very depressing thought. (Dep — fa) (Deep sigh) I sure as hell hope *my* kids don't find the same sort of thing. There'll probably be a complete reaction-formation. I'll probably try and be too close to them, unless I can think this thing through. (Dep + child)

Well, you thought of one of the most positive things when you said that. (Calls attention) *You may never get gratification of this dependency need, and love from your father, to any emotionally satisfying extent.* (Restatement) *But you can establish other effective interpersonal relationships. You suggested one of the possible outlets. You could have a father-son relationship with your own children.* (Advice) *You even thought a step ahead and said you shouldn't engulf them and yourself in a reaction-formation that would be too demanding on them.* (Reassurance)

I don't think I'd ever let that happen. Besides the relationships with them, I could also have relationships with older men, like yourself and my supervisor. That doesn't take the place of father-love, but it helps to ease it. (Dep + ther, auth, Rel)

I expect that many men would say that they have had father-surrogates in their lives. (Reassurance)

I bet also they still wish they had the original article, unless he happened to be a complete bastard. But they'd still want *somebody*. (Dep + gen) (Sigh)

You didn't think of the person toward whom your dependency needs might most logically be directed. (Disapproval; teaching new responses by means of inferred suggestions.)

My wife? I even rejected the thought till now. She puts me in a fine fettle. (Anx — wife)

She rejects those *needs.* (Restatement) *In fact, she seems to elicit protective behavior from you, and dominating behavior. She seems to like it best when you're more controlling.* (Interpretation)

Yeah. But she can also appreciate that there'd be a certain amount of dependency, so long as it didn't go too far, because of my abreacting so hard when I kicked her out; that was a dependent type of thing. (Dep + wife) I told her just how much I needed her, besides the fact that I wanted her as my wife. I told her I'd never had anything that I could hang onto in the past, and that that was one reason why she was so important to me. (Dep + wife)

You see your wife as only a substitute for the relationship you never had with your father. (Clarification)

I'm realistic enough to know that in some ways I think of her in that way. (Dep — fa → Dep + wife)

A mate is almost always something of a surrogate for both parents. (Information)

Well, I used the word dependency needs, and it's broader than just dependency; it's affectional. (Dep + wife) A relationship with your children wouldn't gratify your dependency needs. Lately my wife has been gratifying

that, to a degree. That's *something,* happening. (Dep + wife) (Pause)
I'm stuck. (Dep + ther)

*Well, one interesting thing about our interviews is that it has taken the
resistance much longer to appear for you than it does in many cases.* (Relationship) *I don't think any strong resistance arose until last time.* (Relationship) *Resistances began to accumulate as we started going into deeper
levels.* (Relationship)

Last week I really started to get into something with some depth.

*We're now discussing more intimate questions pertaining to yourself,
rather than to your wife.* (Restatement)

That's right. And I guess I'm really here to discuss myself.

Well, somewhat in both areas. (Structuring)

Yeah. I've strongly felt the need for support in that relationship, (Dep
+ wife) but a lot of things that I've got to work out within myself, I tend
to shove them under.

*Um-hm. There've been real gains. I can see that the situation with your
wife is well past its crisis.* (Reassurance) *In the sense that the crisis was
within you, and when you reached the point that you were ready to issue
an ultimatum, then the crisis was passed.* (Reassurance)

Well, I think I've made a lot of other gains, too. I know, for instance,
in that case presentation I gave in your class, five or six people came up to
me and voluntarily said they thought it was a wonderful presentation. (Ego
+ prof)

I thought you did a very good job there, too. (Reassurance) *And your
relationships with the faculty have been greatly improved.* (Reassurance)
Your synthesis of your feeling about your work shows excellent improvement. (Reassurance) *I'm recapitulating this fact largely so that you don't
feel too depressed about what you may feel are the unexplored and difficult
areas of your problems.* (Information)

I'm not depressed. I'm just wondering how long it will last, or whether
I can get through it. (Dep — gen) I certainly want to. But I've never
blocked as much on anything, before.

I asked my father if he'd seen my woodworking. He saw it, but he
didn't even bother to examine it. I sure didn't get any recognition. No
praise or anything! (Dep — fa → Hos n + fa)

*You showed him that you were a creative person, and he wasn't very
interested.* (Restatement)

That's right. I wonder what the hell I've got to do to have him respond.
(Dep — fa)

Quinn: Twenty-first Interview (10/31)

THE CLIENT characterized this interview as a very resistant one, saying that he did not feel any emotional conviction about the things that were being discussed. Actually, however, some fairly important matters were considered. Major attention was focused on his relationships with his peers, his father, and his wife. One of the principal considerations was his need to have deep friendships. This was probably a reflection of his passive dependency, although it might also have been an expression of latent homosexual needs. The client defended his point of view by taking the position that there were things that "one can't talk to one's wife about," but the therapist challenged this. There was a certain amount of toying with the topic of marital infidelity in such a way as to suggest that the client found some fascination in this topic.

The client expressed concern about relating comfortably to other persons and about his difficulty in group situations; he related this to a strong drive on the part of his father to have him always be very superior in all of his activities.

In terms of affect-themes, a notable aspect of this interview was the fact that affiliative needs occupied more than one-fourth of the discussion. Hostility, anxiety, ego-needs, dominance needs, and dominance presses were the other affect-themes in the interview.

The therapist's techniques were quite varied, with approximately equal amounts of clarification of feeling, challenging and disapproval, and interpretation. He took a somewhat challenging approach to some of the client's ideas in this interview. This may have been the result (or the cause) of the somewhat resistant behavior which the client noted in himself; it may also have been the result of the rather sweeping generalizations which the client seemed to be offering as rationalizations of his attitudes.

When the client complained, in effect, about his resistance and lack of a sense of emotional involvement in the discussion and asked the therapist for a "magic key" to circumvent the resistance, the therapist

suggested that they discuss, at the next interview, the therapeutic relationship, which he called *the* magic key. He sensed that the resistance was a reflection of a change in the relationship. There is quite
a bit of support for this hypothesis in the affect scores for this interview; the client's score was 39, his next to lowest score, and the therapist's was 09, which was his lowest score. Obviously, the relationship
had become poor at this point. When the client expressed dissatisfaction with the topics that had been discussed in this interview, the
therapist suggested that they consider also the topic of dependency.
The therapist felt that the client's dependency needs were becoming
the central issue of the case and that his desire to lean on the therapist
was going to become the main focus of therapy for some time, possibly for the rest of the sessions. Mr. Quinn reiterated his conviction
that his excessive dependency resulted from his father's lack of supporting behavior during the client's adolescence. His dependency
score dropped five points, to 38, and thus into the third, or less dependent, phase of his therapy.

Because the affect scores were so low in this interview, an item
analysis was made in order to determine, if possible, which aspects
of the affect had shifted. On the Client's Affect Scale the numbers of
items scored in the negative direction, classified according to our *a
priori* designations, were as follows:

affiliation (lack of)	7
nurturance (lack of)	8
self-understanding (lack of)	8
independence (lack of)	7
derogatory feelings	5
feeling dominated	2
feeling rejected	3
feeling resistant	9
hostility	0

There seemed to be an over-all sense of less favorable affect. The
only one of the above categories which differed markedly from its
usual frequency in the scale was the feeling of lack of independence,
which was about double in proportion to scores of this type usually
occurring in the test as a whole. It is significant that it was unsatisfied
dependency feelings that seemed to account for the poor affect.

Item analysis of the Therapist's Affect Scale revealed that only
12 of a possible 72 negative scores resulted from negative feelings

toward the client; on the other hand 14 of a possible 34 negative scores resulted from the therapist's estimate of the client's post-interview feelings toward the therapist, 24 of a possible 38 resulted from the therapist's estimate of therapeutic progress during the interview, and 10 of a possible 38 resulted from the therapist's estimate of the client's emotional maturity at this point in therapy. It is obvious that the low score on the Therapist's Affect Scale resulted largely from the therapist's estimate of poor progress in this interview and his perception of negative feelings directed toward himself by the client.

My wife said my father told her, after he looked at my models and woodworking, that he didn't realize that I had so much mechanical ability. That was kind of a minor victory for me. (Dep + fa)

This past Sunday I heard about a Jag that was for sale, and it was a beautiful deal. I was very strongly tempted to buy it, and my wife said it was O.K. to go ahead. So I checked with my father, and he was very much against it. (Dep + fa) So I was going to try to get a loan at the bank, but then I decided we would probably be wanting to start a family in the not too distant future, so I decided against that. Then we saw another Ford that was very cheap and a good buy, but we decided against that, too. Then I got a very nasty letter from my father, telling me I was a fool if I bought the Jag. He brought up the matter that I already owed him so much money. This got me riled up and reversed the good feeling I was having toward him last week. He had a good point, but he didn't have to practically slap me in the face with it. (Hos n + fa)

Our relationship at home has been much better. Once in a while my wife gets a little depressed, but she seems to work it out in her therapy. (Aff n + wife)

I keep repressing that stuff we talked about for the last couple of weeks. I don't know why, but it must be pretty threatening. (Res)

Maybe a better attack would be to approach it as if it were a fresh topic; (Structuring) *that is, what are some things you think ought to be talked about?* (Non-directive lead)

I can't think of anything. I could talk about some things like religion, but I think they're superficial or intellectual. I guess the thing that seems most important is this inability to relate to people deeply. (Anx — peers)

You feel a sort of need to maintain a distance between yourself and others. (Clarification)

Yeah. I think it keeps me from getting hurt. Before this restaurant episode I would trust anybody until he proved otherwise. (Dep + gen) I don't think I'm looking for somebody that's perfect, because that's impossible to find. But with everybody there's always *something* that holds me off. I don't know whether I'm afraid of being laughed at, or rejected, or what? (Dep — peers)

People can reject you if you open yourself up and disclose your real feelings. (Clarification)

But if I never take a chance I'll never know. It's self-defeating.

Maybe you have impossibly high standards or expectations regarding the behavior of others. (Disapproval)

That might be. This business of marital fidelity really gets me. I don't think I'm so rigid in my moral code, but it sure seems to be at variance with an awful lot of couples. (Sex p — $\rightarrow$ Anx — peers)

I would like very much to have a friend. (Dep — peers) Of course, a wife should be a friend, too, but there are certain things that one can't tell one's wife, that you can tell a friend. (Dep — wife $\rightarrow$ Dep + peers)

Such as what? (Question)

Hm. (Laughs, then sighs deeply) Well, I might want somebody else's opinion about some of my cases. (Dep — peers) The fact that my female client conducts her life entirely on a physical plane, going out and sleeping with every Tom, Dick, or Harry she possibly could, and maybe she'll proposition me. (Sex p + het) (Laughs rather vigorously)

You can't decide whether you're afraid your wife would give her consent or be angry! (Interpretation$_6$)

I just don't think it's too wise a thing to talk about with one's wife. I can't think of anything specific that I think I *can* talk over with her, but there're a lot of things that I don't. Typical bull, like went on in college, about dating, and so on. (Hos n + wife)

You're sort of depicting this friend you hope to find as someone with whom you could share confidences even more secret than those you could share with your wife. (Interpretation$_7$)

Well, it isn't just a matter of being secret, because there're certain things I wouldn't share with a friend that I would share with my wife. They're just different. (Pause) But I'd still like to have more than one close relationship where I can share things with friends. (Dep — peers)

You said there were things that one wouldn't tell one's wife, and I'm not sure that the generalization is legitimate; (Challenging) *perhaps you should have only said that there were things that you wouldn't tell your wife.* (Disapproval)

Well, maybe, but if a guy's on a job and there's a secretary who seems to be on the make, he doesn't ordinarily go home and tell his wife. (Aff n + wife)

How do you know? (Challenging)

Well, I don't know. Maybe he does, but I can conceive of this as being rather disturbing to the wife.

It wouldn't disturb her if she knew that he was completely committed to her. (Information)

I guess not. (Long pause) I may be afraid of the reaction I'd get from *my* wife. (Dep — wife → Anx) She said to me before we were married that if I went on a "fishing trip" with some of the girls it wouldn't bother her at all.

But you actually want *her to be bothered by it.* (Interpretation$_7$)

That's right. (Dep + wife) That's one thing I think one shouldn't tell one's wife. I cannot conceive of any marriage partner receiving well the news that one would rather be "shacking up" with someone else. (Aff n + wife)

Well, that's not the example that you gave; you said that some secretary was making a bid for the husband, not that he was "shacking up." (Challenging)

Um-hm. Of course, I would never need to tell my wife that sort of thing, because I wouldn't be doing it. (Aff n + wife)

Well, you made the point that nevertheless you would like to have other relationships; you don't want to be confined to just one deep relationship. (Clarification) *And this is an attitude shared by many people.* (Information) *I'm not trying to imply that if your relationship with your wife were perfect you wouldn't need other friendships.* (Reassurance)

Well, this last semester I've built up a lot of relationships that have not developed any depth yet, but I'm doing a lot more things with *guys*. (Aff n + peers) My wife calls it "my night out with the boys." Another sore point is that she wants a night out with the girls, which I don't mind, but I'm jealous about the other nights. (Dep — wife) She wants to go out then, too. (Dep — wife) (Pause) Something tells me I'm being very defensive.

Are you feeling *defensive? Or attacked?* (Question)

No. In fact I'm not feeling pushed enough. (Dep — ther) I don't think I've really said anything this afternoon at all. (This suggests strong resistance.)

You've said a couple of things: that your relationship with her has certain limits beyond which you can't go, and that you'd like other relationships (Interpretation$_7$)

Yeah. But maybe there isn't the usual conviction behind them. I'm flat emotionally, today. I know when I said I wanted friends I felt *that* quite deeply, (Dep — peers) but right now I don't feel much. (Laughs) I don't seem to trust anyone. I have difficulty in relating to my peers. I feel inferior around them. (Anx — peers) I guess I feel out of water in the bigger groups.

That's a somewhat different problem—the question of your status in a group. Somehow it doesn't quite tie in with your difficulty in finding satisfying relationships. (Challenging)

Everything keeps tying into this situation with my father, but I don't know in what way. (Dep — fa) (Very deep sigh) It's hard going. (Dep — ther)

And it always seems to go back to your father. (Restatement)

Maybe I'll have to settle for less than the best. (Ins) (Pause) I'm sure resistant today. It's becoming uncomfortable. (Res)

In what way? (Question)

Because I'm not producing. Taking up your time when I'm not saying a damn thing. What I'm looking for is some clue. (Dep + ther)

Well, we discussed needs for affiliation with other people. And we also discussed ego-needs. The need to have an adequate status and to be acceptable to other people. (Restatement) *One possible core-idea we haven't discussed, and we probably don't have much time for it today, is* dependency *needs.* (Directive lead) (Long pause)

Well, they haven't been satisfied. (Dep — gen) Maybe my mother actually encouraged them. But she wasn't the strong dominant figure. I guess the stronger the figure, the better, in the case of dependency. (Dep — fa) I wanted someone who was very strong and very secure. I certainly didn't get much of a chance to voice any dependency needs on my father. (Dep — fa) I never really had a chance to get emotionally dependent on anybody. (Dep — gen) (Deep sigh) Here we go again. I'm stuck. (Dep + ther) Perhaps I'm seeing resistance for the first time, first-hand. (Res)

You have the feeling that you're not going into things that you should be considering. (Clarification)

What's the magic key? (Dep + ther)

You're annoyed with yourself for not being able to break into that and get it out into the open. (Clarification) (Pause) *I don't know if we have time to go into it, but I have* one *magic key for resistance, and that is to explore the therapeutic relationship. That's why I'm not sure there is time.* (Structuring) *Probably something is happening in the relationship between us that is threatening you.* (Relationship) *But I wasn't as aware of resistance as you were in this discussion, today.* (Reassurance)

Well, I am, because I'm getting no feeling. (Dep + ther) It has been sort of an intellectual day. In the past I've been very pleased because things I've said have had real conviction, and I don't think there's been much intellectualization. But this today has been kind of divorced from emotion. I'd still like to chew through it. (Anx — self)

Well, let's think about that for next time, then. (Directive lead)

Quinn: Twenty-second Interview (11/5)

THE TWENTY-SECOND INTERVIEW was a rather unique one. Three-quarters of the client's discussion concerned the therapist; half of the affect-themes had to do with the therapeutic relationship and two-fifths were about the client's dependency upon the therapist in the therapy relationship. Following upon the previous interview in which much resistance had occurred, and after which the affect between client and therapist had reached its low point in therapy, this interview devoted to the relationship took a very appropriate direction and was a good example of relationship therapy. In analytic terms the client was beginning to show the development of a transference neurosis, although he insisted that the transferred positive affect was really earned. The therapist interpreted the character of the client's affect, emphasizing that it was a normal phase of therapy and giving examples to illustrate the way in which such strong positive feelings are generally reduced. The client recognized that his idealization of the therapist was probably not realistic, and the therapist confirmed this point. The client attributed his strong positive affect to the lack of a source on whom he could be dependent as a child, but the therapist countered with an alternate explanation. He suggested that dependency was a conditioned response in some cases and implied that this might be true for the present case. The client admitted how strong his dependency needs were.

Some of the therapist's techniques in this interview were rather unique. As we have indicated above, he identified the "transference neurosis." He also went much further and indicated the reciprocal aspect of his own feelings in the relationship, *i.e.*, the drawing of nurturant feelings from himself in response to the client's succorant ones. He made sure that the client was aware that he was revealing this for therapeutic purposes, so as to help the client perceive that any apparent unresponsiveness on the therapist's part was not the result of rejection but rather a deliberate counter-measure designed to help the client grow to be a more independent person. The therapist indicated that it would be a neurotic response on his own part to allow the dependency to be perpetuated. He made the important distinction between the client's goal to find more persons upon whom he could orient his excessive dependency needs and the therapist's suggested method of finding ways to reduce them by sublimating them into nurturant expressions toward other more dependent persons. He also pointed out the conflict between the client's dependency needs, motivated by the pleasure principle, and the social demands upon an adult male; this may be said to be invoking the reality principle in psychoanalysis. The therapist drew from learning theory by pointing out that *in*dependence and nurturance may be rewarding behaviors; here he was enhancing the valence of the socially approved goal (independence), along with his devaluating of the neurotic goal (dependency). Mr. Quinn's PAC-NAC dependency score was at 37. From the 21st through the 25th interviews his score remained almost constant.

In terms of formal classification, 27 per cent of the therapist's remarks dealt with aspects of the relationship, 22 per cent constituted the giving of information, 17 per cent were interpretation, and 14 per cent were clarification of feelings. There were also some supportive responses. He took a very active part in the interview; approximately half of the speaking in this interview came from him.

In terms of affect, this interview had a most dramatic effect: the client's affect score jumped from 39 to 82, placing it back near the mean for him. The therapist's score made an almost phenomenal jump from 09 to 62, raising it from his lowest score for this client to his third highest. Obviously, the therapist was highly satisfied with the client for the turn of events in this interview; instead of merely expressing his neurotic needs, he was attempting to understand them and do something to modify them. The therapist considered this interview to be the turning point of the case, even though it was followed by some regressive interviews; the basic neurotic pattern had been, at this point, identified and attacked.

We were going to try to analyze some of my resistance today—particularly what's going on between *us*. I haven't actually thought much about it. (Sighs) I don't know where to look. (Res)

Well, let's free associate on some of your recent feelings toward me. (Relationship)

I don't know how free the association will be. (Laughs) After our meetings my feelings are always very warm, but last week they were touched by something else that wasn't hostility. I don't know exactly what it was. It was a sort of fear, I think, of your position on the faculty. I don't know if that's enough to inhibit my letting anything out. Probably it does have something to do with it, but there's no way you can get away from that. (Dep — ther → Anx)

There could be two different feelings, the one regarding me personally, and the other regarding your feelings about the possibility that I might do something to you that would punish you by endangering your career. (Relationship)

I don't think there's much concern about the second; it's more the first. (Dep + ther, Rel) I feel that you would definitely respect the confidences of the therapy hour. You would probably disqualify yourself from making career judgments about me.

That's right; that's what I would do. The time when it's hardest to disqualify yourself is when you might want to come to the defense of the client. It's never hard to disqualify yourself from making criticisms of the client. (Information) *One's need to protect the profession becomes more the responsibility of his colleagues.* (Pause) *What you're finding is that you don't want me personally to think badly of you. You want to have my respect and admiration.* (Relationship)

Yes. (Dep + ther)

This puts it at the level of almost pure transference and not of secondary gain. (Relationship)

Yes, but at times like this I find the word transference kind of unacceptable. I tend to define transference as originally defined, as feelings carried over from some other situation and person to the therapist. But I tend to think of my feeling toward you as an *earned* feeling. (Dep + ther, Rel → Aff n + ther)

That's a perfectly legitimate distinction; the term earned feeling, or earned affect, as distinguished from transference, is a more precise usage. (Relationship) *But I think, perhaps, I also was using the term transference with more belief that I was referring to the original meaning of the word than perhaps you accept at this time as being true.* (Interpretation₇)

Perhaps there is, but I don't know where it is, because as far as I can see, the role that you're in now, which is conceivable as being a father-type role, does not involve the negative affect that I perceive I have toward my own father. (Dep + ther, Rel → Aff n + ther)

You have wished so much for a benign, favoring father. In that sense I might be fulfilling the role of the father that you didn't have. (Relationship)

Yeah. The things I've wished my father might have been, I've put onto you. But actually you *have* them. (Dep + ther, Rel → Aff n + ther) (Laughs)

So you haven't projected unreasonably. I've earned all these wonderful things you think about me! (Relationship) (Both laugh)

But actually what I've done, I think, is generalize to you as a whole. I feel that on the outside you're the same way as you are here in therapy, which may or may not be the case. I may be imputing characteristics not actually there, generalizing from a small bit of information available to me to your total life-style. (Dep + ther, Rel)

Um-hm. I really doubt whether I could live up to your in-therapy expectations of me. I expect that if you knew my life in toto, *you would find that it fell short of what you fantasy it as being.* (Interpretation₇) *That's just a generalization that I feel quite safe in making; it would be true of anyone, I suspect.* (Interpretation₇)

I wonder why I do this? Is it because I *want* to see you as a completely benign, and actually loving, individual? Probably it is. (Dep + ther, Rel) And actually, in therapy you haven't been completely that way, although I tend to repress the instances that deviate from that ideal. Several times I felt like you were criticizing me. (Dep — ther, Rel) But I tend to avoid thinking about those times and focus on the times when you've been more helpful or more supportive or actually encouraging dependence. (Dep + ther, Rel) (Laughs; he actually admits, self-consciously, that he has desired to have the therapist let him act in a dependent manner.)

That's a very important phrase, I think. (Calls attention) *You've liked the times when I've actually encouraged dependence.* (Relationship)

Yeah. It's a lot safer. More secure. (Dep + ther, Rel) Even in everyday life, if somebody can tell me what to do, I feel a lot safer than if I have to do it on my own. (Dep + gen) It sort of ties in with the feeling of being a person of unworth, of not being able to get along on my own. That's one thing I want to grow out of. (Dep + gen → Anx; he identifies dependency as a formerly comfortable life-style for him.)

It helps to have someone give you a pat on the shoulder and say, "You're doing it well," is that it? (Clarification)

Yeah. I never *got* reassurance from the people who really counted. That's why I kept trying so hard to do something that would cause somebody to say something favorable about me. It revolves around my father. (Dep — fa)

So you feel a pretty strong need to be given approval and to be reassured. And preferably you want it from a strong, masculine figure. (Clarification)

I think a recent example of this would be when I gave that presentation in your class. I feel funny talking about this. I wanted very much for you to say right afterward, "You did a very good job," or something like that. I was disappointed that your remarks were somewhat milder than what I had hoped for. (Dep — ther, Rel)

I think I did say something to the effect that it was a good presentation. (Reassurance)

Well, I felt I sort of forced you to do it by bringing it up later. I was extremely pleased that you had chosen me to be the one to present the case, of course. It showed some confidence in my work. (Dep + ther, Rel)

But you had wanted to be praised rather strongly for it. (Clarification)

Yeah. It's funny; when other people praise me, I feel kind of embarrassed by it. I think I'd probably find it embarrassing if you'd say something good about me, too. (Dep + ther, Rel → Anx)

Yeah, that's an interesting phenomenon. A lot of people report that sort of thing. It may be associated with the current theory that one should be very good, but one should also not seem better than his peers, if he is to be accepted in the organization. (Information) *You may wanta be a good guy, but if you seem too good, you can't be accepted by the others.* (Interpretation₇)

I don't know. I wonder if I'm actually looking for being the top dog. I like to think of myself as a member of the group. (Aff n + peers)

I've noticed an interesting thing. That if I do show any signs of affection toward you, that you're quite embarrassed—perhaps threatened—or you even tend to doubt them. Perhaps you seem suspicious. (Relationship) (Pause) *But let's go back to this dependency need. What you've said is that it feels good to be accepted and praised by a warm, adult male-figure.* (Clarification) *This is a very basic kind of thing, isn't it? The kind of thing one learns in very early childhood.* (Interpretation₅)

The kind of thing one should expect from one's father. Which normally comes from one's father. And if someone praises me, I want to work even harder. But I guess I've often kept trying, even though I haven't gotten praise. Maybe that stems from the pressure I always had to do well in everything. (Dep — fa → Dep — gen)

This dependency sort of thing is something I seem to be growing out of. I find that I can function as a husband and a provider and be the leader of our small family, and I enjoy it. (Ego + matur) But there's still a dependence on my wife's love. (Dep + wife)

But this is not terribly atypical, is it? (Reassurance) *Most of us must recognize some dependency needs in ourselves.* (Information; the therapist is attempting to teach the client to discriminate between normal dependency needs and those that may be excessive and neurotic.)

But most people have, somewhere in their lives, a father or mother, or somebody that they feel is strong, and someone that they feel they can have this type of relationship with. Or they've *had* it in the past. (Dep — par)

You make something of the idea that if you've once had it, it is a source of strength continually thereafter. (Interpretation₇) *I was about to make the point that ultimately these predecessors must inevitably become weaker, to the point that they no longer can be a source of support. Ulti-mately they may even become dependent on the next generation.* (Informa-tion)

Yes, that's true. Perhaps as I feel more confidence in my wife, I won't have this need to have something from the past that I can fall back upon. (Dep + wife → Ego + self)

I think that's likely. (Approval) (Pause) *Last week you took two po-sitions that rather surprised me. I rather tenuously raised the possibility that we would have to discuss dependency sometime, and you gave it a very different interpretation from mine.* (Challenging) *You indicated some-thing to the effect that we had to discuss the way in which your dependency needs were not being met, which was different from my slant on it.* (Re-statement) *And the other point you raised was that there were things that one had to have friends to share with, because one couldn't share them with one's wife.* (Restatement) *I interpreted this as a similar statement in that you were reporting the need to find sources of support to fulfill your dependency needs.* (Restatement)

Um-hm. I still can't quite see the distinction between your interpreta-tion of dependency and mine.

My interpretation of the situation was that your dependency needs were much stronger than many people's, and our problem was to come to an understanding of their cause and to decide whether they need to be as ex-treme as they are. (Interpretation$_9$) *You were looking for more sources for fulfilling or satisfying your dependency needs, and I was searching for ways by which we could reduce them.* (Interpretation$_9$)

Well, I think it's an accurate interpretation that my needs are stronger than most people's. (Dep + gen) When I first sent my wife away, I had to rehearse to myself, verbally, that I could be sufficient unto myself. (Dep + wife) I know it's true that even if I were able to function quite ade-quately, I'd still have to feel that I had somebody to depend on. (Dep + gen) I tend to think of it as a natural need that one has to have strongly fulfilled and then that one has to wean oneself away from. (Dep − par → Dep + mo surrog)

Now this is one theory on which some therapy is carried out—that cer-tain needs have never been gratified and that the therapy must make up for a deficiency in that area. (Information) *I suppose a great deal of my therapy has operated around the hypothesis that many persons have received in-sufficient love and the therapist must temporarily suffuse them with accept-ance and love to try to overcome the deficiency.* (Information) *But there's an entirely opposite point of view that one might take: that a person may have learned to satisfy his needs by some type of response, in this case dependency responses, and that therapy must be a form of reconditioning where a new type of response can be acquired to fulfill the demands of the drive.* (Information) *It's a little hard to say which theoretical approach one should take in this situation. One is supportive, and the other is more re-educative.* (Information)

I don't know. I got most of the support I received from the maid. Neither my mother or father gave me much sign of affection. With the maid I was very sure of it. (Dep — par → Dep + mo surrog) I can remember feeling a lot of competition with her boy friends. I suppose it was a sort of modified Oedipal situation. (Dep + mo surrog)

She was the mother-figure—not the true generic mother, but in every other sense the real and perceived mother. (Interpretation₅)

Yes. My mother was always off at the club or in some other activity. Even when it came to meal time, I would rather eat in the kitchen with my maid than in the dining room. I definitely had deep love feelings toward her. I even liked to go every place with her. (Dep + mo surrog) Of course her boy friends used to take me out often, too. They were warm, while my own family were cold and distant. (Dep — par → Dep + fa surrog) My maid was a real warm person, a real fabulous person!

It would be almost fair to say that the maid, who was your real mother, was torn from you at the age of about nine when you were taken away after the divorce. (Interpretation₅)

Yeah. It left me without anyone to be dependent on.

I'm thinking that in a way the conflict here is that with your present age and sex dependency is not the accepted role; socially you aren't any longer permitted to show signs of wishing to adopt this role, but your conflict is that you still feel the need to do so. Society expects you to be the aggressive provider, but you still feel a strong predisposition toward being the passive acceptor. (Interpretation₉)

That's right. (Laughs) I was just wondering which is more important, to find out why, or to try and get rid of that. (Ins)

They're not entirely exclusive of each other. (Information)

If I'd find out why, maybe it wouldn't be so important. (Ins)

Well, the passive role must have been very comfortable for you, highly rewarding. (Interpretation₅)

Yeah. It still is. (Dep + gen) (Laughs) It's also now more rewarding, I guess, to be able to do things for myself. (Ego + matur)

You're finding the satisfaction that comes to the adult when he finds that independence has its rewards, too. And even the step farther, when he finds that providing has its rewards. (Clarification)

This brings up the matter of countertransference; I think I owe it to you, hoping that this would not reduce my effectiveness as a therapist, to tell you that I perceive that your strong succorance needs arouse in myself strong nurturance needs. (Here the therapist is discussing the relationship from the point of view of the need-satisfactions which it fulfills for himself, *i.e.*, countertransference.)

I guess we aren't too different; I find myself feeling those nurturance needs toward my own therapy cases. (Dep — gen → Nur + peers)

These are not unrelated. I was hinting at this point earlier. Getting satisfaction through nurturant behavior may be the way the normal adult may compensate for some dependency needs. The adult male may feel it is impermissible to show succorant needs, so some of the nurturance may be a compensation for the dependency. (Information) *As you pointed out, and we often see it, parents often overcompensate for the deficiencies of their own childhood. Children who felt rejected may become overprotecting parents.* (Information)

Um-hm.

But it has its positive aspects. It can be used as a constructive personality force. (Information)

I can see that it would make one a good parent or a good clinician as long as it doesn't go too far.

It wouldn't be healthy for you, if I were to allow this situation to be one where I would play out my own needs to be nurturant and to encourage you to be dependent. I should not try to perpetuate your succorant needs and thus keep you from a desirable maturation. (Relationship) *I have told some clients that the ultimate goal of therapy must be that they come to respect and admire me only as a friend, and also a person who is not perfect, and who makes mistakes too. As someone whose acquaintance they'd like to continue to have, but who also isn't any longer a terribly important influence in their life. A friend whom they can grow to live without perfectly well.* (Relationship) *This doesn't mean they have to come to hate the therapist. I've always been suspicious of those psychoanalyses which ended in a fight between analyst and analysand.* (Pause) *What am I doing here? Why am I telling you this?* (Question; trying to make sure that the client does not misunderstand his intention.)

That's a good question. At times I have felt that you had these nurturance needs and were bending over backwards to go against them. Sometimes you were a little bit harsh. (Dep — ther, Rel) I can't help but say, this is hard to say, that maybe you were trying to therapize yourself a bit. Get it off your conscience. (Dep — ther)

I don't think that's true. I don't think a therapist should feel free to get therapy out of the therapy he is conducting for other people. (Clarification) *No, what I really feel is that transference, when it becomes quite apparent, needs to be discussed, and that to some extent both sides of the matter must be taken into consideration. I think that countertransference should be recognized, also.* (Relationship) *But what I'm most trying to do is to keep our relationship reality-based. To admit what its temporary elements are, and to recognize also what reality is in the situation.* (Relationship) *You see, if you hope, deep down, that I can be a father to you, I must tell you that I can't; it isn't possible.* (Relationship) *I can be a therapist, and a good friend. And this is not a rejection, to tell you this, but an attempt to distinguish between reality and the fantasy of transference in therapy.* (Relationship)

Um-hm. I think this has cleared the air a lot, because I feel on my own here. I'm ready to move again. I think I know what I'll talk about next week. (Aff n + ther; Ins, Rel)

Quinn: Twenty-third Interview (11/12)

THE TWENTY-THIRD INTERVIEW was concerned primarily with the topic of the client's relationship with male peers; he discussed his anxieties about any possible homosexual feelings which he might have toward them. There was some reference to heterosexual interests. All of this discussion was precipitated by the client's alarm over certain compulsions he had experienced to address his friends by somewhat more feminine terms of endearment. The principal affect-themes were affiliative needs, anxiety, sex needs, and dependency needs.

The therapist's principal effort was to help the client to discriminate between terms which might constitute signs of affection and actual sexual feelings toward his friends. The client had been poorly conditioned by his father's use of such terms of endearment rather than the more socially approved forms of masculine salutation. The therapist helped the client to identify the aspect of dependency as one of the major needs he felt in his desire to relate to men older than himself; the client was shown that he could experience satisfaction of these needs with his wife. His PAC-NAC dependency score was 38, showing almost no change.

The client raised the issue of whether he invariably kept people at a distance for some defensive purpose, and the therapist again interpreted that such a defense mechanism might protect him from the need to share more of himself with others than he was willing to do. Interpretation, clarification of feeling, questioning, and giving information were all about equally employed by the therapist in this interview.

Affect was fairly positive in this interview. The client's score was 85, or around his mean; the therapist's score was 59, or his sixth highest score. The interview was friendly, and progress was made in the direction of the client's achieving self-insight. He also obtained reassurance that his compulsive thoughts about his male peers were probably not signs of an abnormal sexual trait.

The thing that I was indicating last week that I'd like to talk about further is going to be difficult to talk about (Dep + ther) It's in the area of sex, and it kind of scares me. On occasion I'd be working with some guy around one of our houses, and I'd go to say something to him, and I'd find myself thinking of an endearing term like "Dear" or "Honey." It bothered the heck out of me, because if I thought about it in relation to some sort of homosexual relationship, I was completely repelled by it. (Aff n + peers → Anx — homo)

Sort of in the form of compulsive thoughts. (Restatement)

Yeah. It didn't occur too often. Actually about four or five times. But it's shaken me up. I just wonder where the heck it came from. In my own mind I thought I had resolved the homosexual business. I still haven't had any homosexual urges since we talked about it. (Aff n + peers → Anx — homo)

Perhaps we really should distinguish between sexual urges and affectional-emotional urges. (Information) *What you're telling me is that you have had some of the latter, but not the former, since that period last spring.* (Clarification) *In a situation where you're sharing some activity with these men, you have these sudden, compulsive, affectional urges toward them.* (Interpretation$_5$)

It hasn't happened since I was in military school, and I called a buddy of mine "Dear" and he told me not to. That was the first time that anyone ever pointed out to me that one doesn't call other fellows by these terms of endearment. I guess I haven't distinguished, because my father has always called me "Dear" or "Honey." You may have pointed out something pretty important. It has always been in a situation where it was just me and some other guy that are doing something together. Some enjoyable work situation. (Aff n + peers)

In a co-operative situation, where some companionship existed. (Restatement)

We might offer to help each other with outdoor chores, like repairing a fence or laying a patio. But also it has occurred with colleagues on my internship. (Aff n + peers)

Anybody with whom you've been sharing a kind of companionate or fraternal role. (Restatement) *You say that your father uses this kind of terminology a good bit?* (Question)

Yeah. I sometimes wonder whether it has too much meaning. It's a different situation. If I had a son, I might use the terms myself. But one doesn't use these terms with one's friends. (Aff n + peers → Anx)

Well, tell me, why do you go hunting with X. and do woodworking with Y.? What needs are being satisfied? (Question)

Well, besides enjoying the activities, I also enjoy the companionship. I went hunting with a married couple, also, but I did think *those* hunting expeditions were lacking in enough close companionship. Just sort of talk-ing and sharing things is what I liked when I went hunting with X. (Aff n + peers)

Companionship, and a close personal sharing. (Clarification) (Pause)
Do you think it's a relevant fact that you never had any brothers? (Ques-tion)

It might be. I know I often wished that my sister had been a brother. And I described this guy in the restaurant as fitting my conception of a big brother. I would have wanted an *older* brother, somebody who could teach me things, show me things, and share things with me. (Dep — fa surrog)

It's interesting that it's an older *brother you wanted.* (Interpretation₇)
How about a younger one? (Question)

Well, I really wanted somebody to show *me* some things. There are an awful lot of things I've had to learn on my own. An older brother would make things a little easier. Again, that puts me in a dependent position. (Dep — fa surrog)

That's what I think is interesting. It seems like only a slight modifica-tion of your feelings toward your father. (Interpretation₇)

Um-hm. Maybe an older brother would be sort of a father substitute. (Dep — fa surrog → Ins)

An affectionate father. A father who didn't have to be so terrifying and austere—one you could talk to in a closer, more intimate relationship. (Interpretation₅) (Pause)

People seek various types of companionship. A man who goes hunting with his dog doesn't hesitate to express love and affection for the dog. He's sure to get plenty of affection in return, but not too much shared compan-ionship, perhaps. (Information)

Yeah. A dog can't talk back. (Both laugh)

The dog can't talk too well, no. Some people share and get a lot of companionship with a wife. Some with siblings. Perhaps more commonly with same-sexed siblings than with opposite-sexed ones, although not al-ways. Some establish a very close relationship with a parent. (Information)
Now it's odd that the only ones that one really feels guilty about showing too much affectional feelings for tend to be the siblings, or a surrogate for them. And yet, it would seem that the laws of learning which hold in one case would just as easily hold in the other, unless there's been some special discrimination also inculcated by some strong counter-conditioning agent. (Persuasion) *I guess you're afraid of two things. You might express one of these terms of endearment and be very much embarrassed, or else you may be worried that they are signs of something within yourself that you don't want to have there, because it's not consistent with your ego-ideal.* (Interpretation₇)

That's right. It's not consistent with my ego-ideal, and I had *thought* that it was pretty much resolved, at least to my satisfaction. I know when I think of sex, I always think of a female. (Sex n + het)

Since last spring, that is? (Question)

Yes. My sexual fantasies concern some gorgeous female. But now I'm worried about these little instances I mentioned. (Sex n — homo → Anx)

Why do you think you need to develop these feelings of companionship? (Question)

(Client sighs deeply) Perhaps because I just don't feel fulfilled, as yet. I don't have everything I need. (Dep — gen → Aff n — peers)

That wasn't quite a fair question for me to ask, because it sort of implies that I don't think they would be necessary if you were well adjusted. (Attenuates) *And yet it isn't natural or typical not to have some needs for companionship with persons of one's own sex. This is almost universal. Up to the point of marriage it's extremely common; after marriage there's probably less expression of such needs. But* most *people do perpetuate like-sexed companionships for the better part of their lives.* (Reassurance) *It's just a question of how much is required and at what point it is perceived as deviant.* (Information)

I don't think I'm looking for anything but the norm. There are a lot of things I can do with a guy that I can't do with my wife. (Dep + peers) She doesn't care much for hunting. Perhaps there are some things like this that she just isn't going to be interested in, that I can share with somebody else. But you can't expect to share everything. (Dep — wife)

I wonder if with regard to these compulsive thoughts that you had, you could find words that would make the thoughts less threatening to you. Are there words of address in our language which men can use to show affection without seeming to express too much endearment? (Advice)

Well, besides their name, I could use something like "Buddie" or "Friend," or . . .

Either the person's name itself, his nick-name, or some diminutive for a name like "Bud" or "Buddie," or something of that sort. (Information)

Which are sort of legal male terms of endearment.

Yes, that's exactly what I was implying. There are certain acceptable terms of endearment, but maybe you don't know these terms. (Information) *The ones that your father has taught you by coincidental learning have been ones that are really appropriate for small children or else intersex terms of endearment.* (Information)

I don't know. It seems like an awful simple explanation.

Yes. It's right, that's just a simple answer. (Restatement) *But what was bothering you was that you were thinking words that might embarrass you because of their flavor of endearment.* (Clarification) *And actually, if you change the words, often this changes the social acceptability.* (Clarification)

The other way, of course, would be to get rid of the need to feel endearment for a person of one's own sex. I don't know whether we can do this, and I don't know whether we should try. (Information)

Well, I don't feel that that's good. If the compulsive thoughts are there, they're gonna come out somewhere. I can't see anything wrong with indicating some sort of endearment with another male as long as it's socially acceptable and acceptable to me. (Dep — peers → Aff n + peers)

If you were to train yourself to think the appropriate word of affection, versus the inappropriate one, you would probably not be distressed about it. (Advice) *The real question is whether this is something that you need to be distressed about. Do you need to be distressed about the feeling or just the word?* (Question; the therapist is teaching the client to discriminate between the thought and the act.)

I don't think I'm distressed about the feeling, it's the word.

The word sounds like something you don't want it to sound like. (Clarification)

That's right.

You aren't ashamed of the feeling, but only the way you show it. (Clarification)

No, but I've been so shocked by the word that I haven't gotten the feeling, either. I keep wondering if I'm not afraid of getting close. I always get hurt in that kind of relationship. (Dep — gen)

Have there been any people who didn't violate those relationships? (Question)

Oh, yes, the fellow who was my best man never violated it. But still I couldn't get that to go to the warm depth that I wanted it to be. I couldn't share as much as he could share with me. The relationships that could be good, I keep myself away from. (Aff n — peers → Anx)

There's another possible inference, and that is that a close relationship makes demands, also, and has expectations. Not only can you get hurt, but you're expected to give something, and maybe it's this giving that you find difficult. (Interpretation$_9$)

At one time I wouldn't have agreed to that, because up till the time of the restaurant episode I was practically known as a doormat, (Dep + gen) but after that episode I really cut down on the giving, and I find out what's in it for me, now.

So there's a sort of conflict. In one way you're a very generous person, and in other ways you're somewhat withholding, somewhat stingy of affection. (Interpretation$_4$)

Maybe I'm afraid of giving something and getting nothing back. If I give something first, I stand to get hurt. (Aff n — peers → Anx)

The person who gives first declares himself, in a way, and also stands to suffer some neglect from not being reciprocated. (Information)

It doesn't appeal to me to admit that, but I think it may be true. A person who's well adjusted wouldn't really worry too much about that. (Ins)

A person who experiences a lot of emotional deprivation may be reaction-sensitive in that regard, however. (Information) *The person whom you describe, who is well adjusted, is the one who is sure at the unconscious level that he will get affection from the world and doesn't have to look out for himself.* (Information)

(Client sighs deeply) I don't see how I'm going to find out unless I do a little bit of reality testing. I still don't know whether I haven't found somebody around here that I could really be close to (Dep — peers → Aff n — peers) or whether I keep throwing up barriers to myself to keep me from getting close to people.

You asked a good question (Calls attention) *as to whether you are raising artificial barriers or whether you just haven't found the right sort of person.* (Restatement)

I guess there have only been two guys in my life that I have felt completely compatible with, and one was the guy in the restaurant, and one was a guy in military school, and both of them disappointed me. (Dep — peers → Aff n — peers)

I would have the feeling that if in the situation of a large potential number of friends whom you might find in a large university like this, that if you haven't found anyone as a friend, that this would suggest that your standards were pretty rigid. (Disapproval)

I don't know whether I'm looking for a really close friend, maybe too close. (Aff n — peers → Anx)

I get the feeling that you're almost looking for one who might be about as close as a brother, or perhaps even as close as an alter marriage partner. (Interpretation₇)

Yeah. And a lot of this could well be from the fact that for so long I haven't had a wife, really. I've had an unfulfilled need for one. (Dep — wife → Dep — peers) I think I have one, now; or at least what could develop into one. But it's possible that this need is just lagging a little bit behind.

One thing that your wife doesn't give you that I think you may be looking for is gratification of the dependency needs. (Interpretation₇)

Yeah. (Sighs deeply) Hm. (Pause) I feel that in our marriage relationship we're dependent on each other, and I wonder if it's in the same sense. It's a companionate type of dependency, rather than a master-servant type of thing. (Dep + wife)

More equalitarian or symbiotic? (Clarification)

Yeah. I really wonder how strong these dependency needs would be if I were completely satisfied with the marriage relationship. (Dep — wife → Dep — peers)

That's a good question. (Calls attention)

But I won't know until I am. But perhaps if I try to do a little reality testing, and if I tried to develop a few friendships, maybe I'd find that I didn't have the need which I seem to think I have. (Dep — wife → Aff n + peers)

I think we should keep in mind that in these relationships what you're looking for is a kind of benign father or a friendly big brother. (Interpretation₅)

I think more a big brother. I wouldn't wanta' be dominated, but I'd want somebody I could share something with. (Dep — fa surrog)

You wouldn't wanta' be dominated or controlled, but you wouldn't mind someone who would take the leadership. (Clarification) (Long pause)

That's what I want, but I don't like it. (Laughs) I don't think of it as being very manly. (Dep — fa surrog → Anx)

So you're really in conflict about your own needs. You have these passive needs, and you also don't like them. (The therapist is clarifying an important ambivalence of the client.)

If there weren't some conflict there, I wouldn't have to worry about it, because I could just be dependent, (Dep — gen → Anx) or I could be what the normal person is, dependent and in a dominant role, varying with the situation. In the relationships I've had, I've been in both roles, and both were satisfying, but there was no depth, again. With somebody who knew something more than I did, I didn't mind being submissive, (Dep + peers) and with somebody that knew less, I enjoyed being more dominant. Sometimes it's sort of reciprocal, depending on what skills are called for at the given moment.

Um-hm. I guess our time's up. I think you made good progress today. (Reassurance)

Quinn: Twenty-fourth Interview (11/19)

THE CLIENT'S discussion concerned itself in the twenty-fourth interview with his handling of his hostility feelings toward his father and his wife. He was puzzled about his need to show a lot of hostility and wondered how much of it was displaced from his father onto his wife.

The therapist handled the interview rather directively. He used direct questions (22 per cent), challenging (19 per cent), information-giving (14 per cent), and interpretation (11 per cent). However, 14 per cent of his responses were clarifications of feeling. The core of his activity in this interview was shown when he explained to the client that he was trying to help him express his feelings of hostility and to understand their true object. Since he detected certain inconsistencies in the client's expressions, he attempted by various challenges or direct questions to help him to see these inconsistencies.

The client's ambivalence about his hostility was the chief dynamic which the therapist was attempting to clarify. Mr. Quinn was both intrigued by, and appalled by, hostile expressions in himself and in others. His basic passively dependent attitudes were in conflict with his needs to retaliate for perceived injustices, particularly on the part of his father, but also to some extent on the part of his wife. Mr. Quinn's dependency score was 37 at this time.

The client's affect in this interview changed very little (81) from the previous mean level score; the therapist's score dropped to 41, which was an eighteen-point drop, and constituted a significant shift, reflecting concern with the client's "retreat into a neurotic symptom," *i.e.,* his hostility feelings.

I don't know whether I've run dry of things to talk about or I've allowed myself to build up some resistance. There are times when I feel quite hostile and aggressive toward my wife, and I displace it onto our dogs. It's a very stupid sort of thing to do. Sometimes we wrestle together, and it's very hard not to hurt her by being too rough. I feel a real need to smash somebody. When I think about it, I wonder why I'm so brutal; what is the source of this repressed hostility? (Hos n + wife)

I personally don't believe much in the idea of a sort of dammed up hostility —a "reservoir-of-libido" sort of thing that has to be discharged— but I believe more in a conditioned response sort of theory. (Information) *That is, I think the hostility has to be getting recharged rather regularly, or it would peter out fairly quickly,* (Information) *although I know it can be carried around for brief periods, or even some days.*

I seem to get a sadistic sort of pleasure out of slugging the dogs at times. I'd really enjoy the sensation of slugging somebody. It seems more like cruelty than just anger. It's not harmonious with my self-concept. I wonder where this sadistic thing comes from? (Hos n + gen)

That's an interesting question. (Calls attention) *Lots of people have a need to displace aggression. When fraternity members initiate freshmen, or when parents are unfairly punitive, I think that's what we'd have to call it.* (Information)

But is it necessarily displacement? When I get pleasure out of hurting my wife, she may actually be the one I want to hurt. Maybe I want to pay her back for having hurt *me*. But I never paid my *father* back. I wonder if at times it isn't actually displaced from him. (Hos n — fa → Hos n + wife)

I'm sort of interested in this wrestling behavior and need to wrestle. How do you account for it? (Directive lead)

Well, it doesn't occur often. Just roughhousing. I've always roughhoused with girls, and boys. I know lots of husbands and wives that have pillow fights.

Could you say that there was not an expression of some hostility in the game? (Interpretation$_9$)

Maybe, but it always starts out as fun.

Is it much different from teasing? (Interpretation$_9$)

Well, it's just a more active process of teasing.

Psychodynamically I suspect the feelings are similar. (Interpretation$_7$) *You seemed to feel a bit defensive about it.* (Clarification)

Well, I didn't think I was, especially. But I don't think it's normal when it goes past the point of becoming hurtful. Sometimes I get the feeling that I'm intentionally hurting her. (Hos n + wife)

Could it be covert anger? (Interpretation$_7$)

I'm not sure. It's a nice acceptable way of getting out some of the hostility you may be feeling. (Pause)

The next time you find yourself in a pillow fight, it might be worthwhile to analyze your feelings at that time. (Advice)

I'm just liable to stop if I did. (Laughs) I really think if no one gets hurt that it's just a good, clean, energetic type of fun.

Do you think that both parties enjoy it equally? (Challenges)

No. My wife doesn't enjoy it at all. (Client then describes wrestling with his father after he had learned some holds at school.) I got him in a hammer lock, and I really put the juice to him. It gives me kind of a pleasure to recall it now. (Hos n + fa)

Whenever you've hurt him, physically or mentally, you've always felt a kind of glee or satisfaction. (Clarification)

Yeah. Probably these were displaced ways of getting back at him. (Hos n + fa)

I don't honestly believe that this is just a perfectly normal behavior between husbands and wives. (Disapproval) *Maybe my sample has been different from yours.* (Attenuates)

Well, maybe *my* sample is biased. I still can't see what's wrong with it, as long as it doesn't go too far. I wonder if it's sort of an aggressive sexuality, kind of like a rape. There's a definite sensuality about it. (Sex n — → Hos n + wife)

I don't know whether the sexual aspect is very prominent. (Information)

Maybe it's just pleasure in dominating. I enjoy being able to beat somebody. (Dom n + gen)

Why do people go to boxing matches? (Question)

I think that's a way of letting out their own feelings. Watching somebody slug somebody. I wonder how you're trying to tie this in to the other. (Hos n + gen)

Do you ever see any plays that depict criminals slugging someone, or SS men beating someone up? (Question)

That reminds me that one of my favorite types of movie is a war movie.

How about hazing in college? (Question)

It was pretty brutal. I went through it just because I had to prove that I could take it too. I don't know whether I ever really got pleasure in watching somebody else getting beaten, but I know I used to try and be there whenever it happened. But it sort of bothered me to see it. (Hos n + peers → Anx)

Why did it bother you? (Question)

Sort of a positive and negative valence to it. I wanted to see it, but when I saw it, it wasn't very pleasant. (Hos + peers → Anx)

You were drawn to it, but also repelled by it. (Clarification)

That's right. I guess it's the same thing that I'm really saying about hitting my wife. I enjoy it, but I don't like it in myself. (Hos n + wife → Anx)

How do you feel toward a policeman who bawls you or somebody else out? (Question)

Usually I'm very scared. That's the first feeling, but then there's sort of a hate. In each instance that we've talked about, in a way it's acceptable for me to show hostility in a sort of legal manner. (Hos n + gen)

I've been trying to help you clarify your feelings with regard to the expression of aggression, both against yourself and against other persons. (Calls attention) *Where you would see that several of your attitudes did not logically fit in with some other ones. . . .* (Challenges)

We might try to determine when it is permissible to justify our own rights. To get satisfaction out of the display of hostility toward others. (Directive lead) *You used the words "legal" or "socially approved." I'm raising the broader issue. How much hostility toward others is legitimate?* (Challenges)

It depends on the situation. The dog doesn't deserve to be hit, when I hit him. And usually my wife doesn't deserve it, either. . . .

I think you're saying that your having received more than your share of punishment, gives you the right to dish out more of it. (Clarification) *The sense of getting even gives you some satisfaction.* (Clarification)

Yeah. (The client, after saying many negative things about his father, told about some of the advantages he has had from having had his particular father; not all of the situation has been disadvantageous.) I've gone to good schools, and he's helped me a lot in this regard. (Dep + fa) There have been disadvantages in having him for a father, but he has been good to me, also.

But all those things don't make up for the lack of emotional security. (Dep — fa → Hos n + fa) (Pause) I guess I keep trying to pay him back. If I could just blow up at him once, I wonder if all that would change. I'm so damn frustrated when I'm around him. There were so many things that I'd like to object to that I can't, except in very nice ways. (Dep — fa → Hos n — fa)

You're saying that instead of these other people, it really is he that you'd like to be punishing. (Clarification)

That's what I wonder. If I could just let it out at him and beat up on him. (Hos n — fa)

I don't think one explosion against him would change a life-style. (Advice)

But if I could develop a consistent reaction pattern like that, responding aggressively to something that frustrates me, it might be a better way of handling it. I wonder if I'd ever reach the point where I could feel really independent. . . . (Dep — fa) I just don't know how he would react. (Dep + ther)

My father was the source of all the problems; he caused the divorce, and that was the beginning of the terrible loneliness that constituted all of my life from that time on. (Dep — fa → Dep — gen) If I show a grudge against the world, it's really a grudge against him. I'd like to punish him.

I am going to express more direct aggression in the future, when it is deserved, and stop expressing so much of this displaced aggression against more helpless recipients. (Hos n + gen)

(The therapist then suggested that the father is no longer the primary source of the client's frustration and that he should probably look for the more immediate source when he feels aggressive.) (Advice)

Quinn: Twenty-fifth Interview (11/26)

THE PRINCIPAL object of discussion in the twenty-fifth interview was the client's adviser, who was for him a very significant symbol of arbitrary authority. Most of the client's affect took the form of anxiety, but there were also expressions of hostility, dominance needs, and ego needs. The client took a position of having been unjustly persecuted by his adviser. He responded with his characteristic pattern of passive resistance.

The therapist employed a consistently challenging (29 per cent) and information-giving (27 per cent) role. He also used some structuring (10 per cent) and directive leads (8 per cent). In this discussion of the adviser, the therapist perceived the client as relying on a longstanding neurotic symptom to cope with a frustrating situation; rather than facing his problem with the adviser by a careful analysis and, if necessary, a confrontation, he withdrew from the situation, using passive resistance. The behavior was not proving successful. Therefore, instead of employing an attitude of sympathetic, nurturant clarification of feeling, which would have increased the client's dependency feelings, the therapist questioned what he considered to be rationalizations and proposed more mature problem-solving approaches.

Somewhat surprisingly, this aggressive attacking of the client's handling of the situation with his adviser did not produce negative affect from the client; his affect score rose to 94, his fourth highest score for the series of interviews. On the other hand, the therapist's affect score dropped seven points, to 34, constituting his fourth lowest score for this client. Again this score was reflecting his perception of the client's behavior as regressive. The client's improved affect toward the therapist can probably be explained as the result of some satisfaction of his dependency needs when the therapist took an active role in proposing alternate ways of meeting his problems. Perhaps also he felt some satisfaction with the insight he achieved, perceiving that his means of handling the matter with his adviser was a neurotic replication of his previous handling of hostility toward his father. His dependency score dropped only one point, to a score of 36.

I hate to say it, but I have nothing to talk about today. I know there's a lot that I should discuss, and I don't want therapy to be a kind of busy work. (Res)

Well, we've had about 23 interviews. That sometimes is the point at which people feel they've pretty well gotten things lined up and can see their way through. (Structuring; suggesting the ending of therapy is likely to be very threatening to Mr. Quinn.)

I don't think that's true for me. I have a feeling that there are a lot of things about myself that I still don't like, and I would like to work through them.

I wish you could blast me out of this doldrum. (Dep + ther) It's hard for me to be objective about what progress I've made and what I've covered. (The client's characteristic pattern of dependency exhibits itself again, here.)

Well, one topic I've thought you could use a little bit of help on is the matter of your relationships with authority-figures, as illustrated by your adviser. (Directive lead) *He recently said to me that you had been goofing off this semester on your thesis. I had the feeling that maybe you were back in your old rut of tending not to face up to difficult situations.* (Disapproval)

Well, you're right that I've been avoiding the matter. I've had two term papers, but perhaps that's just a rationalization. I've been trying to get an appointment with my adviser for over a week, and he says he can't give me one until the day before Thanksgiving. Well, we wanted to leave a day early for Thanksgiving. He seems to be saying that he's going to get even with me now for letting it go all semester. Also, he's now demanding new changes that weren't part of the original agreement. (The client may be attempting to win support in his criticism of his adviser.) (Dom p — auth)

Well, the only way in which we should discuss the situation here is with respect to any aspects of your personality which interfere with an effective relationship with him and need to have something done about them. (Structuring)

I guess the basic problem is the difficulty I have in working with certain types of personalities. I find him so unpredictable, and he's always making fresh demands when you've thought you met all of his requirements. (Dom p — auth)

Isn't this the sort of thing that is true of many supervisors and instructors, though? (Challenges; the therapist is attempting to direct the client in a somewhat reality-oriented consideration of the situation, rather than offering sympathy for what may be a neurotic feeling.)

Yeah. I know you can't fight "city hall"; you have to join them. (Laughs) I'm so teed-off at this research business, I never want to do another research in my life. He said that this was the sort of problem you could wrap up in a weekend, and already I've spent more than a year hacking away at it. To make it worse, he's trying to get me to use a statistical procedure which I know, and everybody I talk to knows, is inappropriate and practically a matter of scientific dishonesty to apply to these data. He's so eager to get certain results, I have the feeling he'd ask me to "fix" the data if he didn't know I'd expose him for it. He's dishonest! (Hos n + auth)

Have you told him you think it's dishonest? (Challenges)

Not in so many words, no. I've told him I couldn't bring myself to use the statistic he wants me to use. I think I have to be true to my own notion of what I think is good research! But this puts me in a bad spot, because he can ruin my career. (Anx — auth)

How can you be sure you're right and he's wrong about the statistic? (A real challenging of the client.)

I've talked with (names four other professors) who all say I'm right. (Dep + auth)

Did you tell your adviser that? (Challenges)

No. I *didn't* tell him that. (Laughs) I'm dreadfully afraid of getting him mad. Which he obviously already is. (Anx — auth)

How does he know that you are basing your opinion on anything but stubbornness? (Challenges) *He may see it as the opinion of a student against that of a professor.* (Information)

It should be obvious to him that he's wrong! Some faculty members are willing to argue with you, but he's completely authoritarian. (Hos n + auth)

I see two possible ways in which this is relevant to our purposes here. (Structuring) *First is the matter of how you react to severe frustration.* (Directive lead) *Second is the matter of how you react toward strong authority-figures.* (Directive lead) *I'm really not disputing the rightness or wrongness of your statements, or of his.* (Attenuates) *In either case, we could consider the matter of the most effective way of your coping with the situation.* (Directive lead) *Maybe he is seeing you as a stubborn kid who won't listen to reason, and you are seeing him as a stubborn autocrat who won't listen to reason.* (Information; the therapist tries to hold to an objective or impartial appraisal of the situation.)

I think probably both of those views are correct. He's trying to pull his rank on me. This reaction to frustration is probably pretty typical of me. I play ostrich and bury my head in the sand, rather than taking positive steps to do something about it. (Anx — auth)

He may be interpreting it as passive, and somewhat unreasonable, resistance. (Information)

But I gave him the statistical logic for saying he was wrong! It wasn't just that I was being a fresh little stubborn kid. (Laughs) I had a real, logical reason. (Hos n + auth)

To what extent is this a contest or struggle of wills? (Challenges)

That's pretty much the way I've pictured it. I wanted to ask you, are you suggesting that I go along with what he proposes? (Dep + ther) But I vetoed asking you, because I don't think you would do *that*. (Laughs with some embarrassment) Perhaps it would make the relationship easier with him, but I just can't be dishonest for anybody.

There may be other positive ways of dealing with it. (Information) *So far you've considered the "ostrich" way, and the "beat-him-down" way, and the "compromise-your-own-integrity-and-give-in" way.* (Interpretation₅) *But he holds all the cards on all three ways. He doesn't have to get the thesis completed, and you do.* (Information; suggesting alternative responses.)

But graduate students aren't little kids in school! I think it's a heck of a thing if it comes to a matter of a contest of wills. I conceive of graduate students as being only a few years different from the faculty. Maybe I just find it hard to accept the idea that that little difference of training makes a big difference between us. (Hos n + auth) Well, this experience has taught me a lot of things that I *don't* want to do on my dissertation, but I'm not sure they're the things it was intended that I should learn. (Laughs)

Do you believe, honestly, that your adviser would deliberately encourage you to fudge your results? That his position is insincere? (The therapist challenges an extreme and improbable position the client has taken.)

I don't think he'd intentionally be dishonest. What might be happening is that he can't see it as fudging as much as I do. I know he wouldn't intentionally say, "Well, let's rig the results."

Wouldn't it be better to go to him and tell him why you're unwilling to do it? That you don't believe he's recommending that you be dishonest, but that you have a lot of evidence to indicate that that statistic isn't permissible? (Advice in the form of a definite suggestion.)

I did that, and it didn't change his attitude. Maybe it needs more clarification; one or the other of us has got to be able to show the other one that he's not right. (Dom n — auth)

I keep wondering how much this is your way of dealing with authority figures. (Challenges) *I keep having the suspicion that you've been through this before with somebody else. You know whom I mean. And that your way of handling the situation was to wait it out.* (The therapist makes an interpretation₇ alleging that the client's response is a generalized reaction from the original authority-figure.) *But in the situation with your father, you probably had a good chance of winning in the end if you just waited long enough, because he probably basically* did *need your acceptance and love, ultimately.* (The therapist gives information attempting to teach discrimination between the two situations.)

Yeah. And my adviser does not. (Laughs) I think this is very close to some of the situations with my father. They're exactly the same types of personalities.

But just as I could never tell my father exactly what I thought, I couldn't act in a completely strong way in this situation. (Dep — fa → Dep — auth) Because I was afraid of having my head lopped off.

Well, it would be unwise to say something like, "Look, you stupid bastard," since the relationship demands a certain degree of respectfulness on your part. (Advice) *Of course, he should not say that to you, either. But I don't think that if he's approached reasonably, he's too temperamental.* (Giving information and some advice)

I did approach him reasonably last spring.

And you made tremendous headway. (Approval)

I guess, but it didn't last.

Actually, when he agreed to see you at Thanksgiving, he made quite a concession, because it's really vacation time. He could have said: "I'm sorry, I'm off duty then." (Challenges)

Um-hm. My immediate thought just then was, "You're trying to paint him in a good light, and I wanta' see him in a bad light." (Hos n + ther)

No. I'm only trying to be objective. (Structuring)

I know. But my first reaction was to be suspicious. It would appear that I have a negative set toward him, and anything that will threaten this negative set, I don't want to accept. I'm sure that he has positive characteristics, but I think it's important that I keep looking for negative things about him. (Hos n + auth)

That's true. That's important. (Approving)

I wonder whether it isn't the same with my father, too. If he does something positive I pass it off, but if he does something negative, I bitch like heck. I tend to remember only the bad things about my childhood. (Hos n + fa; Ins) (The client reveals some insight into his overgeneralizing of negative attitudes.) I guess I've become reaction sensitive. I *look for* rejection and hostility, and this in turn allows me to reject the other person. But why should I want people to reject me? Perhaps I feel that I'm a person who deserves to be rejected—that I'm not worthwhile. (Hos p — fa → Anx)

The most difficult things to see about oneself are those things about which one feels ambivalent. I suspect that's what we have here. (Information) *You see both satisfactory and unworthy things about yourself.* (Clarification)

Emotionally I can't tie up yet this need to be rejected. It seems logical as all get out, but I don't have any great conviction about it. Maybe the intellectual recognition comes first, and the emotional reaction will follow later. I know I *like* this explanation. It satisfies something, and it goes deeper than just logic, because you've said other things that were logical, but they didn't seem to be as "right" as this does. (Dep + ther) It explains these feelings of unworthiness that I've had all along, too. Feelings that I didn't belong, and so forth. (Anx — self)

The deeper convictions that come from earlier periods often are more powerful than the intellectual rebuttals that develop later. (Information)

I'd like very much to talk further about this next week, and I would like to have you help me recall it if I've shoved it down under by that time. I have a feeling I may. (Dep + ther) (Laughs, after making a typically dependent remark.)

Quinn: Twenty-sixth Interview (12/3)

M OST OF the discussion during this interview was directed toward the parents, but a little related to the client's discussion of his enuresis in childhood and to his self-attitudes. One-quarter of the affect expressions were of hostility, one-fifth related to sex needs, the rest to anxiety, hostility press, dependency, ego needs, and affiliation needs. Mr. Quinn expressed much disapproval of, and anger about, his parent's child-rearing methods; he considered whether his enuresis was a symptom of either hostility or regressive urges. He brought up some discussion of his mother's seductive behavior toward him during his adolescence. He seemed to have some trouble accepting the interpretations by the therapist, finding it hard to believe that he could have been driven by such motivation.

The therapist's activity was quite interpretive (34 per cent), with a considerable amount of clarification of feeling and information-giving (19 per cent of each). The therapist tried to work through rather standard analytic interpretations of this material. There was some discussion, also, of Mr. Quinn's tendency to search for rejecting behavior on the part of those persons with whom he comes in contact.

Mr. Quinn showed a few signs of dependency during the interview; he was somewhat hurt that the therapist had not expressed enthusiasm for his insight about his tendency to try to get people to reject him. He thought he might have deserved to be rejected. Although he felt sure that his mother loved him during his childhood, he frequently *asked* whether he was loved. At the end of the interview Mr. Quinn again asked the therapist to remind him of certain topics he wanted to talk about at the next interview. There was no discussion of the therapy relationship during the twenty-sixth interview. The dependency score dropped to 34.

The client's affect score dropped a little in this interview (86), and the therapist's rose to 55. These were not very significant changes.

207

My appointment with my adviser lasted all of five minutes. I suspected that would happen, and it really burned the hell out of me. I can't avoid the feeling that the whole thing was punitive on his part. I did explain why I hadn't gotten to the thesis because of the term papers, and he seemed to accept it. He seems noticeably rather cool toward me, though. (Dom p — auth)

After our interview last week I felt very good the whole day, (Dep + ther) which seemed to indicate to me that perhaps that was an answer: that I was trying to get people to reject me. Even though we once discussed it here before, it just didn't quite hit until our last interview. I was a little bit hurt, last week, that you didn't seem to feel as good about this insight as I did. Maybe you weren't as sure of it as I was. (Dep — ther; it is interesting that the client perceived the therapist's lack of satisfaction with the previous interview; the therapist's affect was *not* as favorable as usual, according to the affect scale.)

I'm still not exactly sure that I can see why I would want to be rejected, unless it was that I felt that I deserved to be rejected. One of the things that sticks in my mind is that the punishment far outweighed the praise, as I remember, at least in degree. Like that business of being tied out in the front yard; that's extremely strong punishment, to my way of thinking. I think when I was young I couldn't discriminate between just and unjust punishment, and I think I internalized a lot of the criticisms. (Hos p — par)

The punishment seems a pretty dreadful thing to you. (Clarification) *You seem to make so much of it, perhaps more than the severity of the punishment seems to warrant.* (Challenges) *Was its meaning to you a severe exclusion from the family?* (Interpretation$_8$)

No, the thing I felt was extreme embarrassment to be publicly displayed there, and obviously because I'd done something wrong. You don't just tie a kid out in the front yard for nothing. (Anx — par)

It was the public aspect of the punishment that embarrassed you. A little bit like placing you in the stocks or something. (Clarification)

And this fear of soiling myself in public was pretty acute. I think my toilet training was extremely strict. And of course this enuresis went on for so darn many years after that. (Dep — gen) I think my mother transmitted to me a tremendous sense of shame attached to these bodily functions. And once I wet my pants in school because I was afraid to ask to go to the toilet, (Dep — gen → Anx) and this led to tremendous embarrassment. I think I was always scared of group situations.

Um-hm. The one interpretation of all of the behavior that you haven't made, but that sometimes is made, is that the wetting and soiling behavior is a form of hostility. (Interpretation$_9$)

Hm. I felt hostile to some teachers, but there was one whom I just loved. I couldn't have felt hostile to her. I guess I can't swallow this hostility thing exactly. (Hos n + ther; Res)

The other possible interpretation that's often made is that it's a desire to regress to a more infantile level. (Interpretation$_9$)

I can't help but think we're making a mountain out of one small mole-hill. (Hos n + ther; Res)

What causes me to tie it in with hostility is the general tenor of what you've been saying for the past few weeks. Especially when we've discussed your method of responding to pressure. Passive resistance. (Interpretation$_4$)

Hm. Well, can little kids rationalize to that degree?

They're not conscious of much of what they do. (Information)

But my feeling was that I was afraid to ask to go to the bathroom. (Dep — gen) That's why I ask whether it would be possible for a little kid to be saying to himself, "This is a good way to be hostile." (Res)

Well, you may be right. It's certainly the most obvious reason, that you were just afraid to ask to go. (Attenuates)

I know I was deeply ashamed of bodily functions. There was a tremendous amount of segregation between my sister and myself. I can remember asking to take a bath with her, but they wouldn't let us do it. (Sex n — het → Anx)

There was a great deal of modesty, almost to the extent of prudishness. (Interpretation$_5$)

Yeah. And I think it caused me to be extremely inquisitive as to how other people were constructed, too. I would try to see my sister or her friends.

Just about that time, when I was near puberty, my mother became somewhat immodest. I could go in the bathroom if she were in the bathtub. She was practically flaunting sex, or something. It was a real sudden change. (Sex p — mo)

Do you have any idea what brought this on? (Question)

One thing that was different physically was the fact that we didn't have two bathrooms any more. But that sounds like too simple an explanation.

It sounds almost like one of two things: either a conscious desire to change because of having been told that she was too prudish in her child-rearing, (Interpretation$_9$) *or the other idea might be an unconscious seductiveness. This was the time when she was separated from your father and hadn't remarried yet.* (Interpretation$_9$)

That's right. I'm sure it was probably unconscious, if it was seduction.

I suppose it could have been a deliberate attempt at sex education. (Attenuates)

Well, then why wouldn't she have let me hear her discuss the sex education pamphlet that she bought my sister at this time? I wasn't allowed to look at the book, either.

This was the time of the first homosexual activity. I wonder if there could have been some sort of unconscious fear of incest on my part. (Sex n — het → Anx)

Or just the normal adolescent interest in sex. It was, of course, about the time of that. (Attenuates)

Another thing which may have intensified something that had already been there was this business about my going in to cuddle with my mother for a few minutes almost every morning before I got up. (Dep + mo → Sex n + het, mo)

That could be a pretty erotic situation for a twelve-year-old child. (Information)

That's what I was thinking. Although I can't think of any sexual ideas I had. But I probably couldn't entertain them if they *were* there. Of course, all of that was changed at the time of the marriage of my mother to my stepfather; that business was cut out fast. I think all of this exposure on the part of my mother would have been bad at that age. (Sex n — mo)

It may tell us more about your mother's dynamics than about your own. (Information) *I'll certainly grant that it may have been unconsciously disturbing to you, though.* (Clarification)

We sort of got away from the discussion of ways in which you might seek to be rejected into a discussion of your "elemental badness," and then into a discussion of your shame about bodily functions, and then into a discussion of your mother's sexual seductiveness toward you. (Restatement)

Hm. Hm. I'm trying to pin down what I might have thought was the thing that I was most consistently bad about. The thing I was punished and ridiculed most for was the enuresis. In this sense, I was a bad child, up till I was at least nine or ten. I wonder if underneath there wasn't some hostility in this. Perhaps a way of showing revenge for the rigidity on their part. I keep having difficulties thinking a child could be so damned intelligent to work up that sort of scheme for revenge. (Hos n — par → Anx — enur)

It's not just intelligence. Any more open aggression would be punished severely, but this way, although there's punishment, it's still possible to believe within oneself that it isn't one's own fault. (Information)

I wonder if it did come from making me conform, back in the preverbal past. How do you ever know? (Dep + ther) I can't help but feel that my parents' relationship to me was based on punitive rather than companionate behavior. I resented it a great deal when they went off on a cruise once and left us at home. I keep getting the idea that I was a convenience to be trotted out in front of their guests, a nice little boy to show off and to have serve the canapes. I can see why I'd want to get revenge. (Anx — par → Hos — par)

Once when I was young I asked my mother whether I was wanted. (Dep — par) She told me that I definitely had been. But what would make me ask that question? Maybe all kids do; I'm not so sure.

You were wondering to yourself or doubting whether they really wanted you, if they treated you this way. (Clarification) *The child who is quite sure he's loved doesn't have to ask.* (Information)

I think I also asked whether I was adopted. (Dep — par)

There seemed to be very little to give you the conviction that you were pleasing to your parents. (Clarification)

Every day I had to ask my mother, "Was I a good boy today, Mommie?" I don't think most kids have to ask that. (Dep — mo)

Um-hm. I guess our time's up.

Yeah. I hate to put responsibility where it shouldn't be, but I'd like to ask you again (laughs) to try and remember as much of this interview as possible and prompt me next week. (Dependency, again)

Quinn: Twenty-seventh Interview (12/10)

THE OBJECTS of discussion in this interview were about equally divided among the therapist, the client himself, and his peers. The most frequent affect-theme was anxiety, with considerable amounts, also, of hostility and affiliation need. Two significant events occurred during the interview: the first was Mr. Quinn's being half an hour late. He justified this by the statement that he and his wife had overslept. The therapist called attention to this as a possible sign of resistance only after there had been a substantial amount of other evidence that Mr. Quinn was quite resistant during the interview. The other significant event was the client's surprise when the therapist pointed out that Mr. Quinn seemed to have an excessive need to establish close relationships with male companions. He denied that he felt this to be true and said he had been pursuing the subject only to please the therapist.

The therapist used a number of direct leads and direct questions, suggesting material for discussion (28 per cent), and a good many interpretations (22 per cent). He employed some challenging and criticizing (14 per cent), reassurance (10 per cent), and discussion of the relationship (9 per cent).

Apparently because of the marked resistance that the client was showing and the misunderstanding that came to light on this crucial question of the client's dependency needs directed toward strong male peers and father-surrogates, the affect in the twenty-seventh interview dropped to nearly its lowest level for both client and therapist (42 and 19 respectively). It also seems quite likely that the client was experiencing resistance and hostility because the therapist had mentioned the possibility of therapy drawing to a close. This is the typical recrudescence of symptoms that occurs when termination of therapy is brought up with a dependent client; the therapist in turn showed his awareness of this regressive phenomenon in his evaluations on the affect scale.

A number of events relevant to dependency and the relationship occurred during the twenty-seventh interview. Mr. Quinn asked some questions about clinic office hours; he also showed a lot of resistance. He arrived late, had great difficulty remembering topics, and asked to be reminded of them. Even when he was reminded, he forgot the topics immediately. He expressed the feeling that he was being "grilled" by the therapist. The therapist suggested the interpretation that perhaps Mr. Quinn's motivation to get better had decreased and that possibly he was finding the therapy so comfortable and rewarding. He denied this interpretation, however. Although his affect scores dropped after this interview, Mr. Quinn's dependency score rose to 45, one of its higher levels.

The rather lengthy discussion of Mr. Quinn's desire to build a strong relationship with another male was taken by the therapist as being a sign of dependency. Although Mr. Quinn denied that this feeling was really very strong, the therapist was unwilling to accept the denial. Mr. Quinn did indicate that he felt that he could discuss most of his problems with his wife. As in any good therapy, he was apparently becoming less dependent upon the therapist.

(The client arrived one-half hour late for the interview and was very much out of breath.) Well, I overslept this morning. I may be a little bit foggy, because I'm still not sure I'm up yet. (Res) I saw my adviser yesterday and turned in the first three chapters of my thesis all written up in final form; he looked at it and said, "Impressive." So now I seem to be on his good side again. I'll find out tomorrow whether the contents are quite what he expected. I asked about the deadlines, but he doesn't seem to be particularly worried about them. We're sure working like beavers to get that thing finished up. (Asked some minor questions about office hours of the secretaries during the Christmas period) (Dep + ther) We're going to be away during the better part of the holiday.

With regard to the material I asked you to help me remember last week, I really don't know exactly what we talked about. I don't know whether that's just fogginess or whether it's the old suppressor working overtime again. (Dep + ther, Res)

Well, we discussed what I would term your proneness for a feeling of rejection and the possibility that you unconsciously seek to get yourself rejected. (Directive lead) *And we discussed the various symptoms of reaction to rejection as a child, particularly the enuresis.* (Directive lead) *And we also spent some time talking about the period of relative seductiveness on the part of your mother, between her two marriages. I think the main theme, however, was this idea that you might want to be rejected, in order to avoid something.* (Directive lead)

Hm. That sounds like you went one step further than I did in my own thinking. (Laughs) Would you formulate that last statement again. I've forgotten it already. (Dep + ther, Res) (Laughs)

That you often subconsciously seek to be rejected, and I added, "In order to avoid something." (Restatement)

Hm. (Long pause) I'm all blank. (Dep + ther, Res) (Pause)

Well, if people are not rejecting, but accepting and loving toward you, what obligation does this place on you? (Interpretation₇)

I've gotta be that way toward them. This is what I don't want?

It's not just a matter of being friendly in a passive sort of way; you become obligated to give something of yourself. (Interpretation₇)

I must be in bad shape this morning. I'm not following you through. (Dep + ther, Res)

Does that seem completely foreign? (Question)

It does right now, yeah. As far as I can get with the formulation we made several weeks ago, I said something to the effect that I reject others before they can reject me. But I can't go further than that, for some reason. (Res)

Do you remember that once when I said that I felt friendly toward you, you had an immediate reaction of thinking to yourself, "Why's he doing that?" (Interpretation₄)

In other words, if I go too far, and give too much, or get involved too much in a situation, I might get walked on. (Pause) This is a very bad morning. (Hos n + ther, Res) (Laughs) I feel like I'm in a case of third degree, or something. (Dom p — ther)

Like you were being grilled. (Clarification)

Yeah.

How do you feel toward me today? (Relationship)

Sleepy. (Laughs rather heartily) Not particularly positive or negative. (Res)

You're almost leading me to make an interpretation or bring up a subject that I hadn't really intended to bring up. (Disapproval) *That was whether you subconsciously overslept this morning.* (Interpretation₇)

Well, that's what I was wondering as soon as I woke up. When the alarm went off, I had had only six-and-a-half hours of sleep. So I was good and tired. But I don't even remember hearing it. It's on my wife's side, and she slugs it so quickly that I don't even hear it. Usually she wakes me up. (Conf; Res)

Let's see where the therapy stands. Let's sort of take stock. I've been intending to do this anyway, because I've been thinking about the way it's been going of late. If we think about the original objectives with which you came here, one was to discuss a marriage situation which was not at all good. (Directive lead) *And the feeling that I now get about that situation is that it's about 90 per cent improved.* (Reassurance) *Another feeling that you brought in was your somewhat "undirectedness," or inability to move toward your professional goal in a satisfactory manner. I would say there is quite a bit of improvement, too. Maybe there was one regression this fall, but you've now overcome that. Your whole picture is one of being much more in control of your own destiny.* (Reassurance) *Then another area that you came to discuss, I think, was that of interpersonal relations.* (Directive lead) *And here there has been some improvement, too, but perhaps you would say less than in the other areas.* (Reassurance)

Definitely. That's the one thing that I don't feel as yet I can carry through myself. (Dep + ther) All of which means that two out of three problems are down, but the motivation is probably down, too. Another thing is, too, that the other things were more on the surface and easier to talk about, and this one is a heck of a lot deeper, and therefore there's a lot more resistance. (Res)

There's been a corollary problem: your feelings of inadequacy, which are pretty strong. (Directive lead) *And here, too, I gather you've made some progress. It's hard to say how much.* (Reassurance)

Yeah.

I've been wondering whether the difficulty you've been experiencing is the result of the fact that the motivation is down to the point where maybe you're coming because of a sense of obligation, but not because you're really getting too much any more. (Interpretation₇)

I don't think that's the case. I've asked myself that question, since I have been having so much difficulty lately, and I still very much want to get these interpersonal difficulties and feelings of inadequacy worked out, because I still feel darn uncomfortable when I get in a group situation. (Anx — peers) And I've been very pleased with the last couple of sessions, because I've thought we were getting to something that was really pretty basic. (Dep + ther)

Or the other aspect of the problem might be that the relationship was in itself so rewarding that you weren't able to face the idea of allowing it to break up. (Relationship)

It's very rewarding, (Dep + ther, Rel) but I'm not such a selfish individual that I wouldn't feel that if your time was more essential to some other individual, I couldn't give it up. I enjoy coming, but still I feel that I come to work, not just to have a friendly conversation. (Dep + ther, Rel) But I don't think I'm ever going to be happy until I can be in a group situation and feel some confidence. (Anx — peers, self)

How much reality testing have you been doing of late on the group situation? (Question)

In one small course where they have discussion groups of four members, I'm one of the discussion leaders. And I can even joke with the instructor and call him by his first name. The thing that disappoints me is my lack of success in forming relationships with individuals. I still hold back. I don't know how much sharing I can safely do. (Anx — peers)

What do you mean by safely? (Question)

Without giving too much of myself and not getting something in return. Or just revealing too much of myself. (Anx — peers)

What are you afraid of revealing about yourself? (Question)

A weakness, I guess. That's mainly it, I think. I could probably do it if somebody revealed something of himself to me, first.

You had this kind of relationship with the fellow in the restaurant. (Interpretation₈)

Yeah.

You had somewhat this kind of relationship with one of the boys in the prep school. (Interpretation₈)

Yeah. My roommate there. And then at college, too. My best man. (Pause)

Nobody locally, however. X. has been the closest, and something sort of holds you apart from him. (Interpretation₇)

Yeah, there must be something there that I'm afraid of. (Anx — peers)

Maybe that's right. Maybe you're afraid of coming too close. (Interpretation₇) *It's actually a little unusual to have a client who is married be this concerned about friendships with members of his own sex.* (Challenges) *What I'm getting at is, why do you have what appears to be a greater need to have close male friends than the average married client does?* (Here the therapist makes a deep-level and threatening interpretation₉)

Do I? (Dep + ther)

You appear *to me that way.* (Disapproval) *Maybe the average male has them and it doesn't bother him.* (Attenuates)

I don't know whether I'm looking for anything that close, now. (Dep — gen) Because I can talk to my wife about a lot of things now. (Dep + wife) But I couldn't talk to her before. It may sound funny, but I've been worried more about it from the standpoint of what you would think if I didn't get them than whether I really wanted them. (Anx — ther; Rel)

It does sound funny in a way, because I've been continuously wondering why you had this strong need, so much stronger than what I considered average. (Relationship)

Well, then I must have misinterpreted what you said, because I thought you indicated that I ought to have many deeper friendships than I have now. (Dep + ther) Ones that I could talk seriously to about my relationship with my wife.

We talked about that at the period when you thought you might be breaking up with your wife. In that context, I discussed other people whom you could turn to for some affectional responses. But it was only in the context of the idea that with your wife gone, you might be a very lonely person. (Relationship)

In which case I would have need of a buddy, again. (Dep — peers) (Pause) A light bulb flashes on! (Pause) As I say, I haven't really been too concerned about it, because I haven't felt the need to talk to anybody in particular on that deep a level. (Ins)

And I was concerned about your apparent continuous need to have some intimate male friendships. (Relationship) *I tended to see it as some sign of dependency and apparent insecurity in your marriage.* (Disapproval)

That may have been true. I really felt that you felt that I should have a close friend, and that's why I have said recently that I should start reality testing, that I should try and get some. (Dep + ther, Rel) That it was just a part of the recommended therapy or something that might do some good.

Well, it's a sort of interesting misperception, (Challenges) *and I do think I gave you some start for that by implying it in the context of the idea of a person who might be breaking up his marriage needing a friend.* (Attenuates)

I can see it now. My feeling is one sort of relief. I don't have to go out and try and find some close buddies! (Laughs rather heartily) Regarding friends, I've just been quite content of late with what I've got. I enjoy hunting or just being with them. (Dep + peers) Just small talk, and nothing too deep. What I can't talk to my wife about, I usually bring in here. (Dep + ther) So my needs that way are pretty well satisfied. My time's up.

Quinn: Twenty-eighth Interview (12/17)

H ALF OF the client's discussion in the twenty-eighth interview was about his feelings toward the therapist. These were a mixture of hostility, affiliative need, and an awareness of gratification of his ego needs. His discussion of the relationship with the therapist focused on his initial annoyance with the therapist's apparent rejecting behavior in the previous interview, when he had raised the question of the termination of therapy and also had challenged the client's excessive need for male companionship and nurturance. But the client also reported a change of these initial feelings of hostility, in that he came more to feel that the therapist was right in raising the question about whether he was ready to end therapy. He was able to experience a growing sense of adequacy in practically everything that he did and began to realize that it was probable that his dependency needs had been causing him to wish to prolong the relationship more than was necessary.

In the area of increasing feelings of self-sufficiency, the client reported that most of his activities were now much more efficient than previously. He also reported that he and his wife had deliberately planned for her to become pregnant, and that both were happy that this had occurred. About one-eighth of the client's responses were devoted to feelings of increasing maturity and a like amount to mention of increased self-esteem; also he could now discuss many things with his wife, which he felt was a more normal form of expression for his dependency.

Again we have an interview in which many of the therapist's efforts (35 per cent) were devoted to exploring the therapeutic relationship. This developed naturally out of the client's presenting of that topic for discussion. The therapist tried to depict the relationship as one involving a growing sense of equality between client and therapist, rather than the previous relationship of dependent client and supportive father-figure. The therapist pointed out that he perceived the client as being less in need of support. He accepted the client's inference that

there were certain skills in which the client was superior to the therapist. He used a few reassuring remarks and a few challenging ones.
There was also a little interpretation and some information-giving.

While the affect in the previous interview had dropped to a very
low level, in this interview it rose fifty-seven points for the client, to
become his highest score (99), and 56 points for the therapist, to become his second highest score (75). Obviously the relationship made
its most dramatic shift between these two interviews. The swift change
from negative to positive affect can be interpreted as the result of the
acceptance by the client of the fact that he was ready to give up his
dependency needs and to operate as a self-directing individual. Both
client and therapist perceived in this the desired motivation toward a
healthy adjustment or the end of the neurotic conflict. Rather than
being overjoyed that they were going to end therapy soon, they were
pleased that the client had attained the desirable goal of achieving
more independence. Their relationship would no longer be the replication of the childhood state but could become the relationship of independent friendly adults.

Although there had been much movement in the direction of growing maturity, there were still a number of residual expressions of dependency. Mr. Quinn asked for information about how to get out of
attending the graduation exercises; he asked whether the therapist believed that the client was too much inclined to worry; he asked whether
the therapist had changed therapeutic methods during the last interview. Then he asked the therapist to tell him whether there were still
some areas which he might need to work on. Finally, even at the end
of the interview, he indicated that he still wished to build a friendship
with his father, although he did describe it as more of a friendship between colleagues rather than a father-son sort of dependency. At one
point Mr. Quinn indicated that he had a strong need for commendation; somewhat related was his desire to have the therapist admit that
there were some activities at which Mr. Quinn was more capable than
the therapist.

At the beginning of the hour, Mr. Quinn had felt some concern
that perhaps the therapist was eager to get rid of him, so as to begin
therapy with another client; later he indicated that he himself was
actually growing ready to conclude the therapy. He even indicated
that he thought he would require only one more interview. He described his feelings toward the therapist as being more those of a
friend or colleague and less those of a son toward his father; the

therapist, of course, strongly reinforced this feeling, indicating that although it would be easy for him to prolong the nurturant-dependent sort of relationship, this would not be therapeutic. Mr. Quinn had apparently worked through a good bit of the dependency problem. His dependency score dropped to 32, the level at which it had been when he began his therapy.

I'm going to have trouble maintaining consciousness this morning, too. (Dep + ther) I was up 'til one-thirty last night on the thesis and began again at six-fifteen this morning. But real progress is being made; I expect to have it done by tomorrow night. (Asks for information about obtaining an excuse from graduation in order to take care of a personal matter; this was another dependent gesture on his part.) Now to the subject matter of the day. After last week's interview I was mad as hell at you, although I don't feel so strongly about it now. I don't know exactly the reason. I remember I said during the interview that I had the feeling I was being grilled. (Hos n + ther) Of course I was foggy, anyway. I felt that you weren't with me, that you were throwing up irrelevant junk. (Laughs) I figured that you had changed your approach somewhat. But I figured that if I asked you about it, you would deny it, and then you'd be lying, and that was terrible. (Hos n + ther)

In what way did you think I had changed it? (Relationship)

In the sense that it was less supportive. (Dep + ther, Rel; his anger at the apparent withdrawal of support reveals dependency.) And also, rather than taking *my* word, it seemed as if you were injecting your own ideas. Last week I considered counseling not much good. But if I asked the question whether you'd changed, you would have to deny it. (Hos n + ther)

Um-hm.

I don't know whether I should ask the question now. (Dep + ther) (Laughs)

Well, I said at least two things that could be very threatening to you. And I anticipated that they would be. (Relationship) *As to whether I've changed, basically, no. I'll present it by analogy. If you were a doctor and were working with a sick patient in a hospital, and he had a temperature of 103 degrees, you would be very sympathetic, and gentle, and allow lots of reassurance. Then if the patient went down to 99 degrees, just a shade above normal, and had been that way for a while, you would start saying that he should eat his meals and make trips to the bathroom, and so forth.* (Information) *What I'm saying is that I perceived much less need for sympathy and support. This doesn't mean that I like you any less.* (Relationship) *It means that your present need is for you to outgrow some of the dependency feelings that you might have toward me. And that was the gist of the interpretive remarks that I made that probably threatened you. The one was to ask you whether you really did feel that you needed much more therapy.* (Interpretation$_9$) *And the other was a rather threatening interpretation that maybe your need to have close buddies, as I was interpreting it, was unduly strong. It may have been a sign of the same thing, of over-dependency.* (Here the therapist interprets two aspects of the client's dependency.) (Interpretation$_9$)

That last one was another bone of contention. Consciously, as I said last week, I didn't particularly see any need to get deeper friendships, and yet I was going to try it because I felt that you felt that I should. You denied that when you said you hadn't meant it generally, but I on the other hand still have the feeling that it could be interpreted generally and not just if my wife and I broke up. And that was one thing that made me mad. (Hos n + ther)

It could be interpreted generally by someone who wanted it to be interpreted that way. (Challenges)

(Client laughs) Well we've got that out.

Well, you see, when for twenty-seven interviews you've been crying out for a close affectional relationship with a strong male figure, then I can't believe that this isn't a basic need for you. (Persuasion) *And I feel that you've had symptoms all over the place.* (Disapproval)

Well, now that you put it that way, maybe you're right. (Dep + fa surrog) (Laughs)

However, I can say that you have a perfect right for an honest difference of opinion on it. (Attenuates)

Yeah. (Sighs) Well, I wonder if perhaps, too, this need may not have been a lot stronger when we first spoke about it. (Dep + fa surrog) But that with developing self-sufficiency it has dropped off. (The client himself recognizes a reduction in his dependency.)

I think that's probably very true. (Reassurance)

One thing that I was reminded of before is that I should be ready for this weaning process. According to your perception I should be. Why, then, did I object so strenuously to being weaned? (Dep — ther, Rel) Why do I still feel the need for commendation, and so on? I still get the feeling that it's stronger than the normal. I know everyone likes to be complimented, but *I* seem to rely on it an awful lot. (Dep — fa surrog) But as to the threat of losing the therapy situation, I still have this need with everybody, and losing the therapy situation itself was, I don't think, quite as threatening. (Dep + gen) That night I told my wife that perhaps I would be dropping therapy sometime in the near future. She said that she felt that I had grown an awful lot. I still have this need for commendation, and where else am I going to work it out but in the therapy situation where I can get somebody else's viewpoint? (Dep — ther)

How much have you been able to direct your dependency needs to your wife? (Question)

A lot, I think. Because she has been gratifying them when I made some sort of test probes. That doesn't mean I'm completely dependent on her, but she bolsters me an awful lot. (Dep + wife) (Goes on to discuss the fact that only a few people threaten him in classes any more. If the class is not too large, he is able to be rather spontaneous in it.) (Ego + peers)

The situation is more or less like the difference between a freshman and a junior. Last year you were a sort of freshman and felt that most people knew more than you did, and now you're finding that you know more than quite a lot of people do. (Interpretation₇)

Just normal maturation, that is. Yes. But part of it may be training. I keep forgetting my age too, which I think enters into this a lot. I just haven't got the maturity that I think a lot of other people have. I need experience. I haven't been around long enough. I need more of this professional, ah . . . (Pause)

Savoir faire? (Restatement)

Yeah. That may be something that just comes with the years.

Well, the time will have to come when you see this school as having little to offer you any more. Not that you reject it, but simply that you've outgrown it. The time will have to come when you see the professors as nice guys, and farther along than you, but not any better than you. (Relationship)

Um-hm. Yeah. I guess that just comes when the views that are held here become somewhat exhausted. I know I have sort of begun to feel that way already. I feel a very, very strong inadequacy of knowledge in psychology, but I don't think I know that much less than somebody who's in a comparable position with me in terms of years of experience.

I guess everybody has some areas where he feels inferior. I would guess that you yourself would feel not too adequate if you felt that you had to give a Rorschach. Is that right? (Hos n + ther) (This may be an effort to derogate the therapist or only a way of saying that even the most secure people have their inadequacies.)

Why do you want me to answer that? (Challenges) *You'd like reassurance in knowing that there are areas in which I don't feel at ease?* (Clarification)

Yeah. Because something gives me the idea that you haven't been using the Rorschach much of late. (Hos n + ther)

That's right. I would feel ill at ease or uncomfortable if I felt forced to do it. (Information; the therapist felt that it was desirable to let the client feel superior to him in this matter, when he obviously had a legitimate claim to superiority, anyway.)

Which means that everybody, no matter how high their position, is probably inferior in something. Other people probably don't worry about it the way I do. (Dep — gen)

What you're saying is very accurate. Everyone feels unsure of himself in comparison with some people. That's an important insight. (Approval) *A related one might be that you no sooner get over one hurdle than the next one is ahead of you. There are always signs of distinction or "passing grades" all along the line. The Ph.D. is far from the last one.* (Information)

The one question I have is whether my worry about this is greater than the normal one? Is it a deeper or more serious worry than other people have? (Dep — ther)

Well, of course you give the appearance of being a pretty confident guy. (Reassurance) *Last year I would have used the word "cocky."* (Disapproval) *We both know that this is not the real you, that you have lots of insecurity feelings.* (Clarification) *But many people don't think it's wise to show other people just how insecure they feel. But everybody has his test situations in life.* (Advice) *But the real criterion is yourself. Do you feel that you have too many to manage?* (Information)

I feel I have too many at the present time, but I don't feel they're too incapacitating. I'm not operating perfectly efficiently, but also they may just drop out just as the result of general maturation. I'm uncomfortable, but I'm not in a panic. (Ego + matur)

I think a little anxiety is a sign that a person is making an effort. (Reassurance) *One needs enough tonus to get started when the gun cracks; he doesn't want to be torpid or languid. But one shouldn't be incapacitated or debilitated by frightening panic or anxiety.* (Information)

I think I am perhaps just a little bit on the over-anxious side (Dep — gen)

Since working like a beaver these last few weeks, I've noticed that I've really enjoyed it. It used to be unheard of for me to work on Saturday, but lately I've been doing it without even thinking about it. (Ego + prof) (A sign of change in attitude and possible improvement.)

You're really getting some satisfaction out of scholarship. (Clarification)

Yeah. I hope I don't drop into the doldrums again. I've often thought in the past that I work best under pressure. But I know this massed crammed learning is not very efficient. If I do work as efficiently as I should, I can produce at a very high level. (Ego + prof)

At this point the motivation has to come from within. (Information)

Yeah. Considering the gratification I get out of real serious effort, I wonder why I sometimes slip? But I'm not so sure that this is atypical. Most people tend to goof a little bit. (Ego + matur)

There's one thing that I think may increase the internal motivation, that suddenly occurred to me. That is that we're pretty sure now that my wife is pregnant. So we're very pleased about that, because we want a child very much. I think we feel adjusted enough now to make this step. This is an added responsibility that I've got to work for. It's not just my wife now, but a child, too. (This would seem to be a sign of maturity in this client; Nur n + child.)

So the motivation is even more strong because of that. It's sort of hard to think of yourself as a parent, I imagine. (Clarification)

That's right. My wife hasn't been too well, but she's been a real peach in helping me with this emergency typing work. I really have appreciated what she's doing for me. It represents a really significant change in her behavior. (Discusses at some length.) (Dep n + → Aff n + wife)

Well, you felt angry with me last week. Why do you think now that you felt angry? (The therapist is testing the client's insight and his feelings about the relationship.)

Probably because you were threatening me at the time, before I'd thought things through enough not to be threatened. (Dep — ther, Rel) But I think that today, in talking these things through and really seeing reality for what it is, and knowing that I'm not in such bad shape as I thought I was, this has sort of dissipated what feelings of hostility there were. Now I conceive of you as being more as a friend than as a father. (Aff n + ther, Rel) Which is a real growth step, I think. (This seems to be a real step forward.) I'm very pleased. Something tells me that after this morning that it may not take any time, so to speak, to wrap up the therapy. (The client now appears to be about ready to end the therapy relationship.) I would like at least one more interview, and what I'd like to do is to try and review the whole thing right from start to finish. (Dep + ther) To sort of get a *Gestalt* on it. Because if I'm able to see the real positive things that have happened, that will give me a lot more confidence. (Dep + ther) I'll be able to carry on, on my own.

How do you feel about this idea of "wrapping up" the therapy? Do you feel that you're getting ready for it? Or do you feel that you're being squeezed out? (Relationship)

No, I think I'm getting ready for it, although last week I felt I was being squeezed out. (Dep — ther, Rel)

Otto Rank, you know, insisted that there were always some terminal pains. (Information)

Yeah. Well, even at the beginning of this hour, I was wondering if you had some other client on the line that you thought was somewhat more pressing than me. (Dep — ther, Rel) But I'm sure that you wouldn't push somebody out that you felt wanted to stay. 'Cause just the wanting to stay would be enough reason to justify therapy. But now I feel that actually I'm ready to leave. If there are areas that I haven't thought about that I should have, I certainly hope you will tell me about it next time. (Dep + ther)

It would be very easy for me to perpetuate the father-son relationship with you, encouraging dependence and getting satisfactions myself from feeling like the parental figure who can solve your problems for you. (Relationship) *But this wouldn't be healthy for you. Or for me, either, as far as that goes. It's better if, like any wise parent, when you're ready to be more of a friend than a son, that this is the way I let the situation become.* (Relationship) *I suspect that every son who grows up through a normal relationship with a parent finds the time when he first feels like a friend or colleague with his parent.* (Relationship) *But this doesn't mean that they stop talking to each other or hate each other. They're just friends at a different level.* (Relationship)

Which is something that I continue to wish for in my own situation with my own father. (Dep — fa)

Twenty years from now the difference in our ages will not be very important any more. (Relationship) *And that's probably true with your own father. You'll both be growing slightly old and worrying about being overweight.* (Interpretation$_8$) (Both laugh)

That's right. (Pause) Well, I guess our time's about up.

Quinn: Twenty-ninth Interview (1/4)

W HILE THE discussion in this final interview covered a
wide diversity of topics, approximately half was devoted to the therapist and the therapeutic relationship. A little concerned the client himself, his wife, his parents, father, mother, sister,
peers, and professional future. The discussion in this interview was
primarily a review of progress, and the client felt quite satisfied with
the changes which had taken place. His attitude toward each of these
persons was much more mature—accepting and affectionate, but not
excessively dependent. Sense of self-satisfaction comprised one-fifth
of the affect-themes. One-third of the affect concerned a sense of affiliation, and one-sixth related to dependency needs (mostly now pretty
well satisfied). There were brief expressions of nurturance needs,
affiliation presses, hostility need, hostility presses, dominance presses,
and vocational concern. The client gave an interesting illustration of
the metamorphosis of the relationship with the therapist. He saw the
therapist first as a god-like figure, then a benign father-figure, then for
a short time as a hostile father-surrogate, and finally as a good friend or
colleague. He recognized that he enjoyed the dependency on the permissive father-qualities of the therapist but that had this been a true
parent-son relationship, he would have been an over-spoiled child. He
characterized the therapy as eclectic—non-directive when it needed to
be and supportive when that was necessary. After this interview Mr.
Quinn's PAC-NAC dependency score dropped to 26, far below that
of any other interview.

On the therapist's part, 30 per cent of his remarks concerned the
relationship, 21 per cent were supportive or reassuring, and 18 per
cent were of the information-giving sort. There were also some interpretations (9 per cent), restatements (9 per cent), and questions (6
per cent). The main efforts of the therapist in this interview were directed toward assisting the client to review his progress and to evaluate
changes which had taken place in the relationship. He also reassured

the client that he had made much progress but that it was possible to return if he felt himself to be in serious difficulty in the future.

Affect in this interview remained quite good. The client's score of 92 was only a little below his score of the previous week. The therapist's score rose one point (76), making it his highest score for the case. Obviously the relationship was at this point a very friendly one.

(The client reviewed his rather pleasant vacation trip during the Christmas recess.) I had trouble with my adviser; you know he had allegedly given me an extension on my deadline for the first draft on my thesis. We worked day and night getting it in, and now I learn that he took my name off the graduation list early in November. But then he said it was really this Christmas trip that was keeping me from getting the degree. (Hos p — auth) At least I will have all the requirements finished this semester.

At the last interview I said I would like to review my progress over the year of therapy. I continue to think that I'm now ready to terminate. My wife reports that she has witnessed changes in me, and she considers these signs of maturity. And you've expressed this idea, and so have other people. But it's rather hard for me to see it myself. One thing which is somewhat improved is that I seem to have a little bit more self-assurance, both in individual and group situations. (Ego + matur)

I guess the most important improvement has been in my relationship with my wife. I was really putting myself in a very dependent position back at the beginning of our marriage, while still trying to look like the leader. (Dep — wife) That is, the relationship was so important to me that I would sacrifice anything to maintain it. Whereas now I think I have enough self-assurance that I can stand alone if I have to. And I think that has produced changes in my wife. So that things are a lot healthier that way. (Aff n + wife)

The same thing with regard to friends. I got kind of confused on how important it was to have a bunch of deep, very close friends. I don't quite feel the need for it any more; I'm quite content with the type of relationships that I have now. (Aff n + peers) Anything really deep, I can talk over with my wife, now, and I've been doing that a lot more, too. (Dep + wife) Also, I've been able to talk with her about my anger at my adviser, (Dep + wife) and that has made me less tense and upset about it.

I asked you before if you would suggest things that I might try and compare. I've pretty much covered all the ones I can think of at the moment. (Dep + ther)

How about your attitudes toward your parents? (Directive lead)

Yeah. Well, I don't think my attitude toward my mother has changed much. I still feel she is kind of a helpless type of person. I love her, but she gets on my nerves. (Laughs) *Now* she's extremely dependent, but I think there has been a change there. Either she is becoming more self-sufficient or realizes that I can't make her decisions for her. (Aff n — mo)

Perhaps you observe her with more compassion and less need-dominated affect. (Interpretation$_8$)

That's quite so. I treat it somewhat matter-of-factly, and so does she, apparently.

Regarding my father, it's hard to decide whether he has changed, or whether my perception of him has changed. Probably it's some of both. I think he has sensed a sort of growing up in me and has reacted somewhat accordingly. For an example again, in his gift giving; I don't react the way I did before. I used to think he was buying affection, or trying to. Now I just sort of think of it as being nice of him. He was extremely generous with us at Christmas. (Aff n + fa) He totters a little bit now, his hip is bothering him, and he moaned a little bit to me, which he never did before. He lets me know he's not feeling well, and he asks me for my opinion about my sister and her husband and how they're getting along. (Nur n + fa)

Then he said about my woodworking that he didn't realize I had so much mechanical ability. He's been giving credit where it was due, finally. I guess that's one way to sum it up. That makes me feel a lot better. I still don't feel I can get *really* close, but this is certainly a much better working relationship than there was before. (Aff n + fa)

And I've noticed a change in my feelings toward my sister, also. Before I was very glib about saying that I didn't like her and didn't give a damn. But it's funny, I feel quite a great deal of pity or compassion because she's such a dud; I tend to want to defend her now when people criticize her. But I doubt whether anything will come of that, because we've been separated so much, and I guess we're creatures of habit. But I think it's a healthy change.

My relationship with my wife's parents hasn't changed too much. I'm still uncomfortable, especially with her father. He's a real crock. Mostly hot air! (Hos n + fa surrog)

About my own self-assurance, I think it has come up tremendously with the work I'm doing in therapy with other clients this semester. (Ego + matur) My clients have made very good progress, and my supervisor is quite pleased with them and praises me a lot. Now I have better ideas as to why I do something in therapy. I think about it before I say something, and I analyze what the effect will be. The clinical "intuition" is there, but it's more systematized now. That, I think, is another indication that I've grown in therapy. The counter-transference in my own therapy cases is better controlled. (Ego + prof) Now I'm pointing out to you all the things that seem to indicate that I'm better than I was last year. But still, I guess I can't look at myself *completely* objectively. Can *you* think of any other areas that perhaps I've overlooked? (Dep + ther)

Well, I think that you're doing a good job of it. (Reassurance) *Perhaps the area of intrapsychic change is the most important, and there you feel more confident and more mature.* (Reassurance) *This is probably the true goal of therapy.* (Information) *Certainly you want your social relationships to work better, also.*

Yeah. I think there's another thing. Scholastically I'm in much better shape. I seem to know more, now, of what I want. Although I haven't made any final decisions on the sort of job I'm going to want some day, but I know what I wanta work toward. My present goal is the Ph.D. By now I'm relatively certain I will get a Master's degree, *some* day. (Laughs rather heartily) But I feel much more satisfied with the work I've been doing lately. I enjoy really studying. (Ego + prof)

It's important that you yourself feel you've done something adequate. (Approval)

I feel that this therapy experience in general has been very rewarding, (Dep + ther) not only from the standpoint of getting more stability myself, but I sort of think of it as a learning situation, revealing how I can keep myself in better shape in the future. I've learned techniques to use in self-analysis. I'll be able to think about myself in a more healthy way. (Aff n + ther)

So it's really been a matter of becoming acquainted with techniques for understanding yourself. (Restatement)

Yes, I don't feel now that there are any real big question marks in *me*. That doesn't mean we've analyzed way back to my earliest memory, or anything like that. But I don't think that's necessary. I don't think I need psychoanalysis.

I wonder if you would want to review your perception of our relationship as it has progressed during this period? (Relationship)

Yes. When it started out, as you observed, I had kind of a god-like adoration toward you, because of your reputation and also from the course I had in therapy with you. (Dep + ther, Rel; he is referring to his *academic* course, here.) When I first came in here, after receiving that bolt from the blue that you sent me, (laughs) I didn't quite know what to expect. I wanted to talk to somebody, but I wasn't sure that it was you. But that note sort of brought me in here, and I was willing to establish a relationship then. (Dep + ther, Rel; this descriptive phrase for therapy is significant.) I thought at the time that I was being honest with you, and I think the questionnaires that I filled out after each interview will indicate that that's what I thought, but as I went farther along and felt more confident in you as a therapist, I started to admit things to myself. (Dep + ther, Rel) Well, even when I first came in, I was able to think of the homosexual episode that I'd had, but I couldn't talk to you about it yet. I would indicate on the questionnaire that there was one item that I didn't feel free yet to discuss. But I was more able to actually think about it to myself, and then the transference got deeper. I don't know exactly where it was deepest, but I can remember going through all the items and getting a *Gestalt* on them and thinking, "Gee, this guy must be really out of this world. How can he be so wonderful?" (Dep + ther, Rel) If there'd been an item, "I wish the therapist were my father," I think I would have marked it true and circled it and underlined it. (Laughs) (Dep + ther, Rel; he reveals an awareness of the overly intense character of his transference feelings.) And I don't know but what this wasn't an earned affect, rather than a transference I was bringing in from somewhere else. I still think of it as being earned. That you were being very helpful. (Dep + ther, Rel) And I'll be darned if I would know from where I could have transferred any positive feelings toward the father-figure. (Laughs) I've had brother-figures, sort of, whom I felt positive toward, but not my father. (Dep — fa → Dep + fa surrog) Well, that sort of continued until the last couple of months, and then it slackened off. Then suddenly it got very negative that one week. I was very angry, and thinking you were being unjust. I'd had little glimpses of feelings like that before, but nothing strong enough that it would have come out on the questionnaire, for example. But that one week, I'm sure it did! (Hos n + ther) The questionnaire has pretty much all-or-nothing type of items, and although you might have seemed rejecting at a specific moment in an interview, if I thought about the whole interview, I couldn't see you as being rejecting. But after we discussed this very negative feeling, instead of swinging back to the opposite extreme, it sort of took the middle position, where I thought of you as being like a good friend, sort of. (Aff n + ther, Rel) I didn't think of you as being a therapist just because it was your job, or I didn't think you just did it because you like having a little boy dependent on you, (laughs) but rather as an individual who wanted to work something through that was a problem for a friend. And that's the way I still feel about it now, which is, I think, probably the way it actually is. (Aff n + ther, Rel) In other words the normal way to think about it. Which indicates that the other two things must have been transference. But as I say, I can't think of where I transferred the positive feelings from, although it's not hard to find the source of the negative ones in my reactions to my father. (Dep — fa → Dep + ther, Rel)

The uncertain elements that you may have transferred from your father were perhaps the satisfaction of the dependency needs. You were never very certain of his affection, except in a rather round-about way. (Interpretation₇) *But I became a benign father, or, symbolically, an idealized father for you.* (Relationship)

And yet, now that I think of it objectively, if you had been my father and were this benign and accepting, I would have turned out to be a hell of a mess! (Dep + ther, Rel) (Laughs) Because, really you were setting no limits, and if I were to have extended this situation into a real life situation between father and son, God knows what I would have ended up as! You weren't saying I was bad, and I would have thought I could have done anything. (Laughs) So it's a benign father in the therapy situation. (Dep + ther, Rel)

In a controlled or limited setting. (Restatement)

Yeah.

Well, that's pretty much a kind of a classic, or ideal, development of what we know about what the therapy relationship should be. It seems to have gone through the typical stages. (Relationship) *Almost like analysis in microcosm. None of the phases lasted as long as they would in psychoanalysis, and they probably didn't go as deep. You never proceeded to any kind of infantile dependency level, for example.* (Information)

Nor did I get to the opposite extreme of hating your guts! (Laughs) I'm not at all convinced that that sort of thing was necessary, for me, that is. (Aff n + ther; Rel)

I agree with you that only in a very few cases is deep analysis probably √ *called for.* (Approval) *You had enough ego-strength that you did not need that great a degree of analysis in order to develop the necessary ego-strength to carry on successfully in life.* (Reassurance) *I would say that deep analysis is needed when the ego-strength is quite weak, but this seems like a contradiction, because presumably analysts don't work with patients whose ego-strength is too weak.* (Information)

I was just trying to type what kind of therapy this might have been. I sort of end up with the feeling that it's sorta like the kind that I use, eclectic (laughs) therapy, non-directive where it's wise to be non-directive, supportive where it should be. (Dep + ther) I have a feeling that you sort of fly by the seat of your pants, too. (Laughs) Knowing what you're doing, but. . . .

Yeah. I wouldn't wanta think that I was just flying by the seat of my pants. (Challenging) *It's eclectic in the sense of not adhering to any rigid "schools" of therapy, but it draws heavily on learning theory. When I have to classify it, I would say it's a relationship therapy and a kind of ego-therapy, and probably one could also use the word brief therapy, although that's a pretty relativistic word. But if I had to put the most important element at the top, it would be relationship therapy.* (Information)

Yeah, I didn't mean to imply that you didn't know where you were going in therapy, (laughs) but rather that you weren't stuck with one school. When you felt you needed to bring in something else, you did it. (Aff n + ther)

One thing that I've been wondering about now. In the future I think I'll be able to handle difficulties which I encounter, for the most part, but I would like also to feel that I could come in and talk about something on a brief basis, if I feel the need to. (Dep + ther, Rel) This would be the feeling that any graduate student should have, I would think, that they could talk to somebody if they were in trouble. I'd hate to think that I'd terminated now, and I was finished, and could never return if I needed to, even if it's just to bitch about the department! (Dep + ther, Rel)

Well, of course you would have the right to come in and talk that any graduate student would have. (Structuring) But second, you would be a special kind of graduate student, which would give you rights somewhat more than that, in that you'll always have once been one of my clients. (Relationship) A therapist never loses some of the countertransference, I think, toward his clients. He probably always has a considerable affection for any of his successful clients, although not in any unhealthy way—or perhaps some hostility toward the unsuccessful ones. (Relationship) (Both laugh) I would put it this way: if you feel that you need it, don't hesitate to come and ask to talk to me. We could use an analogy from medicine; if you just have a headache, it's all right to stop by for an aspirin, and that's probably what I would give you, speaking figuratively or psychologically, but it would be just as reasonable to get an aspirin from almost anybody else, too. (Relationship) But again using the analogy, if you really think that you've gotten pneumonia, don't feel reluctant to bring the subject up! That is, I don't want to encourage the maintaining of a kind of dependency relationship, but I want you to feel that you are a person who has a special amount of welcome, if you need help. (Relationship)

Well, I think also that perhaps of all the people that know me, you know me best, especially among faculty members. If there's some problem, I wouldn't feel ashamed or worried about talking to you about it, because I think you can help me most, since you know me best. Maybe I would turn to you first, even if it were just for an aspirin. (Dep + ther, Rel) (Laughs)

Well, I suppose I should have a certain number of students who come to me for their aspirin tablets, (laughs) just as a certain number go to other people for theirs! (Attenuates)

Sure. Well, I guess that winds up the hour. I really can't thank you enough for working with me. (Dep + ther, Rel)

Well, it's been a pleasure for me too, and I've gotten a lot out of it. Shall we consider this the conclusion? (Relationship)

I think so. But I suppose I'll go through a shock period. (Laughs) So long.

Quinn: Follow-Up Information

MR. QUINN seemed to hold the gains he had made during therapy. His scholastic work continued to be good. He held a number of different positions of responsibility connected with the university, and his work was always evaluated quite favorably. He completed his doctoral work in a satisfactory manner, although a little more slowly than is usual. In this work he showed a little more than average amount of dependency upon his adviser, a different one from the adviser mentioned in the case report.

Mr. Quinn's relationship with his wife remained fairly good. On several occasions his wife showed signs of wishing to repeat her flirting behavior, but Mr. Quinn took a firm position and his wife discontinued the behavior. She herself remained in therapy for several years.

Toward the therapist Mr. Quinn showed a mild amount of dependency, coming to him several times a year for advice in the area of his academic program, but he only once mentioned his personal difficulties, and then just to give a short report of his progress in that area. He did not ask for further therapy.

The matter of Mr. Quinn's relationship with his father was quite interesting. He seemed to be able to build a more companionate type of interaction. When he finished his degree, he took a position in the city where his father lived with the plan in mind that this would make it possible to have a more satisfactory relationship with him. The therapist considered this decision something of a regression.

Part Three

THE CASE OF
JOHN JONES

Introduction

M R. JOHN JONES was a 25-year-old married former graduate student who was teaching in a small college some distance from the therapist's university. However, for the purpose of advancing his therapeutic skill he was conducting several therapy cases under supervision at the university. In his college position he taught several courses, and he also carried a number of counseling cases, some of which occasionally involved work with personal adjustment problems.

Mr. Jones requested therapy on his own initiative. Anxiety about homosexual urges and ambivalence about passive versus aggressive behavior tendencies constituted his main presenting symptoms. He gave the impression of being a normal young man, but he was experiencing strong homosexual urges toward friends and colleagues. His passive-dependency needs and his inadequacy feelings proved to be the underlying causes of these urges. He could be moderately aggressive toward people but was nevertheless a likeable, "clean-cut," boyish person. He had ambivalent feelings toward his father, a school teacher, who was a passive person. Toward his mother he felt much hostility because she was a very dominating individual. He frankly saw the therapist as a strong father-surrogate, in contrast to a former adviser whom he saw as the image of his weak father.

Mr. Jones was one of the most consistent clients of the twenty in our research group in perceiving the therapist as a strong but benign parent-figure. Shortly before his fifth interview, when the therapist was scheduled to visit his former internship hospital as a consultant, the client contrived to have his former adviser also visit the hospital on the same day. He seemed to have a compulsion to have the two men meet each other. In the fifth interview he stated that he had enjoyed having his former adviser see that he, the client, had such an outstanding friend and sponsor as the therapist. He recognized that he identified his former adviser with his father, whom he had always considered to be a weak and unprotecting person, while he considered the therapist to be a strong, protecting father-figure. In many of his interviews he compared the therapist to a strong but benign father. In the special interview that he requested two years after the completion of therapy, he indicated that this was one of the major features of his therapy, and he reported his pleasure from the therapist's having filled this role.

Mr. Jones made reference to homosexual urges toward the therapist in four of his twenty interviews. The first occurred in the fourth interview, when he expressed a wish that the therapist would seduce him. The most significant of his expressions of homosexual interest in the therapist came in the sixth interview, when he projected his homosexual feelings onto the therapist and recognized that this was a projection. Again in the eighth interview, Mr. Jones indicated that he would enjoy having the therapist seduce him. At the time of the twelfth interview, when he had just completed a summer internship and had also had to assume a lot of responsibility in his family during a time of crisis, he expressed hostility toward the therapist, first, for deserting him during the summer when he needed him; then, for being too passive in his therapy. At that point, Mr. Jones stated that he would like to seduce the therapist. It was probably a sign of progress for his sexual fantasies to have changed from a passive and feminine to a more active form.

In addition to frankly homosexual wishes expressed toward the therapist or toward other professors or previous roommates, Mr. Jones reported several homosexual dreams. One of his dreams involved a marine who was interpreted as being either the client's father or the therapist. In the dream the marine stabbed a small Japanese male in the back; such a dream is widely held to be a symbol of a homosexual act. The symbolism is somewhat justified by the fact that several of Mr. Jones' other homosexual dreams or fantasies involved sodomy.

Another time Mr. Jones reported dreaming that he had engaged in homosexual sodomy with his former roommate; he was at first unsure which role he took, at one time in his therapy suggesting that he had taken the more active role while at another time reporting taking the passive role. He found the dream, and the idea, both disgusting and appealing.

A sexual dream relating to the therapist, symbolized in the person of one of the latter's colleagues, was reported in the eighth interview, when Mr. Jones indicated that he had taken a passive role in masturbatory activities described in the dream. In a later interview, Mr. Jones reported having experienced another homosexual dream.

The therapist attempted to help Mr. Jones accept two points. First, that whatever his psychosexual nature, he was a decent person who could live with the less desired aspects of his personality and still maintain self-respect, and second, that his homosexual urges were probably symptoms of dependency needs which were more basic to his ego than the sexual drives.

The therapist felt a lot of affection for Mr. Jones, but he felt that, because of the latter's conscious sexual feelings toward him, he would have to play down any interpretation of his affectional feelings. Although the feelings were paternal, rather than sexual, the client was not yet ready to grasp the distinction, because of his own equating of dependency and sexual submission.

The therapist ranked Mr. Jones as the fourth most successful client. He was able, in twenty interviews, to come to a fairly accurate understanding of his psychosexual and dependency needs and to learn ways of living with them without too marked a sense of inadequacy. He was also able to modify his behavior in sufficient degree that he could feel he was handling the problem, rather than the reverse. He showed less dependency needs, for example, and accepted a more responsible way of meeting the expectations of his marital and professional obligations. He was able to view the therapist as a friendly colleague and teacher, rather than as an all-protecting father or a homosexual lover. Some of the more significant signs of self insight and of change in Mr. Jones' behavior are reported in the follow-up information on his case.

Mr. Jones took the same tests and received all the rankings and ratings which were reported in the case of Mr. Quinn. He was diagnosed as a person who exhibited immaturity reactions associated with feelings of inadequacy and with anxiety caused by homosexual urges. He reported some marital problems, but they were minor in character, except in the sexual relationship, where there was some evidence of a reversal of roles from the more usual pattern, with his wife being the more aggressive partner. He came from an upper middle-class family, and his parents observed rather rigid moral and religious customs, following a somewhat fundamentalistic protestant faith. While Mr. Jones revealed some degree of emancipation from these standards, he also frequently demonstrated a good bit of compliance with them.

Like Mr. Quinn, he was ranked very high on the continuum of altruistic and idealistic value systems espoused, as compared with the eighteen other research clients (see Table A-2 in the appendix).

On the MMPI his high scores were on sexual confusion (MF=73), ego strength (ES=72), dominance problems (Do=73), and problems of control (Cn=71). Among the twenty research clients he ranked third in terms of quality of healthy adjustment as revealed on the MMPI (Table A-3). On the Edwards PPS scale (repeated after every fifth interview), he tended to score within normal range, except for being somewhat low on achievement, orderliness, and endurance needs at the beginning of therapy. His consistently highest scores were on heterosexuality, affiliation, aggression, and succorance needs. His scores increased during therapy on achievement, orderliness, exhibition, introception, dominance, and endurance needs. His scores decreased during therapy on deference, autonomy, succorance, abasement, nurturance, change, heterosexuality, and aggressiveness needs, in that order. (See Table A-4 in the appendix.)

In terms of affect expressed toward and by the therapist, Mr. Jones ranked third highest of the twenty clients in the positive quality of his affect, and he tied for second highest ranking in the positive quality of the therapist's affect toward him. In terms of rankings made by the therapist after therapy, Mr. Jones obtained rankings among the four highest persons on rapport, amount liked by therapist, and success of case; he ranked sixth highest on dependency, fourteenth on hostility, and nineteenth on guardedness. In terms of post-therapy ratings by the therapist, Mr. Jones was rated as friendly in affect, dominating in degree of attempts to control the therapy, open with regard to the amount of his self-disclosure, and well liked by the therapist. He was ranked as eighteenth out of twenty with regard to the therapist's estimate of the amount of maladjustment displayed at the time he started therapy. (Tables A-2, A-6, and A-7.) On the dependency scale derived from the Client Affect Scale, his mean score for the twenty interviews was 32.90, with a range of scores from 23 (last interview) to 47 (middle of therapy). Of the twenty research clients, he placed third from the top in amount of dependency shown on this scale.

On the factor analysis of the twenty clients with respect to their MMPI scores, Mr. Jones' only high weighting (82) was on factor-group I, which contained the more uninhibited (Pd), manic, hysteric type of clients.

On the factor analysis of the twenty clients with respect to their

Edwards PPS scores, Mr. Jones' only significant weighting (61) was in factor-group I, in which the clients were characterized most typically by high scores on affiliant and nurturant needs.

On our factor analysis of the Client's Affect Scale, Mr. Jones had high positive weightings on positive factor groups which were interpreted as comprising clients who were relaxed, self-managing, perceiving the therapist as a friend, co-operative, strong, mature, self-confident, and feeling safe in therapy. He had negative weightings on the factor-groups which were interpreted as comprising clients who felt disliked and were taciturn, dependent, resistant toward interpretations, insecure, or inclined to feel misunderstood.

On the factor analysis of the Therapist's Affect Scale, Mr. Jones had high positive weightings on positive factor-groups which included clients who were perceived by the therapist as relaxed, friendly, enjoying the interview, inclined to make the therapist feel appreciated, open, self-confident, and understanding of their problems. He also scored positively on those negative factors representing clients who were perceived by the therapist as wanting an audience, needing to be pushed, causing the therapist to feel somewhat disappointed, tending to feel guilt about their failure to make enough progress in therapy, and inclined to discuss irrelevancies. These perceptions of the client by the therapist occurred around the twelfth interview. Mr. Jones had high *negative* weightings on the following negative characteristics; perceived as feeling inferior, becoming involved in poor relationships, unsystematic, restless, unrealistic, distant, hostile, aggressive, narcissistic, unmotivated, tending to cause the therapist to feel uncertain, puzzled, and frustrated, hard to understand, and hard to communicate with. To summarize, Mr. Jones generally showed characteristics of clients who were friendly and positive toward the therapist and the therapy. He did not express many signs of hostility, aggression, or other more overt forms of resistance. Similarly Mr. Jones was perceived by the therapist as being a friendly person who was not very hostile or aggressive, although during the middle of his therapy there were some signs of resistance and exhibitionism, according to the therapist's perception of him at that time. Test data on Mr. Jones appear in the appendix.

In the order of frequency, the major sources or objects of Mr. Jones' affect were as follows: therapist, wife, self, father, homosexuality, masculinity, maturity, and heterosexuality. The major affect-themes were: anxiety, hostility need, sex need, dependency, ego needs, affiliation or love needs, sexual pressure from outside, and nurturance. These, too, have been covered more specifically in our discussion about each interview.

The different types of responses by the therapist, listed in descending order of frequency, were: lead-taking, direct questions, clarification of feelings, interpretation, redirective responses, giving education and information, reassurance, discussing the relationship, and restatement of content.

Jones: First Interview (2/10)

M R. JONES oriented the therapy discussion during the first interview toward his father, many of his problems being concerned with his ambivalent feelings about this parent. He had many dependent feelings but also much anxiety and hostility toward him. He expressed concern about his relationship to his department head, whom he saw as a father-surrogate; thus he directed about half of his remarks toward the topic of his father or a father-surrogate.

While he seemed to be a person who was attempting to emancipate himself from the controls of a rather strict home, Mr. Jones showed much reluctance to deviate from the Calvinistic standards of his parents' home. At the same time he professed to have little respect for his father, who was seen as being a weak person, often victimized by his employers, and usually browbeaten by his strong-willed wife. Other topics of some concern to Mr. Jones were his masculinity, his professional adequacy, and his emotional maturity. Thus we are presented with the picture of a person of moderate ego-strength suffering from feelings of insecurity and inadequacy, some of which may stem from his having lacked a strong father-image with whom to identify himself in childhood and adolescence.

In the problem of ego-strength probably lay the the genesis of the strong dependency feelings which were to play a large part in this therapeutic situation. In regard to these feelings, some problems resulted from Mr. Jones' ambivalence; he had many feelings of dependency, but also much need to assert himself. In this sense his was not so much a problem of weak ego as of being a person with a repressed ego struggling for expression. He gave the appearance of being aggressive and argumentative, although, as he later indicated, this behavior was a façade or compensation which he employed for the purpose of concealing the insecurity feelings only slightly hidden beneath the surface.

During the interview the client also expressed some anxiety about

243

whether the therapist might tend to ridicule some of his religious and ethical values, or whether, as a result of the therapy, he himself might lose some of these; he identified some of his religious values as relating to his dependency needs, in that he felt an obligation not to displease a rather personal God upon whom he felt quite comfortably dependent for many material favors. Similarly, he had taken his present job because his department head had previously been his adviser when he was in college, and he felt that this man had a paternal and protective attitude toward him. Likewise, on his internship Mr. Jones almost went out of his way to invite supervision and domination, which he then somewhat resented. His PAC-NAC dependency score after the first interview was 27, much below his mean score on dependency.

The therapist's handling of the first interview was largely one of leading the client to discuss the situation by the use of questions (22 per cent) and interpretation (30 per cent). He also clarified feelings about a third of the time. This involved reflection of most of the feelings of inadequacy, hostility, and concern that the therapist or the therapy might undermine the client's religious values. Interpretation took the form of such things as pointing out the ambivalence which the client did not always notice, or of calling attention to the hostility implied in terms like "locking horns with my father."

The amount of affect in the first interview was moderate, as might be expected. The client's affect score of 07 was almost the least positive of his scores, as is often true in the beginning of therapy. The therapist started with moderately warm feelings toward Mr. Jones, his score of 46 being at the mean of the scores he obtained on the twenty interviews with this client.

I had a hard time taking my present job; the department head is a real father-figure for me. I'm not sure my going there was a real healthy sort of adjustment. The regression creeps out in various ways. He invited us to play bridge, and during the evening my response to him was always "Dr. M." rather than "Tom." His reaction was to tell me the next day to call him by his first name. It smacks too much of the respect-for-father business on my part. It's hard for me to see him as anything but a father-figure. (Dep + auth → Anx — self)

He does make an ideal sort of father. He's got the physical appearance, the maturity, and he's a non-punitive sort of person, and yet he gratifies all of my dependent needs. He's very good at getting things done, but there's still the desire on my part to step in and get things done on my own. I don't have any trouble telling him when I think he's wrong in some situa-

tion. But there's plenty of agreement between us, too. (Dep + auth →
Anx — self)

*Um-hm. I suppose almost everyone finds it difficult to change over to
calling a former professor by his first name.* (Reassurance) *It may be a
typical problem in life to recognize that former supervisory relationships
can become those of colleagues.* (Information)

I think this therapy relationship is going to work out pretty well. But 1
want to be aware of what's happening. I don't want to be too psychological
or to fall into a ruminative, interpretative pattern about it though, where
it will lose its naturalness. (Dep + ther → Anx — ther, Rel)

*The first few times you call him by his first name it'll seem awkward;
almost as though you can expect him to punish you for it.* (Reassurance)
(Laughs) *What do you call your father?* (Question)

"Dad." I'd no more think of calling him "John" than . . . . (Laughs)
See, my boss and my dad went to college together, so my boss became a
very natural father substitute when I went to college where he was teaching.
And now I'm working under him. I had a real lost feeling when I first went
to college, and my boss has a certain permissiveness that my father doesn't.
(Dep — fa → Dep + auth) There are some things my dad can't tolerate.
My father's totally opposed to alcohol. Of course I experimented with it
when I started out in college, and even today my dad doesn't know I drink.
I feel a certain amount of guilt about it; I would feel very badly if he did
find out. It would be real difficult for me to hurt my dad. (Dom p — fa
→ Dep + fa) I don't feel guilty while I'm drinking, but I would feel guilty
if he were hurt. I guess that's pretty typical of the whole relationship with
my father. I guess I protect him. Maybe I tend to see him as a sort of naive
person who isn't aware of what's going on. There are certain issues on
which I won't lock horns with him. I might debate a matter in an intellectual
way, but I would never actually defy him openly. (Dom p — fa → Dep
— fa → Nur + fa)

*Um-hm. When you use the phrase "lock horns," you seem to be describ-
ing another type of relationship from the one presented in the concept of a
person whom you didn't want to hurt.* (Interpretation$_5$)

Well, this is where the aggression comes in. (Laughs) Until you said
it, I hadn't realized that I'd used the term. Perhaps I can't tolerate the idea,
but I couldn't see a situation in which we'd actually lock horns in a strongly
hostile or combative sense. He doesn't fit into the picture I have of a real
authority figure who lays down rules. I accept his ideas because they're
reasonable. He wants me to go to church, for instance, and I've never resented going; in fact, I've liked it most of the time. (Dom p — fa → Dep
+ fa) I don't know whether there's more hostility than I'm aware of. (The
client is concerned that his acquiescence is evidence of an overly submissive
attitude.)

You're suggesting the possibility that your unconscious might have been responsible for your using the phrase "lock horns." (Interpretation$_4$)

Yeah, I'd go along with that as a purely intellectual observation, but I don't get a real feeling response to it. (Res)

What are the little not-very-important things that he's fairly strict about? (Question)

(Client sighs) Well, the alcohol and the business of smoking. He doesn't like my smoking, although I think he's gotten used to it. We sort of thrashed it out. We didn't lock horns on that. (Dom p — fa → Dep + fa) (Laughs)

How did you thrash it out? (Question)

It was pretty passive on my part. They let me know their disappointment about this. I can't recall now the actual situation when this was talked over. (Dom p — fa → Dep + fa)

Um-hm. I would suspect that was the sort of moment in a boy's life that he wouldn't easily forget. (Challenges; the therapist suspects repression of a possibly hostile event.)

I think I promised that I would try to quit, so my initial reaction must have been to knuckle under. (Dom p — fa → Dep + fa) But I don't really think I made much of an effort to do it. If it came up again, I said it was too difficult to quit. I'm remembering it now. I think we're getting into an important area. They chided me not as much about the moral effects, but about how much money was being wasted by smoking, and said that I could pay for quite a bit of my schooling with that money. But I had been working and earning some of my own money, so their argument seemed irrelevant. (Dom p — par → Anx)

I think this money business ties in with my problems in a lot of ways. I probably showed my protest by not being too careful in spending money. I think I was angry with my dad for not providing any better than he did. (Dep — fa → Hos n + fa) We never really lacked for any essentials, but on the other hand, there were plenty of luxuries that I couldn't have. I've never been able to handle money as well as I should. I've never denied myself things I've wanted. I have a pattern in terms of church-giving that I think reflects some of the problem here. We each had a "tithe-box" when I was a kid, and when I'd run short of money, I'd swipe some nickels out of the tithe-box. I think this was a way of protesting: "You're giving it to those damn church people, when *we* need it." (Hos n + fa) My guilt about this is no longer too upsetting, and yet *my* pattern now is tithing. I feel good when I do it. (Dep + fa) No doubt I'm expiating a lot of the guilt for some of the earlier pattern. In our financial circumstances it's a fair sacrifice. (The client admits to having some hostility toward his father, but it is not permitted overt expression.)

It's a pretty big sacrifice, isn't it? (Interpretation$_5$)

Yes, it is.

Did you feel pretty guilty about taking this money? (Question)

Yeah. *Now,* I feel we probably needed the money more than the church people, but I think at the time I felt pretty guilty. It was guilt toward God, not toward the church. (Dep — relig → Anx — self)

You sort of felt, before, that God would be angry with you. (Clarification)

Yeah. There are certain patterns that I carry over from my training. For instance, I felt thankful toward God when I landed the job I hoped to get. (Dep + relig)

You felt that God had been good. (Clarification)

Yeah. And I think I believe this. But this is an area I dislike fooling around with (laughs) in a therapy session. (Anx — ther; Res)

Why? (Question)

My rationalization is that I have a certain set of values that I wanta retain, and I guess I'm afraid that if I lose some of these things, I may lose the whole value system that I have. (Dep + relig → Anx — ther)

Are you sort of afraid that therapy will take it away from you? (Question)

I don't think so. Not consciously, that is. But it's something that I find comfort in. (Dep + relig)

Are you afraid, perhaps, that I will tend to belittle it or scorn it? (Relationship)

I probably am. Yes, I am.

There's a conflict there. You perceive me as a psychologist, and you feel that means that I will have values that would be scornful of some of yours. (Relationship)

I'm not so sure *you* would. But there's still a question. (Pause) I'm blocking now. I've attributed to you a certain set of values, whether they apply or not. In my perception of you I've given you a certain set of moral considerations I think you respect. If I didn't think you had those, I couldn't have told you. (Dep + ther)

I'm a psychologist, but one who appears to be a moral or ethical one. (Clarification; the therapist shows indirectly that he will not threaten the client's values.)

Yeah, I think so. My only question would be, (laughs) now I'm interpreting your behavior, how much you may have reacted against any morality in your background, knowing the way *I* have done that. (Hos n + ther)

You almost said, "How far I'd gone to the other extreme." (Clarification)

Yeah. (Laughs)

It gives you a sense of satisfaction to have these values. (Clarification)

It does. I guess part of the basis for it is connected with the way I want to be dependent. If there is a God, I guess I've got a pretty commercial sort of a God, because he seems to produce whenever I get in trouble. I mean in a financial, physical sense. When I don't see where the money's coming from, something always seems to come up. (Dep + relig) Now the point at which I suspect that this is largely some sort of compensatory device on my part is that I know I'm not adequate myself. I am adequate, but in a real *feeling* sense, I know I'm not. There's that lack of confidence and the need for support. I guess this is tied up with why I'm concerned about having this job with M. It feels real good to be working with him, but at some point along the way I have to achieve some independence and some confidence in myself. (Dep + auth → Anx − self) (The client expresses his dependency needs quite clearly at this point.) Being away on my internship did a lot for me, in that sense. I felt like I was a success. I didn't wanta leave the hospital, actually. I felt the faculty respected me more, then, too. They started calling me by my first name. (Ego + prof)

I get the feeling that you're saying that it's good to have Dad to lean on, whether it's M., or in heaven, or somewhere else. But you also say, with a certain degree of conviction, that you suspect you ought *to be able to feel free of that.* (Interpretation₅)

Yeah, it's the old approach-avoidance situation.

You're ambivalent at this point. It feels good to have M. around, but you have a kind of guilt feeling and tell yourself you shouldn't feel that way. (Clarification)

Yeah. I think some of the things I do and ways I deal with him are attempts to show him that I'm independent. (The ambivalence over dependency is recognized.) He's aware of my dependency, I'm sure. My first semester in graduate school, I used to go back to college and visit him over the weekends whenever I could. (Dep + auth) I'd like to bring him to meet you, sometime. (Dep + ther) Or take him to visit my internship hospital. I guess it's a way of showing him that I have achieved a degree of independence, that there are some things I can do on my own. When I talk to him now, I'm out to spout off what clinical knowledge I have. These are all ways of showing Dad that I'm. . . . (Dep − fa → Dom n + auth)

You're pretty good, too. Or at least you're coming along. (Clarification)
Maybe you feel some needs for him. (Interpretation₉)

I would think so. I used to get a real filial reaction toward him. I think he's aware of it. When I was in stress situations in school, part of my behavior pattern was to run away. Get fed up with classes and take off for a couple of days. On one occasion it was quite rewarding to find his anxious reaction to this. I know I fill the role of a son for him, too. (Dep + auth)

Did you have any feelings of this ever happening in the past before M.? (Question)

I don't really think so. I suppose there must have been people from time to time who have filled this kind of a role for me. No one's ever been quite as successful as he has. I think there have been fathers away from Dad. (Dep + fa) (Mentions a farm he visited as a child, where there was a young man who used to show a somewhat paternal attitude toward him. The client then tells how his family moved about very often during his childhood, and he never was able to become established with a group.) I felt some resentment of that, too. My father had been sick, so I couldn't blame him entirely, but I also know that he wasn't a very adequate teacher, and the school boards let him go more rapidly. But it was a dirty trick on *me,* as far as I was concerned. I was pretty unaccepting of it, and he tried to make up for it, even to the extent of sending me to a private school, to make up for having to drop out of a public school I had enjoyed. (Dep — fa → Hos n + fa)

When he was sick, he needed an operation, and the chances of coming through it weren't too good. During that time on weekends I went to the city where he was in the hospital and visited friends I had there, but I didn't go in to see him very often. I'm sure this must have made him feel bad. I guess this is just another situation in which he was inadequate in the face of some sort of adversity. Either the school boards were giving him hell, or he had a physical defect that he couldn't overcome. When he had to meet situations that he couldn't cope with, I suppose I felt he was an inadequate father. (Dep — fa → Hos n + fa)

He wasn't a very strong hero for a boy. (Clarification)

No, I guess not. But then I was never all boy, either, I suppose. I can remember getting in fights in grade school, and on occasions I got beat up because my father was a teacher. He went to bat for me on several occasions, but this was no way of proving my own adequacy; I felt even worse if he would chase off after somebody who was trying to beat me up. And most of the people expect you to be a patsy, if your father is a teacher. (Dep — fa → Hos n + peers)

When I asked about this ever happening before, you interpreted the question quite logically to refer to father-surrogate relationships, but I was really referring to your running away. (Directive lead)

I don't think I would have gotten into that pattern in college if I hadn't found a buddy in school, the best man at our wedding incidentally, who had the same sort of a pattern. He pulled this one quite a bit, and I decided it sounded like a good idea. But I have had an *escape* pattern for a long, long time. In college it would sometimes take the form of sleeping through classes. In high school it was reading. I still find it hard to sit down and study, but I'll read two novels in an evening. Sometimes I'll use direct aggression when I'm frustrated, but more frequently I'll retreat. (Anx — gen)

One of my supervisors on my internship was a person whom I didn't have any respect for professionally or ethically. For two and a half months I sat there and took it, when I considered he was treating me below my level. I thought I wouldn't make any trouble, but after a while I told him I wanted to be treated as though I had some sort of an idea of what was going on. I saw the threat in his not respecting me for the things that I *could* do. In general he behaved toward me in such a way that I wasn't able to demonstrate my own independence. And likewise I gave the chief psychologist a little bit of a hard time. But we could discuss our differences, and we got along pretty smoothly. (Dep — auth → Hos n + auth)

One of my reactions is an ambivalence which is a kind of dangerous thing. When we were discussing our group therapy sessions, they always wanted to analyze the therapist, and I told them I'd be damned if I was going to be therapized by the whole staff. This put a stop to that sort of thing. And yet when the consultant came to visit, I actually asked him to help me with a transference-countertransference situation I'd gotten myself into. It was almost a masochistic sort of behavior. This inconsistency bothers me. (Dep — auth → Anx — self; the client reveals his ambivalence about dependency.)

Perhaps these are two different kinds of father-son relationships. The one is an accepting father whom you can trust and defer to and ask help from, and the other is the dominating, punitive, authoritarian type of father. (Interpretation$_5$) *He makes you feel rebellious.* (Interpretation$_5$) *It's an interesting ambivalence between passive dependency and aggressive resistance.* (Interpretation$_7$)

It really must have been hell for my supervisors! (Dep — auth → Hos n + auth)

Your response seems to be partly dependent on whether you perceive the father-figure as having respect for you. (Interpretation$_7$)

Yeah. And why is respect so important?

If they treat you with respect, you can admit your weaknesses. (Interpretation$_5$)

I guess respect is a form of accepting me as a mature person. (Anx — auth)

You don't want to be accepted as a junior technician of some sort. You want to be accepted in a mature responsible capacity. (Clarification)

Yeah.

I guess our time's up for today. Is this time all right for you?

Yes. This'll be fine.

Jones: Second Interview (2/17)

THE SECOND INTERVIEW consisted of a great deal of catharsis and guilt about the client's early sex history. This opening up of the sex area may have resulted from dreams Mr. Jones reported in which he interpreted Oedipal desires on his part. Much of his early sex behavior had been homosexual, with his role being the more aggressive one, and he showed a lot of guilt about this. Homosexual dreams continued up to the time of his marriage. Mr. Jones readily admitted having had sexual desires toward his mother, and these did not seem to cause much guilt. However, he reported a great deal of guilt about his having engaged in sex play with his younger sister. He tended to relate his sister's current disturbed state of adjustment to these incidents. Although his sister had been a more than willing partner in the activities, Mr. Jones assumed the major responsibility because he was the older of the two.

During the second interview a good bit of hostility was also expressed toward the parents—toward the father for not being stronger, and toward the mother for being a nagging, dominating person. Some anxiety was produced in Mr. Jones because of his having divulged so much private information; he expressed fear that therapy would cause him to spend too much of his time ruminating about himself. He also had the fear that the therapist would force him to reveal more of himself than he intended to. Resistance was also shown in his criticizing the therapist for not being warm enough in the previous interview. The client raised the question of the existence of transference but thought the second interview too early for this.

In the second interview the principal client affect-themes were hostility, anxiety, and sex need. There were significant amounts of resistance and discussion of the relationship. Most of these feelings were directed toward the father, homosexual activities, the therapist and the parents, heterosexual activities, and his mother and sister.

The therapist's activities consisted of lead-taking (33 per cent), of which a large part was direct questions (25 per cent), clarification of client's feeling (24 per cent), interpretation (14 per cent), discussion of the relationship (9 per cent), and the challenging of statements made by the client (6 per cent). A number of questions were directed at exploring material which was somewhat repressed, such as the exact nature of the sexual activities. Similarly, the challenges were attempts to question improbable memory lapses. Clarification of feelings occurred when the client expressed guilt or hostility, and discussion of the relationship followed the client's mentioning of his feelings toward the therapist.

The change in the expression of affect between the client and the therapist was quite marked in the second interview. Despite the client's complaint that the therapist had not seemed very warm in the previous interview, and despite his resistance devolving from his disclosures of somewhat repressed and anxiety-producing material, his score on the Client's Affect Scale rose 57 points to a score of 64. This was still below his mean score but was a very strong rise. The therapist's score dropped twelve points (score of 34), suggesting a concern about the client's expression of hostility and about the level of his general adjustment as revealed during the second interview. This score (34) was the fifth from the most negative of all the therapist's scores toward Mr. Jones.

On the PAC-NAC dependency scale, the client's score rose ten points to 37, which was in the top fifth of his scores on dependency for the twenty interviews.

What happened last time must have been significant. I've been having dreams, anyway. In one there was a scene in which I stabbed somebody. My impression when I was thinking about it was, "This was Father." It wasn't particularly upsetting at the time. It would be reinforcement for the theory that there is hostility there. Ordinarily I'd be wary of interpreting dreams, but it just seemed so logical. (Hos n + fa; Drm) Then afterwards there was another dream, I can't exactly recall it. Somehow or other there was a Japanese. There was a man with his back toward me, he had a bayonet, and I could see him thrust it in. And then I could see the knife just taken out and slide across the belly, and the knees come up. (Hos n + fa; Drm) The first dream is coming back a little bit now. It's so vivid, here I can actually see the blood pouring out of, I guess it was Father's mouth, but I'm reluctant to say it. It's upsetting now to talk about it. (Hos n + fa; Drm) (Laughs with embarrassment; the client partially senses the possible repressed hostility suggested by these dreams; he does not indicate any recognition of possible sexual significance at this point.)

It kind of got you worked up a little bit. (Clarification)
Yeah.
Why? (Question)
I just don't like to see myself this way. (Hos + fa → Anx — self)
As having hostility toward your father. (Clarification)
In the first dream I'm sure it was. In the second one, I had association afterwards that actually the guy with his back toward me was a marine. And I associate this marine to my father. (Anx — fa; Drm) I told you last time that he wasn't really much of a man. I'm real reluctant to accept this. I'm wondering in a sense if this isn't him fulfilling the role maybe I'd like to see him fulfill. (Dep — fa)
What sort of person was the victim? (Question; the therapist suspects that this was a castration-anxiety dream and that the victim symbolized the client himself.)
Sort of a caricature of the Japanese during the war; a weak, small person. In the sense that I get it, there wasn't even a type of combativeness; the Japanese individual was being taken advantage of. (Dom p — fa → Dep — fa → Hos n + self)
How old was he? (Question)
Well, if we're associating along the same line, I *wonder* if it was me. There was no real association to age. If so, why would I be Japanese? Some kind of inferiority feeling? (Hos n + self)
How old was the marine? (Question)
I couldn't tell; his back was toward me. My association to him would be the stereotype of a staff sergeant. Middle-aged guy, maybe a little paunchy, but still able to move pretty effectively. (Could this be a transference reaction already?) Able to handle himself well in this kind of a situation. If this is Dad aggressing against me, (Dom p — fa → Dep — fa) in what sort of situation is he aggressing? The hell of it is, is this the reality of the situation or just my perception of it?
There is another thing that seems, at least in my introspections, to amount to a classical Oedipal situation. I can very clearly recall dreams of having intercourse with my mother. (Sex n + mo; Drm) And sometimes I believe the association I have to stabbing Dad was that this is the rivalry with him for my mother. If this is so, it's down at the level that I was just never able to accept before. I can go so far with this kind of Freudian theory, and then it just seems to lose any realistic basis. And yet there is the fact of this kind of Oedipal dream. (Sex n + fa; Drm) The part that I'm not too sure about is whether I do see it as a rivalry situation.
When did you learn about sex? (Question)
When I was about ten or eleven. I was about eleven when I discovered what the actual sexual relationship was. And then my reaction was that *my* mother and dad wouldn't do anything like that. I'm quite angry, from time

to time, that they didn't handle me in the way that they did my sister. (Sex n — par → Hos n + par) When my brother was being born, why she had her hand on Mother's abdomen. I was just pushed out of all this. (Dep — par → Hos n — par) When I found out what the scoop was, from a bunch of guys, I though it was unfair.

Did your father ever talk about sex? (Question)

Not openly. He never sat down and told me, "This is what's what." Probably Mother had a more open attitude about it. We can joke about things at the table about sexual matters, and my sister feels a lot freer to do this sort of thing than I do. They're broad-minded in this sense, and yet I think Dad is kind of constricted about it. (Dep — fa → Hos n — fa) They gave me a book at about the age of eleven, something about, *"The Mastery of Sex through Psychology and Religion."* It was one of those books that talks about "self-abuse" and so forth. I had discovered how to masturbate, (Sex n + masturb) actually, and I read it more for its erotic value than for information, because the information it had was mostly erroneous. It wasn't much help. (Dep — par) Probably it aroused a lot more guilt than was necessary.

One of the things I was thinking about last week was that somehow I ought to be talking to you about mother. There's a more obvious conflict there. (Hos n + mo) I'm more prone on a conscious level to take my father's side in things, although there may be unconscious hostility. He's very much the picture, at this point, of not being the strong person, of course. He's the underdog, in a good many ways. (Dep — fa) It's an unkind thought, but I guess Mother's sort of a "Menopause Minnie" who just goes on and on and on about things that irritate her. (Hos n + mo)

Maybe the thing that I resent about Dad the most is that I want him to be the strong figure. To be a real father-figure. As I think of things in recent years, *I've* been the one that's been called upon and asked in a sense to be the father-figure in a situation. (Dep — fa → Hos n — fa) When my sister gets in trouble, it's *me* that's consulted. I'm married now, and I resent this intrusion into my life, now. I've got a family of my own to think about and care for. My reaction is that if Dad was the kind of man he ought to be, I wouldn't have to be bothered. (Dep — fa → Hos n — fa) He could handle this himself.

So he's not a very active figure, for you. Pretty passive. (Clarification)

Yeah. You know, there's a sense of guilt when I'm telling you these things. It seems disloyal. (Hos n + fa → Anx)

You feel like you're being unfair to him. You feel guilty about it. (Clarification)

Yeah. I want you to see him, so you know what kind of a person he really is. (Dep — ther) What the *total* person is.

Um-hm. (Pause) *In this dream about the marine, it seems to me most likely that you were the marine.* (Interpretation$_s$; later the therapist gives a different interpretation of this dream.)

This may be true. For instance, one of my ambitions was to become a marine. When things went tough for me as an undergraduate, I thought I wanted to run away and join the marines. The question is, who is the little guy? (Anx — masc) I don't think *our* relationship has gotten to the point yet where you would actually be involved in this dream. Maybe it's significant that I even think of this possibility. You could be a father-substitute. (Dep — ther, Rel)

Um-hm. It would seem fairly early for that, although you went pretty deeply for your first interview. (Information) *I'm certainly not prepared to say I feel that that connection is definite at this point. We might later decide that we do.* (Information)

I've had frank homosexual dreams that I can recall. One that resulted in castration. Just before I got married. I think if there were this much of a disturbance in this area. . . . (Pause) (Sex n + homo; Drm) If the disturbance were homosexual, I think it would have been of a franker nature than that. (Res)

Tell me about the dream you had with this fellow. (Directive lead)

(Client sighs) As nearly as I can recall, uh, uh, uh, well, Bill was my roommate. I forget who was the passive and who was the active partner in the situation. But the outstanding part of it is the castration at the very end of it, where something like wire-snippers cut off my penis. (Dep — fa → Sex n — homo, drm → Anx) I can remember waking up with my hand on my penis to make sure it was still there. My reaction at the time was that it must be related to my getting married.

It's odd that you should forget who was the active and who was the passive person. That doesn't seem very reasonable. (Challenging)

Well, it may be that I want to forget it.

What kind of activity occurred in the dream? (Question)

Sodomy. And Bill, I guess, was kind of a father-figure for me. (Dep — fa → Sex n — homo) About thirty-two, and married. He was a guy I liked *very* much. He didn't cause me any *conscious* anxiety about my sexuality when I was living with him. He was a masculine sort of a guy. Athletic. (Dep + fa sur → Sex n — homo) My recollection now would be that I was the active partner.

The actual overt homosexual experiences that I've had have been limited to the early puberty period, and it was "off and on" active. There was one main incident with a kid about my age who was much less physically mature. I guess that one lasted for about two or three weeks, and of course there was guilt about that. Or fear of it being found out, more than any actual guilt. We tried to have intercourse between his legs. (Sex n + homo) I didn't have an orgasm, but I can remember straining to try to achieve one. I must confess that in thinking about these things I've been concerned that something of this nature might come up, and I would discover the latent homosexuality. (Anx — ther; Res)

You've been a little bit afraid of that. (Clarification)

Yeah. I would be very upset if I discovered this were true of me. But in trying to check this sort of thing against my reactions to these people, consciously, they don't cause me too much anxiety. There is this much; when instances were reported of a homosexual, in the hospital, I like to think my attitude toward them has been more accepting and more understanding than that of the other staff people. Maybe I'm defending some of the feelings I have myself. (Sex n — homo → Aff n + peers)

You said you thought you would feel quite upset if you found any latent homosexual feelings coming up. Does this imply that you don't think there are any there? (Question)

Well, I know that everybody has latent homosexuality, and I can recognize this dream as a homosexual dream. I think, actually, I'd be concerned if there was the overt impulse to indulge in this kind of thing. As long as there's no concern about wanting to act this kind of thing out, I'm O.K. (Sex n — homo → Anx)

You were telling me about this homosexual experience, and I sort of interrupted you. (Non-directive lead)

The second experience occurred when I was older; I guess probably I was fourteen. My sister and I had gone to visit a friend of ours. I had previously had some sex play with a younger sister of this guy. This time all five of us were involved. We all exposed ourselves. And at night I attempted the same kind of intercourse between the legs with the younger boy, who was about two years younger than I. (Sex n + homo) Actually there was always the heterosexual mixed in with the homosexual sort of thing. I'm going to great lengths to defend myself, now. (Sex n + het)

Tell me about some of the heterosexual activity, now. (Directive lead)

I was very much interested in girls. I guess I discovered what kissing was about then. There was always the fear of going any farther than that. I had very strongly the attitude that I wanted to remain a virgin. It was more of a fear of being seduced than actually seducing. (Dep — gen → Sex n — het → Anx) (This phrase suggests a passive aspect to his personality.) I started dating around that time. Most of these were pretty pure affairs; a few kisses and not much else. It wasn't till I was sixteen that I started doing any petting. This was while I was working at camp, and there was an opportunity there with girls who were also working there. I dated a lot, I think. It wasn't till college that I discovered that there was more to sex. I guess it was during my sophomore year that I first had intercourse. This aroused a lot of guilt, and a lot of fear of pregnancy. (Sex n + het → Anx) (He then mentions several other casual instances of intercourse.)

I guess one of the things I've always dreaded about coming to therapy, and the thing that I was afraid would come up, (Res) is the incestuous relationship between my sister and I. I guess I was curious from the time that she was about ten. There had been intermittent sex play with a hell of a lot of guilt, and when the guilt would wear off after five or six months, sex curiosity would come up again. This happened maybe about five or six different times, up until the time I was eighteen. (Sex n + het; Anx)

When you say sex play, what do you mean? (Question)

There were several attempts at actually trying to have intercourse. I guess there was as much interest on her part as there was on mine, but the fact remains that because I am older, I should be the one that's responsible. (Sex n + het → Anx)

Why should you feel so guilty in telling me about this? (Question)

Because I feel guilty myself about it. If I could say I'd stopped at twelve, or even at fourteen, it wouldn't be so bad. But here I am, a mature individual who ought to know better, and I've still got enough of the super-ego to tell me that this isn't right. (Sex n + het → Anx)

What's bad *about it?* (Challenging)

In my system of values this thing is wrong. I could tolerate it in somebody else. I could probably tolerate it more in any of the other children than I could in myself. (Sex n + het → Anx)

You're simply saying, "It's bad because I think it's bad." (Challenges)

Yeah, I guess I'm very confused. I've never had the attitude that it might *not* be wrong. (Sex n + het → Anx)

It just seems pretty guilt-laden to you. (Clarification) *It possibly didn't occur to you to think that I would ask why you felt guilty.* (Clarification)

No, it didn't. Although it helps.

Would you have felt guilty if you had done this with some other girl? (Question)

No. And I guess the reason that these other sexual experiences aren't so guilt-laden is because of the enormity of *this* offense. (Sex n + het)

But you said that she was getting as much fun out of it as you were. (Challenging)

Probably so, but that isn't reassuring. I felt I had a responsibility to her. (Nur + sib)

So you were betraying a trust at this point. With some other girl, you would be more your own boss, so to speak. (Clarification) *But you were being depended on to look out for your little sister.* (Clarification) *It makes you feel very unhappy with yourself to think that you could fail in that regard.* (Clarification)

It does. I think the thing that increases the guilt is the fact that she hasn't adjusted well. Last year she dropped out of school and went to work, and then went into therapy at my suggestion. And I guess I feel that maybe her adjustment might have been better if this traumatic experience hadn't happened. (Sex n + het, sib → Anx)

You're wondering if maybe you caused it. (Clarification)

Yeah. Although, I suppose this is unrealistic. If I were trying to look at it a little more rationally, I think her problems are somewhat the same as mine, in terms of there being a problem in looking *for* a father (Dep — fa) She seemed to insist on picking out individuals to go with who were much older or were in some way pretty severely maladjusted.

You doubt if you really can be held accountable for all of her difficulties. (Clarification)

If I try to look at it realistically, I know I can't. *Here* I'm trying to differentiate between being rational and rationalizing.

You felt so guilty about it, it was the last thing you could bring yourself to tell about. (Interpretation₅)

I almost feel that I may not have got around to it in this session. (Res)

Well, you're doing real well, I'd say. That's pretty early to be able to report something you feel so much guilt about. (Reassurance)

I'm surprised that I could, when the guilt was so strong. Particularly in view of the feeling I had about you the last time, that you weren't as warm as I'd known you in the past. (Dep — ther, Rel → Hos n + ther) There was a sense of disappointment. Not to the point of any anger, just disappointment.

Um-hm. How did I seem less warm? What about me seemed cold? (Relationship; question)

It seemed like a more formal setting. It was different from sitting down and talking over somebody *else's* problems. (Dep — ther, Rel → Hos n + ther)

Um-hm. You mean there was more distance between us then, is that it? (Relationship; question)

As I perceived it, yes.

You're surprised at yourself that you could bring this out and open up and tell me this when you feel so bad about it. (Clarification) (Pause) *Do you think I will think less of you because of it?* (Relationship)

No, I don't. Because of the way you reacted to it. If I had thought you were going to punish me, I don't think I would have told you. Maybe this is what I want. (Dep + ther, Rel → Hos n — self)

But maybe you kind of like to be able to tell me, knowing that in a sense I would give you forgiveness or expiation of your sense of guilt. (Interpretation₉)

Yeah. (Spoken hesitatingly) If I had thought it would threaten our relationship, I couldn't have told you. (Dep + ther, Rel → Anx)

It's important for you to feel free to tell me what your feelings are. (Relationship) *It's important not to have to feel blocked. Or when you have such feelings, to be able to bring them out, so we can discuss them.* (Structuring; relationship)

I think one of the reasons I was angry with you last week was because of this suggestion that Dad was imperfect. (Dep — ther, Rel → Hos n + ther)

Um-hm. You wondered, who was I to be criticizing him? (Clarification)

I guess that might come close to it. I really hadn't consciously put it in those words, but I guess that's what happened. (Hos n + ther)

You feel sort of protective of him? (Interpretation₅)

I guess I do. Very definitely so. (Sighs) That's an interesting way of putting it. That hits it squarely on the head. One of my ambitions is to get on a school board, and just do everything I possibly can for the teachers. (Dep — fa → Nur — fa)

You feel it's your responsibility to kind of fight his battles and protect him. (Clarification) *Why should a son feel he had to protect his father?* (Question)

He shouldn't have to, unless the father's a weakling. And this fits in pretty logically. The fact that I have to protect him against the school boards, and I have to protect him against Mother. (Dep — fa → Hos n — fa) I want him to be able to handle his own battles. In a very real sense I think it's a battle with Mother. I felt that I was holding back on you last week when I wasn't saying, "Mother's the one we ought to be talking about." (Hos n + mo) And yet, it appears Dad *was* the one we should be talking about.

Well, the relationship with both is important. (Structuring) *Sometimes you talk about your father in a way that most people talk about their mother.* (Interpretation₅)

Sort of a reversal of roles here. (Laughs)

In some ways. To be protected, to be sheltered, to have their battles fought for them. (Interpretation₅)

I guess this is true. The thing is, Mother could reverse the roles in the sense that she can be vitriolic enough to take care of things herself. (Hos n + mo)

The thing that has me anxious now is that I'm afraid I'm gonna work myself into the position where I'm going to start ruminating about these things. Am I gonna talk myself into a homosexual panic that has no basis in my own dynamic picture? (Sex n — homo → Anx → Dep — ther)

Maybe you think I'm trying to talk you into that. (Interpretation₉; relationship)

What I'm looking for, I guess, is reassurance from you that it ain't so. (Dep + ther, Rel) (Laughs) And yet I know that if I do this, I guess I won't be satisfied, although it would be reassuring.

Well, we can be sure that if you talked yourself into something that isn't true, reality will pretty soon up and slap you right back into place. I don't think therapy can talk you into a delusion. (Reassurance)

No, I don't suppose it can. I don't mind thinking of these things when I'm in the therapy situation, and I think it's important that I think about them outside of therapy as I've done this last week, but I don't want it to get to be an obsession with me. (Res) And I'm very much frightened of it if it does appear as though this'll start. (Sex n — homo → Anx → Dep — ther)

You're kind of giving me a good display of resistance now. (Interpretation₅) *It's as if you're saying, "I don't want this therapy to make me think about myself. I'll set certain limits which I'll carefully circumscribe, and if your therapy is going to make me into a ruminative type of person, then I don't like that. I'll think about myself during this hour, but that's all."* (Criticism) (Pause) *I guess our time's up.*

O. K. If I go into a panic this week, I'll call you. (Dep + ther) (Laughs)

Jones: Third Interview (3/2)

SEVERAL FACTORS probably worked together to make the third interview one in which little progress occurred and the one with the most negative expression of affect. The therapist, because of a series of out-of-town meetings followed by an illness of a week, had been forced to be absent for two successive interviews.

Second, the therapist's very bad cough during the third interview gave the client the feeling that the therapist was not able to attend very well. Mr. Jones was inclined to feel a little guilt in requiring the therapist's attention. Third, Mr. Jones had been having difficulty with one of his own clients, brought on by his anxiety about his own homosexual feelings for this client. For these reasons, the client's affect score dropped to −37, his lowest score, and the therapist's score dropped to 07, also his lowest score for the entire series of interviews with this client.

Mr. Jones expressed ambivalent attitudes about homosexuality. One position he took was that he recognized this aspect of his personality, but that he considered it normal; on the other hand, this was something of a rationalized feeling, and he actually had much anxiety. He also recognized that his sexual relations with his wife were not as ideal as those he had visualized in masturbatory fantasies during adolescence. This led him into a discussion of his general inadequacy in sexual, and also in professional, development. He reported many feelings of inferiority and said he tended to limit his activities to only slightly demanding situations, so that he could be rather sure of succeeding.

During the third interview, Mr. Jones gave more expressions of dependency feelings, frequently expressing the desire that the therapist reassure him that he was not "a homosexual." He reported the desire to please the therapist, to be a "nice boy"; he mentioned the presence of feelings of positive transference. He was unable to decide which role in his dreams, the passive or the aggressive, represented himself, for he could remember times in his life when he had shown both of these two behavior reactions. He reported strong dependency needs toward the therapist, just as he had felt them toward his department head. He postulated that his excessive need for love was the result of a love-deprivation during his childhood. His PAC-NAC dependency score rose two points, to 39, which was his third highest score on dependency.

During this interview the client's principal affect-themes were anxiety, dependency, and discussion of the relationship. There were small amounts of discussion of hostility, ego needs, sex needs, affiliation needs, insight, and resistance. The principal objects of the client's affect in the third interview were himself, his homosexual activities, and the therapist. Small amounts of the affect were directed toward his parents, his department head, his peers, and his professional progress.

The methods employed by the therapist in the third interview consisted principally of questioning (29 per cent), interpretation (25 per cent), and clarification of feelings (21 per cent). There were small amounts of reassurance, information giving, and challenging (4 to 7 per cent of each). The questioning was usually an attempt to get the client to explore further some topic which he had opened up; the clarification was of the client's insecurity feelings and anxiety. The therapist's interpretation consisted of attempts to fit the client's discussion into consistent statements of dynamics in the areas of dependency or of the conflict between aggressiveness and passivity. Sometimes he also interpreted unexpressed feelings toward himself.

I found myself resenting a client who was very bossy toward others, and I realized that it was his similarity to my mother which caused the hostile feeling on my part. I find that I begrudge the time that client is taking. I feel that his problem isn't important. He has been very resistant but denies it. I felt a little petulant, because I am doing him a great big favor seeing him when I don't have to and he is denying that it's helping him. (Hos n + peers)

After this business about my homosexual feelings during the last session, I had a frightening thought during my client's therapy; what if I had a homosexual relationship with him, and I were to be the aggressive one. I expected some sort of reaction when I played around with this thought, and yet there wasn't the emotional upheaval that I'd expected. But I felt worried, because I felt that if I was going to experiment with ideas like this, I should at least keep it outside of somebody else's therapy. (Sex n + homo → Anx)

I think the interpretation of that dream about the bayonet business *might* be a homosexual one. Those were small figures I dreamed about. But I find the heterosexual situations more stimulating than the homosexual. It sounds as though I'm putting up a fight against homosexuality for myself. It's an unacceptable thing. (Sex n + homo → Anx; Res)

Is this any more than a routine situation? I recognize that I've had homosexual dreams. I've dreamed of being the homosexual aggressor; overtly this wasn't upsetting. Sure, I have some homosexual urges; so what? I'm making a fairly adequate heterosexual adjustment, and I'm not upset by people who are overtly homosexual. (Sex n + het) I keep having a feeling that we're wasting time on this. Let's move on! (Res) And yet I don't want to make the mistake of moving on to get away from something. I guess in a large sense I'm appealing to you to evaluate this. I guess in a sort of passive submission. (Dep + ther, Rel) (Laughs)

I think there *is* a sexual problem. I'm not sure that the real root of it is a *homo*sexual one. My feeling toward this was the same as your reaction to my incestuous reaction to my sister, namely, "O.K., so what?" I'm not sure but what some time in the near future there might be some anxiety about it, though. I'm not sure how long I'll be able to go on suppressing it. (Sex n — homo → Anx)

I would say that your statement that you have some homosexual feelings, but that you aren't worried about them, is one describing an essentially healthy adjustment. (Reassurance) *That is, if it is really* true. *If you took the attitude that you never had a homosexual thought, I would find it hard to believe. If you took the attitude that you couldn't face the idea of any homosexual feelings, I would consider that indicative of some problem in the area.* (Information) *Is the attitude you expressed your real feeling or a rationalized one? That seems to be the major concern here.* (Question)

I haven't felt *so far* any real overt anxiety about this. I do feel anxiety about *some* of my sexual problems, but I don't think they're in this area of homosexual matters. The thoughts are there, and probably the occasional impulses are there, although I'm not too sure about the impulses. (Sex n + homo)

One thing I've always prided myself on was the fact that my sexual adjustment was good, but I think that's a bit unrealistic. During the point in high school where I'd gotten away from people and spent more time in the realm of fantasy and books, there was always high interest in any kind of sexual urge, and of course in masturbatory fantasies. The books were used to induce masturbatory fantasies. I think I've gotten sort of an unrealistic expectation of what a real heterosexual sort of life might be. (Sex n + masturb)

When I was masturbating, I was in a situation where everything was fulfilled. And since I'm the hero in the event, the heroine is always fulfilled. She always reaches a climax at the same time that I do. This makes me a pretty wonderful, big, masculine sort of person. I was going to say a real Charles Atlas sort of type, but decided against it, because that sounds like a homosexual compensation, or defense. (Sex n — homo → Sex n + het) (Pause; client appears to be thinking very hard here.) In the fantasy I'm always real masculine and able to satisfy where no one else is. And yet, when it comes down to sex relations with my wife, although we both enjoy them, so far she hasn't reached a climax. And this is disappointing to me. That's being slapped in the face with reality; I'm not really the kind of guy that satisfies everybody; I'm inadequate. (Sex n — het) And I don't find myself as eager to have intercourse as I thought I would previous to marriage. I'm satisfied with twice to three times a week, and I had the impression that it would be a twice-a-night sort of thing, which I know was unrealistic.

You had sort of a self-perception as a pretty potent individual. (Restatement)

As I think about it, I don't think the primary function of the masturbation was so much for sexual satisfaction as it was for the narcissism. (Ego — self)

Um-hm. What do you mean by narcissism? (Question)

Making myself a pretty potent sort of person, not sexually, but in terms of ability in general. Feeling that I'm adequate. Adequacy doesn't quite fit, because then I'm just on a par with other people, and actually I want to be much better. In graduate school I wasn't superior any more but was merely scraping along. Actually I felt at the bottom of the barrel here. (Anx — prof) In my present job I'm accepted by the faculty. They see me as somebody who has something to offer. (Ego + self)

But the question now is, why is it necessary to have these signs of achievement? I have chosen to aim at a fairly limited level so I can be the top man in the group; I would never aim at the level of a *big* school. I'd like to get a realistic assessment of what I am capable of. It would be a mistake to leave my present job. Where I'm working, nobody would push me to write papers or that sort of thing or even to pass ABEPP. They'll be glad if I get a Ph.D. (Anx — prof)

I'm irritated with myself right now. I had so much I wanted to say, and I even thought I wouldn't get anywhere on just one hour a week. And yet I feel that I'm sitting here sort of wasting time. (Hos n + self; Res) This sounds like a resistance cure, doesn't it. I've told you nasty things about myself; now that I've gotten these off my chest, I can get the hell out of here! And yet this isn't what I want. I want to be nice and passive and be a good client. I guess being passive is as important as anything. (Dep + ther, Rel)

Why did you say that? (Question)

'Cause this is the way I am, or the way I would like to be, when I can get away from accepting responsibility. I guess that's the way I've reacted to *you*. (Dep + ther, Rel) At one point I want you to tell me, "You're doing fine; as long as you see that connection about homosexuality, that's O.K.; you can go ahead now and get away from that topic." Or I want you to forgive me for the bad things I've done. (Dep + ther, Rel) If I can be passive, I won't get in trouble. On the other hand, if I get aggressive, I almost always get myself in trouble because of the anxiety that results. (Hos n + gen $\rightarrow$ Anx $\rightarrow$ Dep — gen)

That constitutes a major sort of struggle for you, the struggle between being aggressive and the way you want to be and getting into trouble, or being good, and passive, and polite, and keeping out of trouble. (Clarification)

I guess it does, although this is a pretty abstract sort of a thing. When you get down to it, I do want to be a nice boy and be liked. I guess the term "nice boy" is kind of revealing, too. I want you to think of me as a good client. And that is a hell of an attitude to come into therapy with. (Dep + ther, Rel) It really doesn't make too much difference what you think, other than that you like me enough to continue seeing me and helping me. And yet I guess the transference is the one thing that has made it possible for me to say some of the things that I have. (Dep + ther, Rel $\rightarrow$ Aff + ther, Rel)

There are times when you display attitudes where I can't decide whether in the dream you were the little guy who was getting stabbed or whether you were the marine who was doing the stabbing. (Interpretation$_5$) And this may be the basis of the situation, that elements of you want to be the marine and do the stabbing, and other elements want to be the guy who gets stabbed. (Interpretation$_9$)

I never thought of myself as a masochist, and yet there were times when I could want to be punished by my supervisor. (Dep — auth $\rightarrow$ Hos n + self) I guess that's what I feel. Sometimes I'd read a bit, in between seeing patients, and he'd always manage to come in then. Then I'd feel guilty as hell. And yet I'd get disgusted with myself for acting like a little boy. How in the hell have I gotten to be twenty-five years old without growing up any more than this? (Dep + auth $\rightarrow$ Anx — self)

There are times when you've wanted to turn to your department head as a good, loyal, kind, protective father. I've half wondered whether you've wanted to turn to me that way. (Interpretation$_7$)

Yes. (Dep + ther, Rel)

Tell the bad things that you've done and be forgiven for them. But definitely be loved. (Interpretation$_7$)

Now there's a point. (Pause) I had to go to the hospital this week, and my parents came up from ———, which is something that I hadn't expected them to do; I was real pleased that they did. (Dep + par $\rightarrow$ Aff n

+ par) There were two occasions in college when I think I wanted my parents to come, and they should have been there. Once when I was in the hospital, and one time when I was in a show. I think I was hurt more by the fact that they didn't come up at that time than I was by the operation itself. (Dep — par → Hos n + par) And yet, in comparison with other parents who are in our same socio-economic stratum, they're demonstrative enough people. Where have I felt that I've missed out? This is a late time to decide that I haven't gotten enough love and affection. (Dep — par)

You described yourself earlier as quite narcissistic. That's what the narcissistic person is looking for. (Interpretation$_4$)

My assumption has been all along that if I need someone now to show me this love and affection, there's been a deprivation somewhere. Now, isn't this so? I'm not narcissistic because my genes fall that way. (Dep — gen → Dep + ther)

That's right. These signs of what would seem to be more than average demands for love might suggest deprivation, almost inevitably. (Information) *Then, one question is, who deprived you of love?* (Question)

That's just what I'm not sure of. Both Dad and Mother are fairly demonstrative over little things. I don't know. (Pause) In a sense there have been times that things have been taken away from me that I've felt I've rightly earned. (Dep — gen) In a sense I'm blocking. I'm disgusted with myself.

Or maybe you want me to say, "It's all right, I know you're trying." (Interpretation$_9$)

I guess I'm just a vain inadequate kid. I know what I ought to be doing, but I'm not doing it. The thing that comes to me just now is that, "Damn it, I can't even make a success out of my therapy." (Anx — self → Anx — ther; Rel)

So that actually there are a lot of deep insecurity feelings. (Clarification) (Pause) *Well, I guess our time is about up.*

I hope it goes better next week.

Jones: Fourth Interview (3/22)

A GAIN TWO appointments had to be skipped, this time because the very bad weather had made the long trip too difficult. However, the client's feelings in this interview were quite favorable, his affect score rising to 86, an increase of 123 points, which is an unusually large one. The therapist's score rose 34 points to a score of 41, which was a good-sized jump for him, although it only brought this interview up to the rank of sixth from the most negative.

The principal affect themes expressed by the client were hostility, sex need, and discussion of the therapy relationship, which occurred in about half of the client's statements in the interview. There were also some responses showing anxiety, dependency, affiliation need, and resistance. The client's affect was directed primarily at the therapist, with small amounts being directed toward his homosexual feelings, his wife, himself, and his father.

In this interview the client reported his first fully recognized transference dream. This was the first interview in which a large percentage of the affect had been directed toward the therapist; some of it was hostile, some of it dependent and friendly. While he had not reached the point of reporting overt homosexual feelings toward the therapist, he was able to discuss other homosexual feelings; he still tended to minimize their importance somewhat, and yet, at the same time, was able to bring up spontaneously certain evidence supporting their presence, such as his general interest in anal activities. Feelings toward the therapist and concern about homosexuality were the predominant themes of the fourth interview, although they were not yet overtly juxtaposed. Mr. Jones was annoyed with the therapist for interpreting the presence of such a connection in the dream which he had reported.

The interview should probably be characterized as being above average in the amount of resistance expressed by the client. He seemed to be approaching important phases of therapeutic activity and holding them off as much as possible. This often took the form of expressing ambivalent feelings toward the therapist: first anger, then dependency, then competitiveness, followed by a real desire for positive feelings. He felt that he was being pushed, but he also chided himself for not making enough effort in therapy. He expressed the wish to discuss his unsatisfactory sexual relationship with his wife, but then indicated that he desired to withhold this information. This was, perhaps, an important clue to the nature of the repressed material approaching the surface.

In the fourth interview the therapist again used questions for quite a large number of his responses (31 per cent). He also made use of interpretation (17 per cent), discussion of the relationship (12 per cent), and the giving of support and reassurance (17 per cent). The increase in support was a new development in this interview, one which may have stemmed from the increasing evidence of dependency in the client's expressions. The interpretations were not usually of a deep level, but mostly reformulations of the client's interview behavior in a way not explicitly recognized by the client (level 5) and use of a preceding client statement to exemplify an unrecognized process that had been building up during the interview (level 7). The amount of discussion by the therapist of the relationship was among the largest in any interview for this client, but it was still much smaller than the client's very frequent mention of relationship (43 per cent). It was apparent that the relationship between the therapist and the client was becoming a major aspect of the therapy; the client was quite ready to recognize his dependency feelings but only vaguely prepared to recognize sexual feelings toward the therapist. The therapist was well aware of the client's still unconscious sexual feelings toward him, but deliberately focused on the dependency feelings, which he considered more basic. Mr. Jones' PAC-NAC dependency score dropped to 33 after this interview.

The use of questions by the therapist remained in this interview one of his principal tools; these questions were uncovering in character, designed to probe further into ideas only touched upon, or to explore the reasons for certain expressions by the client.

I missed being here last weekend, but the weather was so terrible I don't have too many guilt feelings about not attempting it. You finally appeared in my dreams for the first time, (laughs) but I'm not sure what the significance of it is. Perhaps it relates to my feelings of some guilt about not showing up for the interview. (Anx — ther; Rel) Actually both you and your wife were involved, and it was a scene in which you were showing me a wedding album or a scrapbook, or something like that. (Dep + ther, Rel) It didn't make much sense, because it appeared to be just printed pages. That part of the dream wasn't at all frightening. (The dream just mentioned sounds something like a typical transference dream.) But right after that, one incident developed. There was some scene where a father was involved. I'm blocking now. (Pause) My impression now is that he had killed his child, or at least he had gone haywire, and I woke up with the dead child placed in bed with me. My impression is that the child was a boy. Possibly the father was you, running amuck and punishing me for not coming. (Anx — fa → Dep + ther, Rel) (This dream might suggest hostility toward the therapist, or to the client's father or child, or even toward the client himself.)

One very good thing that you do is that you get right to the heart of things without any fooling around. (Approval)

There are a number of mixed reactions I have yet to the last session. I was disgusted with myself at the time because I couldn't do better, and yet this went away fairly rapidly after the session was over. (Dep + ther → Anx) The feeling of discomfort went away, so maybe repression set in. (Res)

Um-hm. How did you feel toward me? (Question; relationship)

I was upset because of your coughing; I even wrote a note about it that night to your wife on my questionnaire. My feelings were mixed. I felt that you weren't able to attend to me the way you ordinarily do. My dream struck me funnier than hell when I think of it, because my reaction was, "Well that'll serve the bastard right, because he misses a week and then the next week when he comes back he's coughing so hard he can hardly listen to me." (Dep — ther, Rel → Hos + ther)

So you did feel good and mad. (Clarification)

I think I was more angry than I was willing to admit. (Hos n + ther)

Aside from my coughing, what could have made you angry? (Question; relationship; the coughing seems an inadequate reason for the hostility expressed.)

Well, we were talking about the homosexuality. In thinking about this in the interval, there were still mixed feelings while I was talking about this; I wanted to get it out of the way, because it is a threatening thing to me. And it's upsetting to think of myself as having homosexual drive. (Sex n — homo → Anx) But with me it's something else again. After the first session when we discussed this I was fairly truthful in saying that I had felt, "It's there; so what?" This was generalized over from the time that we had talked about the incestuous business with my sister. I think my acceptance was an intellectual insight at that point. I think I was upset that it came up again in the last session. I really wanted help at that point, and although your responses were appropriate, I felt that your coughing interfered. (Sex n — homo → Anx → Dep — ther, Rel)

What kind of help did you want? (Question)

I dont know. I think I wanted to be real dependent. Sort of have you pat me on the back and tell me I was going to be all right, and really play daddy to me. (Dep — ther, Rel)

That's what I mean about our going right to the core of things. (Approval)

I'm glad you say that because there's some more about this homosexual business, and I think I would have let it slide by. Thinking back to the general area of sexual adjustment, when I was an undergraduate, "goosing," I suppose is something that goes on in a good many circles. I know *I* over-did it, myself, and I think this was part of the sexual problem at the time, and related to this homosexuality. There was an over-emphasis on sexual conversation. Jokes had to be a double-meaning type of thing. I must have been fighting like hell to be a male at that point. (Sex n + homo → Anx — masc)

What did you mean that you overdid the "goosing?" (Question)

I think I did it more than most of the other guys that lived in the house with me. It's a moderately well accepted sort of thing, and if the homosexual drive is there, why, you can get your kicks from something like that without getting into trouble. (Sex n + homo)

How do you feel if a guy slaps you on the back? (Question)

It would depend on who did it. The last time I can recall it, I got irritated.

How do you feel if somebody makes a homosexual pass or proposition to you? (Question)

The last time I can recall it, I was working with a patient in the hospital, and it didn't upset me. He had told me about being seduced. I tried to reflect his feeling by saying that it must have been very upsetting. He said, "Oh, no, I enjoyed it." He would sidle up to you in the hall and try to be very friendly. Objectively, I don't think I got as upset about it as some of the other staff members. (Sex p — homo)

When I was a kid about eleven, I can remember being approached at a circus. (Describes an attempted seduction by an adult.) I saw it for what it was, and I was shook up about it. I wanted to get away from him; he was kind of a dirty character. (Sex p — homo → Anx)

Referring back to the "goosing," do you feel you have an interest in that part of the body. (Question)

I think so. I think my preferred position for sexual intercourse would be from the rear. And I like to pat my wife on the fanny.

Does that make you anxious or frightened? (Question)

No, I see it for what it is. I think it would seem pretty logically to be part of the homosexual picture. A nice way of having intercourse without having to do the repugnant thing. I like being the aggressor. (Sex n + homo)

How would you feel about being the passive one? (Question)

Gee, I wouldn't like that. It makes me uncomfortable. This would mean I'd have to be the passive one in the relationship, and this wouldn't appeal to me. At least, I don't like to be thought of as being the passive one. It's much easier for me to tolerate the idea of being an aggressive homosexual than a passive one. (Sex n + homo → Anx)

What was that dream about your roommate right before you were married? What happened in the dream? (Directive lead)

Well, I'm less clear on what role I played in that situation than I thought I was before. The recurring impression is that I was the aggressive one. But I'm somewhat blocked up on that, and I'm not sure. And yet, it would seem that if I had had my penis cut off, *I* would be the passive one. This would make more sense. But the castration was the last incident in the dream. Maybe I was being punished for being an aggressor. (Dep — gen → Sex n + homo)

What came before that in the dream? (Question)

Sodomy from the rear. That's my impression. But that's a real cloudy memory by now.

You say you prefer it from the rear. Why? (Question)

Probably then I wouldn't have to face him.

Might you not be prevented from seeing his penis that way? (Interpretation$_9$)

Yeah, that's true. In the actual homosexual incidents I've been involved in, I was the aggressor. (Sex n + homo)

Does it bother you to talk about this? (Question)

No, I feel pretty flat about it. I've been less bothered since the last session, in recalling this . . . I can't remember what it was I recalled. (Res)

How about the first dream that you told me about, the one about the young marine who was stabbing the Jap. Who might the marine be? (Question)

My first reaction right now is to say that it was you. And I don't know why I reacted that way. It was just my impression. In light of this most recent dream that would seem more likely, although it's awfully early to feel that sort of a thing. (Dep — ther, Rel → Sex n + homo, ther) You know, I think I was working hard to get some sort of transference. Or working to get some countertransference out of you. (Dep + ther, Rel → Aff n + ther, Rel)

You know enough about it to know this might happen. (Reassurance)

How do you mean you were working for some countertransference? (Question; relationship)

Just exactly that. I was real anxious to get to the point where what happened to me would make a difference to you. Actually, last time, while I was angry with you, I was upset *for* you. I felt guilty in talking about myself when you were in such obvious distress because of the cough. And of course this shows my own transference. But from the very beginning I was anxious for a relationship to develop. (Dep — ther, Rel → Anx → Nur + ther)

Why did you feel guilty about not coming last week? (Question)

There must have been something that I was afraid to talk about at that point. There were several things that happened during the week to make me anxious. And I wasn't too awfully satisfied, at that point, with the way things were going. (Anx — ther)

You're implying that you were really staying away for other reasons than the weather. (Clarification)

Yeah. I feel I ought to be here, no matter what happens.

And you might have felt that I would think you were trying to get out of coming back. (Interpretation₇)

Yeah. I think so.

I did wonder. But of course I knew the weather was lousy. I thought it would have been a mistake to attempt it under the circumstances. (Reassurance) *But when it was two weeks in a row, I wondered a little.* (Interpretation₅)

Yeah. And it concerned me that you *not* think that it was resistance. (Dep + ther, Rel → Anx)

Perhaps I was a little bit concerned. That would suggest some countertransference. I had some involvement in wanting to see you work through things. (Relationship)

That makes me feel real good when you say that. (Dep + ther, Rel → Aff n + ther)

I only say it because it's true. I'm not trying to flatter you. (Relationship) *When did you dream that my wife and I showed you a book about our wedding?* (Question; relationship)

I think that was this desire for a countertransference, in the sense of you including me in something beyond the therapy, or as a student. (Dep + ther, Rel)

Showing you a little bit of my private life or my love-life? (Interpretation₇)

I guess so. I don't like that business about the love-life. (Sex n + homo → Hos n + ther)

Why? (Question)

Because of the homosexual elements of *our* relationship. (Dep + ther, Rel → Sex n — homo, ther)

It kind of threatens you. (Interpretation$_5$)

Yeah, I guess a little bit. Well, I guess this is as good a place to have a homosexual relationship as any. (Dep + ther, Rel → Sex n + homo, ther)

Well, if there's something there, it's gonna come out. (Information)

Yeah, I guess so. Well, when I have my first homosexual dream about you, I'll tell you. (Hos n + ther) (Laughs)

Now you're trying to put me off. (Criticism)

(Laughs) I am. There must be some reaction there, because just this desire for something that I don't think is dependency alone may not explain all the need for the relationship. This is probably a place where I could be aware of homosexual feelings toward a person and acknowledge them and get away with it. (Dep + ther, Rel → Sex n + homo, ther)

And not be punished for it. (Restatement)

Yeah. And not have to feel too uncomfortable about it.

That's true. (Information) *You could even try to blame it on the therapy.* (Interpretation$_5$)

Yeah, actually it would be easy for me to react that I had been seduced into therapy. But it was a seduction that I wanted. (Dep + ther, Rel) I was ambivalent about coming into therapy, and then in the second session it felt so damn good, and my reaction was a feeling of a tremendous amount of enthusiasm. I felt that something was really happening, here. Then I felt a tremendous let-down the third week. I was ineffective and felt like kicking myself for not doing a decent job. (Dep + ther, Rel → Anx)

You were sort of mad at me for not picking up this business about homosexuality. We talked about it and then let it drop. (Clarification)

I don't know whether that was it or not. I think I was angry with you for not saying that it really wasn't too serious a problem. I was irritated, because I felt the pressure then to keep on with this thing, whether I wanted to or not. So the problem's still there. It looks like *you're* becoming more involved in it. (Dep + ther, Rel → Sex n + homo, ther)

Does that bother you? (Question; relationship)

Not now, it doesn't. I'm trying to think of you now as a homosexual object. It just doesn't go, one way or another. (Sex n — homo, ther; Rel, Res)

How do you feel about me as a father? (Relationship)

I'd like that. One of the things that upset me during the last session was the fact that I wanted so damn much to be dependent on you, but . . . (Dep + ther, Rel)

You were having to be protective again. At least you went out of your way to say, "If this is bothering you, why we can stop." (Interpretation$_9$)

I hadn't thought of that. I thought probably you were being a martyr. (Dep — ther, Rel → Hos n + ther) (Laugh) It was the helplessness that I felt at that point. (Dep — ther)

You wanted a father you could depend on, and he was acting helpless. (Interpretation₇)

No, *I* felt so helpless. (Dep — ther) The situation at the time was so contaminated with so many things. I hadn't thought of this element of the helpless parent, although this is probably part of the picture. But I myself felt helpless, because I wasn't able to carry out the therapy the way I wanted to. And I didn't wanta get back to the point where I was being so dependent again. It's the dependency versus independency conflict again. I didn't like being put in a position where I wasn't able to handle this. (Dep + ther, Rel → Anx)

But you just said you'd like it if I were your father. (Challenging)

Yeah. There are nice, and distasteful, things about both sides of the picture. (Dep + ther → Anx)

That puts it beautifully. (Approving)

I think I feel more concerned about this element of what happens here than anything else at this point. But maybe by talking about this I'm pushing away this homosexual thing, I don't know. Certainly this is the reason I started out with the attitude that I wanted you to be concerned about me. And it's one of the things I find gratifying about being in therapy. (Dep + ther, Rel → Anx → Hos n + ther) But on the other hand I want to demonstrate in therapy that I *am* reasonably adult. But you're probably gonna have one hell of a rough time before things are over. (Hos n + ther)

This sounds threatening. (Interpretation₅) *Sometimes it almost seems as if we might be competing.* (Interpretation₅)

For the dominant role. I guess so. I'm not so sure of it here as I am in my relationship with my department head. (Dep — auth → Hos n + auth)

In a sense we're not competing, but in a sense there are times when you want me to defend you and love you, and be a father to you, and there are times when you . . . (Clarification)

Wanta cut loose from the apron strings.

At times you wanta show that you're a man, too, *now.* (Interpretation₅)

Yes, I didn't like the tone of voice you used when you said that, because my reaction was that you were talking to a little boy, now. (Laughs) This is really picking the therapist apart. (Dep — ther → Hos n + ther)

I guess that's a projection. (Interpretation₅) *I'm sure I didn't feel that way.* (Relationship)

I think I'm feeling a little bit more aggressive today than I usually do. I took a lot of baloney off of a client this morning. (Hos n + gen)

And you're not gonna take it this afternoon. (Clarification) (Both laugh) *Well, this isn't bad, necessarily.* (Reassurance)

You know I find since I started therapy, not *big* insights but little things popping up all along. With my clients, I see myself sitting in their chair time and time again. (Ego + ther; Ins)

I was thinking that if you wanted to express a lot of hostility toward me, that probably this wasn't deserved hostility, that it was transferred hostility. (Interpretation₇)

Yeah, I guess it is. This is the one thing that I block up on so much. It's still difficult for me to say I'm mad at my father. I keep wanting to say, "No, it's not the old man who's the bastard, it's Mother." And yet we keep walking away from Mother in this thing. (Nur + fa → Hos n + mo)

Um-hm. I guess we have to just keep working. (Structuring)

Now I'm getting impatient, as I was before. My reaction after the second session was, "Damn it, we can't get at this fast enough. Let's meet more than once a week." And yet I don't know that it'd go any faster if it were oftener. (Dep — ther → Hos n + ther)

A good bit of the progress is based on the thinking that you do between the times you come in, you see. (Structuring)

But I haven't done as much thinking in the last two weeks as I did in the week between the second and third session. And it was in the third session that I got all slowed down. Well, that was because of the homosexual business, I guess. (Res)

You're doing all right today. You shouldn't derogate the thinking you've done in the last two weeks. (Reassurance) *You said before that you weren't sure whether the homosexual element was as important as this dominance-submissive element. You said maybe you were just trying to get away from the homosexual. I'm not sure that the sexual element ever is as important as the ego element. I believe quite firmly that sex is used by almost all people as a form of ego-enhancement.* (Information)

Um-hm. And we had talked about this in terms of my really feeling I was adequate and my masturbatory fantasies. This would seem to make sense there. One of the things that I've avoided talking about is the relationship between my wife and I. The sexual adjustment has never been as adequate as it has been in fantasy. She's never really achieved an orgasm. She enjoys sex and is as eager for it as I am. Perhaps a little more. But she never talked about it too much. (Sex n — het) Lately we've been trying techniques to stimulate her a little bit more. But I can't say I'm terribly upset about her not achieving an orgasm. That's a real narcissistic thing to say. Actually I recognize that I get very much excited when she appears to be approaching an orgasm. I don't know how we're going to work that out. I guess it will take practice. (Sex n — het)

Jones: Fifth Interview (4/7)

THE FIFTH INTERVIEW constituted something of a regression both in the client's affect toward the therapist and in his feeling of satisfaction with his progress. His affect score dropped 85 points, to 01, which made it one of his lowest scores. (The therapist's affect score remained at 41, its level of the previous interview.) At the end of the interview, the client complained that he did not feel he was accomplishing anything during the hour. However, our classification of client affect-themes reveals that during this hour many of his responses were classified as demonstrating self-insight. There is apparently a considerable amount of difference between the subjective and objective impressions of the insight and progress.

The client's very low affect score may be explained by a feeling which he experienced during this interview but did not report until the subsequent one: he perceived the therapist looking at his tie pin, as though he were looking at his penis. This projection of a sexual anxiety or desire proved to be quite disturbing to the client; his homosexual interest in the therapist was just below the limen of conscious experience at this point and was something he was vigorously resisting.

The interview was an important one, despite the client's feeling that little progress was occurring. It was the meeting immediately following an extra-therapy encounter which was deeply significant. The therapist had participated in a symposium at the client's former internship hospital, and Mr. Jones had attended the symposium and had contrived to have his department head also be present. He had for some time wanted to bring these two men together, although the dynamics of this desire were not entirely clear to the client. During the symposium the client had asked the therapist a question; the therapist returned the question to the client and then commended him for his answer. However, the client found this interchange very threatening and for some time interpreted the therapist's response as an attempt to ridicule him. In the fifth interview, the therapist attempted to help the client perceive the dynamics of the situation with the two father figures, at least as the therapist had seen it, *i.e.*, that the department head represented the client's weak, inadequate father and the therapist represented his idealized, strong father. There was also some possibility, it appeared, of Mr. Jones' identifying with the therapist as an idealized self. Mr. Jones accepted this, but not with too much apparent conviction. His dependency score was 34, which was close to his mean score for the twenty interviews.

During the fifth interview, Mr. Jones' affect was directed primarily toward the therapist and toward his mother. This fact gives a clue to the major areas of insight. The one was that of his ambivalent feelings toward the therapist, as mentioned above. The other was the matter of his hostility toward his mother. Most of the affect-themes in this interview were expressions of hostility and anxiety. About half of the hostility feelings were directed toward his mother. He reported intense annoyance with her dominating and complaining behavior. He also reviewed, in a very intellectual fashion, the history of his Oedipal feelings toward her. He showed almost no affect during the discussion. Whereas his discussion of his feelings about the therapist seemed to be affect-laden and to contain genuine insights, this discussion about his mother seemed perfunctory and non-significant.

During this interview, the therapist's principal activities consisted of questions (27 per cent) and interpretations (21 per cent). He also employed some discussion of the therapeutic relationship (12 per cent), some information-giving and reassurance (15 per cent), and some clarification of feelings (9 per cent). His interpretations related to the discussion of the client's dynamics in bringing the therapist and the department head together.

We visited my family this past week, and I don't think I was too insightful about what was going on. My conscious response to Dad is still one of liking him, and the one to Mother is still pretty antagonistic. On each visit there's always at least one point when Mother starts unloading all the feelings she has, and I just get terribly uncomfortable. My reaction is one of wanting to get away. (Hos n + par) Damned if I know how to handle those situations. At present I just listen and don't take anybody's side.

The conscious feeling toward Dad is to feel sympathetic. Since your interpretations, I've been accepting the fact that there is some *unconscious* hostility. If he would handle the situations more effectively, we wouldn't have to assume the responsibility of being parents. (Hos n + fa) Also there's a conflict between my wife's mother and mine. I don't know how to handle the situation; it makes me feel inadequate. (Dep — gen) I don't know whether to aggress or not to aggress.

This is pretty intellectual, but I think my hostility probably started back in my adolescent incest dreams about Mother. I don't remember much upset about it at the time. I can recall having fantasies about other boys' mothers, too. I don't know just where this fits in with the aggression against Mother. Maybe I felt too threatened by incest, so I beat her away. Although that doesn't mean too much to me right now. My impression was that in the dreams Mother was accepting of this, if not actually enticing. My earliest fantasies, I guess, were the incestuous ones. Because this would be unacceptable, then there would be a regression to the homosexual. (Sex n — het, mo → Sex n + homo)

I just had this association; it must have been about this time that I had what my parents called night terrors. My sister had them, too. I would dream about something being terribly wrong, almost as though it were something wrong with the universe. This sounds pretty grandiose. And I felt that I was responsible for all this. I know, too, that this was when I first started masturbating, and there may have been a lot of guilt. Even now I can get a cold sweat thinking about it. I would scream out loud, and they would walk me up and down the floor. I *think* by now I've gotten rid of most of the masturbatory guilt. (Anx — masturb)

Last week when you were talking about the case in the symposium at the hospital, you said something jokingly about calling on me to answer a question, and I blocked and felt extremely anxious. I perceived this as a hostile act. I remember looking to see your expression in order to know how to interpret the question. I had a hostile reaction; I guess this is a projection. Actually you were giving me a chance to show *my* stuff. (Dom p — ther → Hos n + ther)

I thought you might feel uncomfortable that day. (Reassurance)

Yes, here I was performing for three father-figures. (Therapist, internship supervisor, and department head. He goes on to discuss various staff members.) (Dep — fa → Dep + ther, Rel, auth) Boy, we're jumping all around today.

You were telling me about these night terrors. (Directive lead)

One interesting thing is that when I cried out, it was Mother who would wake me up. Or at least she was the one I cried for. I guess that's pretty important because what hostility there is to Dad must go back to the period before then. *Now,* my conscious reactions to him are love and affection, but not so toward Mother. (Anx — par) But Mother must have been pretty important at *that* period. I don't know when I started to feel she was an antagonistic person. Maybe it was after my brother's death. Mother talked about wanting to adopt another child. I wonder if I might not have felt that she didn't consider us (his sister and himself) good enough. I had a feeling of being left out. She didn't let me feel her abdomen with the baby in it the way she let my sister feel it. (Hos p — mo → Hos n + mo)

They had a woman's secret that you couldn't share. (Clarification)

I get angry when you say that, because the next step would be that I'm a woman, too. I thought you might have had that thought, too. (Hos n + ther)

I thought maybe you felt jealous. (Information)

I did.

They both could have babies, and you couldn't. (Interpretation$_5$)

I don't think I can accept that interpretation. It's hard to swallow. I don't think I ever had any fantasies about wanting babies. (Anx n + ther; Res)

If you had to give up one of your parents, which would you choose? (Question)

Mother. This is interesting. I've had conscious fantasies about my parents dying, and it's been a blatant thing about what I could do with the insurance. I oughta feel guilty, but I don't. (Hos n + par) (Laughs)

If there is hostility to my father, I don't know why I'm having such a hard time bringing it out. But Mother is the one that causes all the trouble in the family. In recent years I've enjoyed doing things a lot with my father. But I can feel more empathy with Mother, too. Her menopausal problems, for example, must be quite disturbing. (Aff n + par)

Clinically, you can perceive that she has reasons for being this way, but this doesn't make it much easier to put up with her. (Clarification)

No. Her griping embarrasses me.

I don't feel we're getting anywhere in this hour. (Res) My feelings toward you have made me pretty upset this hour. Maybe I'm afraid of where we're going. (Dep — ther, Rel → Hos n + ther, Rel)

Let's talk about those feelings. (Directive lead; relationship)

Yeah. I think this has gotten in the way, today. Last week up at the hospital I almost had a feeling you were ridiculing me. It was an odd situation, really. I had initiated having the department head there, possibly before we started having therapy. But his being there produced an uncomfortable situation. I was afraid you would see him as father-figure for me, and you would perceive my motives in inviting him. (Dep — fa → Dep — auth → Dep — ther, Rel → Anx) I think our relationship here has progressed to a point for me that I don't want to pit the two of you against each other. And yet, in a way, I was showing you off to him. I guess I've been letting him know that I'm capable of handling things in my own way. But when I saw something you said as being ridicule, this seemed like debasing me in front of him. I must have come in here today prepared to be angry with you. (Dep — ther, Rel → Hos n + ther, Rel)

I felt lots of empathy for you last week at the hospital. (Relationship)

I wasn't quite sure whether you knew why you had initiated that situation. (Interpretation₉) *I hoped it hadn't bothered you.* (Relationship) *I also felt some empathy for him.* (Information)

I still feel glad that he had a chance to see you in action. I must have identified with you. And I was anxious for him to see how well *I* was doing in the situation. I think I was deliberately instigating situations where you or he would see me operating in a favorable light. I was really excited about that day, in advance. I was looking forward to it; a big day for me. (Dep + ther, Rel)

Why do you think it meant so much to you? (Question)

I'm not sure. I was very anxious for him to meet you, and to be impressed, and to like you. I was pressing him afterward for his reactions to you. It was something that was going to happen to me that was going to be very nice. (Dep + ther)

Did you feel let down? (Question)

No. I realized that any hostility I felt to you was a projection. I realized that you would never ridicule me, or anybody. In class I used to think you were picking on me, when you really weren't. And last week I felt very proud when you asked me what I thought should be done. And you agreed with my solution. It was almost like giving a good recitation. Evidence that you had enough confidence in me that I would give the right response. I had the feeling you were trying to build up my self-confidence. (Dep + ther, Rel → Ego + self)

Why did you want your department head to see me? (Question; relationship)

Well, you're pretty important to me now. Somebody that I have a pretty strong attachment for. He is somebody else that's pretty important to me, and so I want you to like each other. (Dep + auth → Dep + ther, Rel)

In what way are these two people important to you? What roles do they fill? (Question)

(Long pause) I guess I want some of the prestige that you have, and this is one way of getting it. Which is kind of infantile, but that's it. (Dep + ther, Rel)

Would your department head be your father? (Interpretation₇)

I don't know. I've thought about that. I've deliberately tried to think of him as a father-figure. I guess I'm not sure where I stand with him. He's put me in situations where I've been forced to demonstrate that I can handle things well. (Dep − fa → Dep − auth → Anx)

Could I have been you, in the situation at the hospital? (Interpretation₇)

That hadn't occurred to me. (Pause) I don't get the feeling that you could have been. And yet I empathized pretty strongly with you at one point when the psychiatrist was trying to get you to diagnose his kid's troubles. (Aff n + ther)

Perhaps in the interaction with your department head, the role you were putting me in might have been the role of your own ego. (Interpretation$_9$)

I *guess* that's good. I wanted you to do a good job, and I knew you would. (Aff n + ther)

You identified with me. (Clarification)

It may be that this was sort of a challenge to him. By identifying with you, I might be challenging him. In terms of him not being the only person that's important to me. I'm *sure* that's true. (Dep + ther, Rel $\rightarrow$ Hos n + auth)

The thing is fraught with meaning in a way. You set it up to demonstrate something, and I'm trying to find out what you were demonstrating. (Information)

I wanted him to see a situation in which I can function pretty well. I have to prove to him, too, that I'm no longer an undergraduate. That I am a successful professional person. Although he should be the last one that I have to prove it to. (Dep — auth) (Pause) I'm not sure what kind of a role either of you were playing for me. I wonder why we left the supervisor out of this. At one time he was more important to me than you. (Dep — ther surrog) (Pause)

I guess our time's about up. You've touched on a number of important things today. (Reassurance)

I have a sense of discouragement in the sense that I can't figure out the interrelationships. (Dep + ther) But I feel relieved because I think the anger that I had toward you has been somewhat dissipated. (Aff n + ther)

Jones: Sixth Interview (4/13)

THE SIXTH INTERVIEW was a very important one. The client finally gave expression to his homosexual interest in the therapist, and this was a deeply significant insight for him, although very threatening in its implications. He reported his feeling that when the therapist was looking at his tie pin he was actually looking at his penis. Mr. Jones admitted that this was a projection of homosexual fears, and after interpretation by the therapist, he reluctantly admitted that it was a projection of repressed wishes. At first he felt that such an admission was extremely degrading, but following reassurance by the therapist, he became more able to accept the feelings without so much anxiety or guilt.

The other important feeling expressed by Mr. Jones in the sixth interview was one of intense dependency; he finally gave in to his urge to request support. When the desired reassurance was given, Mr. Jones was surprised at the ease with which he accepted the comfort inherent in the support. He identified this need as one of his major problems and accepted, somewhat intellectually, the therapist's interpretation that the dependency need was probably the more basic one, and the homosexual urges were conditioned means of achieving the dependency relationship. After this interview, his PAC-NAC dependency score again rose to 39, his third highest score for any interview.

Later in the interview, Mr. Jones reported a complicated dream which seemed to incorporate the themes of dependency on the therapist, Oedipal attraction to his sister, homosexual interest in the therapist, castration anxiety, sense of inadequacy, and annoyance with the therapist for releasing Mr. Jones' inhibitions. Interpretations of all of these themes were made by the client himself rather than the therapist.

Naturally, the therapeutic relationship was discussed quite fully in the sixth interview. About a quarter of Mr. Jones's responses were about the relationship. Anxiety, sex needs, and dependency were the principal client affect themes. In this interview the client's affect was

directed about equally at three different objects: himself, the therapist,
and his homosexual feelings.

Most of the therapist's responses were questions (30 per cent) and
clarification of feelings (27 per cent). There were also some interpretations (10 per cent), information-giving and reassurance (13 per cent),
and challenging (12 per cent). The general effect of reassurance was
pronounced; even when the therapist was clarifying feelings or interpreting, the effect was to reduce the sense of guilt involved in the revelation of homosexual feelings. Mr. Jones expressed his intense relief
when he had experienced the catharsis of his confessions. This feeling
was also substantiated by the rise in his affect score of 73 points to a
score of 74. It is apparent that Mr. Jones was inclined to experience
marked shifts in the quality and intensity of his emotions toward the
therapist. In this interview, all the anxiety about homosexual feelings
toward the therapist seemed to be relieved, and a strong upswing in
affection took place. The relationship was becoming more intensely
positive as far as the client was concerned. This was also the interview
in which he asked for permission to be dependent upon the therapist,
and when this permission was granted, he felt intensely satisfied. It
seems likely that his major need was being met at this point.

The therapist showed a slight rise in affect score (46), but this
placed his score only at the mean of affect which he displayed toward
this client. His most positive feelings about this client developed later
in therapy.

Well, this is going to be a hard one to start off. Last week I was confused, and I was upset, and I found myself blocking as we were going
along. And I didn't feel comfortable enough at the time to tell you. (Res)
And the reaction afterward was almost, "Well, I ought to run back and tell
him," but that wasn't too logical. (Dep — ther) But at the beginning part
of the interview, I think probably it was the tie clasp I had on. You were
looking at it, and my immediate reaction to it was that you were looking at
my penis. And it scared me. I *guess* it would be scared. And I found myself hesitating on what I was trying to tell you about, and I kinda
blocked on it, but I tried to carry it through anyway. (Dep — ther, Rel →
Sex n — homo → Anx, Res) And, actually I think this is the thing that
shook me up throughout most of the interview. And it's given me qualms
since. It hasn't been easy to tell you about it. I almost have to force it
out right at the beginning. (Dep — ther, Rel → Anx, Res)
  You felt pretty disturbed about it. Pretty upset. (Clarification)
  Then as I tried to follow it through logically, these were the reactions

I had next. "Well, this is a projection." And I can't report to you now exactly what the other associations were along with it, but the general feeling was, "I'm in bad shape." Projections of this sort are pretty extreme. Before I came in that day, I thought I'd made some progress, and this was almost in opposition to it. I didn't feel I was depending on you too much for support, and then my reaction on going home was really the need to run to you to support me at this point. It was a pretty panicky sort of a reaction, and several times during the week I felt I wanted to suppress it. (Dep + ther, Rel → Anx, Res) I'm sure I *re*pressed it throughout the week. I wish I could think of the other reactions I had after I went home Friday night. (Res)

You must have repressed those. (Interpretation₅)

Yeah. But the sum total of the whole thing is that I thought there was some pretty unhealthy, defensive behavior there. (Anx — self)

What do you mean, unhealthy? (Question)

Well, in the sense of being pathological.

Well, that's just a synonym. (Challenging)

I mean that I was *sick*.

That's a synonym too. (Laughs; challenging)

Psychotic, considerably neurotic?

Do you really think it's psychotic? (Challenging)

Not really, no. But it's a threat of coming close to that. Or severely neurotic.

But that's just a name. (Challenging)

I guess what you're getting at, and I'm avoiding, is that I'm a homosexual. (Sex n — homo → Anx)

You're afraid you are. (Clarification)

That wasn't my reaction at the time, that I'm upset because of my level of adjustment. This is true. My reaction was that I'm afraid of being so upset by what's happening, that *I'm* gonna be a patient. (Dep — gen → Anx)

You're afraid it might actually precipitate into something pretty bad, is that right? (Clarification)

Yes, I'm not too sure that I feel so strongly that way right now, but I did at that time. (Anx — gen)

Why might you have thought that I was looking at your penis? (Question)

Well, I can be very rational about it in the sense that I hoped you would, but this doesn't mean a whole lot. (Dep — ther, Rel → Sex n — homo, ther) And this is the thing that upset me most, to think this way about it. That "He's looking to see if I have a homosexual reaction to him." That is, an erection. And I remember a real paranoid sort of suspiciousness. It scares hell out of me to think of myself in that way. (Dep — ther, Rel → Sex n — homo, ther → Anx)

Why? (Question)

Who wants to be psychotic? Who wants to lose control?

That's probably the important phrase there, losing control. (Calls attention)

Yeah, I guess it is. But there's the feeling that maybe I'm getting into something farther than I wanted to. (Anx — ther)

That maybe you were stirring something up that is a bigger thing than you thought it was. (Clarification)

Yeah, if it wasn't bigger, I wouldn't have gotten all the reactions I did last week. I would have passed it off, except for the kind of relationship that's involved here.

What kind of relationship is it? (Relationship)

It's a pretty close one for me. At least, a real important one. And I have to be able to trust *you,* I guess, to have control. (Dep + ther, Rel → Sex n — homo, ther → Anx)

Why did you say you'd have to be able to trust me; trust me in what? (Question)

If I thought you had homosexual impulses toward me, I'd probably have to get out of the situation. I'm defenseless in the situation, because I tell you everything, almost everything, and it's almost as though there's nothing I could do to defend myself. (Dep + ther, Rel → Sex n — homo, ther → Anx)

What might I do? (Question)

I don't know, but that makes me uncomfortable. Ot at least I felt myself flush. (Anx — ther)

It bothers you. You feel worried. You feel unprotected and defenseless. (Clarification)

I rather expect you to be a pretty strong masculine figure, than one who would have impulses. Although that's not being too realistic, because I would assume that this is a problem that everybody has had, that the impulses are there. (Dep + ther, Rel → Sex n — homo, ther)

What are you trying to tell me now? (Question)

Maybe I'm giving you an alibi, in a sense. I wondered about that when I was saying it. This is uncomfortable to talk about. I have a real hesitancy in laying this out in concrete terms. I can just say that you would make sexual advances to me, but I can't go any further. (Dep + ther, Rel → Sex n — homo, ther → Anx)

Well, I didn't mean that I wanted you to describe the specific advances you were afraid that I might make, although that could be profitable, too. (Attenuates) *Why should you be so fearful that I'd take advantage of you?* (Question)

I've come to count pretty heavily on you at this point. If I thought you would do this, this would be a violation of the relationship. In a sense, and this is projection, too, I felt, you've got me into this mess, now don't let me down *now*. I need *that* much support. In other words, be a friend and a therapist, not a seducer. (Dep + ther, Rel → Sex n — homo, ther → Anx)

A therapist would be not much of a therapist if he were to take advantage of a client, that way, would he? (Reassurance)

No. I guess not. I have no reason to believe that this would happen. But just the thought that it might . . . (Pause)

Or that you might want it to? (Interpretation$_9$; the therapist makes the classic analytic interpretation of projected fears of sexual seduction.)

I wasn't going to say that. But I probably would agree with you. (Laughs) We'll call that resistance. I don't know *why* I can't accept that. (Dep + ther, Rel → Sex n — ther, homo → Res)

All right. Let's assume the worst that we could about you. That you were some kind of a homosexual panderer. Is that the worst that could be said? (Question)

I guess so. Boy, I'm shook. (Anx — ther)

What should be done to you then, if this were true? Should you be . . . (Question)

If it were anybody else, I'd say "be understood." And yet, I know *you're* willing to do this, but the concept is just, is so repugnant. (Dep + ther, Rel) I've had enough training. I know how people should react to homosexuals. How, probably, *I* would react to one.

It makes you feel terrible, that there could even be a hint that this might be true. (Clarification) (Pause) *Tell me about the dream where you dreamed that you had a relationship with your roommate.* (Direct lead) (Pause) *You dreamed that your former roommate was letting you perform some kind of sexual act on him. Did you think less of him after that dream?* (Question) (Pause) *It's kinda tough to talk about it, isn't it?* (Very sympathetically said; clarification) (Long pause)

You don't have to talk till you want to. (Reassurance) (Pause) *Are you saying that it would be impossible to tolerate the idea that you might have a passive homosexual impulse?* (Clarification)

In that sense, no. To have the impulse is one thing. But to say that this is something that I desire is another. And it's on this level that I have real trouble with it. And yet, why would I get so upset at the suggestion that this is something that's likely, if it isn't there? And if it's there, why can't I say so? Why doesn't the feeling at least come, "Yes, this is it?" It would be a relief, I think right now, if I could say that, and feel it at the same time. (Sex n — homo → Anx)

It seems like a degrading idea? (Interpretation$_5$)

Yeah, and I guess . . . I wonder if the thing which doesn't keep me from feeling guilty about this is that I think, well, if I don't really want to, then I need not be guilty. But if I come right out and say that this is something I want, then I *am* a homosexual, and this is a point I can't get to. But my feeling at this point is that I'm not gonna be able to be comfortable with myself until it's resolved. (Sex n — homo → Anx)

It won't be resolved as long as you're thinking in terms of phrases like "a homosexual." (Criticism)

Actually, when I think in terms of my roommate, the idea isn't repugnant to me. I'd like it, I guess. (Sex n + homo)

You could have enough respect for him, and like him enough, that if he were to approach you that way, you wouldn't reject him. (Clarification)

No. I'd probably reject actually going through the act. But the idea isn't that repugnant to me. I'd probably enjoy it. As far as you're concerned, I'd probably enjoy it. Now, why couldn't I say that before? (Dep — ther, Rel → Sex n + ther)

It takes time. You also had to know that I wouldn't look down on you if you said it. That you could trust me to respect you even if you did say it. (Reassurance)

I know I could trust you, or I wouldn't even have brought it up, today. (Dep + ther, Rel)

But you probably had some doubts. (Interpretation₅)

I guess there were. But, now where do we go? Ugh! I guess I'm saying, let me be dependent for about five more minutes. (Dep + ther, Rel)

You can be dependent for a long time. (Reassurance)

I don't know what that gains. I don't know whether that brings a sense of relief, or . . . In a sense, being dependent doesn't seem like such *nasty* business. The association I have to that is, "Well, you're almost back in the womb." (Dep + ther, Rel)

It was real comfortable to feel that way. Accepted and protected. (Clarification)

Almost as though I don't have to knock myself out any more in trying to be *in*dependent. This is maybe what I want. Now I don't feel the urge to kick myself for wanting to be dependent. Boy, I sure have a strong superego. I think I never thought of it that way before. You get to the point where you accept almost anything and anybody except yourself, and there's where you become a taskmaster. (Dep + ther, Rel)

When you said that I can be dependent as long as I want, I just felt as though I want to sit here, inert, and not worry any more. I guess what I'm throwing you into is the job of doing my worrying for me. Or at least protecting me, so I don't have to worry. (Dep + ther, Rel) You know, it's just hard for me to believe that all this fuss about my feelings and desires could be expiated by a confession, "Yes, this is something I want." It's too good to be true. (Anx — ther)

I think sex is not the basic drive of life, but only a symptom of some more important drives. I don't think, either, that all of life's problems might

be resolved by a confession that you might react to a male in a passive way?
(Information)

Or an active way. I haven't admitted that, but it was implied in my
dreams and associations. Now here's something that is being dependent,
but I think it's important. Asking you to interpet this is being dependent.
(Dep + ther, Rel) The dream I had last night must be important, in view
of its timing. The dream had me sitting in on an autopsy, and I've wondered
if the pathologist performing it might not be you, although I can't tell.
(Dep + ther) The dissection had begun, and for some reason, rather
than exposing part of the muscle and exploring, the neck had actually
been partially severed, and then the cadaver got up and began to walk
around. And I was real surprised at this, and afraid. (Anx — ther) And
then the pathologist said, "Well, it's just the nerves reacting to the blade."
And, I don't know whether *I* wrestled with the corpse a couple of times
and tried to throw it down. Boy, this *is* symbolic as hell! I think I must
have. (Sex n + het → Anx) (Freudians would believe this dream showed
evidence of castration anxieties.) And then the corpse got away, got out
the door of the morgue, and somehow my sister became involved in this,
and the corpse was chasing her and another girl and somehow or other
abducted them in a car. About this point, the corpse became an old man
with blood around his neck. But they got away all right. My association is
that the corpse is like my id running loose and doing the things I want to
do. (Sex n + het → Anx) I can't recall any homosexual events in it. But
this may have been repressed. Other than the wrestling with the corpse.
(This would usually be considered a sign of homosexual anxiety or desire.)
It strikes me as funny to think of myself making homosexual advances
toward my id. (Laughs) It occurs to me, now, that you weren't doing
anything to stop this. In a sense you're responsible for my running out of
control. I think this is the way I felt about you last night. I was mad at you.
I guess I'm blaming you for letting the corpse get out of control, or letting
me get out of control. (Dep — ther, Rel → Hos n + ther, Rel)

You're feeling angry with me now for having let you go this far. (Clarification)

No, I don't think so, not really. My conscious feeling about you now is
a pretty complacent one. I feel real good. (Dep + ther, Rel → Aff n +
ther, Rel)

You just feel comfortable. (Clarification)

Yeah, and protected. In the dream everything turned out all right. I
don't know what happened to the corpse, whether it disappeared or got
back on the slab. Everything was under control, again. Maybe I'm just
using the dream as an allegory to tell you how I felt at the beginning, in the
middle, and at the end. (Dep + ther, Rel)

I just feel so damn *good,* with this over, that probably I'm gonna have to be dosed up with anxiety again to move anywhere. (Dep + ther, Rel)

Well, it's partly that you told me a deep secret that you felt awfully ashamed of, and I haven't acted disgusted or rejected you. (Information)

Now it's hard for me to see why I should have been ashamed of them. My impression is that this is tied up with some whole larger thing. This feeling of shame. (Ins)

In a sense, actually the sexual problem is not the main problem, whereas you were thinking it was the worst thing you could talk about. (Information)

Yeah. At least it was the part that was the hardest for me to get out, so far. Why should I feel guilty about this? There are some pretty obvious general answers to it, but the specifics of it are just part of me. I don't get it, at this point. (Res)

I don't know whether *this* is important, but this idea occurs to me now. Maybe the acne I've had accounts for the sense of shame. For no good reason, I associate that with masturbation guilt. I know I felt a lot of that. And there was a feeling of not being quite good enough to be with other people, because of the acne. I still react with anxiety to the phrase "pimply youth." (Sex n + masturb → Anx — phys)

You're talking about the things today that make you feel less adequate and less self-confident. (Clarification)

Everything except maybe the *real* reason why I feel less adequate, and that . . . what is it, or where is it? In what way did my parents condition me that I wouldn't feel adequate? When I first came to this school, I kept feeling so inadequate and wondering, "What the hell am I *doing* here?" (Anx — prof) I may have developed somewhat past that point; the feeling is still there enough that I'm not comfortable here on my own say-so. I've gotta have somebody else to reassure me that I'm doing a good job. And I'm not satisfied with that kind of reassurance from my wife. The reassurance has to be from an older male. (Dep — fa → Dep + fa, surrog) (In other words, only a father-figure can give him sufficient reassurance.)

I wonder what my dad did by way of reassuring, if anything. His reaction has always been that it's just expected that I'll do things O.K. His reassurance doesn't help. I know that the reassurance has to come from within myself. (Dep — fa → Dep — auth) I'm getting circular, here.

Jones: Seventh Interview (4/20)

I N THE SEVENTH INTERVIEW, affect reached a highly positive level for both therapist and client. The client's score rose 23 points to a score of 97, which was his second highest score for the entire series of twenty interviews. The therapist's score rose sixteen points to a score of 62, and this was his fourth highest score during the series. The rise of the client's score seems to have been the result of the cumulative effect of the reassurance offered in the sixth interview and the further acceptance by the therapist, in the seventh interview, of the client's dependency.

In this interview Mr. Jones first discussed his disturbance over the apparent weakness he had come to recognize in his father. He felt protective toward him, but he could not admire him, and he greatly wished for a stronger father. In this regard he mentioned his intense admiration for a very virile and successful uncle and his childhood fantasy that this uncle was actually his father. Similarly he mentioned his admiration for the therapist, and his desire to "show him off" in the hospital symposium reported previously. He found himself imitating the therapist in his therapy with his own clients and also feeling that the therapist's interpretations showed a marked amount of insight. Positive transference was at a high level; at one point he perceived himself and his father as siblings who were rivals for the affection of an idealized father in the person of his department head. At another point Mr. Jones identified with the therapist, noting their closeness in age in contrast to his father and the department head, who seemed much older.

The dependency theme was again quite evident in this interview; at one point the client indicated that he would need to draw ego-strength from the therapist until he reached the point where he was able to build up a sufficient reserve of ego-strength for himself. The client made a point of noting his tendency often to look for a strong supportive father-figure on whom he could lean, and to be quite uncomfortable unless such a person were available to him. His post-interview dependency score dropped to 33 after this interview.

One reason for the client's increase in positive affect during this interview may have been the nature of the therapist's handling of the interview. He asked the usual frequent number of questions (28 per cent), and he employed more than the usual amount of clarification of feelings (19 per cent). Also, in this interview he made a larger than usual number of interpretations (28 per cent), and some of these (one-third) were at the "deepest" (ninth) level in Bordin's scheme for classifying depth of interpretation. One of the interpretations which the therapist dwelt on for some time was the matter of the outward signs in dress and mannerisms which substantiated the idea of the client's needing to demonstrate his virility. Another was the interpretation of the client's behavior in the hospital symposium as attempting to identify with the therapist as the ideal father in contrast to the department head as the weak father symbol. Another interpretation related to the client's need to compensate for his own feelings of weakness, rather than to accept them the way his father usually did. Mr. Jones was able to accept all of these interpretations easily and even expressed approval of the further interpretation that he was disappointed when father-figures were weak, and pleased when they were strong and capable of giving support. This theme was repeated several times, and it seems apparent that the matter of his desire to feel support from a strong father-figure was one of Mr. Jones's main dynamics.

In the seventh interview the therapist also gave some information (12 per cent) and support (5 per cent). The idea was implicit in the therapist's discussion that Mr. Jones was welcome to look to the therapist for as much support as he might feel he needed and for as long as he felt this way.

In this interview, Mr. Jones's principal affect themes were dependency, hostility, and affiliation need. The affiliation need and the dependency were closely related and were mostly directed toward the therapist, while the hostility was directed primarily at the client's father. About one-third of Mr. Jones's responses were classified as pertaining to the therapy relationship; the affective valence of these relationship responses was almost entirely positive. Altogether, three-quarters of the responses in this interview were oriented toward supplying fulfillment to the client's expressed needs, rather than frustration. Regarding objects of the client's affect, about two-fifths of his remarks were about his father, a third were about the therapist, and less than one-tenth about the client's mother. Thus, this interview might well be labeled a "father and father-surrogate" interview. It had the highest proportion of any interview of the client's remarks devoted to his father, and remarks pertaining to the therapist or to the relationship in therapy were similarly numerous. It is obvious that he was struggling with his feelings in this area of dependency on a father-figure, and that the therapist was filling at this point the role of a father, as found in the classical transference. It was as the benign, supportive father, however, that Mr. Jones was using him, and not as the authoritarian one.

It's been a pretty comfortable week. I had to go home this weekend; my dad got in an accident. Observing him in a situation where he's pretty helpless, it seemed to me that he was really enjoying the situation where everyone had to do things for him. (Hos n + fa)
What effect did this have on you? (Question)
Not too much of an effect. I just accepted it. There was some question in my mind how much I was reading into the situation. I feel perhaps I *need* to see this sort of thing. Emotionally, I still see Mother as the fly in the ointment. When Dad gets upset and has headaches, my sister and I get concerned, but Mother, rather than giving him support, picks on him and sort of laughs at him. And this makes us feel that we have to go to his side and give him some support. (Hos p — mo → Nur n + fa)
I guess my rational structure for going down there was a pretty flimsy one. I probably did it more to relieve my own tensions than to help the family. (Anx — self)
Was it a sense of expectation upon you, or one of internal compulsion? (Question)
More of the latter. I don't think it really was expected of me, but more my own drive. I guess it's part of the same super-ego that gives me such a hell of a time in other things. (Dep — fa → Nur + fa)
Suppose your mother had been in an accident, would you have felt you had to go? Or wanted to go? (Question)
I think I would. But not with my sister. I could leave my parents in charge of the situation in that case.
An interesting thing has happened. The State Department (Public Instruction) man felt that Dad should demand a raise from the school board, and Dad didn't want to, because the borough was building a new school. You know I feel a real need for the school board to do the right thing by Dad and a desire that they think well of him. The man from Public Instruction took it up with the school board. I almost feel I'd like to guide Dad in what to say, so that he'll make the right impression on them. That's a real reversal of roles. (Dep — fa → Nur + fa)
You feel quite fatherly. (Clarification)

Yeah. It's really clear now. I'm thinking of him now in terms of being a big *kid*. (Dep — fa → Nur n + fa)

Which of you two is the bigger man? The stronger one? (Question)

I think in the final analysis he would be. If I got in trouble, I think finally I would go to him. (Dep + fa) (Pause)

Last week you were upset because you thought that the previous week I had been looking at your tie pin. I thought about it, and I remember I was looking at it. It seemed to be five Trojans lined up in a row, and I wondered why you had to have so many. (Information; Interpretation₉; the therapist is attempting to relate the client's sense of competition with his father to his desire to feel more masculine.)

They were chessmen. I don't get any associations to Trojans. (Pause) Would you be willing to give me yours? (Dep + ther)

It's not too different from the association I make to the pin you have on today (a steam engine). *You never thought your jewelry was diagnostic, I imagine.* (Information) (Both laugh)

Power?

Power and manliness. (Interpretation₉) *The Trojan is a symbol of virility.*

My hobby is model railroads, so that makes it even better. (Conf)

I notice you also wear masculine, collegiate clothes and haircut. These might be unconscious symbols. (Interpretation₆)

I think they're even conscious. I like to think of myself as a young virile sort of guy. I get a kick out of somebody asking me if I ever played football. (Anx — masc)

You told me that illustration to say, in effect, that there is a lot to support the idea of compensation for feelings of inferiority in regard to your masculinity. (Clarification)

I suppose this is mixed up with what we were talking about last week. You know, I felt so much more comfortable after that discussion. I felt like going down and celebrating at the tavern. (Dep + ther; Rel)

What was it that made you feel so exuberant? (Question)

First, saying this, and getting it off my chest; and second, your reaction: "Well, you can be dependent as long as you want." This is the thing I had been denying to myself all along that I want. And yet, with it was the reaction, "Well, it's there if I want it, but I don't think I really need it, now. I don't think I ever *had* that before. Dad wouldn't have been much to fall back on. (The client's sense of satisfaction in being permitted to feel dependent is evident.) (Dep — fa → Dep + ther; Rel)

There was something else I wanted to talk about. I've been noticing in my therapy that I've been imitating you. I'll copy your techniques. I may even copy your exact wordings. I found myself saying, "Well, let's not play God here, Jones." It almost equates you with God, and that's an extremely unrealistic sort of an equation. (Dep + ther; Rel) But I wonder, is this a hostile way of saying that you've been playing God with me? But I guess I've been demanding somebody that's going to be pretty strong. The more God-like you are, the better I'd be satisfied. I guess I don't have a very objective viewpoint about how I feel about you. Sometimes I idealize you, and sometimes I'm mad at you. Both of these extremes are probably not good. (Dep + ther → Hos n, Aff n + ther; Rel)

You can't see me in a normal perspective at present. I seem to show omnipotent perfection, or else I make you angry. (Relationship)

Yeah. And even when you make me angry, I have to conclude that you're right. At least emotionally, I do. (Hos n + ther → Dep + ther; Rel)

Who is the person who usually seems omnipotent to a boy, but also makes him angry? (Question)

It would be the father. I don't think there's any question in my mind that you've been filling that role for me. (Dep — fa → Dep + ther; Rel)

You know what I thought of just now? My uncle Bob, here is a *real* guy, and that reminds me about the many times that I wondered if he wasn't my *real* father. (Dep — fa → Dep + fa surrog)

Perhaps you interpret this uncle, or even myself, as the ideal *father. It's not just as the father, but as the ideal one.* (Interpretation₇)

Yeah. A kind of a father-figure. (Dep — fa → Dep + fa surrog)

Why did you want to show me off to your department head? (Question)

Because you were somebody that was really competent. (Dep + ther) I was thinking he was the weaker father, and I was proving to him how strong I was, or maybe how strong *you* were, the better father. (Dep — auth → Dep + ther; Rel)

That comes pretty close to what I figured out. (Approval) *You might have been showing the weaker father what the ideal father ought to be like. Or at another level, you might have been showing him what* you *were like* (Interpretation₇) *You might have said, "This is what I'll be like twenty years from now."* (Interpretation₇)

You're young enough that in a sense I can identify with you in that way. Because I suspect he's old enough to be *your* father (Dep — auth → Dep + ther: Rel)

I was thinking that he looks *older than my own father.* (Information)

I think Dad looks up to him as sort of a father-figure. That almost puts Dad and me on a sibling level, which is pretty close to the way I see Dad. (Dep — fa → Dep + auth) (Pause)

This business about identifying with Dad in his weakness really begins to impress me. Where do I begin to get the strength from, now? (Pause) The obvious answer would be that I get it from you. I kinda want to have strength of my own. (The client's dependency causes him to ask the therapist to supply him with ego support.) (Dep — fa → Dep — ther; Rel → Anx — self)

Last week I told you you could have some of my strength as long as you wanted it, and you felt a tremendous feeling of comfort. (Offers help; clarification)

That's right. And that thing about my Uncle Bob impresses me. He was a real virile sort of person, attractive to women, and was a success as far as his business was concerned. He was able to supply physical needs for other people; he was always giving money or gifts. And yet he was humble about it. No wonder I had those fantasies about him being my father. (Dep — fa → Dep + fa surrog)

He seemed pretty ideal. (Clarification)

It is becoming clearer, as we go along, what a weak guy my Dad was. And I'm beginning to resent it, now. I've never gotten that far before. (Dep — fa → Hos n — fa)

You feel a father is, or ought to be, a strong person who can give support and strength and help to you in your battles, but your father was not. (Clarification of his ambivalence)

Um-hm. (Pause) I've often thought of myself as a physical coward. I used to like to hear Dad talk about his experiences when he was in the Navy. At that time I could see him as a pretty virile guy. I can remember cutting my hair just the way he does. And then I guess the break must have come when I discovered that he wasn't really as strong a person as I had thought. (Dep — fa → Anx — self)

It's interesting that the first dream you told me was about a strong marine who was bayoneting a Jap. (Interpretation$_4$)

Yeah, but I'm not sure why. I suggested to you at the time that it might be my father. It might have been a wish fulfillment. (Dep — fa → Hos n — fa)

I think people make a mistake in thinking they have only one *father or* one *mother. They have numerous ones who embody different traits.* (Information) *Therapy often helps them to discover these ambivalences.* (Structuring)

This makes me think now of how I attached myself to my department head in college, and then I came up here and didn't find anybody and was real upset about it. And on my internships I looked for it in different supervisors and became disappointed in most of them. (Dep — fa → Dep — auth)

Father-figures who are weak, and take it, and give in, disappoint you. You want them to be strong, or you reject them. (Interpretation$_5$)

Boy, that's a real help. At least now I'll know why I'm doing it. (Pause) I think I'll have more to think about this week. (Aff n + ther; Rel)

Jones: Eighth Interview (4/27)

THE EIGHTH INTERVIEW was probably one of the most important in the entire series in terms of the therapeutic relationship. The interview started with evidence of resistance that was the strongest yet shown by Mr. Jones; he forgot to fill out the Client Affect Scale. The source of this resistance became rapidly apparent in his anxiety about his homosexual feelings toward the therapist and in his efforts to display masculinity in the manner of his dress. Mr. Jones' homosexual feelings were made fairly explicit in a dream he reported which represented an attempted seduction of him by a colleague of the therapist. Reluctantly, the client came to admit that this dream constituted a fulfillment of a subconscious wish.

Other serious anxieties of Mr. Jones were revealed in his discussion of the somewhat unsatisfactory character of his sexual relationship with his wife. He revealed anxiety about his wife's assumption of the more typically masculine role in the sex act; part of his anxiety was due to the fact that he found this behavior by his wife stimulating.

The most important insight of the interview was Mr. Jones' recognition that his homosexual desires were probably secondary manifestations of his dependency urges; the homosexual act became essentially a seduction of the strong father-surrogate, who, in return for the client's sexual favors, would offer protection and nurturance. Thus, the transference dynamics became evident. His dependency score (33) did not change from the level of the previous interview, however.

Mr. Jones also reported the important insight that a sense of inadequacy was very basic to most of his troubles; this, along with dependency, he saw as his principal source of personal problems. He also felt a deep-seated fear that his relationship with his wife, particularly in the sexual area, might possibly constitute a role reversal of the sexes.

The effect of the resistance showed up in the affect scores, which were less positive than after the previous interview; the client's score dropped 35 points to a score of 62, and the therapist's dropped sixteen points to a score of 46. This made them the fifteenth and eleventh most positive scores, respectively, of the twenty different interviews.

As would be expected from the discussion above, most of the client's affect constituted the expression of sex needs and anxiety. There were also fairly pronounced expressions of hostility and dependency. About a fifth of the responses pertained to the therapy relationship, and a smaller number showed insight on the part of the client. The objects of the client's affect were primarily the therapist and the homosexual needs. There was some expression of affect toward the client's wife, his sense of the inadequacy of his masculinity, and his father. The dependency feelings were directed toward the therapist and the client's father; the sex needs were toward the therapist (and occasionally the wife), and the anxiety was directed toward the therapist, the wife, the homosexual feelings, and the concern about masculinity.

The therapist's principal methods of handling the interview were by means of questions (25 per cent) and interpretations (18 per cent). He also used clarification (12 per cent), reassurance (11 per cent), and information (9 per cent). Even more important, he used some calling of the client's attention to certain matters (7 per cent) and challenging and persuading (4 per cent of each). The interpretations are especially important to notice, because most of them were "deep" ones, going far beyond the client's conscious awareness. Some of the interpretations, challenging, or persuasion attempts made by the therapist, were the following:

Hostility to the therapist is usually the result of resistance.
Fear of homosexual seduction may really be a concealed form of wishing for the seduction to occur.
Dreaming that something occurs must be assumed to constitute evidence that it is preoccupying the dreamer.
Use of anal words by a client may indicate homosexual concern or desires.
Mr. Jones' early stabbing dream was probably evidence of homosexual interest.
The client would probably really like to be seduced and does not consider seduction undesirable.
Passive homosexual seduction of the therapist by the client might constitute a means of buying the therapist's nurturant protection of the client.

Obviously, these interpretations were quite strong ones, and might be assumed to be such as to produce much resistance on the part of the client. On the other hand, the therapist apparently used enough reassurance, information-giving, and support to prevent the client from withdrawing completely from therapy.

I must have been angry with you last week, or something, because that's the first time I've forgotten to send in your questionnaire. (Hos n + ther; Res, Rel)

Um-hm. Did you bring it with you? (Question)

No, I didn't. It didn't even occur to me until I drove up on campus this afternoon. And I didn't know what to do at that point.

You haven't filled it out yet? (Question)

No.

Well, what I'd suggest is, fill it out after this interview, remembering as best you can how you felt after last week's interview. (Structuring)

My thoughts are pretty clear about last week's session. I'm very sorry about that. Boy, I had a real panic reaction, when it occurred to me. I deviated from pattern last week and went straight to bed when I went home. (Dep — ther → Anx)

You said you must have been angry with me. (Relationship)

Well, that would be the standard interpretation for something like that. It's sort of like missing a session. And I don't know why I would be angry. (Hos n + ther; Res)

Your explanation of being angry with me would be the traditional one, particularly since you forgot it the whole week. Hostility or resistance. (Interpretation$_5$)

The thing is, I remembered it Saturday, and I was gonna do it after I did another job, and I even mentioned to my wife that I hadn't done it yet; it's interesting that I put it off, because I usually do it first. (Hos n + ther; Res, Rel)

It occurs to me that toward the end of the hour we started discussing the symbolic ways in which I assert my masculinity or adequacy. My conscious reaction was that it was probably true, but that it's not so terribly serious. That's another way of denying that the interpretation has any meaning. (Anx — masc, Res)

In a way, it is, isn't it? In a way you are saying, "So what?" (Interpretation$_5$)

Yeah. That has been my reaction, too. "This is why I wear these clothes. So what." But *why* I'm doing it *is* important. And yet I enjoyed that part of our discussion. Actually, that sort of thing skirts right around what I'm beginning to think is the core of my problem. What can I do to make myself feel more adequate? That still doesn't explain why I might have been angry with you. Usually I'm able to tell you when I'm mad. (Hos n + ther, Rel)

Did you have any thoughts about me on the way home last time, or coming down here today? (Question)

I thought about you in this sense. I had myself another homosexual dream Friday night (after the last therapy interview). And interestingly enough, I was the passive figure. (Dep — gen → Sex n — homo, ther) I can remember this one very, very clearly and very much in detail. I was lying in bed with B.N. (a colleague of the therapist). And the part of the dream that was threatening was where he had his arm over me, and I had my hand laying so that it was right in front of my penis, and he was reaching down and pushing my hand out of the way, and I was giving him some sort of resistance, not too much, but it was an uncomfortable feeling in that it was the same feeling that I've had when I've actually been approached by a homosexual. In a sense that I'm gonna control the situation, but it's embarrassing, because he's a professor, and I wondered why I felt this way about him. (Sex n + homo → Anx) I like him very much, and he's taken an interest in me, but it seemed unlikely that he would actually be the one that's involved. That *you* would be the one; that it was you, rather than he. (Dreaming about a colleague of the therapist is considered a transference dream by psychoanalysts.) And as I thought about it, I remembered my being concerned about my projection that when you were looking at my tie clasp, you were really looking at my penis, but I wasn't really sure. And I don't think, really, at a real deep level, that I'm still not sure that you don't have some homosexual impulses. (Sex n + homo → Anx + ther, Rel) Now I can say, "Sure, logically, this is projection on my part," but the feeling is still there that I don't know for sure that it's projection. And I was anxious about it the next day, for two reasons. The first one was that I thought I had this damn thing licked, after that real trying interview. I thought, "Oh boy, now I'm free!" And then there was the anxiety after this popping up again that I'm not free; it's still there. But then maybe I can expect this sort of thing to come up from time to time, if the impulses are there. Just saying a few simple words isn't going to get me out of it. But I'm gonna have to deal with it, when it does come up, and give myself a chance to get used to it, rather than. . . . I don't know whether this is just a bunch of verbal baloney, or whether it means something (Sex n + homo → Anx — masc) (Laughs)

Let's see. What you're saying at this point is, "Evidently, now, I do have homosexual impulses that may come up sometimes. And I have to handle them and not deny them." (Clarification)

Yeah. It seems reasonable to me. It's only that I'm not rational about this. (Laughs) There was panic at the point where I woke up and started thinking about this thing. But the more I thought about it, the less it bothered me. (Anx — masc)

There was some panic, some anxiety about it. (Clarification)

Yeah.

But then you accepted it, or you could adjust to it. (Clarification)

Yeah, I feel pretty relaxed with the idea now.

Was there any more to the dream than just that one fragment? (Question)

There was, but I don't recall it. I focused on that one element to the extent that the rest of it has been lost. Then the funny thing was that the night after that, for the first time in a long time, I had a real *hetero*sexual dream. And this struck me as kinda funny. (The client then explained that his sexual urges toward his wife, never very strong, had become more active. He was responding to his wife more, and "giving more of himself." They had developed a new sexual technique. He also mentioned a reduction in the general irritation they felt toward each other.) (Sex n + het, wife)

Let's go back a little bit farther. You said that you still wondered whether I didn't have something homosexual about me. (Restatement)

Yeah. I have less of that, now that I'm sitting here.

The last time you brought this up, about two sessions ago, you wondered if when I was looking at your tie clip I might really be looking at your penis, and how did we resolve it that time? (Question)

We didn't, I don't think. Or at least *I* didn't resolve it. (Laughs)

That's better. (Challenging) (Therapist laughs)

The thing that occurs to me right now, and I guess this may be a hostile sort of an expression, but, "O.K., so maybe you *do,* who doesn't?" I doubt seriously if anything would happen here to upset me. Certainly you've run into this sort of problem before me, I believe, and O.K., so there it is, although I don't really feel quite that calmly. (Anx — ther)

Well, we went through that two or three weeks ago, and I reassured you and said a person would be a pretty bad therapist to take advantage of his client in that way. (Reassurance)

That's right. That reassured me. It didn't to the point of your saying, "Well, I don't have that sort of feeling toward you." And yet, you said you thought there was some countertransference here, and I think if there is, there must be some of that feeling. (Aff p — ther → Anx)

Now then, I tried to push another point, which is a point probably we've repressed here: "Could it be that you want *me to have these feelings?"* (Interpretation₉)

Well, that would be the obvious implication.

If not, why would you have dreamed that I might actually have tried to seduce you? Or at least that B.N. did. (Question) *I'll accept your point that he might be a transposed symbol for me. Or he might not even have to be a symbol of me, but . . .* (Interpretation₅)

At least the wish is there. Or the projection wouldn't have been.

B.'s a colleague of mine, actually. (Information)

Somebody, actually, who I think of as being very much like you.

In personality we are rather similar in many ways. (Information)

So the wish is still there.

Maybe you'd like me to attack you. (Interpretation₉)

I wanta say, "Please don't." (Laughs) I'd be being less than honest if I said, "Yes, I would." (Hos n + ther)

So you're not conscious of a feeling of wanting it. (Clarification)

No. I can be intellectual as hell about it and say, "Obviously, it must be there," but I have a feeling that it isn't. (Res)

Well, I'll give you two clues that are probably significant. (Pause) *I'm hesitating, because I wonder if I tell you the clues, whether you'll turn off the mechanism. I've tended to accept the interpretation that whenever the client uses a lot of anal * words, you may find that this is a homosexual overture. Each time you've talked about this, you've used a lot of those words.* (Persuasion) *But now another clue, and here I'm kind of driving home an interpretation. The first dream you told me, the marine who was about to stab the Jap in the back. And you consistently identified me or your father, or both, with the marine. You never identified the Japanese very consistently. But I consistently thought that you were the Japanese.* (Persuasion)

Well, this makes an awful lot of sense. And I don't feel disposed to laugh it off. I guess the desire is there. Now I'm trying to put it in an actual physical sense. To see how well I'm going to be able to handle it. And I'm disturbed by the idea. And yet it really wouldn't be so *bad*. My reaction now is not one of pushing it away, but one of "So what?" And would I feel any better for having a homosexual relationship with you? (Sex n + homo, ther)

Now you're getting at something more important. (Calls attention) *You said the last time that you had a feeling I was trying to get you to admit you were a homosexual. And I said, "No, I'm not." And I still am not.* (Reassurance)

I think the thing that scared me from saying "Yes" was the feeling that then I would act this out. *I* don't think I will. I would feel guilt if I went through an act like this. (Sex n — homo → Anx) This is the thing that would really make the close relationship that I'm after. This would be

* Some of these anal words have been deleted from this text for purposes of publication.

physical proof of the fact that I *am* important to you. (Dep + ther, Rel) And yet I don't really need this sort of proof. It's not sex for sex's sake, but for what the sexual relationship implies.

Proof of love, is that it? (Clarification)

Yeah. Now, if the marine is you and my Dad interchangeably, this must mean that I've never really been sure that he has loved me. And this makes sense too, because I see Dad as being sort of a withdrawn person. We kiss each other when we meet, but it. . . . (Dep — fa → Sex n + homo, ther)

How do you feel about that? (Question)

I felt very uncomfortable about it when I was in my adolescent period. After I'd been away to college a year or so, I kinda liked the idea. Even if other people observed this. That my Dad and I *were* pretty closely related. (Aff n + fa) (Pause) B.N. could stand for B.N. in that dream, as far as that's concerned. In addition to you. I think that you *are* part of it. But I think I would like a very close relationship with someone like B.N. (Dep — fa → Dep + ther surrog) (Pause) Now what would Dad have had to have given me to have proved that he did really love me?

Now that's important. (Calls attention)

He'da had to be someone pretty strong that I could depend on. This goes back to that business about my feeling his weakness, in the sense of his relationship with the people he works for. (Dep — fa) There must have been clues before that, in terms of the relationship between he and mother. This is the part I have difficulty recalling, before age ten. I remember one time when he chased one kid that had been after me continuously. And then he slipped and fell down and somehow or other made an ass of himself. Even there he was pretty impotent. (Dep — fa) (Pause) I'm just full of anal references today, but I can remember another time when I broke wind in church. I remember his sending me out, and this is a real rejection in which he didn't have guts enough to stick it out with me. (Dep — fa → Hos n + fa)

Did you interpret that behavior as a hostile act on your part? (Question)

No. It was purely accidental. Or at least this is the way I felt about it. If one of my clients were saying this, I'd feel that I would have to think, "No, this isn't the answer," but somehow I keep feeling the really important phases were from age ten on. (Pause)

So he couldn't give you love and couldn't give you strong masculine support. (Clarification) *Do you remember, when I said you could be dependent as long as you want to, how blissful you felt?* (Offers help)

M-hm. It felt very blissful. Or very much at ease. Maybe if I felt at ease being dependent along the way, I could have felt more comfortable being *in*dependent. I could kick myself. Actually I've been pushing myself to be far more independent than I am or have any reason to be. (Dep — fa → Dep + ther, Rel → Anx)

(The client then went on to discuss his earlier anger with his father for not being a dependable, supporting person. He expressed occasional annoyance with the therapist when he felt that he, too, was not being sufficiently supporting. The therapist mentioned that the client had admitted seeing him as a loving father and that the client had also dreamed that the therapist seduced him.)

So that potent fathers, while they have their assets, also have their drawbacks. (Dep + fa → Sex n — homo → Anx)

No, that isn't it, because in the dream, I don't think you see the seduction as a drawback. (Interpretation$_9$)

It made me uncomfortable, and yet I wasn't resisting too much. That's very true.

The potent fathers can give you love, and they can give you something that can be depended upon, and if, along with this, they also expect you to be available for gratifying their sex needs, or they even gratify yours without your having to be responsible for it, that's an easy enough thing to accept along with the other advantages they give you. In fact, that's one way to keep them giving you the advantages. Gratify their sex needs. (Interpretation$_9$)

Maybe I've seen this as the only way I have any tie or any real grip on you, or on him. (Dep + ther, Rel → Sex n + ther, homo)

The only way of holding us. (Restatement) (Pause) *How does a woman hold a man?* (Question)

Sexually. What I'm doing now is searching for another way in which to make a tie bind. (Aff n + ther)

I don't think the sex act itself is very important. It doesn't make much difference, in my opinion, whether you have your sex this way or that way, or masturbation with a woman, man, or something else. It's what it means to you that is important, probably. (Reassurance; Information)

Hm. That helps, for this reason. My wife's preferred way of having intercourse is with her in the upper position. And this essentially means that I'm submitting or placed in the lesser role. (Dep + wife → Anx) Now that I'm giving *her* something, an orgasm, the position doesn't make so much difference. (Nur + wife)

You can hold on to her better that way. (Interpretation$_5$)

Yeah, I can give it, or I can withhold it. Don't ask me why I would have thought of withholding it, because consciously I think there are few things that I have been surer of than the fact that she loves me and will stay by me. (Hos n + wife → Anx) But in observing the relationship between Mother and Dad, a relationship in which *he* has been submissive, this is something I would fight against. (Dep — fa → Anx) This is running away from the relationship between you and I. (Dep — ther, Rel)

Well, it doesn't matter too much. We wanta get away from that sometime. When we've got it worked out. Also, I'm not sure that it's too important which relationship we're talking about, so it's your relationship with some other person. (Reassurance; relationship) (Pause) *I still want to make the point again that I'm not trying to prove to you that you're a homosexual.* (Reassurance)

I don't think you are. The thing that I'm rebelling against is the idea that I have these desires. I'm willing to admit that I wouldn't mind. I'm not willing to admit, yet, that I wanta use this as a weapon. (Pause) Yes, I would, for a tool to keep you. I *would* go that far. I'm kinda leery about coming back next week, to be honest with you. (Dep + ther, Rel → Sex n + homo, ther)

Why, you aren't afraid, are you? (Question)

I *am* afraid of exploring this further. (Anx — ther) (End of tape.)

Jones: Ninth Interview (5/18)

THE NINTH INTERVIEW was a very resistant one, in which the client's affect score dropped to —04, his next-to-most negative interview of the entire series. The therapist's affect score stayed approximately the same as before, at 46, near the mean of his twenty scores for this client. It is a little difficult to be certain about the reason for the resistance, except in a general expression by the client of dissatisfaction with himself and with his progress in therapy. He discussed his sense of lonesomeness because of his wife's having been absent from the home for a week. This was in contrast to the pleasure he had anticipated in the freedom which her absence would allow.

Mr. Jones' feelings of dissatisfaction with himself related principally to two areas. One was general dissatisfaction with himself as a poor provider for his family's needs. The other was the anxiety aroused by his sexual inadequacy; it bothered him that his wife showed stronger sexual desires than he did, although when the therapist questioned him carefully, Mr. Jones admitted that except for intercourse in marriage, his sexual drive was fairly strong.

There was also evidence of resentment on Mr. Jones' part against some of the restrictions and obligations which his wife placed upon him, particularly with regard to prohibition against having liquor or beer in the house and with expecting him to perform a certain number of chores around the house.

An important discussion, which probably contributed to Mr. Jones' sense of inadequacy, was that which took place with regard to his attitudes toward sex. He showed quite a bit of inhibition in this area, much more so than his wife.

Mr. Jones indicated, also, the intensity of his desire to avoid family friction and the fact that he probably tolerated domination by his wife because of the strong need to keep peace. He blamed this need on the anxiety aroused in his childhood by his parents' frequent quarrelling.

305

It is probable that the strong resistance evident in the ninth interview was the result of Mr. Jones' growing awareness of this rather overwhelming body of frustrations and inadequacies. Only a slight amount of hostility was expressed toward the therapist.

Four affect needs were discussed about equally by Mr. Jones throughout the ninth interview: anxiety, hostility, dependency, and sex need. Most of the hostility and anxiety were directed toward his wife, but some was directed toward his lack of sufficient masculinity. The sex needs related to his insufficient heterosexual urges toward his wife, and some anxiety was also related to this area. Toward the therapist he expressed mostly dependency and a little hostility. His dependency score dropped to 29 following this interview.

The therapist's participation in the ninth interview was a little unusual in that 54 per cent of his responses were questions and 24 per cent were clarifications. This was qualitatively different from other interviews in that there was so little interpretation or reassurance. The larger than usual number of questions seemed designed to stimulate responses from the client, who was more passive and reticent than usual. Mr. Jones was being rather resistant, but more in a general sense than as a result of specific hostile feelings toward the therapist. However, the therapist's rather frequent use of questions cannot be said to have been very good handling of the interview, particularly since it involved very little of the dynamics which the therapist considered so essential to good therapy, *i.e.,* the therapeutic relationship.

I think I had better start talking about the relationship with my wife. After my wife's illness, I suggested that she go home with her mother for a while so she could get more rest and not have to struggle so much with the baby and the house. So she's been away for a week. I had some mixed feelings about her after she left for her mother's. Before she left, I wasn't too concerned about having her go. (Hos n + wife) But it didn't take long for the reaction to set in after I came home to the empty house. It was nice to be able to read, but I missed her very much, much more than I thought I would. So I think her visit away was a good thing, in terms of what it taught me about my feelings toward her. I realize how dependent I am on her, now. (Dep + wife)

The areas of conflict between us, if that's what it is, are mostly regarding doing this work around the house which I suppose I ought to do. When we were first married and were both working, I was as much the housewife as she was. And I suspect I was even more compulsive about it than she was. But when she stopped working, she started to pamper me a lot more than she had been, and I enjoyed this swing to the opposite pole. And I began letting slide even those things which I ought to have done at home. (Hos n + wife) I wonder whether it's not the tasks I resent, but what they represent in terms of being married and tied down.

I begin to think again of the dependency versus independency thing, and I'm sure this is much closer to the core of our differences. I say I don't like being babied by my wife, but that's in complete opposition to my telling you that I like to be pampered. (Dep + wife) I like to have the work done by somebody else, but I don't like to be made aware that somebody else is taking over the responsibility for it. I want to be the man of the house. I hate to be fussed over in a physical way, and at times I'm a little resentful of the demands my wife might make in terms of showing affection. (Anx — masc) However, I want her to take over responsibilities like handling financial matters. (Dep + wife) I guess I hate to be faced with the fact that the money that comes in doesn't meet the amount we have to pay out each month. (Anx — prof)

I'm not at all clear about our relationship. Why is there this urge to push her away or to not tolerate too much affection-giving? (Dep + wife → Hos n + wife) I don't know exactly what I'm afraid of. I tend to nail it on one thing: constriction. First, I guess, moral religious beliefs. Thinking specifically of having a bottle of beer at home. We can have a drink when we're out, although she'll feel very guilty about it, but she's pretty adamant about not having any alcoholic beverages in the house. And I look forward to having a bottle of beer. And if only I could go off in the evening without feeling that I had to apologize to her. I have felt responsible for bringing her into the present situation where she hasn't had any friends. (Dom p — wife → Hos n + wife)

Where would you go when you went out in the evenings? (Question)

Up to the fraternity house mostly. Once to a movie, and once to visit a friend on the faculty. I like to play bridge with three of the other fellows; I guess it's a sort of regression. I guess I want to be the perpetual college boy. (Anx — matur)

What do you enjoy about visiting the fraternity? (Question)

I guess being a wheel for one thing. I'm president of their alumni association. Actually I never was a wheel when I was only a member. I was such a goof-off that, although most of them liked me, they wouldn't give me any responsibilities. (Anx — matur)

In the back of my mind all along is what I perceive as less of a sexual desire on my part than on my wife's. Maybe this is part of the picture. If she were away, there wouldn't be those sexual demands. She wants to have sex more often than I do, and yet I enjoy it when we have sex. (Sex p — wife → Anx)

How often does she want intercourse? (Question)

Three or four times a week, whereas I would be satisfied with it once a week. I've never delineated it that clearly before, and I feel kind of embarrassed.

You mean that I might think your sex drive wasn't strong enough? (Clarification)

No, because *I* would recognize the fact that I didn't have a strong enough sex drive. (Anx — masc)

How often would you usually masturbate before you were married? (Question)

Probably once or twice a week, but that was because I didn't have the opportunity when I was living with Bill. If left to my own devices it would have been more often; maybe even once a day. That is, if I were in a situation where it was possible, that was the usual frequency. I think it wasn't really a sexual drive in a physiological sense as that this made me feel like a pretty adequate person. (Sex n + masturb)

There's also the possibility that my wife is satisfying herself by using me in the way that we're having intercourse now. Rather than me doing it, it's she who does it. (Sex p — wife → Anx — masc)

She's the aggressor or initiator, you mean? (Clarification)

Yeah, and the method in which we do it. I wish I could get over my feelings about it, because in an emotional sense I know it's a lot more satisfying than the way we did it before. Even though she is in control, I think my eagerness to have intercourse has increased since we started doing it this way. (Sex n + wife)

I feel our discussion is getting sort of vague. (Res) I guess I really want you to take over more control of it, here. I made a note after the last interview that I was becoming more dependent on you. I think that's what I'm asking for now. I want you to tell me where we're going. But I would kind of resent it if I felt you were taking control too much. (Dep — ther, → Rel, Hos n + ther)

You told me today that your wife makes demands of you that you don't particularly like, in terms of housework and in terms of certain religious or moral scruples she has, and she also makes certain sexual demands of you that are something of a problem, or somewhat threatening. (Restatement)

This would make me appear to be less of a man than I like to think of myself as being. And that's true of most things. If I were really the man that I feel I ought to be, I would want to do these things. (Anx — masc)

Just that in every demand that she makes of me, explicit or implicit, and in my failing to measure up, there is just further proof that I'm not a man. Actually it's the way I see myself in the situation and not so much the objective reality of what she does to me. (Dep — wife → Anx — self)

Why do you think you feel pushed when she wants intercourse once a week, but previously you could masturbate as often as every day? (Question; the therapist is directing the client's attention to the contrast between his strong sexual drive and his feeling of sexual inhibition when with his wife.)

I haven't any real emotional insight into it at all. The logic of it would make me think that I'm less of a man, because I don't act as fully as I might in fantasy. (Anx — masc)

What sort of fantasies do you have during intercourse? (Question)

I think about her body, her legs, and her buttocks. I used to concentrate more on her breasts. Since she's been nursing the baby, this is more distasteful. You know, I was reading Jones' equation of milk to semen, this week, and this struck me very pointedly. That's probably the greatest reason why her breasts are less appealing as a sexual object. (Sex n + het)

I have never mentioned this, but my wife enjoys fellatio, although not to the point of orgasm. And I used to have fantasies about cunnilingus, but I never actually got up to the point of participating in it. But I've come fairly close to it. (Sigh) The sexual organs just aren't quite clean for me. If I knew they were, it wouldn't bother me. But the idea of urine being associated with the same areas is just a little bit too much for me. Actually I'm quite sure I would enjoy it if it weren't for that. Probably it harks back to feeling that sex was dirty, somewhere in my childhood. I think of semen as being dirty. But I don't think of her vaginal lubricant as being dirty. (Sex p — het → Anx)

Are you saying that her vagina seems distasteful? (Question; the therapist was aware of his own pun.)

Yeah. I smile at your word distasteful. *No,* not really any more. (Pause) I'm coming to like the intercourse the way we do it, rather than with me being in the superior position. I enjoy her being active in the pre-sex play. (Sex p + het) I have a feeling that this physical part of our relationship was started on its way to being worked out at the beginning of her having orgasms. This proves that I'm a man; man enough to give some satisfaction. (Sex n + het → Ego + masc)

That's something you want to prove pretty badly, don't you? (Clarification)

I figure I must, considering all the time and effort I devote to it. When I get with an authority figure, I almost defensively start a protest to prove that I'm his equal. (Dep — auth → Hos n + auth) I enjoy going to the fraternity because I'm a big wheel now. I enjoy meeting with the college president and telling him how the clinic should be organized, and I have prestige because my word counts for something with him. (Anx — self)

Do you feel like a man when you do the housework? (Question)

(Laughs) I don't know. I always thought I had this pretty well under control; that I could go ahead and do housework, and other guys just couldn't. But maybe I resent it more than I thought I did. (Anx — masc)

The crazy part of it is that I enjoy cooking, and if we have company I like to take over and make breakfast. So at least I enjoy being the woman of the house for that much of the day.

But you aren't allowed to drink, at home. (Interpretation₄)

In a limited sense, no. I could bring a bottle of beer in the house, and put it in the ice box, and drink it in the evening, but it would precipitate dissension, and the last thing I want *is* dissension. (Dep — wife)

Why do you feel that way? (Question)

There was a time in which drink was the worst possible thing in both our homes. And she's gotten around to the point now where she may have a drink herself when we go out. But she draws a line at the house because of the children. This is a taboo that's just too much for her to break. (Dom p — wife) And actually there's a feeling on my part that I'm not just exactly sure about wanting liquor in the home. Emotionally, I'm still reluctant to go completely away from my religious background, and it would be very embarrassing if either of our parents came and found beer in the ice box. (Dep — par)

It's your *home.* (Persuasion)

But again there would be the family dissension and upset. I wouldn't wanta ever see us get to the place where there'd be the almost constant tension that I think existed in my parent's home. (Dep + wife)

You're really trying to avoid that. (Clarification)

Yeah. And this is the reason I don't want us to argue. It was never conceivable to me that a couple could get along without arguing, until I met my wife's sister and her husband. They'll come to a point of dissension and get a little worked up about it, but they recognize that there's a point of disagreement, and then they kiss and make up, and somebody gives in. I like that. We had so damn much open warfare in *our* (parents') home, or feeling of lack of communication, that I don't want any of this for *my* home. (Hos p — par → Anx → Dep + wife)

So you're kind of on guard to avoid it. (Clarification)

And maybe too far on guard. I know logically it's not good just to bottle up the feeling and sit on it, but I don't want to cause an emotional upset. (Dep — wife)

Jones: Tenth Interview (5/26)

THE AFFECT in the tenth interview recovered considerably and moved toward the more positive end of the continuum; the client's affect score rose 82 points to a score of 78, which was around his mean score, and the therapist's score rose fifteen points to a score of 60, his fifth highest score. The most apparent reason for this marked change would seem to have been an insight which Mr. Jones considered to be very significant. He came to the realization that he tended to project his hostile feelings associated with his mother onto his wife, expecting her to be more aggressive and more socially inadequate than she really was. Several times Mr. Jones commented that this insight was going to make a big difference in the quality of the relationship with his wife, for he would now be able to respond to her in terms of reality, rather than of this inaccurate and projected image which construed her as a mother-surrogate.

Except for his near elation with this one insight, most of Mr. Jones' feelings in the tenth interview were rather depressed. He was anxious about a challenge to his religious orthodoxy made by the dean of his college. He spent much of the interview discussing his inadequacy, both in his earlier life and at the present time. He expressed concern about his wife's lack of social sophistication, and he expressed hostility toward his father for being so passive and inadequate and toward his mother for being so dominating and aggressive. He also resented his own tendency to copy his father's life-style.

Perhaps quite important was the repetition of the dependency theme. He expressed anxiety that the therapist seemed to require him to take too much of the responsibility in the therapy and arrived at the insight that when his feelings of inadequacy were able to be eliminated, it might be that his dependency needs would then be considerably reduced. His dependency score rose to 47 after this interview, making it the highest dependency score for any interview. This was a marked increase over the score of 29, obtained after the previous interview. He showed much positive transference, likening the therapist to a "more human" sort of teacher, who was able to orient himself to more worldly matters as well as to idealistic concerns.

The therapist's handling of the tenth interview differed a little from many of the other interviews. He gave a larger amount of clarification of feeling than usual (30 per cent) and smaller amounts of questions and interpretations (18 per cent of each). There was more discussion of the therapy relationship than usual (10 per cent) and a little more of the re-directing techniques (12 per cent) of calling attention, persuasion, a mild challenge, and a mild criticism. In general it appears that the therapist was a little "warmer" during the tenth interview, although hardly enough so to account for the very marked shift in the client's affect score. We are inclined to believe that the greater amounts of clarification of feeling and discussion of the therapy relationship helped to restore some of the client's more positive affect, but that he was also markedly influenced by his insights achieved during this interview.

The client's major affect-themes were anxiety and dependency, with smaller amounts of hostility and affiliation need. Also, some of the responses were perceived as bearing on the therapy relationship, and some showed self-insight. Mr. Jones' feelings were directed mostly toward his wife and the therapist, but also somewhat toward himself, his father, and his mother.

I've been hard put to keep my mind on the long-range instead of the situational problems this week. Our dean has some question about what my philosophy is, and so forth, and has raised this question with the president before I get moved off of probation and onto a regular contract. I've been all riled up about that. It's pretty anxiety-producing, considering the fact that if I didn't get a contract, there's not much time to get another job for the fall. Actually I have a verbal promise from the president, and I guess there isn't much question that it'll go through. (Anx — prof)

I don't think I really want to bother talking about that today. It'll iron itself out. I've been thinking more about the relationship between my wife and me. One of the things that bothered me when we were considering getting married was that she didn't very well match the concept of the girl I thought I'd like to marry. I thought I'd like to marry a pretty suave or sophisticated individual, college graduate and so forth. But the thing about my wife that appealed to me was the fact that she wasn't so sophisticated that she couldn't enjoy things. She was appreciative of little things which would probably make my stereotype of the average college girl give a big yawn. Sometimes I have a vague feeling of embarrassment about my wife.

(Anx — wife) If we have another couple in from the college, and it gets to be a philosophical discussion of some sort, I'm afraid she might not say the right thing. But yet, I think she's concerned about this, too, and she will ask me afterwards whether or not she's done or said the right thing. And she usually has; if she doesn't have anything to contribute to the conversation, she keeps quiet. But she does step in where it seems appropriate, or asks an intelligent question, often. And she fits in with the wives very well. So my feeling of embarrassment is not very realistically based. I think I would like her to be a little bit more pushy than she is, socially. (Anx — → Nur + wife)

Going back to the dean, whenever I get in a period of situational anxiety, it doesn't take me very long to revert to a very dependent pattern. I have to run around and tell everybody about my troubles. Just telling one person won't do. I don't like myself when I do this, because I feel that everybody ought not to know *my* business, and yet the need is so strong to cast the burden of anxiety on somebody else's shoulder. (Dep — gen)

It's a real demanding kind of thing. I don't want just consolation, I want assistance in an active way that will help resolve the situation. (Dep — gen) Last week, when filling out your questionnaire, I had some resentment that you weren't taking a more active role than you were. And today, instead of acceding to my demands, you're listening but not offering as much help as I probably want you to. (Dep — ther, Rel → Hos n + ther)

What would you like me to be doing? (Relationship)

Damned if I know! As irrational as it sounds, I would probably like you to straighten the thing out, and see that my job was there in the fall. (Dep — ther)

A sort of feeling of dependency. (Clarification)

Yeah. And yet it doesn't bother me now to recognize it as such. I can say, "Well, I'm being dependent on you, so what the hell?" But I still would like to be at a point where I could take the situation in my own hands and do something about it. (Dep + ther, Rel → Anx) And yet there are situational aspects of this thing that I *can't* do much about. It's the old problem of the theologian being leery of someone who has a behavioristic background. The dean used to be a minister. Nobody's approached me directly about the matter; it's all been mediated through the department head. My reaction at one point was being angry that they didn't come and see *me* about it. (Hos n + auth)

It's a question of whether your beliefs are orthodox enough? (Question)

That's part of it, but what gripes me is that I've never conceived of myself as being anti-church. I'm active in church affairs. My beliefs are probably not orthodox, but I'm not *opposed* to the teachings of the church. I might think some of their ideas ought to be questioned, but I don't feel like I'm thinking in an undermining way. I think it may not be the job so much, but I think it may be their questioning of my philosophy that annoys me. (Anx — auth)

How do you mean that? (Question) *You're disturbed about the mere fact of their questioning, more than that they might hold up on your job.* (Clarification)

Yeah. Besides, I'm still young enough to be making up my mind about my beliefs; I'm not strongly enough convinced of things yet that I'm going to say, "This is it." Why should I be forced to make that kind of decision at this point? (Dep — gen)

Maybe you want to keep feeling young? (Interpretation$_7$)

That makes plenty of sense. When I was six or seven, I had all of these problems of personal beliefs decided with finality. But I've never had that same type of certainty ever since. Maybe I keep putting off making necessary decisions. The longer I can put this off, the longer I can stay young and dependent. (Dep — gen) I wish things were more systematic, and you could just go down a checklist. I guess that's just another way of being dependent and asking where I'm going from here. (Dep + ther, Rel)

It bothers you that I'm not taking a more active role in doing things about your problems. (Relationship)

It's seemed like almost a sudden change, although it hasn't really been, I guess. Maybe you feel it's time for me to try my wings a little bit, too. And this is a little bit upsetting after being allowed to be as dependent as I pleased. (Dep — ther, Rel → Anx) I feel I must *talk,* whether I have something to say or not.

You feel under some pressure. (Clarification)

Yeah, a pressure to please you and do what is expected of me. (Dep — ther, Rel → Anx — ther)

When did this feeling start? (Question)

Last week. We *had* missed two weeks, and I wanted a whole lot more response from you after not seeing you for that long a time. I had some concern after last week about whether you believed me when I called up the previous week and said that my wife was sick. And yet I had no reason to believe that you didn't accept this. (Dep — ther, Rel → Anx — ther) Well, that was at the time that we had decided we were going to start talking about the relationship. This would be something I wouldn't wanta face up to. (Dep — ther, Rel → Anx — ther)

It might be carrying over to this week. I didn't perceive my own behavior as being more passive than previously. We did change to a new theme, that of your relationship with your wife. But I remember asking a considerable number of leading questions. I remember having the feeling that you didn't carry some ideas far enough, but that it would be too threatening to you at that time to take them farther. (Relationship)

I hadn't recalled, until just now, your asking them. And yet this is true.

I think I felt at the time that I didn't honestly have any more to say about it. (Res)

I would suspect that it was resistance. (Relationship)

Yeah, I didn't feel satisfied afterward. When we get to the point that something has been explored the way it should be, there is a feeling of satisfaction. In a sense I've been harping on this dependency thing. (Dep — ther → Anx)

Well, I think that's pretty important. (Approving)

But it's an aimless sort of an exploration. My reaction now is to go back to the relationships between me and Dad and Mother and when I *was* dependent on them. (Dep — par) In what ways this was encouraged or discouraged. The concept I always had of myself up until recent years was that I could go away from home and not be bothered about it. I worked in camps for the entire summers and wasn't bothered too much. And of course I went away to school, and that didn't bother me; in fact I enjoyed being away from home. (Dep — par → Ego + self)

So you've actually been fairly independent of them. (Clarification)

I have, and I haven't been free of them. Some emotional consideration makes me react to what I think their dictates would be, even after all this time. The times when I can really notice it are in moments of stress; then I go back to the past. I recall being resentful because my parents didn't visit me at times. (Dep — par → Hos n — par) The first time I went to camp they didn't come up to visit me, and almost every other kid's parents did. And I mentioned those times in college which annoyed me because they didn't come to see me perform in a play and so forth. (Dep — par → Hos n — par)

But then the times when they *have* come, I've been embarrassed about being with my Dad. If somebody curses in front of him, I have a feeling of embarrassment. I never am sure whether or not my folks'll do the right thing. It's kind of looking at them like a couple of country hicks, I guess. And I wish they could be a little bit more accepting of other ways of behavior than their own. (Hos n + par)

Being a little more worldly? (Clarification)

Yeah. I can accept teachers who are also able to be like one of the rest of the world. It's funny, but I almost think of you in that way. I guess that's related to the ideal father. Able to be realistic about life. I guess that could make for difficulty at times. (Here the client shows his positive transference toward the therapist in a somewhat different channel than previously.) (Dep — fa → Dep + ther, Rel)

Why? How? (Question)

I might attribute to you some of the more constricted aspects of my father and start rejecting you. Your being a teacher helps to complicate the problem. And yet there's a lot of appeal about the profession, and I've chosen it for myself, in a sense. (Goes on to describe aspects of teaching that he likes.) (Dep — fa → Dep + ther, Rel → Anx)

People who have the teacher's ideals appeal to you if they can also have a certain humanness that you admire. (Clarification)

Very definitely. There's a real tendency for me to look up to this kind of person. (Dep + fa surrog → Dep + ther, Rel)

If your father could have been a little more worldly, although still somewhat idealistic, you could like him better. (Clarification)

I could be a damn sight more comfortable with him. If somebody would have asked me at one point who was the best person I knew, I would have said Dad, but he's almost too saintly to be comfortable with. He has never indicated to me in any way that he expects me to meet his criteria of perfection, or that he's not satisfied with my behavior, and yet I guess it's an implicit demand. I have to try to live up to his idealized life-style. (Dep — fa → Anx)

You have felt an obligation and a compulsion to meet these requirements, even though he hasn't pushed you. (Clarification)

Compulsion is the word. It's interesting, whenever I get anxious, I go through all sorts of compulsive routines, even such things as avoiding cracks in the sidewalk and sometimes magical rituals like knocking on wood. You know, it would almost follow that someone who I see as being pretty saintly would need protection. And I guess mother plays the role of "screwtape," I don't know. (Dep — fa → Nur + fa → Hos + mo)

That's a pretty significant thing to say. (Calls attention) *What did you mean?* (Question)

I was thinking of "The Screwtape Letters." The Devil's apostle. They're a group of letters from someone of the lower dimensions who is trying to seduce a Christian away from his church. If I were to be religious about it, I would say that Mother is Dad's "cross to bear." (Pause) You know, there hasn't been a whole lot at any point along the way that would make me think that Dad was capable of taking care of himself. Or taking care of his family either, for that matter. I don't know why this looms so important for me. (Dep — fa → Hos n — fa)

Well, an adequate *male does these things, doesn't he?* (Interpretation$_5$)

Yeah. Sometimes it's as if he just isn't there. You have the picture of a man who can't handle his wife and can't support his children. (Dep — fa → Hos n — fa)

You're sort of saying, "Mother is the male of the family." (Interpretation$_7$)

Yeah.

You said, "Father is impotent, Mother is a Devil, Mother is a screwtape." (Persuasion)

In a sexual way, I would see her as the more aggressive one; mother is a bastard. (Hos n + mo)

Mother is the boss, and that makes her a bastard, because Dad's the one who has the right to be the boss. (Interpretation₇) *And Dad is a pantywaist because he lets her get away with it.* (Interpretation₇)

Well, you know, I recognize all of this, and I don't know that it makes a hell of a lot of difference in the way I react to them. (Ins)

How about the way you react to yourself? (Question)

I don't know. (Pause)

Or to your wife? (Question)

Now *there's* something I hadn't thought about, and it's probably a key to what gives here. Boy, that's a doozy. She plays the aggressive role sexually, which is Mother all over again. (Hos n + wife; Ins)

She gives you work to do, jobs, tasks. (Persuasion)

(Laughs) Boy, this is such a repetitive pattern here.

Maybe we're going too fast. At least you can't accuse me now *of being too inactive.* (Attenuates) (Both laugh)

I feel better for some reason. (Pause) Well, this was it! I have two feelings now. One is the feeling that I know what it is now, and now I can look at it and deal with it. And the other feeling is that I'm mad at myself because I didn't see this without having to depend on you. (Dep + ther, Rel → Hos n + self)

You think it makes sense now. (Clarification)

It does. This is one of the strongest "A-ha experiences" that I've had. Mother isn't very socially adaptable, just like I worry about my wife perhaps not being. And she's not open to new thoughts. You know I push my wife into some activities. I've been trying like hell to get her to play bridge, and she was real resistant at first. Now she seems to be enjoying it. I don't imagine I see Mother as any intellectual giant, either. A lot of things I projected onto my wife in terms of her capabilities probably weren't part of the picture. (Hos n — mo → Hos n + wife; Ins)

They were really part of your mother. (Clarification)

Yeah. I'm expecting her to be as inadequate as Mother in some respects, and just as domineering in others. Maybe that's why I get a real charge out of her doing some things that start to break down some of the strong moral codes. Like playing bridge or having a social drink with me. (Hos n + wife)

These seem like a symbol of independence from the old ethic. (Clarification)

Boy, I can't get over that insight that I've been reacting to my wife as if she were my mother. Maybe I'm jumping to conclusions, but my wife seems a lot more acceptable now. There really wasn't that much to fear about our relationship. Maybe I'll think of problems at a deeper level, but at present it just seems that there isn't anything to fear now. (Aff n + wife; Ins)

You can understand it, now. (Clarification)

Sometimes I think I've thought about my wife as a mother-figure in a different sense. Not as somebody like Mother, but as somebody serving as a substitute for Mother in the way that she wasn't adequate, that is, somebody I could become dependent upon. And I was worried about this. (Dep — mo → Dep — wife → Anx)

You want to be the man in the family. (Interpretation$_5$) *And you worry that sometimes you might not be.* (Interpretation$_5$)

Yeah, and that explains something else, too. I'm loath to tell my wife about things that are bothering me. If I did this, I feared that I would no longer be the man of the family. (Anx — masc)

You would seem weaker or more dependent. (Clarification)

Yeah. She keeps telling me how wonderful I am, and I never believe it. Which is some indication of how deep this feeling of inadequacy goes. (Anx — self)

I don't wanta ask too much in one afternoon, but you know we have hit all over the place with these feelings of inadequacy, and yet I don't know that I've ever come to any concrete change because of the insights that have come from this. (Dep — ther) The business of identifying with Dad, who is weak. I guess a lot of the answers to this dependent thing are within why I feel inadequate. (Dep — gen → Anx; Ins) Perhaps as the feeling of adequacy increases, why, the need to be dependent will decrease. (This seems like an insight.) I think the other thing that bothers me about becoming so anxious about this was the feeling that after this much time I ought to have made a little progress. And the feeling that I was experiencing a setback. (Dep — ther → Anx)

You felt you shouldn't have been thrown by it, and it was disturbing to think that this was bothering you. (Clarification)

Yeah. And yet we haven't been at this such a long time. Maybe I ought to give myself a little more freedom with this thing. (Ins)

That's right. This is only the tenth interview. (Structuring)

It seems like more than ten, though.

I guess I have the feeling that you've moved quite rapidly in therapy, (Approval) *but also that there's a lot to be covered yet.* (Challenges)

I guess that's true. I haven't had any impulse to say, "Let's stop this." Sometimes I worry about it a little bit because I'm afraid this is just part of the dependency. (He now seems to recognize dependency as his major personal problem.) (Dep — gen → Dep + ther, Rel → Anx) But I'm sure it's been therapeutic, even as far as it's gone.

I think it's made some changes in you, and you've had some pretty definite insights. (Reassurance)

I like the way I am now a lot better. (Ego + self)

Jones: Eleventh Interview (5/29)

THE ELEVENTH INTERVIEW was a significant one, first, because it was the last interview before the summer vacation, but more important, because it was the one in which Mr. Jones showed the strongest positive affect toward the therapist. It also marked the beginning of what appeared to be the second, and more positive, half of the therapy. Except for a slight lapse in positive affect at the session immediately following the summer vacation, Mr. Jones never returned to his former more negative periods. His score of 99 in the eleventh interview was his most positive. The therapist's score remained at about the same level as in the previous interview, *i.e.,* 58, which was his seventh highest score.

There appear to be several therapist activities to account for this marked increase in positive affect on Mr. Jones' part. Mr. Jones had been rather depressed during most of the interview. There was much anxiety and discussion of unsatisfied sex needs and dependency. Also, for the first time, sexual pressures from outside occupied some of the discussion. Thus, about a third of the interview related to unsatisfied sexual needs or pressures. This material took the form of discussion of heterosexual fantasies of extramarital sex acts, and particularly the form of incestuous feelings which Mr. Jones had toward his sister, with much guilt.

What the therapist did, which seems to have produced the intensely positive affect toward him, was to challenge the legitimacy of the guilt feelings. Using some recourse to logical arguments, he stated a conviction that these incest feelings and actions were quite normal. This had the effect of producing a convincing indirect reassurance. In addition to clarification of feelings (18 per cent), 11 per cent of the therapist's remarks were challenging in nature, 14 per cent gave factual information about sex behavior, and 27 per cent were questions, many of which were leading up to a challenge. Rather than threatening the client, this technique tended to produce a great deal of reassurance. Mr. Jones expressed the feeling that his sex play with his sister

319

may have caused her psychological maladjustment. The therapist countered with the interpretation that the feeling of guilt might really be a desire to be punished and that the form the punishment might take would be sexual inhibition, particularly in the marriage situation, which Mr. Jones perceived as a replication of the Oedipal relationship. Mr. Jones also blamed his father's strongly religious precepts for some of the excessive inhibition on his part.

One other principal insight was developed: that Mr. Jones' need to please his parents was based on his rather excessive need to be dependent and to receive love. This dependency problem was only touched upon in a marginal way in the eleventh interview. The therapy relationship was discussed very little. This is somewhat at variance with our observation that the affect was usually most positive when the relationship was being considered. However, although not discussed in the eleventh interview, it is not possible to say that it was not playing a part. Mr. Jones' dependency was being nurtured in a very definite way by the therapist's rather directive and reassuring approach. The therapist was, in fact, playing directly into Mr. Jones' needs in this regard, even though he did not discuss the matter with him. In this sense, then, the nurturance of his dependency needs may still be perceived as accounting for the aspects of the therapeutic relationship which helped Mr. Jones to move forward. The post-interview dependency score dropped to 36 after this interview; while this was a reduction, his score was still three points above his average score for the twenty interviews.

This is one of the first sessions I've come to that I haven't had a whole lot thought out ahead of time that I wanted to talk about. I think it has something to do with that interpretation of me seeing my wife as acting like my mother. It made a lot of sense. I don't know whether I haven't been anxious to explore all the ramifications of this or whether I just don't know where to begin. (Res) I rather suspect it's the former. Last week when I got home after my trip down here my wife was already in bed, and I read the papers for a while. After I got into bed, I had a distinctly uncomfortable experience. My association is the classical one of the Oedipal situation. I've had incestuous dreams in the past, and they weren't particularly disturbing to me. (Sex n + mo → Anx) I can acknowledge these desires. I'm not too sure where to take off from here. (Dep + ther)

It leaves you at something of a loss; you don't know how to go into that. (Clarification)

My wife's frank comments sometimes leave me upset. For instance, yesterday she was asking me about the urinals in a men's lavatory and whether I don't feel uncomfortable standing there with somebody right along side of me. I seem to remember *that* one especially, maybe because of the homosexual implications. Another thing I think about is the casual double meaning that you find in a flirting situation. I could be pretty adept at this sort of thing, but I'm not that way with my wife, I guess because in that situation it takes on real meaning. Maybe I can't face up to the real meaning. It's like being able to talk a good piece of sexual intercourse and then not being able to come through on it. The feeling of inadequacy is still there. I see Mother as a pretty overpowering sort of person. If my wife is Mother at times, it would make sense to think that I just couldn't meet up to her demands. (Sex p — wife → Anx) I can't think what about Mother's demands could have seemed so terrible. I suppose Mother was always wanting Dad to be more adequate. To be able to stand up and do things for himself. I guess that's true. She was always egging him on to assert himself with the board. (Dom p — mo → Anx)

To be more aggressive, more assertive, more manly. (Interpretation₅)

That's a connection I hadn't made before, that assertiveness or aggressiveness is manliness. That makes sense in terms of my own aggressive outbursts at times. (Anx — masc)

Seeing your wife as your mother, and deciding the meaning of this, might be approached from any one of three positions. One would be in terms of what it means with regard to dominance, and the second would be with regard to dependency, and the third would be what it means with regard to sex. (Information; directive leads)

I feel as though I've been banging my head against the wall on this area of sex. I keep coming to obstructions. Actually I don't know that we've gotten involved in it deeply enough, but my reaction is that we've been spending so damn much time on it that I'm getting a little bit sick of it. (Sex n — gen → Anx) I suppose this is resistance. (Res) I don't know which of the three areas to attack first. For some reason, the area of dependency seems to be the one that crops up again and again. I do want to depend on my wife in certain ways, and yet I'm afraid of becoming too dependent. (Dep + wife → Anx) (Here he expresses his basic ambivalence.) It seems to me that in a way she encourages me to feel that I'm the man of the house. We have a standing joke around the house that *I* must make the decisions. I guess there can be hell sometimes when two dependent people get together. (Dep + wife → Anx) I do fear being dominated by a wife. I fear being dependent on my wife. It's real repugnant to me to see one of my uncles being pushed around by his wife. This was part of my own home situation, too. (Dep + wife → Anx)

This sort of thing makes you mad. (Clarification)

There are a lot of implicit controls, ways in which I'm dominated by my wife. But it's not a domination from without, but from within myself. (Dom p — wife → Dep — wife) I feel real uncomfortable in leaving her for an evening, even though I had every reason to think she'd have a good time. It was almost as though I felt it was up to me to keep looking after her. I guess this is domination by dependence. (Dom p — wife → Dep — wife) It irritates me that she's not willing to move out on her own and make these contacts with other women. (Hos n + wife)

The thing that bothers me most is that when I think of a mother-figure, I think in terms of being dependent on her. I am in a good many respects dependent upon my wife, but I don't think this dependency is as pathological an area as some of my other areas, like the one of the controls that she places on me. (Dep + wife)

Maybe I've been brushing off this Oedipal thing a little bit too lightly. I've been trying to cast around for a reason why the sexual relationship is not a completely comfortable one. The only thing that seems to make much sense at this point is that I can't stand the idea of having intercourse with my mother, or the mother-surrogate. (Sex p — mo → Anx)

Other women are still attractive to me, and I assume the reverse is true of her. Sometimes I tease her about that. I tease her about one of the guys who occasionally comes out to visit us. It's sort of a family joke about his being her boy friend. But I'm not at ease teasing her about other women who might be attractive to me. I guess there's a sense of guilt about it. She's teased me about other women, and I felt fairly comfortable about it. No, *she's* felt comfortable, I *haven't* been. (Sex n + het → Anx)

Do you think you could have relations with other women? (Question)

I'm pretty damn sure I couldn't. The idea appeals to me at times, but the old super-ego wouldn't allow me to go through with it. (Sex n + het → Anx)

How about other men? (Question)

You know, I'd feel less guilt about that. This wouldn't be infidelity. And while other women are sexually attractive to me, I can't let myself have fantasies about other women while I'm having intercourse. This would be a *real* infidelity. I've made a conscious effort to refrain from doing this. (Sex n + het → Anx) There's only been one individual who's affected me very strongly that way since we've been married. It was a secretary at the hospital, and I find her a sex machine, anyway. Everything about her, including her dress and mannerisms, seem to be calculated to be sexually stimulating. I've been trying to think who she might be a substitute for, although I don't know that that's necessary, but I think the most logical one is my sister. There are a lot of physical similiarities. Boy, that's pretty threatening! It's the same old incestuous thing all over again. I thought I had this thing out of the way, but I don't think it is, now. (Sex n + sib → Anx)

The thing that is threatening to you is the possibility that you might still have sexual fantasies about your sister, and this would seem very disloyal to your wife. (Interpretation₇)

Yeah. Maybe all the fantasies I had about the secretary were actually my sister. Wow! That disturbs me. (Sex n + sib → Anx)

What's bad about that? (Challenges)

The same thing as was bad before; you don't go around having incestuous thoughts about your sister. (Sex n + sib → Anx)

You say these things quite categorically. What you really mean is, "I don't believe one ought to do this." (Challenges; the therapist is attempting to teach a discrimination between the client's over-generalized principles and the actual reality.)

"I don't believe my parents would approve" is what I probably really mean. This probably comes a hell of a lot closer. (Dom p − par → Anx)

In a sense you were almost denying a reality when you said, "You just don't do that." It's really precisely what you did do, isn't it? (Challenges)

It is a nice way of putting it a little farther away from me, I guess. (Res) (Laughs) Well, let's get back to my sister. The thing that I recall mostly about our sex play was an intense feeling of guilt or, more likely, an intense fear of being caught. Also, a real strong fear of her becoming pregnant, although actually there wasn't any real intercourse, but I did have orgasms. (Sex n + sib → Anx)

This would be one way you would get caught. (Clarification)

Yeah. This would *really* prove that I was a bad boy. (Sex n − sib → Anx)

What's bad about it? (Challenges)

Parents would disapprove. And their approval means a whole lot to me. Oh, hell, I can't find any objective way in which it *is* a bad thing. But it gives me a bad feeling. And the source of the bad feeling is knowing how my parents would feel about it. (Dep − par)

You still want to please them. (Clarification)

Yes, very strongly.

Why? (Question)

(Laughs; pause) I don't honestly know why, other than that it's very upsetting to me to make either of them feel bad. It's the same kind of thing as with my wife: a sense of responsibility or. . . . (Dep − par, wife)

Dependency? You need their love? (Interpretation₇)

(Pause) You know, I guess that may be it. But I'm not so sure that they would *deny* their love. But it would make them feel disappointed in me. (Dep − par, wife)

And you need their approval. You're sure of their love, but you need their approval. (Clarification)

Consciously I'm sure of their love, although I suspect that somewhere along the way there was reason for me to suspect that. . . .

Maybe they haven't seemed loving when you do bad things. (Interpretation₅)

You know, I'm thinking about the time I broke wind in church; now that strikes me as the one situation in which I had done something bad, and Dad had to reject me in front of the group. So, very likely, going against their wishes could result in a loss of love. (Dep — fa)

You don't like to get the disapproval of the people you look up to. (Clarification)

That's the real truth. It is very, very important to be approved of. And I like to be noticed and to have the feeling that I belong. (Dep — gen) (Pause)

You were talking about having intercourse with your sister. (Restatement) *It seemed bad; you felt guilty or less adequate because of it.* (Clarifition)

The thing that occurs to me now is that I would still like to have intercourse with my sister, and it's not too difficult to admit that. (Sex n + sib) Although I'm not sure whether I may be saying this to get you off my back at this point. (Hos n + ther) (Laughs) But I worry about what this might do to her. I think it would be bad, because it might mess her up quite a bit. I think down underneath I still see our sex play as one of the major reasons for her getting herself into so much psychological difficulty. (Sex n — sib → Anx)

So you still have a lot of guilt about it. (Clarification)

Yeah. It's just damn difficult to throw off this feeling that it's wrong. (Sex n — sib → Anx)

Um-hm. If two puppies are in a pen together, male and female littermates, and they start to explore each other, is that bad? (Question)

No. And I can have a client tell me the same problem, and I can play the same role that you're playing with me now, and it's all right for them to say it isn't bad, but it just "ain't" all right for me. (Sex n — sib → Anx)

Maybe you want to feel bad about it. (Interpretation₉)

Or maybe I wanta be punished. (Sex n + het, sib → Anx → Dep — gen)

Maybe.

Boy, this thing has cropped up before. In a sense, it is something that I've gotten away with. I've never been punished for it. Something tells me that I ought to be. (Sex n + het, sib → Anx → Dep — gen)

You invest sex behavior with an awful lot of magical properties. (Disapproval)

Like stepping over cracks in the sidewalk.

That's right. It seems symbolically important. (Clarification)

That's funny that you say that, because I've had a reaction that the whole thing is overrated. It's an important physical urge, only. (Res) (Pause)

Would you feel terrible guilt if you put your finger in your sister's mouth? (Question; this questioning constitutes a sort of Socratic teaching.)

No. And there's no reason why I should feel guilt about putting my penis in her vagina. (Res)

Would you feel guilt if you looked at her when she was naked? (Question)

I probably would, because I'd probably feel some desire. (Sex n — sib → Anx)

Why is a penis in a vagina so much more sacred an act than a finger in a mouth? (Question)

I don't know, other than that it's just an invested role of magical properties that society gives it. I guess if it weren't for the outcome of possible pregnancy, there would be no such investment. (Sex n — sib → Anx)

That may well be the reason why it was invested with this importance, although that wouldn't explain the assumed importance of the so-called perversions. (Information) *Well, I'm directing a barrage of logic at a highly emotional subject. I don't know that logic really meets the demands of an emotional topic.* (Attenuates)

The thing that strikes me at this point is that there's some more basic reason that we haven't gotten to yet. (Ins) One thing that occurs to me at this point is that both my mother's and my sister's attitude toward sex is a lot more clear than mine or my dad's. (Sex n — het → Anx) This may be another way of identifying with the attitudes that Dad had. (Hos n + fa) I don't think he's ever really been comfortable about sex, but maybe I'm projecting. I can recall Mother and my sister making sexual jokes in the family circle, but never Dad. If my sister could still continue to do that, maybe I'm taking a little too much guilt myself. (Sex n + het) It's hard for me to conceive of my parents having intercourse. Maybe I thought Mother and Dad were too good for this sort of thing. (Sex p — par → Anx)

You do carry around a big load of sex guilt. (Interpretation₇)

I sure do, and I wish the hell I knew what the roots of it were. Or what would make me able to be more free about it with my wife.

It occurs to me that if I find out that I'm not going to get external punishment, it would seem that after a while there ought to be enough reinforcement that the guilt wouldn't have to continue. (Sex n + het; Ins) Some of the reactions that you keep giving me in this respect ought to encourage me to believe at some point along the way that maybe I ought not to feel that sex is as dirty as I try to perceive it. (Dep + ther)

The reason I kind of pushed you to dwell on this, so much that you said today that you were sick of talking about sex, is that I have wondered if it wasn't related to your previous statement of some dwindling in your sex desire. (Information) *You indicated that your sexual intercouse was much less frequent than your masturbation used to be. So I wondered if there are some sex-guilt feelings operating to inhibit your sexual behavior in your marriage.* (Question)

I don't think there's any question but what there are. But my question, right now, is, what *is* it that I fear? I guess if I knew what I was afraid of, I'd know where it came from. It's annoying because it's all so damn vague. It would be nice to be able to recall a group of incidents that would account for it, but I'm afraid there aren't any. (Ins)

Perhaps your mother was able to make your sister feel that her sexuality was normal, but your father wasn't able to make you *feel the same way.* (Information)

Yeah. And if I were to establish some sort of sexual role, he would be the one that I would pattern after.

He seemed to be unwilling even to think about sex, let alone talk about it or do anything about it. (Information)

I don't think I'd get as angry now if you suggested that it was Dad that I wished was dead, rather than Mother. It's beginning to make sense, now. (Hos n + fa)

Jones: Twelfth Interview (9/29)

FOLLOWING THE summer vacation, the initial affect during therapy became considerably more negative. The client's score dropped to 35, his sixteenth score out of 20 on a scale of positiveness, and the therapist's score dropped to 27, his seventeenth score. Both client and therapist, thus, were near the least positive levels in their affect toward each other. Mr. Jones expressed the feeling a number of times that he had been deserted by the therapist during the summer when needed and that he had wanted to be dependent on the therapist. He expressed annoyance with the therapist for his more non-directive periods. Somewhat related to this idea was Mr. Jones' seeing the therapist, when he was in one of these "impotent phases," as being similar to his father. There was a lot of transference in this attitude, and Mr. Jones even described a feeling he had that the therapist's physical appearance resembled that of an "inhibited school-teacher" like his father.

One of the decisions which Mr. Jones wanted the therapist to make for him was that he might be allowed to stop seeing a client whose extreme dependence was very annoying to him. This annoyance with dependency reminded him of his annoyance with his father for the same thing; here the dynamics were clarified by the expression of the idea that the reason Mr. Jones resented his father's dependency was that he himself wished to be dependent upon his father, rather than the reverse of this situation. His dependency score (37) remained approximately the same as in the previous interview.

There was only one element of self-approval expressed by Mr. Jones in this interview. He was very satisfied with his handling of a scrape which his sister had gotten herself into, although again he resented his sister's dependency.

One other main theme was covered in the twelfth interview; Mr. Jones had given further thought to his feelings about some of his homosexual urges and had decided that he could tolerate this aspect of his personality. He was able to go further in the direction of self-tolerance and to say that he could even contemplate with enjoyment the prospects of engaging in a homosexual seduction; in this regard, he showed more active and less passive sexual feelings than had been apparent in earlier interviews. He did report, however, conscious fantasies and anxieties about castration which had bothered him since adolescence. These were of a rather unrealistic sort. It may be possible that while Mr. Jones alleged that he was more able to tolerate his homosexual fantasies, his guilt feelings or "super-ego" expressed themselves in the form of the castration anxieties. As a result of recognizing some of the homosexual urges, Mr. Jones wondered whether he was really a well-enough adjusted person to pursue psychotherapy as a profession. Although he expressed some doubt about this, he never conceded any real intention to stop his psychotherapeutic work, and the therapist felt that he was seeking reassurance about his fitness to conduct therapy.

The therapist interpreted quite boldly Mr. Jones' discussion of a new acceptance of homosexual urges as being a possible sign of a desire to be seductive, rather than an increased self-acceptance. This interpretation was somewhat resisted by Mr. Jones at first, but shortly thereafter he admitted quite freely that he did fantasy such an idea. Actually, interpretation was used rather heavily in this interview (23 per cent), and some of the interpretations were quite "deep" in character. The use of clarification of feelings was about average (24 per cent), and the number of questions was considerably less (14 per cent) than usual. There were a number of challenges and calling attention (13 per cent), and nine per cent of the responses dealt with the relationship between therapist and client.

Mr. Jones' principal affect themes were anxiety and sex needs, hostility, and dependency. About a fifth of the responses pertained to the therapeutic relationship, indicating that both the therapist and the client were now tending to focus much of the therapy interaction on the matter of their feelings toward each other. In fact about a fifth of the client's remarks were about the therapist. The only category of remarks which occupied more of the client's attention was that of his homosexual feelings. The twelfth interview was one of the main ones to deal with that topic, along with the sixth and eighth interviews. It was the dominant concern of the twelfth interview. A closely related topic was the concern he expressed about whether he was sufficiently masculine; thus, about four-fifths of the discussion was related to this central issue of sexual identification. The therapist's method of handling this material was somewhat like it had been in previous interviews. He tried to get Mr. Jones to accept the homosexual feelings but also not to build them up in importance. There was not too much discussion of the dynamic of the seductive behavior serving as a way of winning nurturance by a strong father-figure. Mr. Jones' need structure appeared to be changing, and dependency seemed to be reducing. The therapist considered this a healthy change.

It's been a good summer in a good many ways. There were problems that arose during the summer, and some insights that I thought I'd gained, but I can't recall them now. (Ego + self) There was a serious family crisis involving some improper behavior on the part of my sister near the end of the summer. (Anx — sib) (He discusses the incident in detail.) I had to take charge of the situation, which meant spending about a week in various sorts of negotiations and supervisory activities, etc., and telling everyone, including my parents, exactly how to behave in the situation. As you might suspect, Dad was pretty willing for me to take over whatever had to be done. (Hos n + fa) Dad reacted as usual with the notion that this represented failure on his part, so he wanted to talk to me, so as to try to get some psychotherapy or at least reassurance, which I just dreaded. We talked about it, and I tried to be helpful, and I recognized at the time that he was being dependent on me, in his typical way, and that it made me angry. I still feel that the less I have to do this sort of thing, the better I feel. (Hos n + fa) I have a feeling that in a way I might have gained something from it—maybe something of being able to live with and accept him as being this way. (Ego + matur)

I resented the physiological panicky feeling that I thought I had gotten over during this last year and which came back when things were at their worst. I guess my ego was in my stomach at that point. (Anx — gen) I was resentful, too, of my sister imposing herself in my life-space. My wife and I are now virtually her guardians, and I am responsible for her behavior, at least in a psychological sense. She's moved to our town, although she isn't living in our home, but she's in a position where any indiscreet behavior on her part can jeopardize my professional position. (Hos n + sib) Although I must admit that her present adjustment has been exemplary. (Aff n + sib)

But you worried that she could become a problem to you. (Clarification)

Yeah. It occurs to me that maybe the reason I'm telling you about all this is that I'm pretty proud of the way I handled the situation. I'm saying, "Look, I'm a good boy." (Dep + ther, Rel) (Laughs) I think I must have been pretty mad at you for not continuing on with my therapy during the summer. (Dep — ther, Rel → Hos n + ther, Rel)

You felt that by not seeing you, I was letting you down. (Relationship)

Um-hm. I think I really did want to continue on with it during the summer. There must have been mixed feelings; I was glad not to have to make the trip every week. But it would have been nice if you had been available. (Dep + ther, Rel)

Does this perhaps represent a certain ambivalence within yourself. (Clarification)

Yeah. I've thought in recent weeks that in a good many ways I identify you much more closely with my Dad than I thought I had. I think the times when I get angry are times at which you appear to be impotent the way Dad is. (Dep — fa → Dep — ther, Rel → Hos n + ther, Rel; This would appear to be a manifestation of a classic "transference neurosis.") This is pretty hostile, I guess, but I think that sometimes in your physical appearance you might be mistaken for the same kind of inhibited schoolteacher that he is. That *is* hostile! (Hos n + ther, Rel) (Laughs)

I can hardly resist saying, "You can call me any names but inhibited!" (Relationship; Structuring) (Both laugh) *But I see what you mean.* (Attenuates)

I get mad at you at the times when you don't step in in an authoritative way; I like you better when you're being real dynamic and interpreting all over the place! (Dep — ther, Rel → Hos n + ther, Rel) (Both laugh)

You like to have me be forceful and aggressive and sort of dominating, and when I'm more passive or nondirective, I seem to be shirking an obligation or responsibility. (Clarification; Relationship)

I must have been more angry with you than I realized. (Hos n + ther, Rel)

We talked some last spring about my being an ideal father-image and fulfilling roles that your dad wasn't able to fill, and it would seem that when I seem more like him, more passive or inadequate, that then you feel annoyed. (Relationship)

(Client sighs deeply) I just wish to hell he could take care of him*self.* Maybe at one time, maybe even still, I feel, "And take care of me, too." (Dep — fa → Hos n + fa)

You've hit at something fairly significant there, (Calls attention) *that if he could take care of himself, he could take care of you, too.* (Clarification)

I've got other people I could turn to, now, if I need anybody, including you, and the department head. (Dep + ther, auth; Rel)

You don't feel you need to be dependent on him, *and you just wish he wouldn't bother you with* his *dependency.* (Clarification)

Exactly. I don't think there's much question but that *I* still need to be dependent. But I guess I've about given up on him as a source of support. (Dep — fa)

But you're angry with him that this is so. (Clarification)

(Pause; client sighs deeply.) It's hard to get back in the groove today.

I think I'm still dissatisfied with you. (Hos n + ther, Rel, Res) I still must be irritated with you for not being more dynamic. In a sense I'm telling you, "Look, I've done all these things for myself this summer, now you take over for a while." I guess that clears the air a little! (Dep — ther, Rel → Hos n + ther, Rel)

You kind of resented my leaving you in the lurch this summer, and right when things were bad, too. You had to take all the responsibility and be the primary source of strength in the environment, while I had deserted you, which is just what he *usually does.* (Clarification; Relationship; Interpretation₇)

That's true. This is kind of a diversion, but there's something else I wanted to talk about before I left today. It's connected. I have a therapy client now who is a real homesick kid. I was seeing him every day, and I expressed the opinion that he might as well be sent home, for he was just too unhappy and immature to keep him in school. (Hos n + peer) Well, the department head and I have been arguing this back and forth, (Hos n + auth) and he feels I must keep working with him, and I shouldn't be concerned about a possible failure. That I at least ought to give it a try. Well, part of the trouble is that I have a hell of time with these extremely dependent individuals. (Dep — gen → Hos n + peers) The department head said that if for no other reason, I should keep working with him for the sake of getting more experience in handling this sort of problem. But I am still reluctant about it. The department head suggested that we leave the decision up to you. (Dep + ther) One thing that occurred to me was that this was just like dealing with Dad, and that seems to me like a *partial* insight, but maybe it's pretty intellectual. (Dep — fa → Dep + ther)

What does it mean to have someone depending on you? (Question)

(Client sighs) Being dependent on me doesn't fully express it. I'm often gratified if I feel a client is dependent. However, when I really have to be a *father* to them, I think this is the point at which I can't tolerate it. When they're not willing to accept *any* responsibility. (Dep — peer → Hos n + peer)

Someone being passive, or impotent, or incompetent even at making a small decision, or to take any *responsibility, is very irritating to you.* (Clarification)

And this is very much the way Dad behaves. He was completely happy to have me take over all the responsibility. (Hos n + fa)

Well, that isn't the manly way to act, is it? It's a kind of baby way to act. Or perhaps kind of feminine. (Interpretation₇)

Yeah. (Long pause)

The man who acts dependent or feminine irritates you. (Interpretation₇)

Now this is arousing some anxiety. Maybe this is the reason I was anxious about coming in. (Dep — gen → Anx) (Long pause) This explains some other things, too. During the summer one of the medical interns wanted to do some psychotherapy, so I suggested we do some co-therapy, and I guess he was really an aggressive female. Quite a bit of dependency about him, and I became quite irritated with him. (Sex p — homo → Hos n + peer)

Let's see if we can go into why it should bother you for a man to act in a feminine way, or a passive way. (Directive lead)

Well, the obvious is that I react in some sexual way toward them. And yet I didn't think that this was so upsetting any more. What happens, I think, is this. It's one thing to make the intellectual admission that there are some homosexual ways in which I behave, but to face this kind of thing seriously is still threatening. (Sex n + homo → Anx)

You can be intellectual about it, but to say it with any meaning, and about yourself, is hard. (Clarification)

Yeah. And yet I know I *do*. You know, the idea of sodomy has a certain amount of appeal to me, whereas before I think I'd have given you the reaction that this was pretty repugnant. I don't know whether this is progress of a sort or not. (Sex n + homo: Ins)

You think it might be progress that you can find that idea stimulating. (Restatement)

I feel kind of good about it; kinda pleased. (Ego + self) And I have sort of a "So what" reaction, but it's more sincere this time. (Pause) Do I see these people as being seductive? (Sex p + homo)

That's a good question. (Calls attention) *Which role do you find more appealing, the passive or active?* (Question)

Active. Using *them* as the feminine partner. Before I couldn't have told you. I would have blocked on which role I wanted. (Sex n + homo; it is probably a favorable sign that the client's homosexual fantasies appear to have shifted from a more passive to a more active role in the sex act; this would suggest an increase in the more normal aggressiveness of the male.) (Pause) This explains something else, too. This is something I've never done before with a client, but after I read about him in the reports from his professors, I thought, "Boy, this would be a good one to try some hypnotism on." And I built up some good rationalizations for it. He had a functional tremor, and organicity had been ruled out. So I think I did a nice job of seducing the boy. (Sex n + homo → Dom n + peer) (Pause) I don't think I was going to tell you about it. (Res)

Why? You felt a little anxious about it, or ashamed of it? (Clarification)

I am ashamed to tell you that I attempted to hypnotize somebody. From a theoretical standpoint it's not a good idea to do it to somebody who's already extremely dependent. And yet I went ahead and did it anyway. I guess I told myself that I wanted to see whether I could do it. (Dom n + peer → Anx — ther)

You're sort of implying that you did this, in a sense, for some gratification of your own, that you were enjoying being somewhat seductive. (Clarification)

It *was* for my gratification. And if not seductive, at least I was being powerful. (Dom n + peer)

Are you telling me that you thought you could contemplate with satisfaction the idea of having intercourse with one of these passive males? (Interpretation9)

(Sighs; pause.) The idea hadn't overtly occurred to me with *this* kid.

When you said it hadn't occurred to you with this *kid, it sounded as though you were implying that it had occurred to you with regard to* some *kid.* (Interpretation5)

Yeah, it did. That client I was seeing up here last year. I consciously contemplated it, and it wasn't too distasteful. (Sex n + homo) Maybe this has something to do with this thing that's been bothering me. It's something that I've been very reluctant to bring up with you. That is, ought I to continue to do psychotherapy? And also, is this really something that I'm interested in? (Anx — prof)

Why do you wonder whether you ought to? Because you're afraid that you're doing it for an inappropriate purpose? (Question)

Yeah, and it never occurred to me until today that it may be in terms of wanting to seduce my clients. (Sex n — homo, Ins)

It's certainly an important question. (Calls attention) *I don't think we could answer it, today. But we might consider it.* (Structuring) *Probably most therapists don't give it sufficient thought.* (Persuasion)

The thing that's really upsetting about considering this is that I've spent a hell of a lot of time and anxiety so far in trying to learn to be a psychotherapist, and it's not something that's gonna be very easily laid aside. If you were to tell me now that I shouldn't be one, I would resist very strongly. (Anx — prof)

You want me to tell you that it's O.K. to go ahead. (Interpretation5)

It would be reassuring, but it wouldn't really make much difference I think. I've gotta convince *myself* one way or the other. Or be convinced. (Hos n + ther) This business about seducing clients would be a damn good explanation of why I find it difficult to warm up to them. Maybe you're right in this business that I'm afraid of getting too close. (Sex n + peers → Anx, Ins)

Therapy involves a certain closeness or intimacy that could be something you couldn't control. (Interpretation7)

I must be afraid to say that I couldn't control it. (Anx — ther; Ins)

I'm still not quite sure why you were pleased to tell me that you could contemplate the idea of seducing a male. (Question) *Would it be a way of telling me that you weren't too threatened by a homosexual idea? Could it even have been sort of seductive, a way of telling me that you were available? (Interpretation₉)*

That might be. I had an association of seducing you and found it not unpleasant. There's something to this idea that seducing an individual is a good way of holding on to them. (Dep — ther, Rel → Sex n + ther, homo, Rel)

In fact, I think we came to the conclusion that that was the purpose of seducing people. (Information) Or at least a purpose. You contemplated the idea that you could enjoy seducing me, too. (Clarification)

I could hold on to you. There are some anxieties associated with this idea, though. I have the sensation that I'm not going to be very comfortable on the way home, today. (Dep — ther, Rel → Sex n + ther, homo, Rel) (Laughs)

I think you tend to symbolize very often in sexual terms. (Attenuates) It would be interesting to know what seducing people does mean to you. (Question) I expect it means more than just orgasms. (Interpretation₇)

It means guilt. Damn near any association I have to any form of sexual play involves guilt, whether it involves my seducing or being seduced. Whether it involves incest, homosexual play, or pre-marital activity, it's all guilt. (Sex n — gen → Anx)

I thought you would respond that seduction might be a symbol of power, control, or potency. (Interpretation₉) Or you might have responded that it might be a symbol of love-seeking. (Interpretation₉)

Or a symbol of being castrated. Actually *losing* potency. (Anx — masc) I was reading Reik this summer, *Listening with the Third Ear,* and I enjoyed that. And one of the phobias I have is about swimming. This is rampant with symbolism, but there's always the fear of snakes in the water. My first association to the snake was that maybe I'll be sexually exploited by some males; but it's not that, it's the fear of losing something. I fear being castrated by this snake, he's going to bite my penis off. When in reality it should be the vagina that would bite my penis off. (Sex n — homo → Anx — masc) But I guess too, in that dream where I was castrated for having intercourse with Bill—that's interesting, Bill Snyder, Bill X. (laughs) —when I had this dream I was castrated, it was sodomy, and I rather suspect that in some way the other penis castrates mine, in spite of the fact that I'm the *active* partner. (Sex n + homo, ther → Anx — masc, Rel) Maybe Father will castrate me. (Anx — fa; The client is fully aware of the elements of "transference neurosis," as revealed in the reference to the therapist.)

I don't know why you should say, "In spite of the fact." (Challenging) The castration is punishment for the act, not in spite of it. (Interpretation₉)

But another association I have is that I always feared the stopper being pulled out of the bathtub while I was in there, and the water going out, and I associated this to a newspaper story of a snake coming up the pipe. And this gave me something concrete to hang on. This snake was going to castrate me. Now whether Father's penis stands for Father, or what, I don't know. (Sex n — gen → Anx — masc)

Well, this is all pretty rich symbolism, and nobody can know, at this point. It fits certain classic pictures. Perhaps it's too classic in some ways. (Challenging; the therapist did not interpret the obvious symbolism of the client's identification with the female role at this point.) *You're sophisticated enough in Freudian dynamics that you might subconsciously invent these ideas, too, or these dreams.* (Challenging) *It'll take time to find out the real meaning of them.* (Structures; the therapist felt that the client was using Freudian symbolism to escape serious ego-damaging thoughts about himself.)

I'm trying to get these things over to you so they can get across while I think about them. I can recall having dreams about having a car; even in recent months, maybe even weeks, I dreamed about having a Model A. Before I learned to drive, I remember dreams of having a car, and after I learned to drive, then I was in control. After I was sexually potent, why I became a real driver. (Sex n — homo → Anx — masc) (Laughs) Reik's talking about the car being feminine symbol, and yet, when I had talked to *you* before about it, about my roommate's car, you called it a phallic symbol. I'd always thought of it as being rather masculine, and then I began to wonder about it being feminine. (Sex n — homo → Anx) The fact that the dream recurs makes me feel that it's important. (Dep + ther, Rel)

It's important, but certainly very difficult to interpret. (Challenging) *It would require a lot of collateral thinking; it could be about either sex, perhaps.* (Structuring; the therapist was a bit disturbed by the client's jumping around among sexual symbols in an unsystematic manner; this seemed to be an avoidance mechanism.) (Pause) *I guess our time's just about up. We seem to be right back into the midst of things again.* (Approval)

Yeah. I think, after talking with you, that maybe I ought to try to continue on with this boy I have in therapy now. (Dep + ther → Ego + self)

Jones: Thirteenth Interview (10/2)

THE THIRTEENTH INTERVIEW might be called "the neurotic and resistant interview." Resistance and the desire to hold on to some of the client's more neurotic behaviors seemed to characterize its dynamics. Mr. Jones expressed the desire to relax in therapy and not to have to work at it. He asked for permission to be more dependent on the therapist and compared himself to a small boy asking his father to "make everything all right" for him. He also was irritated with the therapist's passivity, and he said he was afraid of some of the insights which might be turned up in therapy; he particularly feared that his marriage might be damaged by something he would discover about himself. His dependency score rose to 43, his second highest score for any interview.

Late in the interview, Mr. Jones asked whether the therapy relationship might be comparable to that of a marriage. There were, in fact, numerous signs of transference, such as this question and his calling the therapist "Daddy." His fear that the therapy might be comparable to a marriage was related to a concern that perhaps his behavior might constitute an attempt at seduction of the therapist.

There was quite a bit of discussion of the therapy relationship and of what Mr. Jones and the therapist expected of each other. Some of this discussion was slightly hostile, and some was very friendly. Mr. Jones also expressed the feeling that he had made progress during the interview. This impression was borne out by the rise in his affect score from 35 to 68, which brought it up to around his mean score. His optimism was not shared by the therapist, whose affect scored 18, his next-to-lowest score for the entire treatment.

Mr. Jones' "complaints" were focused mostly around problems related to the marriage relationship. He was very critical of his wife for being too dominating and sexually aggressive. There seemed also to be some disagreement with his wife about financial and religious matters; he felt guilty for not being able to provide well financially. His wife felt irritated with him for giving such a large part of their income to the church. His attitude about religion showed some ambivalence; despite his rather pronounced devotion, he had periods of resentment of authority, particularly in religious areas. He considered himself too moralistic in the area of sex and blamed much of his own moralism on his father's excessive moralism and religiosity. One insight occurred when he arrived at the conclusion that his rather extreme sexual inhibitions stemmed from his sexual insecurity. This insecurity made him feel less adequate as a male.

Two persons occupied the major portion of Mr. Jones' discussion: his wife and the therapist. The only other topics involving significant affect were the client himself and the question of his masculinity. The major affect expressed was anxiety; next in frequency were dependency, sex pressure from his wife, and his own sex needs. About one-fifth of his discussion bore on the therapy relationship, but most of this evidenced signs of resistance.

The procedures of the therapist during this interview were not greatly different from some of his other interviews. He used more interpretation (28 per cent) than usual and less clarification of feelings and questions (15 per cent of each). Challenging and other techniques were about the same as usual. The interpretations were not very "deep"; only three were above seven on the scale of depth of interpretation. But the therapist did tend to defend the sexual behavior of the client's wife, obviously showing that he considered her attitude more healthy than Mr. Jones'. None of this seems to have been resented by the client, and his affect score rose from the level of the previous interview. It was the therapist who was convinced that the client was resisting the therapeutic task.

I had a dream, and I haven't decided whether to tell it to you. I think I'm blocked about telling about my relationship with my wife. (Res) The dream was pretty vague, and I only remembered part of it when I woke up. My wife was irritated with me this week because I wouldn't get her some things she wanted. She really had a right to ask for them, but we have so damn little money that I have to be penurious. A salary of $3500 a year is pretty crummy. She doesn't think we should continue to give a tenth to the church, the way we do; she feels I should take care of my family first. (Hos p — wife) This brings up the whole damn thing of my decision not to have a neurotic wife. I was thinking about a girl I had been dating in college; she was real dependent, and I was very much attracted to her, but I don't think I ever really wanted to marry her. I know she had a strong physical appeal for me. There was a real conflict, and after I finally broke off with her, I kept coming back and coming back. The sexual appeal was just almost too much to be denied. (Dep + girl → Sex n + het)

Another thing, I feel that we ought to have family devotions more often. We always had these in my own home, and there were times when I was critical of it and even embarrassed by it. I must amplify and distort some of her neurotic traits. I keep being disturbed about her not having anybody to talk to. I am constantly making a conscious effort to arrange for social affairs. I feel it's my responsibility. She doesn't have any neighbor nearby that she can talk to. It occurred to me that maybe these social arrangements are a good way of keeping her from being too dependent on me. (Dep p — wife → Anx)

You don't remember what it was that she was upset with you about. (Directive lead)

No, I don't. I know it wasn't sexual. There *is* something, however. She has a habit of putting her arm around me in bed. Well, I do it first to her, and then if I'm sleepy and she's not, she'll put hers around me. I'll find that irritating and wish that she would roll over so I could go to sleep. (Sex p — wife) But last night it felt rather comfortable. Maybe she was letting me be the baby again. (Dep + wife) (Long pause)

I have a feeling you're being like a client described me at one time. He said I just sat there like a sponge. I'm throwing this stuff out, and you're kind of absorbing it and not doing anything about it. And I'm irritated because you're not. (Whenever this client is entering a resistance phase, he shows quite a bit of hostility toward the therapist; Dep — ther, Rel → Hos n + ther, Rel)

Almost as if you were giving me all these gifts, and I'm not responding, is that it? (Interpretation₇) *What's your feeling about me right now?* (Relationship)

I guess I want you to make me feel that she is not neurotic. I want you to make me feel better. I guess I feel sorry for myself. I feel I want to tell you these things so you *will* do something. I've reported just about every feeling I've had since I've come in. (Dep — ther, Rel)

What do you want me to do? (Relationship)

I don't know. I feel like saying, "I want you to make it all right, Daddy." I guess I've had the reaction that if I hadn't come back to therapy this fall, I wouldn't be in this mess, now. And yet I know damn well that realistically I *would* be in the mess. (Dep — ther, Rel → Hos n + ther, Rel)

It's a little bit painful to open things up again. (Clarification) *You've been telling me that the relationship with your wife has not been too comfortable of late.* (Restatement) *I seem to remember that before when you were discussing things about your relationship with your wife, you were pretty uncomfortable.* (Interpretation₄) *Evidently this subject is pretty threatening to you.* (Interpretation₇)

Actually, I can't ever remember any time when my wife and I have had an argument. We've adjusted so well to each other that there is really no need to express our differences. It's kind of like a beautiful picture of a nice smooth pond, but every once in a while something pops up beneath the surface that isn't so tranquil. (Aff n + wife; Res) I guess the thing I want you to tell me is that this is something that occurs in every family. That I oughta shape up and accept the fact that from time to time we are going to have differences. I guess I'm worried about the possibility of us going into something here that would break up the marriage, which would be a *very* upsetting thing. (The client may fear discussing a recurrence of his feelings of dissatisfaction with his wife or of his homosexual or extramarital urges; Anx — marriage → Dep + ther, Rel)

Do you want it to break up? (Question)

Certainly not consciously. I know I have had intermittent dreams that I can recall, in which the marriage hasn't taken place, and I was going around with somebody else. (Hos n + wife)

Do you remember you thought once about how it would be fun to have your wife away for a while so you could go out with the other guys? (Interpretation4)

You know, Sunday I went up to the fraternity house and sat down and watched the football game on TV. (Aff n + peers)

We talked about the fact that there were certain things she expected you to do that irritated you, and there were certain things you couldn't do because she wouldn't tolerate liquor in the house. (Interpretation4) *Then you mentioned the fact that, and this may be very similar to your mother, she wants you to have more family devotion and prayers.*

And in that respect she resembles Father. The more I think about it the more I feel that it's easier to brush Mother aside and see Dad as the fly in the ointment. (Hos n + fa)

It really registers fortitude when one can face the fact and say that his marriage isn't all that one might like it to be. It could be quite upsetting if somebody calls it to your attention that marriages aren't always perfect. (Reassurance; attenuates)

Why must I maintain, though, that it is perfect? I have a feeling that I'm getting an awful lot of superficial insights today, that I'm not really getting answers. (This sounds like resistance to the insights being uncovered in the therapy.)

Maybe there's something more important you want to talk about. (Interpretation7)

(After long pause) The thing that occurs to me is that there are a lot of things that my wife says that are almost like something a schizophrenic says. It's almost an unconscious expression. For instance my penis has a name; it's always Peter. She likes to hold my penis. When we first got married, she thought it would be wonderful if she could hold my penis while I urinated. I suppose she wants to recover the penis she's lost. (Pause) Maybe that's why that was upsetting to me. Maybe I thought she was sick. And she's often told me about dreams which, if I had had the same kind of dream, I could not have told it because I was aware of the meaning. (Hos n + wife)

I can't say that I see anything schizophrenic about the examples that you just told me. (Challenging) *Maybe you feel that it's important to see them that way.* (Interpretation₉; the therapist feels that the client's anxiety about possible psychotic behavior on the part of his wife is a projection of his anxiety about his own attitudes toward sex.)

Your saying that makes me want to ask you what kind of label you would use. (Dep + ther)

Perhaps I ought to let you *work that out.* (Structuring) *You must have thought her behavior was unhealthy; I'm not at all sure that it was.* (Criticism)

Well, I think it's very important that this makes me uncomfortable.

I think that is *more important.* (Calls attention)

She's so much more at ease sexually than I am. (Insight) The other day in the living room, I had just come home from college, and she was horsing around, and for some reason or other she lifted her leg and said something about "P——" (slang for vagina). And I thought this was uncouth and vulgar and a dirty way. (Laughs) Evil is in the eye of the beholder. (Sex p — wife → Anx — masc) (Laughs)

It sounds as though she's a lot more spontaneous about sex than you are. (Disapproval of client)

Sure is. Maybe if you'd see her as more neurotic, I would be more comfortable. (Dep + ther, Rel)

She seems rather healthy about it. (Challenging) *Why should it make you mad if your wife makes sexual overtures to you?* (Question)

Maybe because I don't quite make the grade. (Pause) I can say that intellectually very easily, and recognize the fact that it's probably true, but it doesn't mean a damn thing to me. (Anx — masc)

I wonder, does she seem sort of sexually demanding to you? (Question)

I think I mentioned before that she does. (Hos n + ther)

If she cuddles up to you, this may mean that you're going to have to have intercourse. (Interpretation₅; the therapist is taking up the theme of "spouse phobia" again.) *The adequate sort of male is expected to respond to what you called her horsing around.* (Interpretation₅)

Yes. (Pause) I can't seem to take this very seriously. Right now I can't get involved in it. (Res) (Pause)

What are you thinking? (Directive lead)

I was thinking that you're behaving today in the way I wanted you to

last week. And yet I don't want to get mixed up in that stuff again. (Dep +
ther, Rel → Anx, Res)

*If therapy means that we're going to explore your libido, you're not
sure you want it.* (Clarification)

No, that's not it. When you said that, it was really pretty threatening.
I wanta be here and be comfortable. I don't wanta work at it. (Dep +
ther, Rel)

*You don't want me to say something that sounds like "Produce or get
the hell out," and you also don't want me to make you give me all these
gifts in order to keep me interested, is that it?* (Interpretation₇)

And yet I haven't been able to get any place with the leads you've been
throwing me. It's hard for me to remember now what we were talking about.
(Acknowledges his resistance.) It was my wife and her sexual behavior.
(Pause) I had a client who had a pretty sexy wife, and he liked to perform
fellatio once in a while, and it was reassuring to hear a client say that.
(Sex n + het)

It didn't seem as dangerously unhealthy if he did it. (Clarification)

I can't figure out where in the world all this began. My parents' conscious attitudes, I suppose. My association was that I wanted to have intercourse with my mother. My association to that is that I wish to hell there'd
been a father around. (Dep − fa → Anx) (Pause) Maybe in a sense I have
a right to be dependent once in a while, in the sense that I've never had a
chance to be. (Dep − fa → Dep + ther, Rel) (Pause)

We had been talking about your sexual attitudes. (Directive lead; the
therapist's rejection of the dependency theme, in favor of the sexual one,
was an attempt to thwart the client's resistance but was inconsistent with
his belief that dependency was the underlying problem.)

Up until the time I came into therapy, or at least until the time I was
married, I thought of myself as being pretty sophisticated about sex. And
it's pretty startling to find out that I was as inhibited as I seem to be. (Sex n
− het → Anx) This is one reason I might be angry with my wife, and
that's for pointing out to me so clearly how inhibited I am. In a sense
there's been some advancement in the times that I anticipate intercourse,
and I'm the aggressor more frequently now than I was before. (Sex n + het)
I see now that my thinking of intercourse as being rather messy is significant. I must have had one hell of a primal scene. (Sex n − mo → Anx)

*I rather doubt whether this kind of attitude comes from primal scenes;
my own suspicion is that it comes from a long, but carefully subtle, indoc-
trination.* (Challenging)

Maybe it does. It's funny, though, I've often tried to think back to
remember if I'd ever witnessed my parents having intercourse, and the only
time I can think of when there might have been a possibility was back when
I was about 14 and I walked in on them, but I couldn't be sure. I've often

looked for it. (Sex n + het) I can't think why I'd want to look for it, other than maybe to prove to myself that Dad *was* a man at one time or other. (Hos n + fa) (Pause) I'm kicking up a hell of a lot of dust today; I'll be glad when it settles down a little. (Both laugh) I guess I want to prove pretty badly that I am a man. (Anx — masc)

I couldn't quite interpret the phrase "kicking up a lot of dust." Did you mean throwing up a screen? (Question)

Or slinging a lot of crap around. I guess it's like water that seems smooth on the surface, but underneath it's pretty riled up. (Anx — self) (Long pause) I have a feeling now that I'd just like to sit back and relax. I honestly can't say whether I've been struggling to put up a screen, or whether I've been telling you things that are important. (Dep — ther, Rel)

If you feel like relaxing, it tends to suggest that you've gone through quite an ordeal, and you're pretty spent. (Interpretation$_9$) *You feel sort of satisfied.* (Clarification)

You said before that when the client makes a lot of anal references you think he's being sort of seductive, and I think that's true. I'm telling you these things now in hopes of hanging on to you; seducing you to let me stay. Consciously, I want to do this thing right. (Dep + ther, Rel → Sex n + ther, homo) (Laughs) I'm a pretty anal character, compulsively piling up the ashes in one corner and telling you what a good job I've done. Most of these kinds of things are damn complicated! Crap! (Anx — self → Anx — ther, Rel; Res)

You're running into a pretty difficult phase right now, I think. (Reassurance) *You're feeling pretty mixed up on things about sex at present. The last time you told me you'd like to seduce me, and then at times you're very angry with me, so that I think that there is a lot of symbolic enactment of your feelings about our relationship going on at present.* (Interpretation$_4$; relationship) *This problem is complicated by other things: you're anxious about discussing anything that does imply any threat to your marriage relationship, and that is probably also related to the signs of fear you show about any threat to your masculinity that is implied.* (Interpretation$_7$; the client's resistance is being explained to him.)

Are you thinking that maybe I'm equating in some way the relationship between you and me with the relationship between my wife and me? (Dep + ther, Rel)

Possibly. (Information)

You know, that made me feel better for you to summarize the situation in an intellectual kind of way. If the intent was to ease my feelings, I think it's done that. (Dep + ther, Rel)

No, the intent was to put it into therapeutic perspective. (Information) *Showing you that what's happening is a part of the therapy process. You're not quite as mixed up as you think you are, because this is a stage of therapy which we can anticipate will happen.* (Reassurance)

Maybe my stumbling around now has to do with the relationship. Maybe I've discovered that I can't seduce you. (Dep — ther, Rel → Sex n — ther, homo)

Jones: Fourteenth Interview (10/11)

THIS INTERVIEW would probably be classed as a rather inactive one on the basis of study of its content, but in terms of client and therapist affect it was a very positive one. In fact the client's affect score of 96 was his third highest score, and the therapist's score of 74 was his highest for the entire treatment. Both client and therapist must have been reacting to the client's statements indicative of progress in maturity of handling some of his problems, and of his reporting the discontinuance of his "transference neurosis," *i.e.*, his tendency to fantasy a sexualization of the therapeutic relationship. The client claimed that all his sexual feelings for the therapist had disappeared, that he also had stopped projecting sexual motives onto the therapist's behavior, and that his sexual relationship with his wife had improved considerably. From a retrospective overview, it would be possible to consider these signs of marked improvement to be something of a symptom cure, or a "retreat into health." At the time, however, both therapist and client seemed to think that a good bit of progress had occurred.

Actually, there was not much activity in the fourteenth interview; Mr. Jones engaged in a good bit of resistant behavior. This was particularly evident in his lengthy discussion of his annoyance with one of his clients, whom he was finding uncomfortably dependent. He seemed to want to make the interview into a supervisory conference. In general, the therapist tried to divert the discussion back to consideration of the client himself.

That Mr. Jones was resistant in this interview was evidenced in his comparing the therapy to the process of going to a dentist and "playing around with a raw nerve." Later he indicated that the interview had not seemed very therapeutic, and he thanked the therapist for "not using the drill."

Despite the client's general diffidence in the interview, some fairly important matters were covered. One was his reiteration of the insight in which he recognized that his homosexual impulses served mainly the purpose of nurturing his dependency on a strong supportive father-figure. With this understanding, he no longer found the idea of attempting to seduce the therapist a repugnant one, and he had ceased to be preoccupied with thinking about this. He still expressed resentment of his father's failure to offer him adequate nurturance while he was a boy. He recognized that he was still somewhat dependent on the therapist, and he showed some panic when the idea of stopping therapy was even mentioned. He did, however, accept the interpretation that *in*dependence can also be a satisfying experience. His post-interview dependency score dropped to 31 in this interview and remained fairly low from this point on.

There was some evidence that the relationship with the client's wife had improved. Mr. Jones claimed that his sexual relationship was better. He also commented that he had ceased to worry about his wife's being neurotic—that it was all right for her to be neurotic if she felt the need to be. Quite pertinent was the fact that when his wife asked him what his problems were, he told her and felt a great deal of satisfaction as a result of this. It seems possible that as his relationship with his wife was improving, he was finding it possible to confide more in her, and as a result, his dependence on the therapist was diminishing.

One of the areas to which a good bit of attention was devoted was Mr. Jones' concern about his general feelings of incompetence; he stated that he now felt that his main problem was the overcoming of his many self-doubts but also that he had improved in this regard as a result of his therapy.

A matter that was probably somewhat irrelevant, and which was introduced mainly by the therapist, was that of Mr. Jones' attitudes of anti-Semitism, which arose in connection with his difficulties with his client. The overemphasis on this problem was probably mostly the result of the therapist's need to try to modify Mr. Jones' attitudes, rather than of any felt need on the client's part.

In general, the "self" was the major topic of client affect in the fourteenth interview. The discussion of peer relationships came second, and that of the relationship with the therapist was third. The affect took the form of a great deal of anxiety and hostility, with dependency and feelings of self-satisfaction occupying slightly lesser roles. A small portion of the responses referred to the psychotherapy relationship.

Therapist activities did not differ significantly from those used in the thirteenth interview, except for a slight increase in the amount of challenging, calling attention, and persuasion (14 per cent of the therapist's responses).

I must confess this is one week I haven't done much thinking. When I was sitting there waiting, I had a strong impression like I was waiting in a dentist's office, waiting for the man to go to work. (Hos n + ther, Res)

Your analogy suggests that you find it a painful operation. I hesitate to use the term extraction. (Clarification; interpretation$_5$) *The idea might be conveyed, in your analogy, that a person puts himself under the domination, or in the power, of the therapist.* (Interpretation$_9$)

And there's the potentiality of playing around with a raw nerve. Last week wasn't a comfortable session for me, although I felt fairly comfortable on the way home. I think this is one of the few times that I've come in without anything that I've wanted to talk about. (Res) I did have the one impression after I left that I didn't have to bother any more about trying to seduce you; that the idea wasn't repugnant to me, so it wasn't really necessary to be concerned about it any more. Particularly in light of your discussion of transference. On the way up today, I did think of the possibility of a transference cure; there hasn't been any conscious anxiety during the week, in spite of what happened. (Ego + matur, Res)

Let's see if we can analyze a little bit further this idea that you didn't feel it was necessary to be worried about having to seduce me. (Directive lead) *Was it that you no longer felt the need to?* (Question)

The sexual element has disappeared, I think. And there isn't the projection any more. I don't project my sexual urges on you any more, which makes me feel a lot more comfortable. Even when I realized that this was my own idea, although I didn't report it to you, I often had the feeling. (Dep — ther, Rel → Sex n — ther, homo) I didn't tell you, because I thought it would be a sign that I wasn't making progress. (Dep — ther, Rel)

Several times you indicated it unconsciously. (Interpretation$_9$)

I wonder if we could go back to something. I'm still having a rough time with my homesick client; I have a real ambivalence about what should be done with him or to him. He's excessively dependent, and the thing that makes it a hell of a job for me is how much I'm involved in the situation and am distorting. (Dom p — peer) I've pushed, and I can't get him to move into anything else. I've tried to let him be dependent in the hopes that this would cause him to talk about something else, and I haven't gotten very far with him. I've had strong feelings of empathy toward him at times. I feel he's suffering a terrific amount of pain. (Aff n + peer) He doesn't want to change; he wants to be miserable. His attitude is that he doesn't want to get to like it in college, or he'll have to stay all year. And I've had the feeling that he might get along better at home. (He discusses the client's dynamics for ten minutes; he apparently wishes to turn this meeting into a supervisory interview; this indicates continuing resistance.)

Considering him intellectually as a therapeutic problem, what does he mean to you? (Question; an attempt to get the material back to the client and his own problems.)

Well, he's resisting what I want him to do, and that irritates me. In a sense he's a failure for me; I'm unable to get through to him. I wanted to drop him, I guess, or send him home, because he may represent a mistake to me. (Dom p — peer)

He represents something of a failure. (Clarification)

And I guess there's also the question of who's going to run this psychotherapy, me or the department head. (Hos n + auth)

He's forcing you into something that you don't want to do. (Restatement)

But I can argue with him about it. I'm not keeping the kid in school. And every time the bastard complains, I feel like I'm being cruel for not giving in to his wishes. (Nur n + peer)

If your child was sick, and you had to administer some awfully unpleasant medicine, but it would make her well, would this bother you? (Interpretation$_5$)

No, it wouldn't, provided I thought there were a good chance of getting her well. But this is one situation in which I don't have much faith in myself. (Dep — auth) The thing that scares me about the damn kid is that he sounds schizy as hell at times. He says, "I want to just drift off. I have my own world."

Maybe you're having to keep him from going into schizophrenia, not keep him from going home. (Interpretation$_5$) *Perhaps he's asking more of you than you feel you can give.* (Interpretation$_5$)

He may be. But what bothers me is not that he's asking so much, but that I don't want to give it. I don't wanta mother him. Maybe I don't think it's worth the effort, but at present it just looks so damn hopeless. He wants to see me any time of the day and expects me to be right there whenever he wants me. (Dom p — peer; the client goes on to discuss annoyances caused by his client or his parents.)

Of course, you can't expect all your clients to be all-American boys. (Disapproval) *It's essentially because they aren't that kind of person that they are clients.* (Information) *The question would be in just what way this guy threatens you, because it's more than obvious that you are threatened by him.* (Interpretation$_7$)

I can't get him to *move.*

I'll admit that there are cases that therapists can't get anywhere with, and I'm not trying to propose any "Rah-Rah-for-therapy-you-can-do-it-if-you-try" solution. (Information) *But I would worry if every time a case got resistant, you felt you had to drop it.* (Disapproval) *Therapy can be rough going.* (Information)

You know, I've never asked him how he feels about me. Maybe I ought to try this. I wonder if I don't tend to bend over backwards and try to be God-like. (Anx — self)

Sometimes to get over this kind of hurdle, it's best to face your own feelings and admit them. (Advice; the therapist has become resigned to having the present interview be a supervisory one, although he still hoped to keep it somewhat therapeutic for the client.)

I don't think *anything* would drive him out. He just loves to come and talk to me.

What about this Jewish business, does that bother you? (Question; this matter had been hinted at previously.)

It does. And I think it was a hell of a while before I was willing to recognize it. (Anx — self)

How does it bother you? (Question)

(Laughs) The fact that I'm prejudiced.

In what way? (Question)

I suppose that I see him as being aggressive. Now here's something important. He was pretty much of a sucking, clinging parasite. (Dom p — peer)

You probably have a fairly small percentage of Jewish students in your college. (Interpretation$_4$) *How does your family feel about Jews?* (Question)

They're prejudiced.

Have you ever known any wonderful Jews; Jews that you could love? (Question; the therapist hopes to persuade, by means of Socratic questioning.)

I think if D. (a Jewish supervisor) could have been available a little more often, I could have. And I think my first reaction to Y. (another supervisor) was negative because he was aggressive and Jewish, and I wanted to run things my way, not his. But I was fond of him later. I never think of him as Jewish. (Aff n + peers)

Are you saying that if a person is really nice he can't be a Jew? (Question)

(Laughs) Maybe so.

But you still have certain feelings. (Clarification) *I suspect that in your background a person who deviated very far from the prototype of a middle-class protestant white was somewhat threatening.* (Interpretation$_5$)

I got really irritated in reading Reik when he kept concentrating on his Jewishness. And Freud. I kept saying to myself, "Well, it isn't so damn important." And yet obviously it is. (Hos n + auth)

I sort of enjoy the joke that Jews have on Christians, that their ideal was a Jew. This is one of the amusing ironies of society. (Persuasion)

I never though of that before.

The basic issue is that some clients can be pretty damn unlovable. And every therapist has to find out for himself how unlovable a client he can take. It's all right to have limitations, but one has to know what they are. (Information)

I've never thought that he can't be helped. I just wanted somebody else to do it. And yet I've actually helped more difficult clients. (Pause)

You know, I feel funny about the time we've spent today; in a sense it's been like an informal sort of chat. There hasn't been much therapy, I guess, which may be why I felt so damn comfortable doing it. You've let me get away from discussing myself today. (The client now admits his own resistance during this interview; Aff n + ther; Rel, Res)

We've been talking about you, *however.* (Challenges)

I suppose so, but not in a way that's very deep or threatening. I guess maybe I'm grateful to you for not using the drill today. (Dep + ther, Rel)

And I've been talking to you as one therapist to another, too. (Relationship)

That's right. (Dep + ther, Rel)

And I've also indicated implicitly that I think you can work with this case. (Reassurance)

You know, I don't have the feeling now that I ought to quit doing therapy. I've had this transient feeling, and I think I ought to square away whether it's the result of several incidents of failure or whether it's a general feeling. I've come from a peak last night where I helped a client over a real rough spot, and I feel pretty good about what I did. (Ego + prof)

You've presented this question several times. And once at the hospital you told me about the time when you blew up at a client. (Calls attention)

Who was of this same type.

Aggressive. (Clarifies) *Maybe this is something you have to work on; how to handle aggressiveness. Find out what your level of tolerance of aggression actually is.* (Advice)

You know, when things get rough, I almost hammer away at a client until he aggresses at me, because in effect I've told him to be aggressive. And I feel good when the aggression comes out. I guess it's a masochistic sort of thing. (Hos n + self) We've never gone much into why aggression upsets me. I don't like competition. That's one reason I haven't liked graduate school, at least until this last year. (Hos p — peers)

You're uncomfortable in a competitive situation, or where there's aggression being shown. (Clarification)

I think I see another barrier coming down. (Ins)

It's funny, my first stereotype of you was that you were probably a scrappy little guy. (Challenging)

The hell of it is, I think it's true. I'm orally aggressive, anyway. But I shy away from physical aggression. (Anx — masc)

That might suggest a deeper level of meaning. Scrappy guys are sometimes guys who protect themselves from aggression by a verbal onslaught. (Interpretation₇)

I've never been very successful in any fights I've had. I've had to defend Dad's honor. If he'd throw some kids out of his class, they'd come around and pick on me. (Anx — self)

Well, I suspect for most therapists, aggressive clients are a lot harder to take than accepting ones. (Reassurance)

But why do I experience this enjoyment in seeing the clients be aggressive to me? In the hospital, one was a sociopath who was always threatening to pick me up and throw me against the wall, and it didn't bother me. There was a verbal expression, but no real fear of physical punishment. (Hos n + self)

There are different ways of being aggressive. Maybe the actual physical threats are not as aggressive as. . . . (Information)

As the ego-threat. That makes a lot of sense. Like this professional squabble with the dean last spring. And this fall the gal in the office implied that I might not get my office back this year, as though I wasn't important enough to take note of. She doesn't respect me for what I can do. (Anx — auth) It helps me a lot that I feel I have been accepted by the president. (The client finally decides to focus the discussion more on himself; Dep + auth)

You've talked quite often about these deep feelings of personal inadequacy. (Restatement)

I have the feeling this is getting closer to the core of the whole problem. In a sense the problem over what I felt was homosexuality is simply a means of establishing dependence on somebody. (Dep + gen → Sex n + homo, Ins) And the business of being dependent or independent is just a striving, in a sense, to prove that I can make the grade. (Anx — self → Dep + gen)

The other problems have seemed secondary to this one. The real problem is really "Am I an adequate person, and am I going to be an adequate psychologist?" (Clarification)

And I think I am.

Last year you had some doubts about whether you had a right to be in graduate school. (Interpretation₄)

I think I feel those doubts less now than I ever have. And yet there's no substantial increase in insight as to the source of these doubts. Other than that I had a father who's a pretty lousy example; sort of sponge-rubber pillow. (Dep — fa → Anx — self) I have a feeling today, and I don't know whether it's legitimate or not, that I'm finally growing up. There's just this one tiny doubt in the background. (Ego + matur)

You don't want to be swept off your feet by a temporary euphoria. (Clarification)

Yeah, that's right.

How did you happen to be telling your wife what you thought of your-self? (Question)

She said: "I've often wondered, what *is* your problem?" And I told her, and I experienced some real relief in telling her, and I could have told her the same thing almost any time but I never did. (Dep + wife → Ego + self) And incidentally, since talking about the sexual relationship between my wife and me, there's been at least a cathartic cure, and I've been much more comfortable in the situation with her. I'm less concerned about whether or not she's neurotic. Or rather, I feel it's O.K. for her to be neurotic if she wants to. I think I know why it was bothering me for her to be neurotic; if she's neurotic, then she's not a very stable source for my dependency needs. (Dep — wife → Anx) In that sense I've been willing to invest enough in *you* so far, that if things go rough, I think I can count on you. But I don't think it's gonna happen, but I can, if I need to. (Dep + ther, Rel)

I've often noticed that when a person has a good relationship of confidence with a wife, he no longer has much need for therapy. (Information)

Hm. Maybe I'm going in the wrong direction there. (Laughs)

The things you talked about last night had a real bearing on your starting to feel today that maybe you've got control of the situation. (Clarification) *Of course that's only one part of it.* (Attenuates)

I was gonna say, don't throw me out yet. (Dep + ther, Rel → Hos n + ther) (Laughs)

You were talking today as though some day you're gonna tell me that you're ready to leave. (Interpretation$_7$)

Yeah, but I don't want to tell you that yet. (Dep + ther, Rel)

If you did tell me that, I would probably tell you it would be good not to make that decision yet. (Reassurance)

But you know there is a feeling . . . I was concerned last spring after there were what I thought had been a few rough interviews, I had the feeling that I'd made an awful lot of progress, and you said you thought I had, but there were things I should work on in the fall, and I was very grateful to you. (Dep + ther, Rel) And I feel as though we are getting somewhere closer to the problem. That's a damn good feeling. (Ego + self) (Pause)

That is, that independence can be nice too. (Interpretation$_9$)

I think so.

Jones: Fifteenth Interview (10/17)

THE FIFTEENTH INTERVIEW continued to show the very high client affect score of the fourteenth (score of 96), but the therapist's affect score dropped to 51, which was his eighth highest score. The client remained quite pleased with the progress that he felt he was making, and commented that both the present interview and the fourteenth had been very helpful sessions. The therapist's judgment showed more reserve about the situation in this interview than it had in the fourteenth.

This interview could be described as the "family relations interview." About half of the discussion concerned the client's wife, and about one-tenth each concerned his own feelings toward himself, anxiety about his masculinity, the question of possible homosexual feelings, and feelings about the therapy and the therapist. The predominant type of feeling in this interview was anxiety, although there were some feelings of hostility, sex need, and affiliation needs and sex pressure from his wife.

Mr. Jones attributed some of his anxiety about the family situation to his reluctance to accept the responsibilities of marriage and being the head of a family. He felt that he was forced to give more to his marriage than he wanted to. He had a strong need to "play the play-boy" by spending more time with the boys or by occasionally dating other girls.

Some of Mr. Jones' anxieties stemmed from his feeling of inability to provide financially for his family to the degree which he felt he should, and this reminded him of his father's impotence in most situations. However, he recognized that perhaps most of his feelings of inadequacy in the marriage stemmed from his sexual inadequacy; he was disturbed by his wife's sexual aggressiveness and by his own inability to respond sufficiently. He admitted that he found masturbation more satisfying; he also was able to fantasy a situation in which he was seduced by an attractive woman, indicating a basically passive psychosexual nature.

352

On the other hand, Mr. Jones expressed a desire to be able to take more sexual responsibility in his marriage and admitted that his sexual difficulties were probably more his fault than his wife's.

Two other concerns were expressed by Mr. Jones about the marriage relationship. The one was his concern that his wife might be socially and intellectually inferior to himself. The other was his awareness of the fact that the two of them were more comfortable when in the presence of other persons than when by themselves.

Relative to the therapy, Mr. Jones expressed satisfaction with the way it was going, although he felt that some of the insights had been intellectual rather than emotional. He also indicated a recognition of the fact that he must try to develop an independence from the therapy, if possible. His dependency score rose by only two points, to 33, after this interview.

During this interview, the therapist adopted a clarifying role much of the time (27 per cent). However, he also asked many questions (31 per cent) and gave a fair amount of interpretation (16 per cent) and information (11 per cent). The interpretations were designed toward opening up a recognition of "deeper" motivations in the area of sexual behavior, particularly of the unconscious homosexual mechanism which was causing much of the client's "spouse phobia." Mr. Jones was not very responsive to this lead.

Last week's session left me with a good feeling, but with a sneaking suspicion that I really was running away from something. (Res) Today I want to talk a little bit more about the relationship between my wife and myself. It's something on which there haven't been too many answers yet. I think I ought to be able to express my feelings more freely with her. The amount of guilt that I feel at times when I stay away from home is more than it ought to be. And perhaps I worry too much about my wife, herself, in the sense of seeing that she has something to do. (Hos n + wife → Anx) I think I ought to be dependent on her, but I am concerned with the fact that I *am* dependent. (Dep — wife → Anx)

You would like it if you could feel more freedom to say how you felt about things, and even how you felt about her. (Clarification) And you also wish you weren't as concerned about whether she's well adjusted or not. (Clarification)

Yeah. I think that now I'm less concerned about this business of adjustment, but there's still a concern about whether she's happy and contented. I think part of the problem is that maybe the responsibilities of being a husband and a father weigh a little bit more heavily on me than I allow myself to realize. (Dep — gen)

I might ask in what way you perceive them weighing heavily? (Question)

It's self-imposed; I'm forcing myself to give more of me to my marriage than I want to. Sometimes I feel maybe I go too far and do more than other people do, and yet there are other things in which I don't do as much as I should. (Anx — wife; does this suggest the phenomenon of "spouse phobia" or fear of the sexual relationship?)

What are you thinking that you give that you don't want to? (Question)

You know, I really don't know. (Pause) I'm having trouble putting my finger on anything now. Maybe I'm tied down more than I want to be and made responsible more than I want to be. (Anx — matur)

I was going to ask you, if you feel tied down more than you want to be, what would you rather be doing if you had your choice? (Question)

I don't know, I suppose that in a sense it would be going out with the boys. I'd like to stay at school in the afternoons and watch football practice, for instance. (Aff n + peers) There are occasions, too, when I see a pretty girl, and I think I'd like to date her. I think this area is a little bit tinged with guilt as well. (Sex n het → Anx) I don't mind teasing my wife about other fellows, and I don't think I get particularly jealous, because I'm pretty confident about how she feels about me. But I guess maybe I'm not quite so confident about how I feel about her. (Anx — self)

You're not quite sure you feel as strongly about her as you think maybe you ought to. (Clarification)

Yeah. (Pause)

You're not worrying too much about the possibility of her being interested in other fellows. (Clarification) *This could result from two possible causes; first, that you were pretty sure she wouldn't be, or second, that you didn't care if she were.* (Interpretation$_9$)

Talking about the latter alternative, we have one friend who is about six-foot-five, real good-looking, and I think probably *the* one individual I tease my wife about the most frequently. I've thought about it from time to time, that in the course of teasing her I'm sure that she finds Ed attractive and that he appeals to her. But my reaction has been pretty much that of "So what, there are women that appeal to me." And we have a good time together. (Aff n + wife) And I suppose she might find another one of our friends as being attractive, the husband of a couple we see about once a week. But we have a good time, and it doesn't upset me. (Aff n + wife) I'm pretty sure I would be *very* upset if I thought there was any danger of our marriage breaking up or of her becoming seriously interested in somebody else. That would hit me pretty hard. But the element that really bothers me was why I felt guilty. (Anx — wife) I will get extremely uncomfortable when my wife mentions my former girl-friend. Or if any of these friends mention my girl-friend, it makes me real tense and uncomfortable. I think I have come to the conclusion recently that this business with her hasn't worn off as much as I thought it had. (Anx — self, wife)

The things you say you'd like to be doing, if you weren't a family man, would be going out with the boys or dating some girls. (Restatement)

None of it seems too insidious to me. This is what strikes me: why *should* I feel guilt about *these* things? Except that they keep me away from my wife. I think maybe, too, there's the element that I feel maybe I ought to be sharing more with her. Perhaps this encompasses a larger problem, that I oughta share more of myself, period. (Anx — wife, self) If I don't feel like saying something when she talks to me, I might just not bother to say anything. (Hos n + wife)

This is what you've said several times in different ways. You're kind of reluctant to be giving yourself. (Interpretation₄) *The things you mentioned that you might be doing are the things that a young bachelor would do, or any young man who hadn't accepted a family, having fun with other people.* (Interpretation₇)

I guess maybe that's the reason I've been insistant on her doing things with other women. I was real pleased about it. I thought it was good for her, but really, it was good for me, because then I can do some other things without feeling so much guilt. (Aff n + wife)

It gives you somewhat more freedom. (Clarification)

There's a real reluctance sometimes at the end of the day to going home. (Again the idea of "spouse phobia" seems to be implied; Sex p — wife)

What does going home signify; what does it require, that you want to avoid? (Question)

The idea of being tied down, and being responsible, or accepting responsibility. (Dom p — wife)

Responsible for what? (Question)

Oh, my wife and daughter. That sounds pretty vague.

In what way are you more responsible for them when you're at home than when you aren't there? (Question)

(Deep sigh) Well, I think it sounds so damn simple to say "the chores," but that's part of it. (Dom p — wife)

So it's husbandly obligations. (Restatement)

And I think, too, that sometimes I resent it that my wife doesn't do all that she should. Hell, I go out and bring in the laundry, and I do some of the dusting and pick up the living room, and I take on a pretty wifely role and do things that I wish *she* would do. (Hos n + wife)

Um-hm. Do you ever tell her that? (Question)

No. That's a thought. (Laughs) I feel now like talking to her about that. Or telling her that I, too, sometimes think that *she* overlooks some of her responsibilities. Maybe it would clear the air a little bit. (Hos n + wife) (Pause) There was something else I was thinking of, but I've forgotten it. (Pause) Oh, I remember. In a psychological sense I guess it isn't too damned important, but one of the things that I connect with my Dad's impotence is lack of money. (Dep — fa → Anx) And something that upsets me, and that I've avoided, is making out a budget. I wish I never had to *worry* about money. The fact that I'm not bringing in all the money I should. (Dep — gen)

Is the thing that upsets you that the money seems too little when you make up the budget? (Question)

It's really the guilt that I'm not bringing in more. And also I know that I could probably be a little bit more careful with my own spending. Hell, like when I come up here, if I have a buck in my pocket, I have to stop off at the dairy store and get myself something to eat on the way home, whereas I could pack a lunch and save some money. She's more careful about the money than I am. I resent having to make those sacrifices; they're the same ones I've had to make all along. (Anx — matur)

You'd like more freedom; you resent a certain self-discipline that your marriage requires. (Clarification)

I guess I want to just be a playboy. That may be a clue to something; it's not altogether facetious. I never had a chance to play the playboy. Poor John! (Anx — matur) (Laughs)

Some of the things that you resent having to do are the obligations associated with a more adult role. (Interpretation₅) *Is this why you kind of avoid going home?* (Question)

I think that must be it; this is part of the same syndrome that you mentioned about the boyish clothes I wear. (Anx — masc)

The need to maintain the youthful freedom. (Clarification)

And yet I would have to say that the happiest years of my life have been the present ones. That's interesting; there's not as much fun when we are just at home together as there is when we are with other people. (Anx — wife)

It's more satisfactory to be with other people than just to be with her. (Clarification)

I guess that's right, although it's a hell of a thing to have to admit. (Pause) One of the things that came to mind was that my wife wasn't worthy of me. (Hos n + wife)

In what way? (Question)

In the sense of being less socially adept, or stimulating, or less intelligent.

Are you saying that you find the time with her somewhat boring? (Question)

That could be. There's a sense of guilt in acknowledging that.

If I were Dollard, I would have socked you long ago with the question of why you didn't bring up the main *husbandly obligation.* (Challenging)

I guess I have to say there's still some resistance there. There's still some reluctance. (Res) (Sighs)

Dollard, of course, believes, and I think he's probably right, that most of these other things are rationalizations for the main one. When he describes "spouse phobia," as you probably know, he indicates that a spouse probably finds these other things irritating because he finds the main one threatening. (Information) *You gave me the almost certain cue to it when you said that her company isn't bad when she's with other people.* (Interpretation$_9$) *What is expected of a husband and wife when they're alone?* (Question)

Hm. Why does this still occur? (Sighs; long pause) There still might be a pretty strong sense of inadequacy. I initiate the sex more often now. But there's still this damn prudishness. (Sex p — het → Anx)

Who initiates it the most at this point? (Question)

Perhaps it's still she. (Dep + wife) I'm not sure. I think I'm blocking here. I just wish I knew where in the hell I got all of this inhibition. I've done a beautiful job sometimes on helping other people in their sexual relations, and it's unnerving to discover all this in myself. There's still a prudish reaction. (Sex p — het → Anx)

Tell me about that prudish reaction; what is it that she does that upsets you. (Directive lead)

Well, (sighs) frequently she'll expose herself, and this shakes me up a bit. There's always a sense of irritation whenever she is the one that's initiating intercourse. I think I have the feeling that *I'm* the one that ought to be doing it. (Sex p — wife → Anx — masc)

People don't like doing things they ought *to be doing.* (Information)

No, that's true.

Her initiating it causes you to feel somewhat less adequate. (Interpretation$_5$)

Less of a man. A real threat. (Anx — masc)

You feel less manly, less potent, and your ego suffers. (Clarification) *If you stay away from home, there's less of this problem.* (Interpretation$_9$)

Yes. I'm glad you said it that way, because of course the whole thing was there implicitly, but the connection I had wasn't that concrete. (Anx — masc)

Do you think you have a weak sex drive? (Question)

I think the overt sexual drive has diminished, certainly, since I got married. I masturbated a lot more often than we ever had intercourse. (Sex n + masturb)

Does that imply that masturbation was more rewarding, or intercourse was more difficult, or both? (Question)

Masturbation was more rewarding. Probably because in the masturbatory fantasies I was always an adequate male, a real potent man, rather than . . . . (Anx — masc) That's interesting because in a sense I think the fantasies would be more the kind in which I would be seduced or tempted by a woman. And my wife behaves exactly in this way, and I resent it. That doesn't make sense. (Sex p — wife)

It does if you see that the personality is ambivalent. (Information)

I perceive her tempting as a demand that's gotta be satisfied, by God, now, no ifs, ands, or buts about it! Rather than as my being able to come to a decision whether or not I'll let her have sex. (Sex p — wife → Anx — masc)

You see her as wanting something of you that you don't want to give. You feel obligated to do it. (Clarification) *You're ambivalent in that you both want to be the dominant male and . . . .* (Interpretation$_5$)

And dependent. (Dep — wife)

Or an ambivalence between dominance and passivity. (Interpretation$_5$)

I don't know why I have such a tendency to see things as either black or white. Why can't I accept the shades of gray? I'm just not quite up to the point of admitting that I feel ambivalent or even inadequate in sex. (Anx — masc)

Do you feel more comfortable going home at times when she's menstruating? (Question)

(Sighs) I don't know, it may well be. I'm sure there's a sense of relief when she starts. I feel that I can relax. (Sex p — wife) The ambivalence is there; I need her, and yet I don't want the responsibility. (Dep — gen)

You seemed to get a certain amount of satisfaction out of discussing the possibility of her being interested in these two other fellows. (Calls attention)

That's true. (Long pause)

Some men like their wives to be interested in other men for one of two reasons: one is vicarious interest in the men themselves, and the other is a sense of freedom it gives them. (Information)

I think both are there. Bob and I have a routine, one that he started, and we call it "queer talk" (homosexual banter). The girls get real upset when we start talking to each other this way. But I think that's a nice, almost conventional, overt way of expressing that. (Sex n + homo)

A socially approved way of expressing affection, keeping it ostensibly at the joking level. (Clarification)

And I consistently describe Ed as a darn good-looking kid. And of course if they would satisfy her sexual needs, then I wouldn't have to worry about it. (Pause) Why am I taking all this so calmly? (Sex n + homo)

You feel you ought to be upset by it. (Clarification)

Yeah. (Laughs) I guess maybe my laughter would indicate that maybe

I *was* upset by it. I almost had the reaction, "Oh well, if it's homosexual, it's all right." (Sex n + homo) (Pause)

I keep thinking about this process of therapy; what do I have to do, sit here long enough until I've absorbed enough of Snyder, and then I can feel adequate and go home and be a man? Although what am I gonna do, identify with *you* for the rest of my life? Or does it just happen that when I feel that I can try out my own wings, why, I get to the point where I *feel* that I can do things myself? (Dep + ther, Rel → Anx)

Reality testing should be a reinforcing experience. The hope of therapy is that you can make some transition from here to the reality situation and that the success with reality will reward you. If therapy rewards you but reality doesn't, this sort of learning won't stick. (Information)

And yet I had the feeling that while this is practical as hell, maybe it doesn't really mean much that when I delay going home I think, "Well, am I afraid of having intercourse?" If so, I have the feeling I'll be able to go home. (Anx — masc) Certainly, I oughta be able to share more with her without getting punished for it. This is something I oughta try, and it should help. I had the feeling that doing these things doesn't make me feel like more of a man, and yet it *will*. In the sense that it may be rewarded. (Anx — masc)

You'll know *why you're doing things; you won't be doing things for reasons you don't understand.* (Reassurance)

I guess this idea, that if I find marriage boring and the answer to it lies within myself in that *I'm* bottling up, makes the whole thing seem a lot more hopeful. (Ins)

Something you can do something about, rather than it being her fault. (Clarification)

Yeah. That makes me feel pretty good. (Ego + self) In many ways this has seemed kind of intellectual today, rather than some intense kind of physical upset that I've had at times. Maybe there's a sense of disappointment. Maybe this oughta be real dramatic. (Hos n + ther) And yet I have a feeling we've accomplished so much today. (Aff n + ther)

It may be intellectual because some of it was my interpretation, rather than some insight that came from you. I do remember that we went over most of this once before. (Information)

Yeah, evidently it didn't register very much. The proof of the insight will be how much of this I remember next week. (Ins)

Or how much of it carries into your regular life. (Information)

Um-hm. I have a feeling now that I'm anxious to get home and tell my wife a little bit about some of the things we've talked about. (Dep + wife) There are still some things that I'm going to withhold, but I don't feel bad about that.

If they're things that need to be communicated because they'll improve the relationship, we would hope in therapy that you would move in the direction that you would be able to do it. But if they're things that don't need to be communicated, and you tell them, this would appear to be a neurotic dependency, and the therapist would hope that it would go the other way. (Advice)

That *helps,* too. Last week was helpful, also. (Aff n + ther)

Jones: Sixteenth Interview (11/1)

THE SIXTEENTH INTERVIEW continued the very positive level of affect that had been occurring in the last few weeks. The client's score dropped only a little, to 91, and the therapist's score rose to 71, which was his third highest interview score. This interview was devoted primarily to the "self" and the therapy or therapist. However, a small part of the discussion concerned the client's wife. Anxiety was still a highly predominant emotion, but expression of affiliation needs and ego-satisfactions increased markedly over previous interviews, and hostility dropped considerably. About a quarter of the responses also concerned the therapeutic relationship, and slightly fewer showed insight, making this interview one of the more insightful ones.

Mr. Jones expressed much pleasure with the progress he had made in the last two interviews. However, he was somewhat ambivalent as to whether his adjustment had really improved, or whether he was experiencing a "resistance cure." Perhaps Mr. Jones' euphoria stemmed largely from the satisfaction he had obtained in talking with his wife about the topics discussed in the previous interview. She had been quite responsive, and his own feelings toward her had increased in tolerance. He also was pleased because he felt he had acquired a habit of self-examination, which brought him intense satisfaction. He began to raise the question of when the end of therapy would be likely to occur, although he quickly accepted the therapist's implied suggestion that he might wait for at least four or five more interviews to see whether his improvement was genuine, rather than a flight into health. Actually, Mr. Jones found it necessary to show some dependence upon the therapist with regard to expressing an opinion about when he should stop therapy. He indicated that he had strong positive feelings toward the therapist and wondered whether the transference would ever die out. At another point he stated that he would have liked a more intense personal relationship. His ambivalence showed in that he indicated much satisfaction in identifying with the therapist, but he also described his treatment as "a half-baked psychoanalysis." Similarly he said he would like to have a close colleague-confidant, but he wondered whether his desire to analyze his problems was a sign of neurotic dependency. He showed marked dependency by indicating that he had thought of asking the therapist to come to his campus and help him sell his counseling program. He blamed most of his trouble on a tendency to distantiate himself from people and attributed this tendency to a fear either of a possible homosexual attraction to them or of annoyance aroused by having people dependent upon him. His dependency score dropped to 27, his lowest score thus far.

Some negative feelings toward the therapist were demonstrated by Mr. Jones' wondering whether the therapist had any problems.

With regard to therapy techniques, this interview was most significant for a large increase in the amount of clarification of feelings by the therapist (44 per cent). Information-giving also increased above any other interview (15 per cent), and there was one very long structuring passage by the therapist which accounted for 15 per cent of his responses. Interpretation was considerably reduced (7 per cent) from the usual level. The long structuring passage came at the time when Mr. Jones asked whether he should be thinking that therapy was about to end. The therapist expressed his real ambivalence on this point. He had the feeling that there was much important material with which Mr. Jones had not dealt sufficiently, but he was also aware of the signs of growing independence, a trait which he very much wanted to foster. He was debating, to some extent, whether to be satisfied with brief therapy and its somewhat superficial insights or to push Mr. Jones into a deeper sort of analysis. His real inclination was toward the latter, although he was not sure that it was really necessary in this case. Mr. Jones' problems were not ones that he would have too much difficulty living with. It is interesting that, although Mr. Jones accepted the therapist's advice to continue in therapy for a short time, he actually came for only four more interviews. Thus, he himself made the decision not to explore the more unconscious levels of his personality, and the therapy remained "brief adjustment therapy." His general later adjustment suggests that this decision may have been a good one, although there is always the tantalizing possibility to consider of how much *more* successful and self-actualized a person he might have been had he decided to go deeper with his self-analysis. Both the therapist's ranking and the MMPI had evaluated him as the third-best adjusted of the twenty clients in the research study. The therapist had also ranked him as about the third most successful of the twenty cases. Two years later he felt that his adjustment was much improved, and that the therapy had contributed much to this. But there were insights about this client which the therapist felt he himself had arrived at, which the client never reached. And, although Mr. Jones had been rather successful in overcoming many of his signs of dependency, he had only partially eliminated the symptom of homosexual urges. By a pragmatic test his therapy was a rather successful one.

I think if I had to pick one outstanding session, probably the last one was it. I felt we really approached something significant, and then I gave it some reality testing. (Aff n + ther → Ego + matur) I felt on the way home that I just couldn't wait to get home and talk to my wife about it. And she reacted very positively toward it and toward me, and I don't recall having felt so comfortable in a long time. (Pause) Everything hasn't been perfect since then; there are still times when I have to force myself to talk at home, but at least I've tried it several times, now, and find I can do it much more often. (Aff n + wife)

You're trying out relating to her and responding to her, and it's been somewhat rewarding. (Restatement)

I also explained to her the element of why I was so concerned about her getting out and doing more things. I don't think it's really too important to me any more whether she *is* neurotic or not. (Aff n + wife)

The other thing I was thinking about on the way up today, I was thinking how much, or rather, where, this need to help people comes from. I think it's part of my wanting to do therapy. And then when somebody's too dependent on me there's the opposite reaction, and I question whether I ought to be a therapist. (Anx — prof) You know, I don't think I'm going to have much to say today. (Both laugh) I haven't said much so far. (Res)

You feel you've got things pretty well worked through at present. (Clarification)

I guess the thing I'm beginning to wonder is whether I'm getting close to the end of therapy, or whether I'm kidding myself. I think there are a lot of problems that I haven't found an answer to. I'm sure there are still people that irritate me no end, for instance. (Anx — matur) At times there has been the defensive idea that I'm not really too fouled up. And then following that, there has been the acute realization that there has been real upset and things that had been pretty aggravated, and yet now there's such an increased feeling of comfort that there doesn't seem to be any real reward in going on further. (Anx — self) And if I did, where should I go from here? (Dep — ther)

You're feeling so satisfied that you can't quite see much motivation to continue, or even the direction in which you would work, if you continued. (Clarification) (Pause)

The interesting thing is that, in spite of the fact that I have the feeling that maybe I'm getting pretty close to the end, maybe I'm not as close as I think I am, because I still want your opinion. There's enough of a dependency there that I want to know what Dr. Snyder thinks about it. And as far as *our* relationship is concerned, there's a pretty large amount of transference, particularly after last week. I have a real feeling of gratefulness. (Dep + ther, Rel → Aff n + ther, Rel; the client admits that he still has dependency feelings and positive transference.)

You feel reluctant to break off this situation. (Clarification)

It's so damn hard to figure out whether breaking it off will be another growing experience for me, or whether there are things that I'm avoiding at this point. If there are, I'm not conscious of them. (Dep + ther, Rel → Ego + self)

I've gotten into this kind of habit that I think is a healthy one, too. And that is, examining why I do certain things. When a discussion is going along in one of my classes, it doesn't hurt me to admit to a class that my previous point of view might have been overly idealistic. (Ego + matur)

You're finding that you're more accepting of yourself without feeling threatened by things that might previously have seemed to be admissions of weaknesses. (Clarification)

In a sense there's almost an overbalancing in the other direction. I'm showing what a wonderful psychologist I am by having these tremendous insights into myself. I begin to understand and appreciate a little bit, now, why an analysand goes around all the time talking about his analysis. I think if I were asked by a student now if I had been in therapy, I wouldn't feel too much reluctant to tell it. (Ego + matur)

There must be some tension in talking about this, I'm blocking. (Pause) I'll *be* dependent and ask you, is it possible that I've accomplished enough at this point that I can feel close to the end? (Dep + ther)

Well, that's a very difficult question to answer. I'm asking myself the same question. I'm not sure that I can decide with any certainty. (Structuring) *The alternatives are that you really have made real strides in self-understanding, or on the other hand that this is a kind of resistance cure going on and the neurotic pressure is reduced enough to allow you to find life more tolerable the way it is than you would find the discomforts associated with the therapeutic uncovering process.* (Information) *And that gets into the whole question of what our conception of therapy is and what our therapy goals are. I believe that I myself have changed over the years in this regard; I'm somewhat ambivalent. I now see dropping out in less than twenty interviews as too rapid a conclusion.* (Structuring) *But this is obviously a different "level" of therapy from what analysts are talking about. Perhaps I'm only carrying on "brief, adjustment therapy," rather than a deep insight therapy.* (Structuring) *I am inclined to encourage clients who have felt like leaving after only about fifteen or sixteen interviews to stick around for a while, just to see if their attitudes changed.* (Structuring) *I think the most important consideration is how* you *feel regarding* your *needs in the situation. I might see unresolved problems that you don't.* (Structuring)

I'm pretty sure that there are still problems that I have that I haven't solved. One of the real questions in my mind is, have I achieved a sufficient level of insight to be able to find some of the answers myself. And the other thing is that with the kind of rewarding experience I've had in the last two weeks, there's a very strong possibility that maybe the elation is a temporary one. Although something on the other side is that I've stopped wanting a close personal relationship with you. (Ego + matur → Anx — self)

The last time you indicated that that personal need was gone, that strong need to feel close had disappeared. (Restatement)

Now there's no question in my mind that whatever prestige I could get from you I will use, but on the other hand, it's not the intense dependent kind of thing. (Dep + ther, Rel) I have a fair feeling of success in what I'm doing now. (Ego — self)

The criterion of success in therapy is that your *needs are being well met.* (Information) *It sounds as though you feel that they are.* (Clarification)

I think they are. I'm sure I haven't gone quite as far in terms of getting the deep level of insight that will give me some of the insight into clients that I need. But that probably isn't an adequate motivation for coming in for therapy. (Ego + matur)

You don't feel it's enough of a reason. (Clarification) *And besides, you have to make the long trip every time, which would seem like a nonrewarding experience if you weren't getting some other satisfaction out of the therapy.* (Information)

I suppose that affects it to some degree, although I think it's a fairly minor consideration. Another reason is that outside of therapy I haven't done anything scholastic, and I've used the rationalization that when you're in therapy you can't do anything else very creative, because all your efforts are going into the therapy. (Hos n + ther) (Pause) I've taken what you've told me as sort of an implication that maybe it wouldn't hurt to stick around for a few more interviews, and I think I feel that way, too. There's a reluctance to give up the contact with you. (Dep + ther, Rel)

We could set some definite date and say we'll keep it up till then and see how you feel at that time. Perhaps we might plan to keep it going until Christmas, for example. Or we could leave it less formal and just continue indefinitely. (Advice)

I think I ought to know by Christmas whether or not I'm ready to stop.

That's about four or five more interviews. That gives you a little over a month to test out the situation. (Information)

I guess in looking over the past few interviews, I recognize that these things sort of come in spurts. I'm more impressed by what happens in the spurts than I am during the periods of lull. My wife and I both have a real feeling for our relationship now. She is responding, and so am I. I must be a fairly cantankerous character to live with at times. (Aff n + wife) I have a pretty good feeling about things today; I feel pretty secure. I have the feeling that I am somebody, and I don't have to apologize for being around any more. (Ego + matur)

There's been a great reduction in the feelings of inadequacy. A great increase in sense of self-confidence. (Clarification)

One of the problems that I've been faced with as far as my role on the campus is concerned is how to get across to the student body, and actually to the faculty, what I'm doing that can be a help to them. One thing that occurred to me, among others, that might help me do this would be to ask you to come down there and give a talk about it. (Dep + ther; a very dependent suggestion.) But I've actually discarded this idea; I'm not sure just why. I think part of it was that the department head suggested that it was something I ought to do myself. And I got the impression from him that I could accomplish it on my own without help. It is kind of a nice feeling, although I must admit that I would really very much like to have you come down. (Dep + ther, Rel → Hos n + ther) There are very mixed feelings about you at this point. There are times when I've wondered about what kind of problems *you* have, or I've made observations in a hostile way. There are times when I've seen what I thought were neurotic traits on your part, and this bothered me to some extent. But I can feel comfortable now in assuming that you have some neurotic traits. I don't know why you wouldn't, since everybody does, but it's kind of O.K. (Hos n + ther, Rel)

Before you sort of expected me to be perfect, some sort of paragon, and then you found that these expectations weren't all justified, that I seemed to have some human characteristics, too. Now you find that you can accept these human weaknesses. (Clarification; relationship)

I guess the thing that got me off on this is, I wonder if transference ever really dies out? I suppose it wears off in time, after the therapy is discontinued. I'm pretty sure there's going to be a sort of halo effect that I will have for you. Perhaps for a very long time. (Dep + ther, Rel → Aff n + ther, Rel)

You're saying you wonder whether there can be a time when you don't really need me or care too much about me? It's hard for you to imagine that this could be true. And yet, from your own experiences with others, you suspect that this would be quite likely. (Clarification)

You know, I think I feel cheated in one sense. Maybe I've been cheated;

I've had a half-baked analysis. (Negative transference is now quite evident.) It occurs to me especially in terms of thinking about stopping. I think I have the feeling that I could have achieved the satisfaction that I have right now without this therapy. (Hos n + ther)

You're sort of angry with me, perhaps for two reasons. For one, you feel that you haven't got as much as you might have, that the therapy might have been a deeper sort, and second, I get the idea that you're angry with me that you didn't get as close a relationship or as deep a transference as you might have gotten if this had been analysis. (Interpretation₇; relationship)

That's true, but then I can see your side of it. I wouldn't be as comfortable as I am right now if it had been a real intensive relationship. (Dep + ther → Anx) In a sense it would have kept me neurotic rather than making me feel that I can make out on my own. I would have had to be kept neurotic in order to keep me in therapy and to keep me moving into deeper levels. I'm not sure what these deeper levels are, but when I read something like Reik, I become aware of it. (Anx — self)

So you're somewhat ambivalent. Sometimes you feel that it's much better this way, and sometimes you feel it isn't. (Clarification) *I gather that sometimes you feel deeply grateful, and other times you feel kind of short-changed.* (Clarification)

And this is what's so confusing about it. When I say something like this, it kind of indicates that I want to stay on in therapy and really go into this deeply. Is this a neurotic kind of dependency? (Dep + ther → Anx) Or is it a realistic appraisal of the situation? I guess in part it's realistic, in that there hasn't been real depth. But there *has* been at times. I think, for instance, I could have gone all the way through therapy and been satisfied without exploring this business of the homosexual feelings. I feel kind of proud of myself for having weathered through that. (Ego + matur)

But then I'm puzzled at times as to why I've come to feel competent and adequate the way I have. I've been aware of the source of the inadequacy, (sighs) and yet, what is happening that I do feel this way, now? I think part of it stems from identifying with you. Whether these two things are enough to add up to a lasting kind of an answer, I don't know. (Dep + ther, Rel → Ego + self)

You're saying that therapy seems to have made some difference, and yet you can't see anything that would have done it, and you wonder if it's real. (Clarification)

Boy, I *do* have real ambivalent feelings. I'm sure that if I stopped today, there would be a question in my mind and real anxiety on the way home that I should have stayed in therapy and seen what would develop. (Anx — self → Dep + ther) (Long pause) Another reason for not leaving therapy is getting out of practice with this business of looking for causes, and also, knowing how much I've lifted bodily out of my own therapy and injected into the therapy of my clients. That's been very nice in the sense of enjoying identifying with you; I really like to play Bill Snyder when I sit in the other chair. (Dependency in the form of identification; Dep + ther, Rel)

You know, one of the other reasons that there's reluctance to end therapy now is that I remember another guy who had therapy for about fifteen weeks and went around talking about all the insights he had, and yet he had a complete lack of understanding of himself, and everybody considered him still a deeply neurotic guy. And my reaction was of wondering whether I would wind up like him, bragging about the therapeutic change that nobody else could see. (Anx — matur) There are two reasons that I can see why I freeze up like this. One is that I really don't enjoy doing therapy too much, and I know I don't at times when I am like this. The other reason might be that they're leaning on me too hard. I'm getting now so that I can spot this; when somebody's leaning on me, I get a sense of irritation with the client. (Hos n + peers) I can usually sort it out in my mind quickly enough and recognize that this is the cause. Then it doesn't interfere too much with the therapy. Occasionally when I run up against these difficulties, I wonder if I ought to be working in the field of therapy. One task I ought to set for myself between now and Christmas is to find out whether or not I'm a therapist. (Anx — prof)

Whether you really do want to go into this field. (Clarification)

Also I feel the need of someone to talk to who's interested in these things. The department head is willing to listen, but he's not an informed listener, and there can't be any exchange of ideas; I have to do all the giving in that situation, and he can only listen. It would be helpful to me if I had someone I could discuss these things with. I need an informed colleague. (Dep + ther)

It's pretty desirable for a therapist to have colleagues whom he can discuss his therapeutic problems with. He needs a "control supervisor," or at least an informed colleague. (Information)

I guess most of the analysts don't have anyone to talk to. Well, I like my job a lot. I'll have to work on that problem.

Jones: Seventeenth Interview (11/7)

THE SEVENTEENTH INTERVIEW was one in which a marked amount of resistance was evident. Some of the major signs of resistance were the following feelings expressed by the client:

1. He was slow about filling out the questionnaire after the interview and admitted he felt less need to please the therapist than he previously had,
2. He admitted his feeling that he would have preferred to have had a psychoanalysis,
3. He saw his previous enthusiasm about his improvement as being over-optimistic,
4. He tried to repress thinking about therapy during the week,
5. He dreamed that the therapist (or a therapist symbol) had been critical of his intelligence,
6. He showed annoyance when the therapist offered an alternate interpretation of the person in his dream,
7. He questioned whether to go deeper into therapy or to stay at his "present level of personal satisfaction,"
8. He felt less positive affection toward the therapist and recognized that they could probably never be close personal friends,
9. In his cryptographic dream, he made the interpretation that his therapy may have constituted a victory over the therapist (or over the client's father).

On the other side of the question, there were some positive feelings, in that Mr. Jones expressed several times the idea that some progress had occurred in therapy.

During this interview there were a number of signs of general or specific anxiety; the major ones were the following:

1. He showed concern about his intellectual adequacy,
2. He was hostile toward his wife for making sexual advances which he considered sadistic; however, he also felt guilt and anxiety about this feeling,
3. He had fantasies of physical aggression toward his wife,

369

4. He feels revengeful when his own sexual appetite is greater than his wife's,
5. Whenever he feels inadequate, he identifies with his father,
6. His anxiety about his masculinity leads him to compensatory fantasies,
7. He resented the lack of adequate recognition of his professional competence,
8. His lack of sufficient salary has caused him to engage in minor prostitutions of his professional skills,
9. He has wondered whether to change to a less desirable position in order to earn more money, but felt that he should adjust himself to a low earning-power.

One feeling gave Mr. Jones a sense of some adequacy, however; he sometimes found that his sex drive was greater than his wife's.

Anxiety, then, and hostility were the principal forms of client affect during this interview. There was some ego-satisfaction, however. About a fifth of the responses dealt with the therapy relationship. The affect in the interview was directed particularly toward the client's wife, the therapist, his professional adequacy and his maturity, his masculinity, and his father. The interview seemed to be a sort of summing up of all the things that bothered the client. His affect score dropped from its very high level of the last interview to 68, which was a little below his modal score. His dependency score (29) represented almost no change. The therapist's score dropped markedly to 18, coming down from one of his most positive scores to his eighteenth. There is no doubt that the therapist perceived the signs of general maladjustment and discontent which the client was feeling in this interview. His therapy did change significantly from its usual style. Clarification of feeling accounted for 22 per cent of his responses. The amount of interpretation was increased to 38 per cent, and there was some information-giving (7 per cent) and challenging (5 per cent). Most of the other techniques did not change much from usual. Some of the deeper interpretations which the therapist made were the following:

1. Staying away from home may have been a means of escaping the unpleasant fact that he was not earning enough money,
2. Lack of earning-power might remind the client of his parents' situation in his childhood, and bring back unpleasant memories,
3. The person described in the dream sounded more like the client's department head than like the therapist,
4. Helping him to plant young trees might symbolize counseling young college students,

5. His feeling of having achieved a victory over his father might stem from his freedom from the desire to have his father take care of him,
6. His father's acceptance of his ideas might make him feel more manly,
7. His wife might find his sexual behavior somewhat frustrating.

Some of the more significant examples of information, persuasion, and challenging were:

1. Indicating that it is easier to contemplate the idea of being castrated than that of being sexually passive or feminine,
2. Suggesting that people often engage in sex play that would be physically painful under other circumstances,
3. Indicating to the client that his preconscious ideas should be more accessible in deeper stages of therapy where the transference is the strongest,
4. Suggesting that it is preferable to couch ideas in psychological rather than in physical terminology,
5. Suggesting four ways by which he could adjust to the situation of not earning enough money.

Thus it is apparent that the therapist took a rather active part in attempting to influence the course of the client's thinking during the interview. While 22 per cent of his responses were classifications, 49 per cent were more active interventions.

The last two weeks I guess I've had mild guilt feelings of varying degrees about this business of filling out the questionnaires for you. The one this week, I repressed the fact that I had to do it, and I didn't get it done until last night. (Hos n + ther, Res) I'm not exactly sure why I'm doing this. One of the things that occurs to me is that it isn't too important to me any more to stay in your good graces by doing this. Before, I felt that if you were doing all this for me I ought to do that for you, and now there's not that kind of a pressure to do it. I still feel guilt about it, though, when I let it go. (Dep + ther, Rel)

You're feeling less sense of obligation toward me, and less feeling of responsibility there, in the last two weeks. (Clarification)

I guess that's part of it. I have a feeling that there's more to it than that. After a week's thinking about the thing, I think probably I was a little over-enthusiastic last time about my estimate of the progress I'm making. I'm pretty sure there has been some positive progress. (Ego + matur) But on the other hand, I can't help but recognize from time to time that everything isn't going exactly as I would want. That there are relapses in this business of relating to my wife. (Anx — self) And I thought quite a bit more on the way up here, today, about what was going on, than I have for some time. I guess there's been a tendency to push the therapy out of my mind during the week, at least more so than previously. (Res)

I had an interesting dream last night. The thing that kind of tickled me about it, when I got up, is that it was a real Theodore Reik kind of a dream. This cryptogram kind of business. There was singing, I was doing the singing, and it was some . . . I'm not quite clear, I've been trying to bring it back, but the phrase that I was singing was, I think, "An Allyson is one," and I had a very concrete association to June Allyson, almost as though I could kind of see her, or I was singing this to her, but of course the "Allyson" and the "An" is really "analysis" and the "one" was o-n-e (spelled out), 'cause I was singing that, but the question comes up in my mind if it wasn't w-o-n. I'm trying to figure out just what the hell I've won. (Anx — ther, Drm)

Um-hm. That's pretty neat. It would have taken me many years to have figured that out. (Approval) *As you were singing it, the phrase itself had no particular meaning?* (Question; the therapist avoids showing some of the skepticism he feels about cryptogram interpretation.)

No. There's a real need to interpret this in the sense that I've come out on top, and yet why is this important enough to sing about it? Of course, the fact that I was singing suggests an enthusiastic kind of a gesture, a cheerful one. (Ego + matur) And yet, immediately after this dream, comes the recognition that there are things to be accomplished.

The idea that something is won implies that there had been a battle with an adversary. What or who is the adversary? (Interpretation$_5$; Question)

I suppose *you* might be the adversary, although the hell of it is it's contaminated in this sense: Dad and Mother were up on Tuesday to pick up my sister and take her home for a visit, and I don't know whether therapy has enabled me to win out over my father or not. (Dep — fa → Dep + ther, Rel) I suspect there's a pretty good possibility, because the discussion we got into that evening was about psychotherapy and psychology in the colleges and high schools, and we were debating determinism versus free will, and I could express my views to him and he could accept them. (Aff n + fa)

Are you saying that he accepted you as a man, now, rather than as a son who could not have independent ideas. (Interpretation$_9$)

Yeah, I guess that's it. Although Dad hasn't really been giving me that sort of problem as much as he has this business of him forcing me to be a man before I was ready to. (Dep — fa)

He's forced you to be free of him. In that sense you may have won this battle. In that now you don't care any more. Perhaps you've won in the sense that now you don't care that he doesn't let you be dependent. (Interpretation$_9$)

Yeah. There was one other separate dream that I'm pretty sure occurred last night. It's vague as hell, except for a few details. One incident involved me driving along with a car, and somebody made some sort of a violation which I think must have come close to hurting *me,* and I see a policeman, a state trooper in a car, and I yell at him to go after the guy that did it. (Hos p — peers → Hos n + auth) And the other part is a guy, a farmer, who is selling me some trees that had been planted, and I think telling me what the process was, and complaining about a stupid Irish farm-boy who he has to explain everything to in order to get him to do it right. I'm pretty sure the farmer is you. (Dep — ther, Rel → Anx) A funny thing I wanted to check on today, I've never perceived you as having a particularly ruddy complexion, but I think perhaps you do (projection due to transference), and I remember distinctly the farmer having a ruddy complexion. He was older than you and had gray hair. But I'm pretty sure that the farmer was you, and this concept of showing *me* how it was done ties in pretty closely with you showing me the way. (Anx — ther, Rel) Of course, the trees are a pretty obvious kind of a symbol, though interestingly enough they were new trees.

The description you give of me sounds a little bit more like your depart-ment head than me. (Interpretation$_9$)

Hm. (Pause) Gee, I felt I had that all nicely worked out. I don't know what kind of a context that puts on it. (Hos n + ther)

Well, I may be wrong. (Attenuates)

Now I'm beginning to wonder if it was important at all. My reaction now is to toss it aside. At least I can't see much in it that means anything. (Res)

An older man shows you how he has planted trees and complains about the stupid Irish boy who can't help him. (Restatement)

That may fit in more with the interpretation of the department head. I'm still not too sure how bright I am. (Dep — auth → Anx — self)

Does that make you the stupid Irish boy? (Question)

I had kinda thought about that. (Anx — intel)

You're helping him plant the trees, but not doing it very well. (Inter-pretation$_7$) *Young trees; trees are a kind of male symbol. Young trees might be equivalent to young college boys.* (Interpretation$_9$) *Of course I'm helping you plant them, in that sense, too.* (Interpretation$_9$)

Yeah. It's kind of funny that these dreams would remain in conscious-ness, now. Particularly in view of my view last week of this as being a half-baked analysis, and my fence-sitting attitude of not knowing whether to go really deep or to terminate at the level of some personal satisfaction. (Hos n + ther; telling the therapist about these dreams may constitute a testing of the limits by the client, in order to determine whether he can persuade the therapist to change the treatment to a psychoanalysis.)

Normally the dreams would be most prominent at the times when the transference was also the more acute. (Information)

I hadn't thought of that in that sense. There may be some negative transference at this point. But I think my view of you is more realistic, now. I don't think you and I ever could be good friends on a social level. For one thing, because I've been in therapy with you. And then I think that I don't know that our interests are much along the same line, outside of therapy. I'm not so sure that the recognition of some negative traits in you is so much a hostile sort of observation or simply more realistic. (Hos n + ther)

You suspect you simply tended to ignore the negative factors before. (Clarification)

Or project something onto you. I guess I'm still pretty ambivalent about what I want to do about this thing. I'm dissatisfied, too, in the sense that I feel as though I'm spending a lot of time talking about the technical aspects and not enough about my own problems of adjustment. I want to terminate therapy, and I expect there's some reluctance to go on to other things as long as this is in mind, because I get the feeling that anything new will just drag me down deeper. And then in the last day or two I've had the reaction that if I have this time left, I ought to make good use of it instead of just. . . . (Anx — ther)

There are several things that occur to me that are pretty important. One was (sighs) last Friday afternoon. I stopped over at the department head's office late in the afternoon to talk over with him one of the clients that I have. And just when I was leaving, my wife called and wanted to know when I was coming home. I knew darn well she was irritated; she hung up hard! And I just couldn't wait to get home; I had to drive down there as fast as I could and try to smooth things over. And she was really mad about it. You would think I would be irritated because she called me at work, but I feel irritated with myself for pulling a stupid thing like that. Plus the realization that I probably wasn't at the point yet where I was anxious to get home. Or else I wouldn't have allowed myself to fool around chewing the fat the way I did. So there's an awareness of something of a setback in my adjustment to her. (Dom p — wife → Anx)

You feel you've regressed. (Clarification)

Yeah. I hadn't gotten the full impact of that until just now. It's still kind of disturbing that there are still times when I don't want her to bother me. One thing that's real irritating is that she'll say, "Oh, I love you," and then make this real aggressive painful kind of an attack. Pinching and thumping. I think this is upsetting for two reasons. One is that I see it as a sort of sadistic kind of thing on her part, and the other thing is the threat that something like this might precipitate our having intercourse. I don't mind it when we're actually having intercourse, in fact I kind of enjoy it then. But the most frustrating part of it is that when I try to call her off or let her know that it really does hurt, before I get a chance to do this she'll start whining, "Oh now, Honey, take it easy." And she's actually imitating what my reaction would be if I had a chance to say it. And it's frustrating as hell to deal with! She's aware of the irritation on my part, and yet there's not a whole lot of attempt on her part to stop it. (Sex p — wife → Hos n + wife)

She's ridiculing you for your tendency to recoil from her seductive advances. (Interpretation$_5$)

Yeah, she's apt to grab me by the waist, or grab ahold of a roll of fat and sort of grip into it, and (laughs) it's actually painful. (Sex p — wife)

When you're actually committed to sex, this doesn't bother you; it bothers you when she's attempting to arouse you and you don't want to be aroused. (Clarification)

Yeah. Right now I have the reaction that "What the hell, this isn't all my fault." She fits in the picture here some place, too. It's almost as though I were coming to you for support for my side of the story. (Dep + ther) (Laughs)

Why do you feel like holding back? (Question)

Back from thumping her one? (Hos n + wife)

No, that wasn't what I was thinking of. (Challenging) (Both laugh)

(Laughs) I knew what you were thinking. (Hos n + ther, Rel)

Perhaps you'd really like to hit her. (Interpretation$_7$)

(Pause) When she gets aggressive, I'd like to aggress back. (Hos n + wife)

Lots of sexual acts are perceived as being aggressive, especially by people outside of the sexual situation. (Interpretation$_7$)

Yeah. And I expect it as part of the sex play. As you say, when she's doing it, I'm not committed. But actually she doesn't treat me as painfully in the sex act as she does at these other times. (Hos p — wife)

Perhaps there is some aggression there. (Attenuates)

Well, this is what I was trying to get at. My reaction is to interpret this behavior as some kind of sadistic or neurotic activity. But I guess that could logically be true, because it's almost as difficult for her to tell me that she's mad at me, as it is for me to tell her. (Hos p — wife)

Maybe she finds you frustrating. (Interpretation$_9$)

Well, I expect that would be true. And in a sexual way as well as others. (Sex n — het)

You're suggesting that in her aggression she may be saying, "Why don't you be more sexy." (Interpretation$_5$)

Your saying that takes me back to that feeling that I'd like to give *her* a good crack. There have been times, too, more recently, when I've been the aggressor sexually. And there has been something less than enthusiasm on her part. And actually it made me feel kind of good: "Well finally, old Johnny is gettin' to the point where he wants to get his piece of - - - once in a while, too." (Sex p — wife → Hos n + wife)

You're pleased with yourself that your sex appetite could be a little bit stronger than hers at times. (Clarification)

Or that the sex act doesn't seem so distasteful. Although there is this sort of competitiveness about it, too. Sort of: "Let's see who's got the penis around here!" (Hos n + wife)

"Who's got the more masculine sex role?" (Clarification) (Pause)

I don't seem to be able to do much with that. (Res)

I was trying to take it away from just possession of the sex organ to include the whole matter of personality characteristics. I was trying to make it more poignant that way. (Information)

That's the way I have of beating it, by turning it into a physiological matter. (Res; Ins)

I think it's easier for people to think about having penises or not having them than it is to think about being sexually passive. Nobody can dispute the fact that you have a penis, but you might feel more vulnerable on the passivity question. (Challenging)

Every time an incident comes up like the one last Friday, it kind of asserts that she runs the place and that I don't, and then in a sense I become my father, instead of somebody who is adequate and controlling. (Dep — wife → Anx)

Why do you think you didn't go home until late on Friday? (Question)

Well, there was a lot of shopping I had to do; it was payday; we were going to have company that evening. I'm pretty sure there wouldn't have been time for intercourse anyway, despite her teasing. (Anx — prof)

You don't think it was fear of sex. Perhaps it had to do with money. (Interpretation$_7$)

That might be. It always is a problem, and as usual there wasn't enough money for what we wanted to buy. I had to go back home and get more. (Anx — prof)

This is a point you're pretty sensitive about. (Clarification)

There's not a hell of a lot I can do about it, other than accept the fact of my income, which is difficult to do, particularly when you're faced a couple of times each month with its inadequacy. (Anx — prof)

Well, you can fail to go home in time to go to the store. (Interpretation$_7$)

(Laughs) And let her worry about it. This seems kind of innocuous, yet it's pretty important in terms of the stress that comes up from day to day.

Why should the amount of money you have seem especially important to you? (Question)

(Sighs) Well, if I can't supply the things my family needs, then I'm not being adequate. (Anx — self)

It's a symbol of status and ego adequacy. (Interpretation₅) *Your paychecks wouldn't seem very rewarding, and especially if you grew up in a family where this happened a good bit of the time.* (Interpretation₈)

And this is another sense in which I'm repeating the old man's cycle. There's a quandary. I feel happy doing the work I'm doing now, and yet it also involves me asking my family to make a sacrifice. Actually my wife is willing to make it and doesn't complain about it, and yet it points up an inadequacy on my part. Why in the hell should we have to debate whether or not my daughter should get a new pair of shoes this month? Money isn't important enough to want to make a lot of it, but it's important enough to want to be able to pay the bills. If I could just do that, I think I'd feel satisfied. (Anx — prof)

You don't feel you have to make a big income, but you feel bad when you know your family has to worry about whether their standards of living are adequate for comfort and health. (Clarification)

I think it represents, too, how adequate I am, in terms of what kind of rank I have. I'm just an assistant professor, with the equivalent salary, but the college chaplain and the director of religious education, who have no more graduate work than I have, hold the rank of associate professor and make six or seven hundred dollars more than I do. (Anx — prof)

It's a status symbol. (Interpretation₅)

And that was true for my dad. A guy with no better education had a school job that paid more. (Hos n + fa)

It symbolizes frustration for you. (Clarification)

And in a sense, too, I find myself making almost what I consider ethical violations in order to get a couple of extra bucks. I've been doing some psychological tests for a business in town, and I know they don't use them in the way that I think they ought to be used. (Anx — prof)

You even see yourself as compromising your principles for some extra money. (Restatement)

The question that's in my mind is, where this leads me. Do I get to the place where I can accept the fact that I don't make enough money? Am I going to be content with less, or am I always going to want to make more? (Anx — prof)

Well, it could lead in three possible directions: first, you can be content with less; second, be unhappy with what you earn, but not do anything about it; and third, make a change that makes it possible to get more. (Information)

I see as being the healthiest kind of response the being unhappy with it but content to stay where I am. (Ego + prof)

Um-hm. When you say healthy, you mean that this is the one that suits your personality best. (Interpretation₅)

Yeah. At least I don't like to think of myself as giving up something that's real important to me in order to do something that I won't like as well but just to have more money. (Anx — self)

You like this work a great deal, and there's a conflict between whether to stay at this work that you like, or get into something that pays more but that you're not at all eager to do. (Clarification)

I'm pretty sure I'm going to stick with this. The objective really, I guess, is to get to the point where I can tolerate the low income. (Anx — prof)

I might suggest another alternative, which is to figure out ways of getting more money out of it. (Advice)

Yeah. This is something that has occurred to me. I think this is involved in the status matter. That is, holding them up for more money, so that they'll appreciate me a little more. I was too eager to go there and took the job at too low a salary. (Anx — prof)

Jones: Eighteenth Interview (11/15)

THE EIGHTEENTH INTERVIEW was a "working" one, in which a number of rather important matters were covered. Most of the discussion concerned the client's wife, or his attitudes toward himself. In general, there was a decrease in the amount of hostility, anxiety, and dependency displayed by Mr. Jones. And correspondingly, there were increases in the amount of ego-satisfaction and sex needs expressed. Some affiliation needs and sense of external sex-pressure were also reported. The contents of the interview covered four main areas: problems of hostility, sexual problems, dependency problems, and insights or personality changes achieved.

Some of the main problems concerning *hostility* were the following:

1. Felt much irritation with his wife for lack of neatness, for "making him jump through hoops," and for sexual aggressiveness,
2. Resented his client's dependency,
3. Was annoyed with the therapist for pressing the consideration of psychological, rather than physical, problems (such as passivity versus "castration"),
4. Was irritated with himself for allowing his homosexual and voyeuristic needs to affect the therapy he was conducting,
5. Was annoyed with himself for having extra-marital sexual fantasies,
6. Was annoyed with himself for being so inhibited in sex,
7. Was irritated with his mother for being so dominating and aggressive.

The *sexual* problems included the following:

1. Was anxious because of the recurrence of homosexual fantasies about his client,
2. Is reluctant to engage in intercourse, but this makes him feel inadequate,
3. Is afraid that intercourse will not be successful,
4. Would rather masturbate; in masturbation he can fantasy very successful incidents,
5. Wants to develop more sexual aggressiveness in his marriage.

Problems of *dependency* were expressed as follows:

1. Still finds himself wanting to depend on his wife,
2. Accepted the interpretation that his puritanical attitude about alcohol is the result of a desire to please his parents, thus indicating dependency upon them,
3. Still wants the approval and acceptance of the therapist. (His dependency score dropped to 23 and remained low for the rest of therapy.)

Some of the *insights* achieved or signs of personality changes were as follows:

1. Has become more aggressive about the use of alcohol; could now tell his parents that he drinks beer,
2. Does not want to go to extremes in trying to dominate his wife,
3. Recognized that he must stop equating the upper position in intercourse with psychological and sexual dominance,
4. Has been thinking about the ending of therapy; now feels less need to remain dependent upon the therapist,
5. Recognized that some problems still exist in the areas of sex, lack of aggressiveness, and the relationship with his wife.

The affect scores during the eighteenth interview returned to very high levels, indicating an improvement of the relationship over the previous interview. The client's score was 91, and the therapist's was 60; both of these were the fifth highest scores of each.

During the eighteenth interview, the therapist employed procedures more typical of most of his therapy than the few previous interviews had been. There were a large number of questions (37 per cent) and clarification of feelings (29 per cent), and some interpretation (14 per cent) and calling attention or persuasion (8 per cent). These examples of interpretation, persuasion, or calling attention focused around suggesting for the client inferences about his behavior of which he was relatively unaware. For example, it was suggested:

1. That the client's use of the phrase "whiphand," with reference to his mother, was significant,
2. That the client might prefer masturbation for other reasons than that he could have fantasies of being the successful lover, *i.e.,* the absence of the feared female,
3. That the client's description of intercourse made it sound like something of a chore,
4. That the client perceived intercourse as if it were rape,

5. That the client's long training might make it difficult for him to accept his wife's taking an active sexual role,
6. That merely asserting an idea often enough to himself would not necessarily make it more believable to the client,
7. That his concern about alcohol actually stemmed from his parents' disapproval of it,
8. That it would be better to forget about whether the act of intercourse will be successful, and to just participate in it,
9. That it would be better not to discuss with his wife certain aspects of their sexual relationship which might be damaging to her ego.

Well, I guess this is one of those weeks that had its low points as well as the high. Sunday we came home from church and the apartment was in a fairly messy state, and I was real irritated. I'm compulsive enough that I thought we had to get it cleaned up. And my wife wanted to sit down and read the paper. And it wasn't till after it was all cleaned up that I was able to talk to my wife about it. (Hos n + wife) There was a sense of irritation, and along with that a real feeling of failure for not having been able to talk with her about it earlier. We did talk about it, and she was good about it. Maybe eventually I'll get to the point where I say what irritates me at the time that it irritates me. (Anx — self) Since that time my wife tries to keep the house more straightened up. (Aff n + wife)

I don't think I saw the connection at the time, but there's irritation that we don't have a decent vacuum cleaner, and we don't have the money to buy a new one. We're terribly short financially right now, and we have a number of extra expenses coming up. We really need the fees from some of the testing I've been doing outside. (Anx — prof) I'm not really sure what kind of a decision I'm going to make about what to do in this financial matter. I'm a little more amenable to the idea that I won't be staying on my present job forever. Before, I couldn't tolerate that idea. There's a need that I have now to achieve some measure of success at what I've chosen to do. There's something of a realization that maybe I don't have to be content with mediocrity. I have a feeling I can be a good teacher. (Ego + prof)

You're saying that, before, you felt you couldn't hold more than a half adequate job, but now you're not sure that that's all you want for yourself. (Clarification)

No, and the thing that brings it out is realizing that I'm changing my set on some of these questions.

The other bad factors during the week involved what therapy I've been doing. (There is some description of rather routine interviews with one client.) The other boy, who was in the hospital, I wanted to tell you about this, but I blocked on it. A lot of his problems have been sexual, and we've gotten around to a point where I felt that with all his paranoid ideation, there must be some homosexuality there, and he had some pretty upsetting dreams including one in which his wife was having intercourse with another man. I thought he was ready to tolerate an interpretation of some homosexual involvement at that point, so I made it to him, and he accepted it. And I pumped him more and made him go more into detail than was necessary, and I think it was a kind of voyeuristic thing on my part. And I felt upset by it afterwords in that I'd do something that was unethical. (Sex n — homo → Dom n + peers)

And this reminds me that I still get irritated about my wife's mauling me. (Hos n + wife) And yet I think I had an insight into that, too, in that this week she made some statement to the effect that if I loved her enough or was affectionate enough toward her, she wouldn't do that. And I think this is something that I have suspected all along but have been unwilling to recognize. There's something that I need to do about our relationship, and that's to be more affectionate toward her. (Aff n + wife) There's still not enough satisfaction in the sexual relationship at home to prevent this kind of thing. (Sex n — het → Anx)

You find yourself being left unsatisfied. (Clarification)

Not in a physical sense. I think it's the lack of ease. I still do not feel comfortable as I think I ought to. (Anx — self)

In what way do you feel uncomfortable? (Question)

This I don't know. (Sighs) When I was thinking about what we had to say last week, I know now that I was getting around to the point of accepting more what you had to say. (Dep + ther, Rel) I was pretty resistant; I think I was even somewhat resentful of some of the interpretations. (Hos n + ther, Res)

Which ones? (Question)

I didn't get the import of the difference between . . . I didn't wanta be dragged back to the point of going over this whole thing again. I think that was the major source of irritation. I felt I had these things worked out. (Hos n + ther) I'm referring to the matter of my wife's sexual advances and my own reaction to them. And I saw the superficiality of this business of my saying that it's a question of who has the penis, and the question of who has the masculine role. (Ins) And I related this to my home situation where there's no doubt but what Dad had the penis, but there's a real question of who has the masculine or the commanding role. (Hos n + fa; Ins) And the other thing that occurred to me, I always thought of it as an asset of his, that this business of during mealtime why he'd be up and down getting things, and now it occurs to me that this is really a quite feminine role. (Hos n + fa) And that he had to jump through hoops for Mother, and I guess there's still the residual feeling that my wife makes me jump through hoops for her. (Dep — wife → Anx)

You're anxious about this question of who has the more masculine or more dominant traits. (Clarification)

Yeah, the more dominant ones. What happens sexually between us is confounded by this, in terms of who is the aggressor. But one of the things that I think has led me off the track is real concern about the *sexual* role, and not about whether I'm gonna run the house. Or am I going to be browbeaten like Dad was? Maybe I'm evading the sexual issue, but I still feel that the real question is one of dominance. The person who's dominant is adequate. If I'm dominant there, I'm adequate all the way around. (Dom p — wife → Anx — self) I'm beginning to feel adequate at school now, and if I stay away from home, maybe it's because in a sense this is the one place I'm not adequate. And it's true that I'm not. I still don't know quite how to cope with my wife's mauling. (Hos p — wife) I say that if I give her more affection she won't do it, but I have no proof of this. (Dep — wife → Anx)

The way you usually cope with it is to complain or make her stop. (Calling attention)

Or show some irritation; it's sort of a passive-aggressive reaction. (Hos n + wife → Dep — wife) You know this fits, too. Maybe I saw this before, but it didn't fit then in the way it does now. The reason for my aggression against authority is because Mother was the authority in our family. Just to make sure that nobody else gets the whiphand and beats me into submission like Dad was. (Hos n — mo)

There's a real struggle for control and a need to demonstrate to yourself that you control the situation. (Clarification)

I have a feeling that I'm fitting a lot of pieces together today. And it's not as intellectual as it has been for the last few weeks. Sometimes I almost have an impulse to take notes during the week, so I can remember better. (Ego + ther)

You used an interesting figure of speech when you spoke of your mother having the whiphand. (Calls attention)

It almost sounds like she does have a penis. The thing that occurred to me then was that she does have the beard. That's a funny one. She certainly did have a lot of masculine characteristics. (Hos n + mo)

And your father had a lot of feminine ones. (Interpretation₅)

The structure was pretty definitely reversed. He was really castrated by her. She even called Dad an old maid. (Hos n + mo)

It's that being castrated that you fear. (Interpretation₉)

By the whip, huh? That kinda left me blah. (Res)

Yeah, it was a straight typical Freudian allusion. It might have been better if what I'd said was, "What you fear is a replication of the situation where the woman runs the place and denies the man his proper right of controlling the situation." (Clarification)

Um-hm.

We use this phrase "castrating female" when it's only become a stereo-type of something that's fairly different. We really are referring to a woman who controls and dominates a situation. (Information)

Yeah, but you know, I've thought about aggressive women being cas-trating females, and this is a pet phrase for me, and if you had called my mother a castrating female, this would have really hit the nail on the head. Because it does describe the type that I think of, and it describes *her*. (Hos n + mo) I guess there is the fear there of my wife being a castrating female, a real aggressive kind of woman, when quite obviously she isn't. I say she isn't, and yet I must perceive her as being this way. I perceive some aggression, especially in the process of that mauling. (Dom p — wife) And at other times, too. Although in general her role is more of a dependent one. And there's an ambivalence on my part there, too, because I don't want her to be *too* dependent. I want her to be able to do some things for herself, so that she can help me when I need help. (Dep + wife)

This behavior you describe as mauling, you've told me about the physi-cal aspects of it, but I'm trying to see it in perspective with regard to its psychological meaning to her, and to you. (Question)

You know Steig has a cartoon called something like "An Affectionate Woman," and it shows a man sitting in a chair with a woman with her hair down over his eyes and sorta draped over him, and this struck a real chord with me. It's almost me sitting there immobilized by all this love and affection. Trying to be as objective as I can, I think there's this element in my wife. (Dom p — wife) And I don't feel quite equal to this. Part of it's a neurotic need on her part, but I should be able to go half way in meeting her needs. She gratifies a lot of my neurotic needs. (Dep + wife → Aff n + wife)

You find it difficult to do it for her. (Clarification) *I wonder why?* (Question)

I suppose it gets around to this. . . . This is getting to the point where the homosexuality did at one time, where I'm just damn sick and tired of hearing about it. (Res) But it almost comes to the point that I'm going to have to have intercourse with her, and there's a reluctance on my part to do it. (Sex p — wife → Anx)

Why is there a reluctance to have intercourse? (Question)

Sometimes because I think there are other things I would rather do.

What would you rather be doing? (Question)

Relaxing, reading, solitary kind of things. I think we were married for over a year before she was able to have an orgasm. I'm sure that during that stretch there was a feeling on my part that I wasn't making the grade. (Anx — masc)

So having intercourse was a sign of failure for you. (Clarification)

To some extent.

Why do you think reading is more attractive than having intercourse? (Question)

Well, it's a way of escape. A defense. And on some occasions I think I'd almost rather masturbate than have intercourse. (Sex n + masturb)

Why? (Question)

In intercourse I think I see her as being the aggressor. She takes the upper position, which would reinforce that idea, and I'm almost a passive recipient. (Sex n — wife → Anx — masc) Or so it seems to me. And in the masturbation fantasy it is reversed, and I am the aggressor and the real adequate powerful male. (Ego + masc)

Intercourse does not seem like carrying out that role for you. (Clarification) (Pause) *There might be other reasons why masturbation would seem more attractive than intercourse.* (Interpretation$_9$) (Pause)

There is in the sense that I can fantasy girls other than my wife. Although it's been so long since I masturbated now that I wouldn't know who the object would be. (Sex n + masturb)

When you have intercourse you always fantasy about her? (Question)

You know, I can't consciously recall fantasying during intercourse. But pretty much my attentions are upon her, and upon both of us as the climax approaches. (Sex n — het)

You're sort of preoccupied with having it be successful. (Clarification)

Yeah. There's a strain there (laughs with some embarrassment) rather than having. . . . (Sex n — het)

That sounds like it's something of a chore. (Interpretation$_5$) *Or you're worrying about the success of the act itself.* (Clarification)

And yet with each attempt working out almost entirely successfully, you would think there would be reinforcement. I would have little objective reason to doubt that it would work out successfully. But evidently the fear is always there that I won't measure up to it. (Sex p — wife → Anx)

There's another aspect of masturbation that might be less threatening. That is if the feared female isn't present. (Interpretation$_9$)

Then I don't have to worry about being the aggressor any more. (Dep — wife)

You can go at your own pace, and you don't have to please her. She can't criticize you for being inadequate. (Interpretation$_5$)

Which she wouldn't do anyway. But it's true that I might feel that she was, even when she wasn't. I would certainly feel the inadequacy in any event. I'm not quite sure what I should *do* about this. (Dep — ther) Other than that I take your advice and make her think she's about to be raped. It's interesting that I should think of that. (Dom n + wife)

It's interesting that that's the thought that you have. (Calls attention)

I think that's pretty true, too, I perceive it as an attack. This is just another way in which she is dominating me. (Dom p — wife)

If she gets on top, you tell *yourself that this doesn't make any difference, but what about all the attitudes you may have built up over a long time about which is the "male" role.* (Persuasion) *Have you ever known a male to boast about a woman lying on top of him?* (Question)

I think maybe on one occasion. With a woman that I pictured as being in the male position most of the time. It would seem to me if I could get to the point where I could accept the fact that she isn't trying to take over domination, that this would bother me less. (Dom p — wife)

How can you get yourself to accept that? (Question)

Probably by asserting myself more.

You aren't going to believe it just because you say it, are you? (Persuasion)

No, it's gotta be the same kind of thing as telling her that I am. The only danger here that I see is going off the opposite end. Maybe this isn't a real danger, (laughs) because it's gonna be difficult enough for me to do. (Dom n + wife → Anx)

You're a little afraid of going too far. (Clarification)

Plus the fact that there's a reluctance to give up what dependency I have. (Dep + wife) (Long pause) In reality I do leave a lot up to her in the way of final decisions. I accept her decisions a lot of the time. And I'm fearful of violating some of these. (Dep + wife) For instance the matter of beer or alcohol in the house. I feel I've gotten farther with her by going easily on some things. I buy beer now when I want to, and I wouldn't want to have liquor in the house myself. (Ego + matur)

Why? (Question)

I think I still retain enough of my puritanical background. (Dep + par) I'd be kind of leery of how much drinking might be done. I tend to see hard liquor as being a. . . . Plus the fact that there appears to be a difference between the kind of person who drinks hard liquor, and the person who just has a glass of wine.

What is the difference? (Question)

Well, the highball seems to be a crutch, while with wine it's just a taste, it has less of an effect, and I guess it's less puritan. (Laughs)

Less the kind of thing you've been taught was proper. Less the mores of the group you were a part of. (Interpretation$_5$) *Perhaps also less what your parents would approve of.* (Interpretation$_7$)

That's true. You know, when my folks were up last week, I was thinking before they came, about what's the difference if I have a glass of beer in the house. I always get rid of anything I might have before they come up, but I think now if the situation were to arise where they were to ask about it, or if it were to seem natural, I could tell them about it. I couldn't have done that previously. (Ego + matur)

Well, that's progress. Progress on the independence goal. (Approval)

You know, I think that's one of the reasons that it was of concern to me to start thinking about discontinuing therapy. The thing that occurred to me on the way up was a kind of reluctance to think about that, now that December's coming up pretty rapidly. (Dep + ther) But I also had this reaction that it's really another step forward in establishing independence. (The client is now conscious of his desire to increase his independence.) I don't have to ask Snyder for affection and support. If I can do this and handle it, I'll feel pretty good about myself. I think really this week for the first time I came to the realization that I probably will be able to get along without using you as a crutch. Or using you as a source of dependency-gratification. (Ego + matur)

That's the goal of good therapy, isn't it? (Reassurance)

I guess so. I think it would be the major goal of *my* therapy. My major goal in life, really. (Insight) I almost have the feeling that if I continue on past that point, I would start looking at it as a didactic therapy. (Ego + matur) I'm sure there are problems that I haven't solved, and there's a lot of reality testing to be done, especially in the business of my relationship with my wife and in this business of aggression, and in the sexual relationship. But on the other hand I have the feeling that I have some of the tools to work with, now. (Ego + self) It's true that one of the motivations has been that I can come back to you and report success to you. There's still a search for approval. (Dep + ther) But there's a lot of satisfaction that comes just within me that makes getting your approval less important.

It's more important to have your own approval. (Clarification)

And in the past I haven't been able to see that I could achieve things and just feel pleasure in my own sense of satisfaction just for the achieving of them. Before, I had to have somebody else giving approval. (Dep + gen) (Long pause)

I wonder what you're thinking. (Question)

I have the same feeling I had a couple of weeks ago when I wanted to go home and try this out. I think I'd better tread lightly because I may be inclined to misuse this feeling. (Laughs)

Just exert authority for the purpose of exerting it. (Clarification)

I kind of have the feeling I'd like to talk about this with her. I think I could in the sense of the way I saw Mother and Dad, and it wouldn't have to be too threatening to her. (Aff n + wife)

Some talking might be appropriate, if it wasn't designed to further your neurotic needs at her expense or by injuring her ego. It could be constructive. I'm not sure how appropriate it would be to discuss the question of your perception of her in the sex role. (Advice)

This is the one area I was thinking about that I would want to avoid. For one thing, I'm not her therapist. I have the hope that this area will come along as I test out the other. I don't see that there's any point for me to assume my concept of the male position. (Ego + masc; Ins) It would mean that she wouldn't have the satisfaction in intercourse. I think I should be able to be satisfied to be content and enjoy the way we have intercourse. (Sex n + wife) And that the reason that I don't is not because of a sexual. . . .

It may be because you're thinking about the adequacy of the act, rather than being directly involved in the act itself and participating rather than observing. Rather than being involved in the sexual fantasies, you may be thinking about the insecurity aspect of whether it's going to work. (Information)

Jones: Nineteenth Interview (11/29)

THE NINETEENTH INTERVIEW was rather different from many of the others in that the therapist assumed a much more active role in the therapy. In the transcription, his speech occupied 38 per cent of the lines of manuscript. The number of supportive responses rose from an average of about 6 per cent to 19 per cent. Redirective responses were also high: persuasion and criticism (5 per cent of each), challenging (3 per cent), and calling attention (2 per cent). Giving advice and information constituted 14 per cent of the material, which was a high frequency for this therapist. On the other hand, the use of interpretation was considerably lower than usual (7 per cent), and the number of questions asked was only about average.

Despite the large use of therapist intervention in the interview, the affect scores changed very little; both dropped slightly, so that they were still above the mean score.

The analysis of the content of the nineteenth interview is quite interesting. About a third of it pertains to sex needs and another third to discussion of the "self." Affiliation needs, discussion of ego-satisfactions, dependency, and hostility comprised the rest. About a sixth of the client's responses concerned the therapy relationship. Sex was the main theme of the interview; what the client talked about most was his concern about his homosexual feelings, which seemed to be exacerbated by the therapy he was conducting with a client who had some homosexual problems. Mr. Jones was at times greatly depressed that he was unable to rid himself of these feelings, but at other times, he held to the point of view that he could expect these feelings to occur sometimes, and he could adjust to their presence without becoming upset by them. His ambivalence was marked. At times he described himself as a person who definitely would prefer homosexual to heterosexual relationships, but at other times he expressed strong desire to develop more predominantly heterosexual interests.

When this discussion was at its height, the therapist took a rather important step; he indicated to the client, by means of an analogy to certain food appetites, a feeling that it might be impossible for the symptom of homosexuality to be completely eradicated for this client. He suspected that the appetite was an over-learned behavior pattern. This implied that the client would need to adopt a goal of learning to adjust to the homosexual feelings while doing everything possible to enhance the valence of the heterosexual responses which he did experience. It also may have provided the motivation for the client's feeling that there was no longer much reason to remain in therapy. That is to say, that he would have to settle for an adjustive and re-educative kind of therapy rather than a reconstructive or reorganizing type.

Another strong intervention by the therapist came when the client was discussing the strength of his sex drive and compared it unfavorably to that of some of the young men he knew in the fraternity. The therapist was quite critical of Mr. Jones' applying to himself any external criteria of masculinity. Here the therapist was directly attacking Mr. Jones' neurotic insecurity.

The principal objects of client affect during this interview were the "self," the therapist, the client's homosexual urges, his lack of sufficient masculinity, his lack of maturity, and his wife.

Since this interview was a crucial one, and so near the end of the therapy, it was especially important that the therapist decided to take such an active part in directing its course. At this point, he had decided that the elimination of the homosexual symptom was impossible for Mr. Jones and that he would be leaving therapy fairly soon. The therapist felt, therefore, that he should take stronger supportive and persuasive measures to build as much ego strength as possible, so that the client would be able to deal with his inadequacy feelings in this area in a less emotional and more rational way. The major examples of support he offered were the following:

1. Latent and quiescent problems often exacerbate themselves when the end of therapy approaches,
2. Deeply conditioned appetites are likely to remain residual in the personality, like over-learned skills; you may not be able to unlearn your homosexual appetites,
3. If the physical sex drive is allowed to accumulate sufficiently, it is bound to overcome your psychological inhibitions which exist toward marital intercourse,
4. You need not be concerned about the strength of other people's sex drive but only whether your own is sufficient to take care of your own marital responsibilities,

5. You have been moving in the direction of your goal of a more satis-factory heterosexual adjustment,
6. We may be getting farther in the direction of solving your problems than you think.

Some of the more re-directive statements by the therapist were the following:

1. A learned appetite is like an over-learned neuro-muscular skill and often cannot be entirely unlearned (Persuasion),
2. Therapy isn't brainwashing; even imprisonment doesn't eradicate most homosexual appetites (Persuasion),
3. Having to consider how sex will work out would be less rewarding than just being able to experience it unsubjectively (Advice),
4. If you're driven by a desire to compete with other young men in strength of sex drive, you're asking for trouble (Persuasion).

There were also some occasions of information-giving which were supportive of the ideas presented above. Despite the therapist's strong use of such interventions of a persuasive, supportive, or informing nature, Mr. Jones' post-interview dependency score remained very low (25).

We went to my parents' home last week, and things went pretty well with the parents. There was no pressure on their parts to have me step in and solve problems, which I was grateful for in a way. (Aff n + par)

The other thing that I have had on my mind was another homosexual dream I had after our last interview, probably the first one I had since 'way back before I was married. There wasn't any real anxiety about it. I kind of have the impression that maybe I can relax and enjoy it, accept it in a way. (Sex n + homo) I don't know whether I can expect this kind of dream occasionally. This is the one thing that has me concerned, whether it is still a problem or whether I've gotten to the point where I can accept it enough to recall it. (Anx — masc)

You're not sure whether your dreaming that kind of dream represents ability to accept it and not repress it or whether it represents an area of conflict. (Clarification)

It may in some sense represent a conflict, in that one of my clients has been trying to work through a homosexual problem. You remember I told you about this voyeuristic kind of thing. Perhaps in what I'm encouraging him to tell me, rather than showing an interest in the heterosexual devel-opment, there's the possibility of my identifying with his wife rather than with him in the situation in a covert kind of homosexual fantasy. I wasn't too much aware of that before, but that's a possibility. (Sex n — homo)

The dream itself is rather unclear. I can recall two prone figures beside myself, not much in the way of the sexual act itself, and that one of those figures, instead of having a penis, had a flap, I guess sort of a castrated male. This may tie in with a decrease in sexual desire on my part for my wife. It occurred about this same time, and a reluctance to have intercourse that bothered me, because I thought I had been making some progress in this regard. (Sex n — homo → Anx) The desire for intercourse has increased since then.

That was what I meant the last time when we talked about this, and I asked you what you might rather be doing than having intercourse. (Information) Because you didn't go into it, I didn't pursue it, but in terms of the things you've told about yourself at times, the possibility existed that you might rather be having homosexual intercourse. (Interpretation₄)

I can probably accept that on an intellectual level. It's interesting that it keeps cropping up. In a sense it's upsetting, but not as much now as it was the previous time. (Anx — gen)

Why is it upsetting? (Question)

Well, it would seem like a relapse. I guess also I've had in the back of my mind the idea that probably I was getting close to the end, and this suggests that maybe I'll have to continue in therapy longer than I'd planned. (Res) Unless it's one of these things that Reik talks about as being old scars that give pain even though you understand them.

Often when you're contemplating the end of therapy, as you're implying in this example, old problems exacerbate and the symptoms reappear. (Reassurance)

This is another thing that occurred to me, too. While there's a conscious desire to end therapy, one of the reasons for the dream may be to have a new problem and present you with another reason for staying. (Dep + ther)

Perhaps you were thinking this, too. I could raise the question whether it is realistic to expect therapy to eliminate this need, whatever it is, that causes these occasional upsurgings of homosexual feelings. Perhaps this is an appropriate analogy: suppose that you loved a particular kind of food, like candy or cake, and then a doctor told you that you shouldn't eat it because it wasn't good for you. And you learned to adapt yourself to a diet without this food. Would you be astonished if every once in a while you would dream about cake or candy? Or if you saw a cake you might have an uncontrollable urge to eat some of it. (Reassurance) Now, is there anything that you could do by any therapeutic or conditioning process to arrive at the point where you never had the slightest interest in cake? (Question) Maybe you could become so damn sick from cake that it would have absolutely no reward value for you and just made you feel ill to think about it.

What I'm implying, of course, is that these homosexual feelings are an appetite, a learned response to a basic drive combined with a given cue or stimulus. (Information) *Suppose you had always written with your left hand, and then you were forced to use the right hand; nevertheless, part of your neuromuscular system would include a skill with your left hand that you would probably never entirely lose. There would be times in your less conscious behavior when you might find yourself writing with your left hand, or dreaming of doing so.* (Persuasion)

Kind of a staggered-interval partial-reward sort of situation.

I don't know whether you could ever completely extinguish this; whether we have strong enough forces ever to completely extinguish deeply learned behavior, or rather, to de-condition it. Therapy isn't brainwashing, and even putting a man in prison for homosexual acts usually fails to achieve this de-conditioning. (Persuasion)

You know, I have several reactions to what you just said. One is a pleasant one, and I suspect that maybe the other one is hostile. The one is that you're indicating to me now that my judgment that I'm getting close to the end is the right one. I think you feel somewhat the same way I do. (Ego + ther) The other reaction was almost an automatic interpretation of your analogy in terms of the problem that I'm dealing with now as a homosexual one, and your analogy was one of cake, and eating the cake. There was a mixed feeling whether or not to express it. (Hos n + ther)

I think you should express it. (Relationship) *I'm not sure whether you're trying to reverse the therapeutic process and analyze me on the basis of my expressions here.* (Question)

It's hard for me to decide whether I'm being hostile in this or not. Maybe I'm just telling you that I'm ready to take over for myself. (Ego + matur)

Why did my analogy of eating cake bother you? (Question)

I don't know whether it bothered me or whether I saw it as being kind of funny. One thought that occurred to me was that I projected homosexual impulses onto you. I think that would be a sort of hostile weapon for me to use against you; I think psychologists who analyze their friends' behavior in social situations are really being hostile, and my feelings might have been similar. (Hos n + ther)

Why did my analogy of cake suggest homosexual behavior? (Question)

It wasn't the cake, it was the idea of eating. I don't have any associations with cake.

Why did that make you want to project homosexual feeling onto me? (Question; relationship)

I'm not altogether sure that it did. I think I was more concerned with having insight into you than anything else. It's almost as though you were free-associating for me instead of me doing it for you. I guess it was an

attempt to understand what this guy Snyder's really like. (Hos n +
ther)

*Well, actually I think of eating as the best example there is to illustrate
appetite. I think of sex as an appetite.* (Information)

Yeah. In a sense the way that I use homosexuality is to establish a close
liaison with some male figure and for orality, and for giving me love and
affection. (Dep — ther → Sex n + ther, Rel) And I think, too, it's an
attempt to identify with you, somehow. I think I've had this kind of reaction with other men before. (Aff n + ther)

*There was another thing inherent in the therapy, and that was that I was
in essence saying that I doubted whether* any *therapy can completely eliminate this problem, or rather symptom. And that might make you quite angry.*
(Interpretation₅)

(Sighs) Disappointed, perhaps. I can gauge the anxiety that I have
fairly well, I think, at this point, and there are twinges when I don't do a
job well or I goof in some way. It's much more rapidly dissipated now than
it was. There's still a lot of dread in having anxiety. (Anx — self, ther) I
can experience anxiety in situations where it isn't justified, like when I first
took my present job. I feel secure now on the job, but I think that if I
should ever decide to change to another, I can pack up and leave without
being too upset by it. And before therapy I don't think I could have felt
that way. I wouldn't have felt that I was able to hold down any other job
than this one. That seems to be running away from what we were talking
about before. (Ego + prof)

*Well, it's not discussing that dream, or your feelings about it, your
homosexual fantasies.* (Disapproval) *But I wouldn't say it wasn't important.*
(Reassurance) *You feel that you're now in better control of your anxieties.*
(Clarification)

The one situation that does leave me anxious or upset at times is the
one of not making headway with one of my clients. And this, I think, is because I consider it a real personal failure. (Anx — prof)

*In some cases, perhaps it isn't your fault. They may be the result of ele-
ments that you can't control.* (Reassurance)

That's probably true. I think the strongest sense of failure still lies with
this kid who's so dependent and homesick. He comes in regularly as clock-
work, and I still dread the hours. I told him again this week that from time
to time I got irritated with his dependency. (Anx — prof)

What does having people dependent on you mean to you? (Question)

It's not just having them depend on me; I think I can accept the dependence. In fact, I like them to be a little bit more dependent than they
are independent. But if there is dependency, without *any* attempt on the
part of the client to understand himself. . . . (Dom p + peers → Hos n
+ peers)

It's the plain, all-encompassing, over-all, helpless kind of dependence that you can't stand. (Clarification)

Yeah. And the inability to produce any results. What's so discouraging is that he's a hell of a bright boy, who gets a straight B average, so he *ought* to be able to learn something about himself. (Anx — prof) I guess this is a blind alley in our discussion. (Res; Ins)

You got away from the topic of your sexual difficulties, and the sexual problems with your wife. (Disapproval; directive lead)

I don't imagine I like the concept too much of my possibly preferring a homosexual partner to my wife. That doesn't sit well. And yet, damn it, it seems to fit. Or at least it explains quite a bit. (Sex n — homo → Anx) Probably that was the reason I attempted to interpret *your* needs, rather than sticking to my own. (Hos n + ther; Ins) Maybe the solution lies in my wife's expression, "I wish I had your peter," and maybe what I ought to do is give it to her. (Dep — wife) But there's the problem that it really does raise, that with this preference for a male partner, am I ever going to be sufficiently rewarded with a female partner? Or is this a continuing problem, and I can never become conditioned to prefer the female partner? Perhaps I've gotten to the point where I can say, "O.K., these are homosexual feelings that I have, and when they come up I'll deal with them."(Sex n + homo) But that doesn't completely solve the problem, in the sense that certainly one of my major goals is to have satisfying sex with *her.* But the feeling occurs to me, "Damn it, why don't you let things die out, rather than stirring up trouble again?" (Hos n + ther) And I guess that must have been the reason for my resistance. It's difficult for me to honestly see a rapid adjustment to this kind of thing. To enjoy sexual relations with my wife completely. (Sex n + het)

Well, we talked about ways in which sex with her was less rewarding. For example, if you have to think a lot about the adequacy of your performance in the act, rather than just experiencing the situation unsubjectively, and you had to worry about whether it was going to work out . . . (Advice; the therapist is suggesting a method of improving the client's experience of the sexual act.)

But if it's just experiencing it, this sounds like a pretty passive kind of activity. As a male, one of my concerns is to see that she's satisfied in the situation. (Anx — masc) There are physiological and psychological adjustments that *most* people have to make, in order for both partners to achieve an orgasm. Why shouldn't she have the same satisfactions in intercourse that I do? And yet I suppose there is this element of strain on my part. (Aff n + wife)

It seems like something you have to work at rather than enjoy. (Clarification) *I get the feeling that for you intercourse is an undertaking, or project, or duty.* (Interpretation$_5$)

(Sighs) I guess that may be true.

How long a time interval would you have to let pass before it ceases to become a duty and becomes a thing you really desire? (Question)

I guess a week.

What I'm getting at is that the intensity of the sex drive itself probably would eventually mount to the point where you were able to overcome psychological reasons you might have for some resistance. It's an appetite, a hunger, in most people. (Information) *But you said that, when you were masturbating, you did it almost every day, which suggests that your drive isn't too weak.* (Information) *Presumably the time will come for almost anyone when the drive becomes powerful enough to overcome psychological barriers.* (Information; reassurance)

That's certainly reasonable. I think I feel that way at the end of about a week. I guess too there's the factor that as a real manly kind of a male I ought to be demanding it two or three times a week. (Anx — masc)

Where did you get that idea? (Question; challenging)

Damned if I know; from the boys in the fraternity, I suppose. I guess I really need to prove myself in this area. (Anx — masc)

The only question that needs to concern you is whether she wants it more often than you do; not that of how often the young, deprived hot-bloods in the fraternity think *they would like to have sex if they had a constant source of it available.* (Reassurance) *If you're driven by any competitive desire to be as masculine as some other guy, and you interpret masculinity as being measured by frequency of intercourse, you're asking for trouble.* (Persuasion)

Yeah, it's interesting, the guy that I was thinking about while we were talking about this was my sister-in-law's husband, who's always implying that his appetite is very strong and that they satisfy it quite frequently. He meets his family needs sexually, socially, and financially, in ways that seem to me much better than I do mine. (Anx — masc)

You feel pretty inadequate in comparison to him. (Clarification) *I suppose we can assume that he's as sexually adequate as he says he is.* (Challenging)

Well, his wife implies it, too. (Pause) You know something else that I've repressed until we started talking about it. I think for the first time in over a year I've masturbated. The first time was the day after my last visit up here. I was very reluctant to tell you about this, but this makes a little bit more sense to me now that, as I said, there was decreased sexual activity with my wife, and then when the desire did arrive, she was in her period. Maybe the physiological effect may have something to do with the reduced drive. (Sex n + masturb → Anx)

You feel you were using another outlet for the sex drive. You had a decrease in physiological need, by discharging it through masturbation, and

so you feel it's logical that you're not going to want intercourse as much.
(Clarification)

Well, the thing that concerns me is why I would rather masturbate than
have intercourse. (Anx — masc)

I think we talked about that a little bit the last time. (Calls attention)
It may be easier. (Information)

Plus the fact that I wasn't too anxious for a heterosexual relation.

What were the fantasies you had when you masturbated? (Question)

About this secretary. She seems to be the prime figure in my sexual fantasies. I think she may be a substitute for my sister, although I don't any
longer have conscious sexual fantasies about my sister. But I find *that*
interpretation tolerable. (Sex n — het)

Why did you feel anxious about telling me that you had masturbated?
(Question)

I thought it constituted a real regression on my part. It was a sign that
I had failed. (Anx — ther)

Why does that seem like failure? (Question)

Oh, it's certainly not progress toward an adequate relationship with
my wife. (Anx — masc)

Well, it would probably draw off some of the heterosexual drive. (Attenuates)

You know something. For me to look at her or to perceive her external
sex organs at one time was pretty repugnant. (Sex p — wife → Anx; a
probable sign of "spouse phobia," "split *imago*," and latent homosexuality.)
And this has diminished considerably. Now I'm at the point where I actually
find that exciting. (Sex p + wife)

The fact that it's exciting is good, isn't it? (Reassurance) *The fact that
you have been developing in that direction; if your goal is toward a heterosexual adjustment, then this is real progress.* (Approval)

The way I finally got around to telling you about this: I want to draw
things to a close, and at the same time I don't want to waste the time I'm
spending here. If I didn't tell you, I'd feel as though I'd cheated in some
way. I've had conflict about how to use the remaining interviews. But also
I feel if I'm gonna spend the time it takes to come up here, I might as well
use it advantageously. (Aff n + ther; Rel; Res)

*Also I expect that it requires a good bit of courage on your part to tell
me about something like this that you looked upon as regression or failure.*
(Clarification)

I feel a little bit discouraged today, but I think it's just from seeing the
immediate picture and not being able to fit it into an over-all picture. (Anx
— matur)

Things don't look as good as you'd hoped they would, maybe. (Clarification)

Yeah. I'm afraid I've set up pretty strongly for myself the goal of terminating by Christmas, and I have some apprehension about maybe having to continue beyond then. (Anx — matur, ther)

Maybe we've done more today toward solving the problem than you've perceived. (Reassurance)

Maybe I've recognized some of the key issues more than I had been before. (Ins)

I would suspect, for instance, that your telling me about this thing that you had been blocking on is itself a sign of progress. (Reassurance)

Um-hm. There aren't many, if any, things that I've consciously been able to conceal or withhold during the time that we've been together. I guess this is some sort of tribute to the kind of relationship we've had. And also probably some indication of how dependent I've been. (Dep + ther, Rel → Aff n + ther; Rel; Ins)

Yes, you've been very frank. There hasn't been much repressing and screening, and masking, or sallying around important issues. Which has made things move rather rapidly. (Approval)

Jones: Twentieth Interview (12/6)

THE FINAL INTERVIEW was one where very positive affect existed. The client's score of 90 was his seventh highest, and the therapist's score of 72 was his second highest. The client's affect took a number of different forms: anxiety and ego-satisfactions, hostility and dependency, need for affiliation, and need to demonstrate nurturance. The objects of this affect were also rather widespread: the client himself, the therapist, the therapeutic relationship, the client's maturity, his parents, his sister, and his peers. The hostility, anxiety, nurturance, and affiliation needs were directed primarily toward the client's sister and his parents. There was some anxiety about his self-concept and about his maturity. Most of the dependency and some of the affiliation needs were directed toward the therapist.

Being a final interview, much of the content seemed to constitute a summing up of the progress achieved on various fronts. However, Mr. Jones' discussion can be divided logically under four main topics: (1) an incident in connection with his sister's difficulties, (2) his reactions in competitive situations, (3) general signs of improvement in his adjustment, and (4) the client's feelings about the therapy and the therapist.

Some of the ideas expressed with regard to his sister's "escapade" were the following:

1. He was pleased that the community was not judging him in connection with his sister's behavior,
2. He recognized that his sister was rebelling against a symbol of maternal authority, which he perhaps also symbolized for her,
3. He felt protective and nurturant toward his sister, but was annoyed with her for endangering his relationships at the college,
4. He recognized that at times he had been just as badly mixed up as his sister was now proving to be,
5. He perceived that his rebellion against authority took the form of a passive withdrawal, whereas his sister's rebellion was more outward and hostile.

399

With regard to competitive situations, Mr. Jones recognized that he had always had some trouble in this area. He felt that his desire to teach a course for a group of ministers might be something of an attempt to get even with the clergy, toward whom he had always been required to be very respectful. A colleague irritated him by trying to take over his plans for the ministers. He felt some anxiety about letting control get out of his hands, and this was also apparent in his behavior toward his family: he felt himself to be defensive against the idea of copying his father in the latter's tendency to permit the control of the family to be taken over by his mother.

Mr. Jones reported quite a number of different signs of improvement in his behavior since the beginning of therapy:

1. His sexual adjustment was better; he was allowing himself to be more spontaneous during intercourse,
2. His wife teased him about becoming more dominating and aggressive,
3. His wife had been more co-operative and less dominating toward him,
4. He felt that he had handled the situation of his sister's difficulties exceptionally well,
5. He no longer felt so much need to associate with "the boys,"
6. He is not as anxious as formerly about his wife's adjustment when they are separated.

The largest number of responses in the interview concerned the therapy interview, or Mr. Jones' feelings toward the therapist:

1. He wondered whether the therapist was trying to "taper off" the therapy,
2. His behavior in telling about all of his improvement may have constituted "telling Daddy what a good boy I've been!"
3. He had come to feel less concerned about having the therapist think well of him,
4. He felt that he was about ready to terminate therapy; he then felt some anxiety when this idea was reflected by the therapist,
5. He still felt that he would like to depend on the therapist to guide him professionally, to recommend him for APA membership, and, while not being on his doctoral examining committee, to serve on his dissertation committee,
6. He recognized that he hadn't thanked the therapist for his help, and he expressed gratitude,
7. He had never felt that the therapist was experimenting on him,
8. He liked it best when the therapist made interpretations.

There was nothing unique about the therapist's procedures during the final interview. Clarification of feeling occurred most frequently

(28 per cent). Procedures utilized about 12 per cent of the time were structuring, interpretation, giving support, and giving information. Less frequently utilized procedures were discussing the relationship (9 per cent), asking questions (7 per cent), and calling attention or challenging (4 per cent). None of the interpretations were very deep in character. They tended to go only slightly beyond the overt theme expressed by the client. The discussion about the relationship and the offering of support were perhaps the therapeutic techniques with the most dynamic potential. The discussion of the relationship took the form of reflecting the client's feeling of mild anxiety about closing the therapy, of indicating that the therapist had also found the therapy a rewarding experience, and of stating that the therapist had never been "experimenting" with the client. The reassurance or support took the form of indicating willingness to recommend the client and to serve on his dissertation committee, of indicating that, if he was showing a desire for independence, he was moving in the right direction, and of reassuring him that his anxiety about leaving therapy was a very natural feeling to have. Mr. Jones' dependency score after this interview (23) was his lowest during therapy, although he had also had that score two interviews previously.

I guess I might as well start off with the sad story first. My sister managed to get herself into a scrape again; it sure has aroused a lot of the old anxiety again. At first I was afraid she'd have gotten stupid drunk, or jumped off a bridge, or something like that. Her boss called me in and asked me what I thought they ought to do, and they were pretty understanding about it. She won't lose her job, fortunately. Somehow this time I didn't feel that it was all *my* fault; in fact, I felt more on the boss's side than on hers. (Hos n + sib) There are some things to be said on my sister's side, for that company's labor relations aren't very good, and the cause she was espousing has some merit to it. (Aff n + sib)

It's fairly complicated for you, and your status is somewhat jeopardized by being related to someone involved in these activities in the same community. (Clarification)

That's for sure. She's fighting a system, and by virtue of my position in the community I'm perceived to be partially on the side of management. She says I don't need to feel involved or to accept any responsibility for her actions, but the community won't let me get by that easily. I was ready to let her stand on her own two feet about the situation, but I got dragged into it without being able to prevent myself from it. (Hos n + sib)

You felt compromised by the situation and her activities. (Clarification)

Yes. In a sense I felt good about the fact that this has been able to happen and nothing serious has happened to me as a result; I'm being judged on my own merits, and there hasn't been any talk of my possibly being an embarrassment to the college because my sister's something of a troublemaker in the community. (Ego + matur) While the whole mess was occurring, I did have the reaction of feeling that I was just damn sick and tired of worrying about my family's problems. I felt as though my sister had gotten herself into this scrape and she damn well ought to get herself out of it. I'm not sure whether that's callousness, or whether it's just being realistic. (Hos n + sib)

Why do you think she did it? (Question)

I'm pretty sure it was a protest against authority; I think it's all a generalization of her attitude toward Mother. In a way I'm put in a sort of semi-parental role with her, and when she does things that I think aren't very wise, I tell her so, so I think she could be rebelling against me in some ways, too. There's no reason why I should have to act as *her* super-ego. But she doesn't seem to be able to control her own actions, and I'm her big brother. It sounds like my attitude toward Dad, doesn't it. (Dom n + sib)

Protective, yes, but he seems to have plenty of super-ego. (Interpretation₅)

I'm concerned about the reactions of the college. Does the college population think that I have an alcoholic sister? What sort of sexual behavior are the campus gossip-mills cooking up about her? (Anx — peers) It's very difficult for me to define where my responsibilities end as far as she is concerned. Technically, she's of age. Emotionally, she's not. She wants freedom, and yet when she has it, she sure kicks hell out of the limits. I make a strenuous effort not to play therapist with my sister, although when she gets in difficulty I try to counsel her in what way I can. (Nur n + sib)

You try not to play therapist, but you do have to try to be a big brother. (Clarification)

That's really what I'm trying to do, I suppose. It's a protective role. And I serve as a go-between with the authorities. One thing that occurred to me is that at various times I've been almost as fouled up in my own way as she has. Trying to find out what makes me tick, and trying to handle my anxieties. Why should the two of us turn out as different as we have, at least as far as behavior is concerned? My defenses apparently are different from hers. I'd rather withdraw than aggress. In some ways her aggression seems like a healthier kind of behavior. She raises hell and lets people know how she feels, while I'll just go off in the corner and not say anything. It hurts me, too, that I'm probably more passive and feminine, whereas she would be more masculine and aggressive. (Anx — masc)

I seem to remember your telling me that you used to take off once in a while, when you were in college. (Interpretation₄)

Yeah.

If you went on a binge, people wouldn't get as upset, because you were a boy and not a girl. (Challenges)

I didn't think of that. I feel as though you're telling me, "Don't be so damn smug." (Hos n + ther)

I think I was pointing out, more, that rather than the behavior being so very different, there is a striking similarity in it, really. (Interpretation$_5$)

Um-hm. I wasn't as actively aggressive, I think, although I did threaten to punch the chaplain in the nose one time! (Hos n + auth) (Both laugh)

Apparently you never did like chaplains. (Both laugh) *Do I need to ask why?* (Interpretation$_5$)

You know, I've wanted to offer a seminar for ministers in the community who would be interested in counseling, and I've wondered why I want to teach the ministers particularly. It goes back to my father's being a deacon and forcing me to be so respectful to all his minister buddies whom I detested. Of course, it also happens that the ministers have indicated an interest in having such a seminar. (He discusses in some detail his plans for such a seminar.) (Hos n + fa)

I have trouble with competitive situations. (Another professor wants to "assist" in teaching the seminars, and the client feels that this colleague will try to take over their direction.) Whenever I worked with a co-therapist on my internship, I always had to try to show that I was the senior therapist. I often inject competition into situations that really don't need to be competitive. I always have to be the leader. Here's an explanation that might make sense. Thinking of our own home when I was younger, Dad allowed the control to get away from him and allowed himself to become the passive, feminine member of the family, and this may be what I'm afraid to have happen. (Dom n + peers, par)

A form of masculine protest, sort of. (Interpretation$_5$)

I always thought masculine protest occurred in women.

It's been pointed out that more men may show it than women. (Information)

I guess I'm gonna have to step back every once in a while and say, "Look, not every guy you know is. . ." (Ins)

We haven't talked at all about what we were talking about last week. This past week I'm sure we've been more active sexually; I don't know whether it's just so I could come back this week and tell you so or not. (Dep + ther, Rel → Sex n + het) I suspect that has something to do with it. But it's been fairly enjoyable. There is still some resistance on my part. I don't think it's quite as severe as it has been. (Res) I've been paying less attention to whether we're doing it right in order to achieve the maximum results, and it's gone better. (Sex n + het) I don't think that this means that there's been a cure yet, but at least I've tried it, and it works. My wife has teased me several times about being the lord and master of the place. I guess there is some sense of resentment behind it, and yet she seems in a sense to be pleased. And maybe even a little bit more acquiescent than she might have been before. (Dom n + wife)

You're being more aggressive, and you're both rather pleased with it and accepting it rather well. (Clarification)

I'll expect relapses from time to time. I seem to be real pleased with myself today, don't I? (Ego + self)

Well, when you first came in you were a little upset and said that things had happened that had been pretty disturbing. (Calls attention) *But then you seemed later to feel that it had been a good week. I wonder whether what you're saying is that, except for the event of your sister's getting into trouble, things went pretty well for you.* (Clarification)

Yes, and essentially I didn't have much control over the part of it involving her. The fact that it worked out all right has given me a good feeling. And as a matter of fact, after it was over I didn't even think about it much, until I was driving up here today. (Ego + matur) There were some other problems in the fraternity that probably kept me somewhat occupied, although they didn't bother me at all. You know something. I haven't been in the house for a meeting at all this year. It didn't occur to me what it might mean until I just mentioned it. (Ego + matur) (Laughs)

I think you're a little pleased with yourself that you're able to tell me this. (Interpretation$_6$)

And when we've had the one boy out to the house this year, the one that I said was a darn good-lookin' kid, he's come out with his date to play bridge. So there isn't this need to go out with the boys any more. Maybe I'm looking at my world through rose-colored glasses. Everything seems to be so damn cheery, there must be a fly in the ointment somewhere. (Ego + matur)

You're afraid that there might be a relapse. Or that you're ignoring the more unfavorable aspects of the situation. (Clarification)

I probably am doing that, and yet along with it, I have a real sense of accomplishment and a feeling of enthusiasm for what's happened. And I probably have in my spare moments tried to sit down and evaluate what changes there might have been in my behavior as a result of therapy. (Anx — matur) You know, I'm wondering right now whether you're letting things slow down. (Dep + ther)

You wonder whether I'm letting things taper off in order to not get anything started up at this time. (Clarification; relationship)

You pick the damnedest times to clarify feelings! (Hos n + ther) (Both laugh)

Well, I was actually considering answering the question. No, I wasn't conscious of letting it taper off. I was conscious of thinking about something

you had said and debating to myself whether it was important enough to re-
flect it, or interpret it, or just to let it go. (Structuring; information)

There's some of *this* feeling I have, too, that perhaps in acting the way
I have during the hour I've been saying to Daddy, "Look what a good boy
I've been, and how much progress I've made." Which isn't exactly an inde-
pendent way of operating. (Dep + ther, Rel)

I think it is. It depends on the motivation. If the intent is to say, "I'm
doing all right, and you see, I don't need you much any more," this is inde-
pendence. If the intent is to say, "I've done the things you want me to do,
now will you reward me by telling me what to do next," that's different.
(Reassurance)

You know something. In the time that I've been telling you this, and
right now, I'm not particularly concerned what your reaction is going to be.
A couple of weeks ago I would have been, and I was concerned about how
you felt about whether or not I ought to come in some more. I see now that
I oughta terminate therapy. (Ego + matur) Probably if you indicated very
strongly to me that I ought to stay, I would think about it seriously. But
you would have to be pretty strong in your indication before I would consider it. I have the feeling that you'd have to have a pretty healthy argument.
(Hos n + ther) Likewise, I'm not as anxious for you to tell me that I *am*
through, because this is a judgment I've arrived at. I'm more certain of it
than I was a couple of weeks ago, and I feel good about being able to make
the evaluation myself. I think something you said last week indicated that
you thought I *had* achieved a certain amount of success. But at least this
much of the decision I'm ready to make on my own. (Ego + matur; the
client's increasing self-assurance is a healthy sign in his case. His self-
determinism in selecting his own values is a form of progress.)

So you see that you're pretty well finished, now. You feel you're pretty
well the way you want to be, and you're satisfied. (Clarification) *I'd really*
have to give you an argument to convince you otherwise. (Restatement)
You don't even care whether I am inclined to agree with you or not.
(Clarification)

I feel dependent on you to this extent, that I'm still running into problems in the therapy I'm doing. I would value your judgment, your opinions
in those situations. But I think perhaps more as an authority in the area of
therapy, rather than as someone simply to be dependent upon. (Dep +
ther, Rel) And the other thing that's been running through my mind is
something that I hesitate to bring out because I think it jeopardizes in a sense
the therapy, and yet, let me think for a moment about it. (Pause) I have to
have five references for membership in the APA, and I had considered asking you to be one of these. I feel very certain that you would do it if I asked
you to do it. (Dep + ther) But I don't think that it would be quite ethical

for me to ask you to do it at this point. (A rather mature attitude, showing independence.) For one thing I would be fearful of using it as a way of testing you, to see just how much you approve of me as a psychologist, (Ego + matur) but the reason that I would rather use you than I would somebody else is that I can't be exactly sure how the others would react. I *think* they are favorably inclined toward me at this point. (Dep + ther)

If you were deeply involved in therapy at this point, I would rather not be asked to commit myself on this, and if, also, I had some doubts about your qualifications, it would be embarrassing, because I wouldn't want the evidence of my doubts to influence the therapy. But since I think you are no longer deeply committed to further therapy, or that you're pretty well out of it, and since I don't have any doubts, I would be quite willing to recommend you. As a former teacher of yours, rather than as your therapist, I am glad to do it. I don't think at this point it can either jeopardize or enhance the therapy situation for me to do that. (Offers help; the client actually did test the relationship, and the therapist felt it valid to show positive approval in this regard.)

I made my decision, and now I. . . .

And now I threw you back into feeling ambivalent. (Clarification) (Both laugh)

Well, I'll put it this way: if the form comes from the APA for me to fill out, I will neither be annoyed nor pleased. And the same if it doesn't come. (Offers help)

Something else that I've been thinking about is whether or not I oughta terminate therapy today. (Ego + matur, ther)

Well, I was wondering whether or not I should ask you, because you were saying for some time the things that . . . (Structuring)

That a client says in a final interview.

Then that's probably the way we should handle it. (Structuring)

I get a real funny feeling, now that you've said that. (Dep + ther)

You have some reservations. (Clarification)

Yeah, there's some reluctance. Possibly that even predominates, at the moment. (Dep + ther)

It's been a satisfying relationship for you, and you have some positive vectors toward me, as I have toward you, and we can't have as much interchange with each other outside of therapy as we have had here, and so this gives you a certain twinge of regret. (Relationship) *One would normally feel regret, too, when he was leaving his parents' home, which had been satisfying to him, but he wouldn't feel real pain about it. The regret wouldn't be so intense that he couldn't do it. And we aren't ceasing to know each other.* (Reassurance; relationship; the therapist was attempting to make the "separation trauma" less painful.)

If we have just a few minutes left, I'd like to mention one other thing.

I've considered this almost since we've started working together, and that is the matter of your being on my doctoral committee. I'm not sure how well I'm going to be able to tolerate this, in orals, for instance. I would value having you on my committee in terms of advice on a dissertation, but I'm sure I would be upset to have you be present during my orals and asking questions in such a way that you were putting me on the spot. It would seem like a reversal of our relationship, and kind of hard to take. I may change my mind in the future; at present I would prefer that you weren't on the committee. Is this sort of thing ever changed? (Aff n + ther, Rel)

Why don't I just ask to be taken off of the committee? That's very easy to do. (Offers help) *Your reason is perfectly valid, and I have used it other times.* (Reassurance)

Will I be able to use you as a member of my thesis committee? (Dep + ther)

That depends on the nature of your study entirely. If it's in my area, the answer is "yes." Otherwise, it wouldn't be feasible.

The thought has just occurred to me that I've never directly said "Thank you," although it's been very much in my mind. (Aff n + ther)

I've found the therapy rewarding, too. That's why I do it. And you've made a contribution to me by helping in my research project. This is my experimental laboratory, and I learn things here. Although I wouldn't want you to feel you were a guinea pig. (Relationship)

No, of course not. You know something that's never occurred to me till now. I haven't wondered even from the beginning whether or not you were using a "technique" with me. I haven't felt that way. Although logically I might have expected it. (Aff n + ther)

Well, I'm exploring certain procedures, but what I'm really first interested in is the relationship. And second, I'm interested in the effect on the relationship of certain specific procedures. But I never use a procedure without the conviction that it is a good one to use. I don't just deliberately manipulate something to see what happens. (Reassurance) *I'm exploring the use of some procedures, particularly interpretation.* (Information)

Which, incidentally, I liked. (The client gives one last evidence of some dependency feelings here; Dep + ther, Rel)

Jones: Follow-up, Three Years after Conclusion of Therapy

M R. JONES did not enroll for courses during the next three years; however, the therapist saw him several times at professional meetings, when he was very friendly. Three years after the conclusion of therapy, he requested an appointment, ostensibly to discuss his returning for further graduate work. (Therefore, the therapist made no attempt to record the session.) After a brief discussion of this topic, it became apparent that the client's primary purpose in requesting the interview was to report his progress since the end of therapy. He stated that he felt he had matured much since he had left therapy. His relationship with his wife had been much better; they could discuss with each other the feelings they have, and this had occurred at times. They had several more children. They were getting along better sexually, and the client desired sex more frequently than at the time of therapy, as did his wife. He stated that he still avoided doing the household chores that his wife expected of him.

Mr. Jones stated that he felt willing to leave his present job some day. He said he gets along well at work and feels less dependent on his department head. At times he will even argue with him, although in a friendly, rather than a hostile, manner. He has been quite active in mental hygiene work in the community, and in church work. He had decided that dependency was his real problem at the time of therapy, and he stated that he feels he needs a God to turn to at times. (Turning to a Heavenly Father for support?) Mr. Jones indicated that, although many of the memories of therapy had melded into a diffuse impression and he was unable to remember some of the details, several principles did remain with him. The first was that he had felt shocked with himself for allowing himself to project his homosexual feelings onto the therapist. The second major conclusion he drew in therapy was that dependency was his main problem and that homosexuality was only the mechanism he used for winning affection from father-figures. His third conclusion was that the therapist had served as a strong father-surrogate and, as Mr. Jones put it, had "skillfully walked a tight-rope between being strong enough and not being too dominating." He felt that he had learned in therapy certain tools for handling his problems by the process of self-analysis.

The client mentioned, regarding homosexuality, that he had had one situation which had bothered him. He had been counseling a student who later had to be hospitalized. The student's mother contended that a homosexual relationship had developed between her son and Mr. Jones. Mr. Jones said that he realized that he had built up a strong countertransference toward this student. He had found himself dreaming that he also was being hospitalized. He stated that his present attitude toward being a therapist had changed; whereas he had formerly wanted to be one of the world's best therapists, he was now less interested in conducting therapy and more interested in teaching. He still liked academic counseling but not the handling of the deeper sort of personal adjustment problems for which therapy seems more appropriate.

About a year after this follow-up interview, the client asked the therapist to write several letters of recommendation for him. Subsequently, he took a position at a college in a large southern city, where he would be near a major university, so that he could enroll part-time for further graduate work.

References

APFELBAUM, B. *Dimensions of Transference in Psychotherapy*. Univ. of California Publications in Personality Assessment and Research, #2, pp. 90. Berkeley, Calif.: Univ. of California Publications, 1958.

BERNFIELD, M. JUDITH, and GUTHRIE, G. M., "Experimental Control of Dependency by Posthypnotic Suggestion,"*J. Clin. Psychol., 15,* 1959, 114–115.

BESWICK, D. G., and COX, F. N., "Reputed Aggression and Dependence in Children," *Aust. J. Psychol., 10,* 1958, 144–150.

BLYTH, D. D., "Dependence, Independence, and Other Factors Related to Veterans' Reactions to an Offer of Psychotherapy," *Dissertation Abstr., 20,* 1960, 2899.

CAMPBELL, MARY M., "The Primary Dimensions of Item Ratings on Scales Designed to Measure 24 of Murray's Manifest Needs," *Dissertation Abstr., 20,* 1960, 4161.

CARUTH, ELAINE G., "The Relationship of Dependency to Verbal Learning without Awareness," *Dissertation Abstr., 20,* 1959, 748–749.

COUCH, A., and KENISTON, K., "Yeasayers and Naysayers: Agreeing Response Set as a Personality Variable," *J. Abnorm. Soc. Psychol., 60,* 1960, 151–174.

DOLLARD, J., and AULD, F. JR. *Scoring Human Motives: a Manual.* New Haven: Yale Univ. Press, 1959.

FITZGERALD, B. J., "The Relationship of Two Projective Measures to a Sociometric Measure of Dependent Behavior," *Dissertation Abstr., 20,* 1959, 2380–2381.

GISVOLD, D., "A Validity Study of the Autonomy and Deference Subscales of the EPPS," *J. Consult. Psychol., 22,* 1958, 445–447.

HARDISON, J., and PURCELL, K., "The Effects of Psychological Stress as a Function of Need and Cognitive Control," *J. Pers., 27,* 1959, 250–258.

HELLER, K., "Dependency Changes in Psychotherapy as a Function of the Discrepancy between Conscious Self-description and Projective Test Performance," *Dissertation Abstr., 20,* 1960, 3378.

HELLER, K., and GOLDSTEIN, A., "Client Dependency and Therapist Expectancy as Relationship Maintaining Variables in Psychotherapy," *J. Consult. Psychol., 25,* 1961, 371–375.

HILER, E. W., "The Sentence Completion Test as a Predictor of Continuation in Psychotherapy," *J. Consult. Psychol., 23,* 1959, 544–549.

JONES, E., WELLS, H., and TORREY, R., "Some Effects of Feedback from the Experimenter on Conformity Behavior," *J. Abnorm. Soc. Psychol., 57,* 1958, 207–213.

KAGAN, J., and MUSSEN, P. H., "Dependency Themes on the TAT and Group Conformity," *J. Consult. Psychol., 20,* 1956, 29–32.

LEVY, L., "A Study of Some Personality Attributes of Independents and Conformers," *Dissertation Abstr., 19,* 1959, 1823.

MASLOW, A. H., and MITTELMANN, B. *Principles of Abnormal Psychology.* New York: Harper and Bros., 1941.

NAVRAN, L., "A Rationally Derived MMPI Scale to Measure Dependence," *J. Consult. Psychol., 18,* 1954, 192.

NELSON, J. W., "Dependency as a Construct: an Evaluation and Some Data," *Dissertation Abstr., 19,* 1959, 2149–2150.

PETERSON, A., SNYDER, W. U., GUTHRIE, G. M., and RAY, W. S., "Therapist Factors: an Exploratory Investigation of Therapeutic Biases," *J. Counsel. Psychol., 5,* 1958, 169–173.

RAUSH, H. L., SPERBER, Z., ZIGLER, D., WILLIAMS, JOAN V., HARWAY, N. I., BORDIN, E. S., DITTMAN, A. T., and HAYS, W., "A Dimensional Analysis of Depth of Interpretation." *J. Consult. Psychol., 20,* 1956, 43–48.

SCHEIDEL, T., CROWELL, LAURA, and SHEPHARD, J., "Personality and Discussion Behavior: a Study of Possible Relationships," *Speech Monogr., 25,* 1958, 261–267.

SNYDER, W. U., "An Investigation of the Nature of Nondirective Psychotherapy," *J. Gen. Psychol., 33,* 1945, 193–223.

SNYDER, W. U., and SNYDER, B. J., *The Psychotherapy Relationship.* New York: The Macmillan Co., 1961.

WILLIAMS, JOAN V., "The Influence of Therapist Commitment on Progress in Therapy," *Dissertation Abstr., 20,* 1960, 4727–4728.

ZUCKERMAN, M., and GROSS, M. J., "Suggestibility and Dependency," *J. Consult. Psychol., 22,* 1958, 328.

Appendix

TABLE A-1

List of Items in the PAC-NAC Dependency Scale, together with Item-Analysis Information

Item #	Task #1 Σ	N	Task #2 r	Ratings A-p	J-1	J-2	Weight	Item
† 3	29	8	.6355**		+		2	Today many of the things my counselor said just seemed to hit the nail on the head.
† 8	45	13	.5458**		+		2	Today I was quite aware of my counselor, his every word, his tone of voice, his facial expressions.
† 11	27	7	.5336**		++		2	Today I felt that I owe it to the counselor to change or grow.
† 15	7	5	.5661**				2	Today I felt a need to keep the conversation moving during the counseling hour.
22	6	2	.4333*	+	++	+	1	Today it seemed as though my counselor had a great deal to offer me.
† 23	15	4	.6416**				2	When I was in the counseling session today, I forgot things I had meant to tell my counselor.
† 32	19	6	.5474**	+	++	++	2	Today I felt that I wanted to rely on the wisdom of my counselor.

A-p = *A priori* scale items
J-1 = Judge #1
J-2 = Judge #2
* = .05 level of significance
** = .01 level of significance
+ = relevant
++ = very relevant
† = items which survived the cross-validation.
N = the number of interviews in which the more and the less dependent client groups exhibited a discrepancy of 3 or more in the number of persons answering "yes,"
Σ = the algebraic sum of the discrepancy scores referred to under column N.

TABLE A-1—Continued

Item #	Task #1 Σ	N	Task #2 r	Ratings A-p J-1 J-2	Weight	Item
† 39	9	2	.5156*	+ ++ +	2	Today I looked to my counselor for help as if he were my father (mother).
† 47	28	8	.4815*		1	Today my counselor made me see myself as I really am.
† 52	17	4	.4506*	+ ++ ++	2	Between interviews, when a problem comes up, I feel that if only I could talk with the counselor everything would be all right.
† 53	30	9	.3850*	+ ++ ++	2	Today I feel that I just couldn't manage without these counseling hours.
55	12	4	.3850*	+	1	Today I felt that my counselor helped to make the process of problem-solving quick and easy.
† 59	27	7	.6374**	++	2	Today I wanted my counselor to like me very much.
† 68	14	4	.3764*	+	1	Today I tried to be more "mature" in order to please my counselor.
71	28	8	.3681	+	1	It is easier for me to talk with my counselor than with most other people.
75	24	7	.3899*		1	Today I felt that my counselor and I are strangers in many ways.
† 79	6	2	.6545**		2	Today I felt very pressed by my counselor.
82	21	7	.4369*		1	Today my counselor seemed very satisfied with me and with the progress I made.
85	20	8	.4633*		1	I know my counselor understands me even when I don't express myself well.
89	35	9	.5872**	+	2	After the counselor said something, I just couldn't think of anything else to say for awhile.
† 94	0	0	.4289*	+ ++ ++	2	Today I felt I could count on my counselor to assume the responsibility for solving my problems.

TABLE A-1—Continued

Item #	Task #1 Σ	N	Task #2 r	A-p	J-1	J-2	Weight	Item
96	9	3	.4742*				1	Today I felt like I was being put on the spot.
97	4	1	.4307*	+			1	Today I looked forward to talking with my counselor.
† 98	30	8	.6469**	+	++		2	What my counselor says is deeply important to me.
† 99	32	11	.4431*				1	I think I am developing a better relationship with the counselor than with other people in my life.
†106	50	8	.4761*	+	++	+	2	Today I feel that my counselor feels responsible for me.
114	3	1	.4451*	+	+		1	Today I felt that my counselor is a strong person who knows what he is doing.
118	26	7	.5840**	+	++		2	Today I was eager to hear what my counselor would have to say.
124	12	4	.3776*		++		1	Today I wished I could spend more time with the counselor.
†130	7	4	.4695*				1	Today it was hard for me to talk about myself.
†135	30	9	.6012**				2	I feel that my counselor wants me to tell him a lot more than I am telling him.
138	4	1	.3926*				1	My counselor knows a great deal about me.
140	12	5	.3991*	+	+		1	Today I felt that I was anxious to develop and maintain an emotional "flow" or contact with my counselor.
†143	31	9	.6062**		++		2	I want from my counselor the kind of personal relationship I have never had but have always wanted.
147	4	3	.3910*				1	Today my counselor was able to "see" me as I see myself.
148	0	0	.3850*		++		1	Today my counselor seemed so wise and correct I felt rather overpowered by him.

TABLE A-1—Continued

Item #	Task #1 Σ	N	Task #2 r	Ratings A-p	J-1	J-2	Weight	Item
†149	20	5	.5983**				2	Today I wished we were talking about something different than what we were talking about at the moment.
†153	34	10	.5567**	++			2	Our counseling relationship is so satisfying that it is hard for me to think about leaving it.
†156	12	3	.5073**	+			2	The things my counselor said and did today gave me confidence in him.
†158	44	9	.6304**	+ ++	+		2	I feel that I rely very heavily on my counselor.
†159	21	7	.5303**		+		2	I wish I were more like my counselor.
160	16	5	.4750*				1	Today I found it difficult to think of things to say.
†164	8	2	.6242**	+ ++ ++			2	Today I really feel very lost and confused and want all the sympathy and comfort and reassurance that my counselor can give.
165	23	7	.4980*	+	+		1	Today my counselor's calmness was most reassuring.
†166	27	8	.7128**				2	Today my counselor made me think for myself.
168	32	8	.6128**	+	+		2	I really got "wrapped up" in what was going on in the counseling session today.
171	3	1	.4031*				1	Today my counselor frightened me.
†173	14	4	.5063*	+	+		1	Today I regard the counselor so highly that I really dislike to differ or disagree with him.
175	10	5	.5059*				1	Today it took a long time in the interview for me to get started talking about important things.
183	13	3	.4002*				1	Today my counselor met me on my own terms.
189	15	6	.4450*	+ ++			2	The simple fact that my counselor is willing to listen to my troubles was comforting today.

TABLE A-1—Continued

Item #	Task #1 Σ	N	Task #2 r	Ratings A-p	Weight J-1	J-2	Item
†197	0	2	.3738	+ +		1	In an important sense, I feel that I "give my soul" to the counselor.
†198	20	6	.4521*			1	Today my counselor was able to see and feel things in exactly the same way as I do.
†199	20	6	.5274**	+	+	2	Today I feel deeply grateful to my counselor.
200	3	1	.3632	+ +	+ +	1	I would like to spend all of my time with my counselor, and most other hours are meaningless—uncomfortable.

TABLE A-2

Actuarial Data, Test Scores, Rankings, and Ratings on Clients Quinn and Jones

	QUINN	JONES
Actuarial Data		
Age	22 years	25 years
Diagnostic category	Immaturity	Immaturity
Homosexual problem?	yes	yes
Marriage problem?	"	"
Inferiority problem?	"	"
Parents' social class	Lower upper	Upper middle
Parents' religion	Protestant	Protestant
Initial complaint	Marriage probs.	Inadequacy probs.
Test Scores		
Increased scores on EPPS (First to final)	ach,exh,aut,suc, dom,end,het	ach,ord,exh,int,dom, end (aff unchanged)
Decreased scores on EPPS (First to final)	def,ord,aff,int, aba,nur,chg,agg	def,aut,suc,aba,nur, chg,het,agg
High scores on MMPI	Pd 77, Mf 77, ES 74	Mf 73, Do 73, ES 72, Cn 71
Rankings		
Rank on idealism (out of 20)	1	2
Rank on altruism (" " ")	1	3
Rank on EPPS change (" " ")	4	11
MMPI rank (" " ") (low score means favorable)	7	3
Rank on PAC-NAC* (out of 20)	2	3
Rank on PAC-NAC increase	9	6
Rank on PAT-NAT** (out of 20)	1	2.5
Rank on PAT-NAT increase	7	6
Rapport, 12/57 (out of 20)	1	4
" , 4/59 (" " ")	1	2
Hostility, 12/57 (" " ")	20	14
" , 4/59 (" " ")	19	17
Liked best, 12/57 (" " ")	1.5	3.5
" " , 4/59 (" " ")	1	2
Dependency, 12/57 (" " ")	1	6
" , 4/59 (" " ")	6	7
Success of case, 12/57 (out of 20)	2	4
" " " 4/59 (" " ")	1	3
Guardedness, 12/57 (" " ")	20	19
" , 4/59 (" " ")	19	17
Estimated rank on maladjustment, one year after therapy	19	18
Ratings		
Type of affect toward therapy	Friendly	Friendly
Type of affect from therapist	Well-liked	Well-liked
Type of "control" shown	Passive	Dominating
Type of self-disclosure	Open	Open
Classifications on Leary's circle	Co-operative-conventional	Responsible-hypernormal
Second " " " "	Docile-dependent	Managerial-autocratic

* PAC-NAC = Client Affect Scale
** PAT-NAT = Therapist Affect Scale

TABLE A-3

Quinn's and Jones' MMPI Scores

Scale		QUINN Raw Score	QUINN Centile	JONES Raw Score	JONES Centile
?	— Items omitted	0	50	0	50
L	— "Lie" score	1	50	0	50
F	— Validity	4	50	3	50
K	— Plus-seeking tendency	15	55	14	53
Hs	— Hypochondriasis	10	48	8	41
D	— Depression	18	53	17	51
Hy	— Hysteria	18	53	17	51
Pd	— Sociopathic	30	77	21	55
MF	— Sexual inversion probs.	34	77	33	73
Pa	— Paranoia	6	44	9	53
Pt	— Psychasthenia	29	62	25	54
Sc	— Schizophrenia	26	57	27	59
Ma	— Hypomania	21	60	20	58
A	— Anxiety	12	50	9	46
R	— Regression	12	43	11	40
ES	— Ego Strength	59	74	58	72
Dy	— Dependency	28	59	18	48
Do	— Dominance	16	53	23	73
Cn	— Control problems	29	61	33	71
Re	— Responsibility	19	47	20	49
St	— Social status probs.	24	64	23	61
Pr	— Antisem. Prejudice	08	43	08	43
Rp	— Role-playing	19	51	23	62

TABLE A-4

Quinn's and Jones' EPPS Scores on Various Testings *

Scale	QUINN								JONES					
	1	5	10	14**	15	20	24	29	1	5	10**	11	16	20
achievement	48	53	61	53	63	56	51	53	31	29	44	44	58	58
deference	41	41	36	36	38	36	38	36	47	44	52	58	41	41
orderliness	38	47	40	40	45	43	40	36	38	43	43	43	49	45
exhibitionism	40	46	46	43	49	49	52	52	52	57	55	57	60	60
autonomy	36	29	33	40	33	27	42	45	54	51	49	49	51	49
affiliation	64	66	59	59	59	55	52	43	62	66	64	59	52	62
introception	65	59	65	57	56	54	54	52	42	48	48	44	50	50
succorance	61	63	61	63	68	70	65	65	59	55	55	53	61	55
dominance	35	35	43	45	45	51	55	59	55	63	61	59	61	61
abasement	56	54	47	43	50	52	52	47	47	39	37	39	31	29
nurturance	60	64	62	60	56	64	52	56	60	56	56	56	56	58
change	47	36	40	40	40	32	34	34	45	38	36	49	43	43
endurance	43	47	49	45	47	49	43	47	32	36	34	37	39	37
heterosexuality	49	49	49	58	45	52	56	60	65	63	58	52	49	54
aggressiveness	61	57	53	59	55	57	59	59	59	61	61	55	50	50

* The only correlation between various occasions that dropped below .50 was that of Quinn on first and last testing where r. = .30 ± .26 (see *The Psychotherapy Relationship*).

** A three-month summer vacation occurred between Quinn's 14th and 15th interviews, and between Jones' 10th and 11th interviews.

TABLE A-5

Quinn's Client and Therapist Affect Scale Scores

	PAC	NAC	PAC-NAC	Corrected PAC-NAC (—15)	Rank Order	PAT	NAT	PAT-NAT	Rank Order
1.	52	86	—34	—49	29	79	56	23	26
2.	93	25	68	53	22	76	41	35	24
3.	96	19	77	62	20	77	37	40	22
4.	101	13	88	73	12	77	36	41	20.5
5.	104	7	97	82	2.5	80	31	49	17.5
6.	104	7	97	82	2.5	81	25	56	9
7.	101	11	90	75	11	81	26	55	11
8.	101	8	93	78	6.5	79	25	54	13.5
9.	95	15	80	65	17.5	79	20	59	5.5
10.	101	8	93	78	6.5	78	27	51	16
11.	102	11	91	76	10	82	24	58	7.5
12.	88	35	53	38	25	79	30	49	17.5
13.	95	22	73	58	21	81	23	58	7.5
14.	102	8	94	79	4.5	81	21	60	4
15.*	102	10	92	77	8.5	78	23	55	11
16.	91	27	64	49	23	77	34	43	19
17.	92	43	49	34	26	77	24	53	15
18.	98	19	79	64	19	79	25	54	13.5
19.	95	15	80	65	17.5	66	52	14	28
20.	91	31	60	45	24	74	38	36	23
21.	85	46	39	24	28	69	60	09	29
22.	97	15	82	67	15	81	17	64	3
23.	99	14	85	70	14	79	20	59	5.5
24.	100	19	81	66	16	77	36	41	20.5
25.	101	7	94	79	4.5	74	40	34	25
26.	100	14	86	71	13	82	27	55	11
27.	82	40	42	27	27	71	52	19	27
28.	105	6	99	84	1	84	09	75	2
29.	102	10	92	77	8.5	83	07	76	1

* The fifteenth interview followed a three-month vacation.

TABLE A-6

Jones' Client and Therapist Affect Scale Scores

	PAC	NAC	PAC-NAC	Corrected PAC-NAC (—15)	Rank Order	PAT	NAT	PAT-NAT	Rank Order
1.	67	60	07	—08	17	83	37	46	11
2.	90	26	64	49	14	74	40	34	16
3.	52	89	—37	—52	20	70	63	07	20
4.	98	12	86	71	8.5	75	34	41	14.5
5.	66	65	01	—14	18	77	36	41	14.5
6.	95	21	74	59	11	76	30	46	11
7.	103*	06*	97*	82	2	82	20	62	4
8.	91	29	62	47	15	78	32	46	11
9.	66	70	—04	—19	19	78	33	45	13
10.	98	20	78	63	10	82	22	60	5.5
11.	105	06	99	84	1	80	22	58	7
12.**	80	45	35	20	16	72	44	28	17
13.	93	25	68	53	12.5	70	52	18	19
14.	103	07	96	81	3.5	83	09	74	1
15.	103	07	96	81	3.5	79	28	51	8
16.	101	10	91	76	5.5	84	13	71	3
17.	91	23	68	53	12.5	73	53	20	18
18.	101	10	91	76	5.5	83	23	60	5.5
19.	98	12	86	71	8.5	80	30	50	9
20.	101	11	90	75	7	81	09	72	2

* The PAC-NAC for the seventh interview was filled out eight days late, and following the subsequent interview; its validity is uncertain.

** The twelfth interview followed a three-month vacation.

TABLE A-7

Quinn's and Jones' Mean Scores for Tenths of the Therapy Process on the Client Affect Scale and the Therapist Affect Scale, together with Ranks of the Tenths

PAC-NAC

	QUINN		JONES	
	Mean	Rank	Mean	Rank
1	37.0	10	35.5	9
2	94.0	2	24.5	10
3	87.7	3	37.5	7
4	79.0	6	79.5	4.5
5	86.3	4	37.0	8
6	64.0	8	67.0	6
7	59.7	9	82.0	3
8	82.7	5	93.5	1
9	74.0	7	79.5	4.5
10	95.5	1	88.0	2
$\overline{X}$	76.0	—	62.4	—

PAT-NAT

	QUINN		JONES	
	Mean	Rank	Mean	Rank
1	32.7	9	40.0	8.5
2	48.7	7	23.5	10
3	56.0	3	43.5	6
4	52.7	5	54.0	3
5	57.7	2	52.5	4
6	50.0	6	43.0	7
7	19.7	10	46.0	5
8	54.7	4	61.0	1.5
9	36.0	8	40.0	8.5
10	75.5	1	61.0	1.5
$\overline{X}$	48.4	—	46.5	—

$\overline{X}$ of both on PAC-NAC = 69.2
$\overline{X}$ of both on PAT-NAT = 47.5

Me ... *C-NAC*

Adams		3.89
Baker		35.09
Clark	s*	30.97
Davis*	wood	14.21
Evans*		20.94
Gilbert	*	21.94
Hill		

* Better

Com ... *Scores*

Inter-views	NINE BETTER CLIENTS		ELEVEN POORER CLIENTS		ALL TWENTY CLIENTS	
	# of S's	Mean Dy	# of S's	Mean Dy	# of S's	Mean Dy
1–3	9	25.18	11	14.81	20	19.48
4–6	9	26.80	11	15.46	20	20.56
7–9	9	27.38	11	17.61	20	22.01
10–12	9	30.18	11	15.18	20	21.94
13–15	9	32.18	10	18.56	19	25.01
16–18	9	27.91	9	17.01	18	22.47
19–21	8	28.73	8	18.50	16	22.46
22–24	6	27.05	7	17.70	13	22.00
25–27	5	32.52	7	16.20	12	23.00
28–30	5	28.82	4	14.90	9	22.63